A HISTORY OF GERMAN JEWISH BIBLE TRANSLATION

A HISTORY OF GERMAN JEWISH BIBLE TRANSLATION

ABIGAIL GILLMAN

THE UNIVERSITY OF CHICAGO PRESS
CHICAGO AND LONDON

The University of Chicago Press, Chicago 60637
The University of Chicago Press, Ltd., London

Published 2018
Printed in the United States of America

27 26 25 24 23 22 21 20 19 18   1 2 3 4 5

ISBN-13: 978-0-226-47769-5 (cloth)
ISBN-13: 978-0-226-47772-5 (paper)
ISBN-13: 978-0-226-47786-2 (e-book)
DOI: 10.7208/chicago/9780226477862.001.0001

The University of Chicago Press gratefully acknowledges the generous support of the Center for the Humanities and the Elie Wiesel Center for Jewish Studies at Boston University toward the publication of this book.

Library of Congress Cataloging-in-Publication Data

Names: Gillman, Abigail, 1964– author.
Title: A history of German Jewish Bible translation / Abigail Gillman.
Description: Chicago ; London : The University of Chicago Press, 2018. | Includes bibliographical references and index.
Identifiers: LCCN 2017036448 | ISBN 9780226477695 (cloth : alk. paper) | ISBN 9780226477725 (pbk. : alk. paper) | ISBN 9780226477862 (e-book)
Subjects: LCSH: Bible. Old Testament—Translating—Germany—History. | Bible. Old Testament—Versions, Jewish. | Bible. Old Testament. German—Versions. | Bible. Old Testament. Yiddish—Versions. | Bible. Old Testament—Criticism, interpretation, etc., Jewish—Germany. | Judaism—Germany—History—Modern period, 1750–
Classification: LCC BS941 .G55 2017 | DDC 221.5/3109—dc23
LC record available at https://lccn.loc.gov/2017036448

♾ This paper meets the requirements of ANSI/NISO Z39.48-1992 (Permanence of Paper).

For my parents

שתיבדלו לחיים ארוכים

Aug 1, 2018
For Diane
a wonderful
friend + mentor.
Long live Ludwig
Philippson!!
Abig[illegible]

Ich erinnere mich keinem Menschen begegnet zu sein, dem ich dieses Verhältnis zur Bibel zugetraut hätte, so wie es Rembrandt in dem Bildnis seiner Mutter, die Postille lesend so rührend schön dargestellt hat.

I can't recall ever meeting a person I would have thought capable of having this relationship to the Bible such as the one depicted so movingly, so beautifully by Rembrandt, in the portrait of his mother reading the postil.

—Bertha Pappenheim to Martin Buber, 18 March 1936

CONTENTS

PREFACE

The Bible is the Book of the World.
—Abraham Geiger, 1857

לוּלֵי תוֹרָתְךָ שַׁעֲשֻׁעָי אָז אָבַדְתִּי בְעָנְיִי
Were not Your teaching my delight / I would have perished in my affliction.
—Psalms 119: 92 (JPS)

In German belles-lettres, the adjective *ewig* (eternal) calls to mind the "eternal feminine" in the last line of Goethe's *Faust*, a song by Gustav Mahler, and a duet in a Wagner opera.[1] But for German Jewry in the modern period, *ewig* described one Being above all: God. In a bold gesture, Moses Mendelssohn rendered the proper name of God as *der Ewige* (Eternal One) in his translation of the Pentateuch.

Moses Mendelssohn's Pentateuch was reprinted countless times, and its popularity inspired many others to try to match his accomplishment. The large majority of these new translations retained *der Ewige*. *Der Ewige* was further incorporated in prayer books, sermons, and all forms of religious literature across the German-speaking Jewish world, in Austria-Hungary, Poland, and Russia. Insofar as we can speak of *the* German Jewish Bible, *der Ewige* was its signature. One German word influenced how generations of Jews across Europe would address God and think about God. Mendelssohn was the Moses of modern German Jewry, and *der Ewige* was the Name he bequeathed to his compatriots when they asked him, as the Israelites did of Moses, *ma shemo?* By what name shall we address our God in our new German language?

> But Moses said to the Deity, "Suppose I come to the sons of Israel and say to them, 'Your fathers' deity has sent me to you,' and they say to me, 'What is his name?' (*ma shemo*)—what should I say to them?" (Ex 3:13, Anchor Bible)

Practically every biblical translator identified with Moses, and this verse shows why. Standing in the wilderness alongside the still-burning bush, Moses inquires after the Name of the Deity on behalf of the nation he has just been asked to lead. Since Moses grew up in Egypt, he may in fact have been ignorant of the Name. Or, perhaps he was testing the voice calling to him from that burning bush, and the Name was the shibboleth, the word by which God's identity would be verified.[2] Either way, Moses's question shows he was already attuned to the vast divide separating God, the Israelites, and their forefathers. Alas, Moses did not receive the clear answer he had hoped for. The conversation goes from bad to worse. The more God tries to persuade Moses to take up the divine mission, the more discouraged he becomes. Moses knows all along that what is being asked of him is impossible, and finally persuades God to that effect. Aaron is appointed to be Moses's spokesperson; the translator gets a translator. Forty years later, as the Israelites prepared to enter the land, it is again Moses who sets out to "expound this teaching" (*be'er et ha-Torah ha-zot*) (Deut 1:5, JPS), which Rashi interprets as "render in seventy languages"; perhaps this explains why *Be'ur* is the term that Moses Mendelssohn chose for the commentary to his translation.[3] Every German Jewish translator identified with the biblical Moses, because of the impossibility and the necessity of the task at hand.

But how did Mendelssohn choose *der Ewige*? What other options were available to him? On what grounds was his innovation retained or rejected? *A History of German Jewish Bible Translation* tells the story of myriad small decisions and their repercussions. But the starting point of this book is anything but minor: the fact that between the eighteenth and twentieth centuries German Jewish luminaries produced an astonishing number of Bible translations—sixteen different translations in roughly 150 years, not counting revisions and partial translations.[4] These works were not for religious observance, since the Hebrew Torah retained its primacy in Jewish worship, in a fundamental difference with Christianity where translations of the Old and New Testaments became "second originals." The motives for translation lay elsewhere. In a time of rapid social and political change, Bible translation promoted educational, linguistic, and cultural as well as religious goals. Translations produced by the German Jewish minority over three centuries served many of the same purposes as translation in the majority culture: to cultivate and educate the reading public, both women and men; to foster national identity; to foment the unions of self and other, ancient and modern, national and foreign (Hölderlin); and to promote the agendas of twentieth-century modernism, such as the traditionalist return to the past and spiritual renaissance.

The greater context of these German Jewish translations was the return to the Hebrew Bible by Jews throughout western and central Europe beginning in the eighteenth century—a widespread campaign that took the form of scholarship, sermons, visual art, and literature, as well as translation. The Jewish religious and national *Urtext* was also "the book of the world": a bridge to Christianity and an established part of the European canon. The hope was that engaging with the Hebrew Bible would make it possible for Jews to remain Jews as they entered society at large. The development was analogous, in scope and significance, to the physical progression of European Jews out of their segregated existence into the public sphere.[5] Like the new stately synagogues, the reborn Bible had to retain its traditional functions, yet appeal in new ways. Even movements that disparaged traditional religion, such as Haskalah, Reform, and Zionism, reclaimed the Bible.[6] To do so was not merely to imitate Protestant Christianity, as Shavit and Eran point out: Jews did not return only to a written book, but to "the Bible as a system of ethical principles, history and literature," which was continuous with their nascent self-understanding as a "living historical entity with a mission in the world."[7] Modern Jewish intellectuals took up the challenge with urgency and ingenuity. Translating was not just one strategy among many; it was to engage with the essence of Judaism, in Leo Baeck's phrase. Translators faced intense scrutiny. In the age of biblical criticism, the integrity of the Masoretic text was under attack. Each element, from the appearance of the page (layout, design, illustrations), to the rendering of the divine Name, to the inclusion or exclusion of commentary, was potentially controversial. Each translator was at pains to rationalize his or her particular approach to translation; covert agendas were at variance with public pronouncements. Translating the Hebrew Bible was a way to work through theological and ideological problems. It was also, to quote the Psalmist, a source of play and delight; a "goal worth any pain."[8]

A History of German Jewish Bible Translation analyzes representative German Jewish Bibles as part of an evolving cultural project. I do not discuss each and every translation produced by German Jews, nor do I treat individual translations as unique artifacts, as their authors might have wished them to be studied. Because it is only a slight exaggeration to say that each translator aspired to be a Jewish Luther—in other words, to produce a Bible translation that would launch a revolution, or, at the very least, that would revivify Judaism in his or her time. (Franz Rosenzweig's opening caveat in his Mendelssohn essay, "Mendelssohn's historical significance is well known," was not a compliment.) The translators' aspirations notwithstanding, it is precisely the historicity of these translations that makes for a compelling story—that *is* the story. I arrive at their historicity in a number of ways. First, I contextualize each work with reference to the author's career, prior translations, and agenda. Second, I divide the history into four waves of translation that correspond to periods and/or well-known phenomena in the history of German Jewry: the Yiddish and German Haskalah in the seventeenth and eighteenth centuries; the academic movement called Wissenschaft des Judentums (the scholarly/scientific study of Judaism) in the early nineteenth century; the bourgeoning of distinct religious movements, Reform and neo-Orthodoxy, in the middle and late nineteenth century; and the age of Jewish modernism and dissimilation in the 1920s and '30s. As much as history helps to frame the translations, the works themselves complicate the historical narrative. Within each wave, I juxtapose two or more translations that were designed to achieve similar goals, but used diverse, sometimes even opposing, strategies to do so. These untraditional pairings bring to light tensions within each period, as well as affinities across generations. As Henri Meschonnic writes, comparing retranslations of the great ancient texts brings the experimental poetics of translation into focus. "C'est là qu'on peut confronter un invariant, et ses variations. Leur pourquoi, leur comment." (This is where one can confront an invariant and its variations. Their why, their how.)[9] Finally, whenever possible, I draw connections to the English-language context and to twenty-first-century concerns.

This study stands on the shoulders of the few treatments of the topic. Two book-length studies, neither one in English, are compulsory for those seeking to grasp its depth and breadth. William Weintraub's monograph *Targume Hatorah Lelashon Hagermanit* (the German Translations of the Pentateuch) devotes some chapters to individual translators (including Luther), and others to knotty linguistic topics; Weintraub's philological insights are an essential supplement to these chapters.[10] Hans-Joachim Bechtoldt's *Jüdische deutsche Bibelübersetzungen vom ausgehenden 18. bis zum Beginn des 20. Jahrhunderts* catalogues each translation project, displaying the history in expanded view.[11] A number of essays conceptualize the history of German Jewish Bible translation or particular episodes thereof, including W. Gunther Plaut's "German Jewish Bible Translations: Linguistic Theology as a Political Phenomenon" and Hermann Levin Goldschmidt's chapter "Jewish Quest for a German Bible" in *The Legacy of German Jewry*. Other studies—Jonathan

Sheehan's *The Enlightenment Bible*, Yaakov Shavit and Mordechai Eran's *The Hebrew Bible Reborn*, Alan T. Levenson's *The Making of the Modern Jewish Bible*, and Richard I. Cohen's "Urban Visibility and Biblical Visions"—shaped my thinking about the Bible as a cultural asset. The extensive body of research on the translations of Moses Mendelssohn and Buber and Rosenzweig has been invaluable. I have attempted to bring a new perspective on these well-researched projects by widening the historical contexts in which they are commonly studied, and, at the same time, sharpening the focus on each translator's vocation. Three other sources deserve mention at the outset. Hans Joachim Störig's *Das Problem des Übersetzens* (1963) does more than assemble canonical prefaces and statements about translation; it conveys the breadth and depth of a "translator culture" in Germany, wherein "Gottsched, Wieland, Bürger translate Homer, then Voss. Goethe translates Voltaire and Benvenuto Cellini. Schiller translates Shakespeare and Racine. Schlegel translates the Bhagavad Gita. Tieck translates Don Quixote. Schlegel, Dorothea Tieck (daughter of Ludwig), and Baudissin produce an important Shakespeare translation."[12] Antoine Berman's *The Experience of the Foreign: Culture and Translation in Romantic Germany* (1992) constructs a fascinating metanarrative about the role of translation in the forging of German cultural identity. Berman frames his study with two invaluable points. First: translation means something different in each case; second, two questions must be asked in every case: "What are we if we are a nation of translators? What is translation, and what is a good translation, for the people we are?"[13] Finally, the German Jewish "translator culture" acquires new meaning in Naomi Seidman's *Faithful Renderings: Jewish-Christian Difference and the Politics of Translation* (2006), a pioneering work of Jewish translation theory.[14] Seidman compares Christian and Jewish translation practices from the targumim and Septuagint to Anne Frank and Elie Wiesel through the lens of postcolonial theory, showing that the Jewish minority consistently mimics the linguistic ways of the Christian majority, but always with a difference. Seidman makes the fascinating claim that Jewish translations "demonstrate the asymmetrical relations between cultures rather than symmetrical relations between texts." It remains to be seen to what extent her insight that the Jewish translator in Christian society is a mistranslator applies to the figures in this study.

I began writing about German Jewish Bible translation to test Plaut's thesis that two German Jewish Bible translations formed the bookends of German Jewish culture.[15] In an essay from 2002, I compared the translation project of Mendelssohn with that of Buber and Rosenzweig: the first, prosaic, idiomatic, disambiguating in the extreme; the second, literal, Hebraic, foreignizing in the extreme.[16] In all apparent ways, I wrote, the later translation overturned the first, and it announced this overturning by framing the text with an unmistakable design element: white space. I also observed that the Buber-Rosenzweig Bible remained implicated, and not only through negation, in the tradition Mendelssohn had initiated. Indeed, the two projects have much in common. They shared the central priority of making the music of Torah audible in a new way for a new generation of Jews, placed philosophical and theological matters front and center, and developed innovative approaches to translating the Divine Name.

The present study expands my earlier analysis in several respects. First, I incorporate six major translations of the nineteenth century—known mainly to specialists—that form the core of the tradition. These translations are the first fruits of Mendelssohn's initiative and forgotten precursors of Buber and Rosenzweig's approach. They also shape contemporary approaches to Bible translation.

It is not only the middle but also the so-called endpoints of the tradition that my book reconsiders. To be sure, Mendelssohn remains the precursor translator par excellence, who shaped the practice of the translators who followed him. He was credited with all the good and blamed for all that went wrong. Recent scholarship has shown that Mendelssohn was not so much the father or founder of the Haskalah as a participant in trends already underway. Even Mendelssohn's *Be'ur* belonged to a trend, which included Christian Enlightenment Bibles, as well as two *modern* Yiddish translations—the Judeo-German Bibles printed in Amsterdam in 1678 and 1679. The fact that Mendelssohn criticized these Yiddish versions in his preface tells us that they appealed to the same population—in other words, part of the same wave. The parallel tradition of Judeo-German or Yiddish Bible translation continued to shape the religious lives of German Jews, and thus remains part of the history of German Jewish Bible translation. The Yiddish women's Bible, *Tsene-Rene*, remained an important source of Torah for generations of Jewish women in the Ashkenazi world, including German-speaking Jewish women, into the twentieth century. The fact that even in the twentieth century a review tried to make the case that the *Tsene-Rene* was not appropriate for modern girls suggests that it remained popular.[17] The appeal of a Yiddish Bible did not fade when German-language education became mandatory. For these and other reasons, Bertha Pappenheim's initiative to translate the *Tsene-Rene* into German in the 1930s is another "bookend" of the tradition. Pappenheim was a social activist, feminist, educator, writer, and translator, a close friend and colleague of Martin Buber, and a lecturer at Rosenzweig's Freies Jüdisches Lehrhaus. Correspondence reveals that Pappenheim's translation project was undertaken in tandem with Buber and Rosenzweig's translation efforts. Hers was a feminist, Orthodox alternative to their approach. As in every wave, these two projects attempted to achieve similar goals through different methods.

Why did modern German Jews produce so many more translations of the Hebrew Bible than any other Jewish community? One answer is that distinct phenomena and values in German Christian society and in Jewish society dovetailed to create the conditions for an unprecedented series of translations—values such as ennoblement through culture, self-expansion, and fidelity. Germans valued *Bildung*—education and self-formation through culture, and to culture—to the same degree that Jews valued the study of Jewish texts.[18] Is culture at its best *not* a kind of Torah, ennobling and edifying? Translation played a key role in creating the corpus of works that shaped German literature and culture; but only a certain kind of translation "marked by fidelity" to the style and language of the source text would serve this purpose.[19] Jews also understood the "cardinal virtue"[20] of fidelity because of their attachment to the Masoretic text of Scripture. Modern German Jewry did not embrace secularism; they remained attached to Judaism and to the Hebrew Bible, even as they became deeply enamored of German language and culture. And this only begins to explain why the history of German Jewish Bible translation contains so much more than the story of how the German Bible became the Jews' "passport" to German culture, making possible the collective crossing from Yiddish-speaking Ashkenaz into modern Germany. This book shows that German Jews *never stopped* being a community in transition; each generation experienced anxiety of influence and sought to update or upgrade what they had inherited. In other words, during this period, Jews and Germans obsessively asked, *what are we if we are a nation of translators? What is translation, and what is a good translation, for the people we are?*

The modern Jewish approach—if one may generalize—was a merger of rabbinic and romantic sensibilities. It was rabbinic in the sense that it shared the essential impulse of rabbinic exegesis, and perhaps even more important, it affiliated with rabbinic discourses to gain internal legitimation. As Gerson D. Cohen notes, "All German Jewish scholars—even those who proclaimed loudest that Judaism was the most authentic representation of the Biblical faith and ethic—understood full well that it was not in Scripture itself so much as in its exegesis that the message of the Bible achieved any real impact on society."[21] Bible translation was a religious enterprise, undertaken in dialogue with Christian translation practices and with contemporary cultural and aesthetic trends. It was Romantic in the sense that translation was an imaginative and ideological enterprise influenced by poetry, aesthetics, nationalism, and Orientalism.[22] The pages of these Bibles confirm that they were designed to be sites of interpellation in Louis Althusser's sense, allowing readers to read from left to right or right to left, from the bottom of the page upwards and from margins to center, thereby engaging with one or more facets of a reader's identity at will. This book tells that story forward and backward, using precursors, reception, and the afterlives of these Bibles to gauge their impact.

The primal scene of German Jewish Bible translation is not the Tower of Babel in Genesis, but an apocryphal tale about Exodus. According to a midrash, God had to resort to the Egyptian language to give the Israelites the Decalogue:

> "I (*anokhi*) am the Lord thy God." (Exod. 20:2). Rabbi Nehemiah said: What kind of word is *anokhi*? It is an Egyptian word. In Egypt, when a man wishes to say to a friend "I (*ani*)," he says *anokh*.[23]

The Israelites had forgotten Hebrew during their four-hundred-year-plus sojourn in Egypt. How would God communicate with them? How would they receive the laws and commandments? The God who had redeemed them from Egypt with signs and wonders, split the Sea of Reeds, and sent manna from the sky had a further obstacle to overcome, and translation was the solution. The midrash continues:

> How may God's need to use an Egyptian word for "I" be explained? By the story of a mortal king whose son had been captured. The son spent a long time among his captors and learned their language. Finally the king wreaked vengeance on his enemies and brought his son back. But when he tried to talk with his son in his own language, the son did not understand. What did the king do? He began to speak with his son in the language of his captors.
>
> The Holy One had to do the same thing with Israel. During all the years Israel spent in Egypt, they learned the Egyptian speech. Finally, when the Holy One redeemed them and came to give them the Torah, they could not understand it. So the Holy One said: I will speak to them in the Egyptian tongue. Thus the Holy One inaugurated the giving of the Torah by using the word *anokhi*, which is a form of the Egyptian *anokh*.

By this account, translation is not a punishment but a reward. God was the first translator, and the revealed Law, the foundational text, was always already translated. God's "I," *anokhi*, is a *Fremdwort* (loan word), a trace of the very un-logocentric reality that throughout Jewish history, translation was deeply interwoven with the word of God, and deployed time and again to reconnect the people and their Scripture.

A NOTE ON TRANSLATIONS AND YIDDISH TRANSCRIPTIONS

All translations are mine unless otherwise noted.

Moses Mendelssohn transcribed his German translation of the Pentateuch into Hebrew characters. Werner Weinberg transcribed it back into Latin letters in JubA vols. 9–12, and he explains his method and orthography (and those of Mendelssohn) in the preface to volume 9:1 (VII–XXXII). All quotations from Mendelssohn's translation in the present work follow those of Weinberg.

The spelling of premodern Yiddish exhibits much variation; furthermore, an understanding of its pronunciation is incomplete. This state of affairs presents a challenge when one is faced with presenting the language in Latin letters. Our solution has been to bring text from Blitz and Witzenhausen following the transliteration system standardly applied to Modern Yiddish. We hope this will render the quoted material generally recognizable to the reader familiar with modern or older forms of Yiddish and/or German, and will assist those wishing to consult Yiddish reference works (whose orientation is typically toward the modern language).

ABBREVIATIONS

Alter: Robert Alter, *The Five Books of Moses: A Translation with Commentary* (New York: W. W. Norton, 2008)

AZdJ: *Allgemeine Zeitung des Judentums*

BR: Martin Buber and Franz Rosenzweig, trans. *Die fünf Bücher der Weisung* (Berlin: Schocken, 1925)

BT: Isadore Epstein, ed., *Hebrew-English Edition of the Babylonian Talmud*, trans. J. Rabbinowitz (London: Soncino Press, 1984)

GS: Franz Rosenzweig, *Der Mensch und sein Werk. Gesammelte Schriften.* Edited by Rachel Rosenzweig and Edith Rosenzweig-Scheinmann, together with Bernhard Casper. The Hague: Martinus Nijhoff, 1979

Hirsch/Levy: Samson Raphael Hirsch, German translation and commentary, *The Pentateuch*, translated into English by Isaac Levy, 2nd rev. ed. (Gateshead: Judaica Press, 1982)

IB: Ludwig Philippson, ed. and trans., *Die israelitische Bibel: Enthaltend—Den heiligen Urtext, die deutsche Übertragung, die allgemeine, ausführliche Erläuterung mit mehr als 500 englischen Holzschnitten* (Leipzig: Baumgärtner, 1841–58)

JPS: *Tanakh: A New Translation of the Holy Scriptures. According to the Hebrew Text.* (Philadelphia: Jewish Publication Society, 1985)

JubA: Moses Mendelssohn, *Gesammelte Schriften, Jubiläumsausgabe*, ed. Werner Weinberg (Stuttgart: Friedrich Frommann, 1990)

KJV: King James Version

Luther: Martin Luther, trans. *Die Bibel, oder die ganze heilige Schrift* (Berlin: Britische und Ausländische Bibelgesellschaft, 1924)

OBS: Orthodox Bible Society

INTRODUCTION

The German Jewish Bible in Context

TORAH TWICE, TARGUM ONCE: RABBINIC AND MEDIEVAL CONTEXTS

A cultural history of translation normally studies how and why a nation or language community acquires and absorbs foreign works. This phenomenon was enormously important in the German context, where Martin Luther made the Greek New Testament and the Hebrew Old Testament into one German book and started a language revolution, and where, a few centuries later, intellectuals from Herder to Goethe, Schlegel to Hölderlin, promoted the synergy of "one's own" and "the foreign" by way of translations and myriad other genres of adaptation. But what happens when a nation relies on translation to reacquire its own core text? Can this also be a type of self-expansion through the encounter with the foreign, as occurred in German Romanticism? Is it possible for a nation to become estranged from itself, from its own foundational text, to such an extent that translation into a foreign language enables it to repossess that text in a new form? Is this perhaps the subtext of Franz Rosenzweig's quip to Martin Buber, "So, we will missionize"?[1]

Indeed, Ashkenazi society had lost access to the Bible in Hebrew. The *Torah* in Hebrew retained its central place in liturgy and synagogue worship, as a source of teaching, rituals, and values shaping daily life and across the life cycle. But the *Bible* in Hebrew was not the primary source of Torah for the average Jew in Central Europe between the thirteenth and eighteenth centuries. Jews did not learn biblical grammar. The Scripture they studied was heavily mediated by rabbinic commentary, traditional interpretation, and midrash, and accessed mainly by way of rabbinic texts, through repetition and memorization of selected verses (by boys), and reading vernacular narrative Bibles at home (by women and girls). To put it more precisely, it was not the Torah, but the twenty-four books comprising the Jewish biblical corpus that had become foreign.

Nor was translation held in high regard. In Jewish society, as perhaps in any community, translation has a different "value in different historical contexts. It does not have an absolute, trans-historical meaning."[2] The practice of translating to remedy the forgetting of Biblical Hebrew dates back to ancient history, to the Babylonian exile in 586 BCE. In one of the last biblical books, Ezra the Scribe returns with the people from Babylonian exile in the sixth century BCE and organizes a public reading of the Torah in a language they could understand. Ezra was also the first to transcribe Hebrew letters into a script these returnees could read—the vernacular script called *ktav ashuri*, Assyrian script. With the closing of the biblical canon, translation became associated with the (newly) regulated methods of rabbinic exegesis: the most ancient Jewish translations into Aramaic, called *targumim*, were interpretive translations that also acquired a sacred character. Skip ahead a few more centuries, and medieval commentators such as Rashi, writing in twelfth-century France, quoted those targumim, printed on the page of Scripture, as the starting point of exegesis. And yet, for much of the period prior to the Haskalah, Bible translation was not framed as something creative, advantageous, salutory: the first step to Torah, or "the first step to culture." In premodern times, Jews were not proud of translations of the Hebrew Bible, which were associated with exile, loss, forgetting, earthquakes, and idolatry. Their use was strictly regulated, and out of fear, caution, or superstition, most translators downplayed their motives for translating and tried to conceal the complexity of their project. Perhaps the general lack of interest in Jewish translations of Scripture owes to a residual association of translation with shame and ignorance. Jewish historians have for the most part relegated the topic of translation (biblical and otherwise) to the margins. In studies of German Jewish history and culture, translations, even those by major figures like Mendelssohn, Philippson, and Hirsch, are rarely analyzed as historical documents, as sources of information about cultural, religious and linguistic practices and trends. The spring 2016 edition of *AJS Perspectives*, dedicated to translation, is a most welcome sign that times have changed.

To my understanding, translating the Hebrew Torah was problematic, if not heretical, for one main reason: it forced an impossible choice between the words and the sense of the Torah. Whereas Christians (following the dualism of Greek thought) separated letter and spirit, Jews had a monistic view of the sacred text (and of the human being). To choose sense over language or language over sense was simply not an option. The Talmud attempts to understand what exactly is meant if someone refers to himself, in the course of making an oath, as a reader and translator. "R. Judah said: If one translates a verse literally, he is a liar; if he adds thereto, he is a blasphemer and a libeller. Then what is meant by translation? Our (authorised) translation."[3] Rabbi Judah's utterance may the earliest admission of the untranslatablity of Scripture, or the impossibility of doing justice to the Torah in another language: no human being is capable of navigating between the Scylla of literality and Charybdis of idiomatic rendering when it comes to a revealed text. Only the "authorised translation," the Aramaic targum, was permitted. This revered translation even came to be printed in the pages of the second edition of the Rabbinic Bible in 1530.

Another talmudic passage claims that the day the Torah was translated into Greek was like the day the golden calf was built; this would equate translation with idolatry.[4] But in reality, the ancient position was nuanced. As we have already noted, translation became legitimized out of necessity. In the centuries after the return from Babylonian exile, Jews have spoken Aramaic, Greek, Arabic, and Judeo-German, or Yiddish; Hebrew, the language of the Bible, ceased to be the Jewish vernacular. But hearing the prescribed readings from the Torah on the Sabbath and festivals was a religious obligation for every Jew, female and male, not just for the intellectual elite. Translation was required to enable members of the community to fulfill their religious obligation. Initially, as early as the time of Ezra (fifth century BCE), only oral translation was permitted in the synagogue; this was the job of the *meturgeman*, the translator or interpreter.[5] Still, only one biblical verse at a time was read and then translated, to prevent translation from acquiring "a life of its own," as Nehama Leibowitz put it.[6] Many other passages in the Talmud express unease about translation. One tells of the earth quaking and a heavenly voice descending in reaction to the targum of Jonathan ben Uzziel, lest certain secrets pertaining to the Messianic age be revealed before their time; here is an early confirmation that translation can, indeed, unlock a secret power residing in the words of Torah, what Rosenzweig later called its "world historical influence."[7] Another passage reports that the Bible can be translated into any language, but the tiny parchment scrolls with biblical verses placed inside the *mezuzah* (doorpost) and *tefillin* (phylacteries) must appear in Hebrew. The Talmud includes an account of the Septuagint, along with a series of verses that the Septuagint mistranslated. Rabban Gamliel issued a decree that the Bible may be translated into Greek only, using as his prooftext Noah's curse to his grandson

Canaan: "Let Japheth dwell in the house of Shem."[8] Naomi Seidman asserts that this account shaped the rabbis' reception of the Greek Bible, which was positive up until the point when the Septuagint became the foundational text of Christianity.[9] Permitting only one "authorized" translation solved the problem, but the rabbis went further and elevated it to a sacred hermeneutic (*siman*)—signs given to Moses on Mount Sinai to enable him to decode the written text.

Targum became required reading in the synagogue, where it was recited in alternation with the Hebrew original. The exact formulation of the requirement provides a fascinating insight into the relation of Scripture and translation in the talmudic period: I refer to the custom of *shnayim mikra v'echad targum* (twice in the original and once in translation): "Rav Huna bar Yehuda says in the name of Rabbi Ammi: 'one should always complete the reading of one's weekly Torah portion with the congregation, twice from the *mikra* and once from the *Targum.*' "[10] More than any other, the practice "Torah twice, targum once" exemplifies the rabbis' attitude towards translation: they ritualized the practice in a way that prevented equivalence between, or equal time for, Scripture and translation. They made sure that in a given week, contact hours with Scripture exceeded the time with translation by a two-to-one ratio. "Torah twice" seems to guard against instrumentalizing the contents of Scripture, or the notion that the Hebrew words are a vessel for some otherwise transmissible content. Understanding the text is important, but secondary to the performed reading and ritualized listening.[11] In later times, when Aramaic was no longer a Jewish vernacular, the prescription was adapted to require some translation, be it the *Tsene-Rene*, Mendelssohn's *Be'ur*, or in lieu of translation, Rashi's commentary; the custom continues to be observed to this day.[12] With the institution of carefully regulated, public Torah reading in the synagogue, the *meturgeman* translated each verse into the vernacular after it was read aloud in Hebrew; he was not allowed to look in a book while doing so.[13]

Nehama Leibowitz argues that these oral translation practices continued "unbroken" from ancient to medieval times in synagogues and in educational settings.[14] In the medieval *heder*, teachers read a word or phrase out loud followed by a "translation," which, as Erika Timm points out, was really only what was needed to understand the word in its context.[15] Such was the curriculum for boys aged five to ten in Ashkenaz. Sephardic and Italian schools, in contrast, had introduced systematic instruction in Hebrew grammar in the late Middle Ages. Education manuals from thirteenth-century France and Germany instruct the teacher to allow students to translate the Bible into their own language. In one such tract, the writer refers to Onkelos, Saadia, and the custom of "Torah twice, Targum once," rendered in German as "zweimal im urtext und einmal im targum."[16] However, despite the prohibition against written translations, transcription became necessary due to the dispersion of the Jews and the impossibility of locating a *meturgeman* for each and every community. Once multiple versions could be printed, it became possible to canonize an authoritative Judeo-German version that would be faithful to the traditional understanding of the text. This is the origin of what came to be known as *chumesh taytsh*.

THE SECOND CHARIOTS: OLD YIDDISH BIBLES

Ashkenazi Jewish society was trilingual, with one spoken language and three written. Hebrew, called "the holy tongue" (loshoun koudesh), was used for prayer, rabbinic responsa, exegesis, kabbalistic writing, and scholarly and business communication among the elite. Aramaic, the first Jewish vernacular, was also the language of the Babylonian Talmud; knowledge of Aramaic in Ashkenaz accorded one even greater prestige than knowledge of Hebrew. Yiddish, written and spoken, was a fusion of a Romance language (*lo'ez*), Germanic dialect, Hebrew, and Aramaic. "This fusion is not to be conceived as a simple additive combination of the various components, but rather as a complex system which gradually gained autonomy from the languages that were present at the beginning of the fusion process, so that ultimately it became a language in its own right."[17]

Jean Baumgarten writes that complaints about the "forgetting" of Hebrew by traditional Jews appear around 1500 in Poland and around 1600 in documents from Bohemia and Germany, ostensibly because the German elementary school teachers came from Poland. I return to the first question: what does it mean for a society to forget its core text, its Torah, even though it is read weekly in the synagogue and studied daily by members of all classes? Despite almost universal literacy, ordinary Jews were excluded from intellectual life. Teachers were ignorant; Hebrew grammar was taught inductively, and pedagogy emphasized repetition and memorization. Only a very small percentage of Jewish men continued studying after their bar mitzvah, leading to the creation of a Jewish intellectual aristocracy and the "professionalization of knowledge." Those who did continue learning full-time studied the Talmud and neglected the Bible.

With modernization and the printing press came the technology to combat the ignorance of the masses. Old Yiddish literature arose between the fourteenth and sixteenth centuries, with the earliest written Yiddish work dated 1272. In the sixteenth century, Yiddish authors criticized the poor methods of education and sought to repair the rift. The earliest books were translations of selections of the Hebrew Bible used in liturgy (the Pentateuch; the Haftarot, or readings from Prophets for Sabbaths; the Five Scrolls; and the Psalms, which were well known because they were sprinkled throughout daily prayers). The printing of religious texts in the vernacular was both tolerated and prohibited: tolerated as a "palliative for the uneducated and a stopgap against the misunderstanding of the divine word";[18] prohibited because this risked tampering with the divine word, opening the door to distortions, and challenging the hegemony of rabbinical authorities to elucidate Torah. But popular demand for translations was so great that the authorities could not oppose them. By the sixteenth century, Baumgarten writes, this "space" within Jewish culture had been "conceded" to new genres of writing for the uneducated Jew. In 1543 and 1544, in Konstanz and Augsburg respectively, two translations with similar vocabulary were published, both by Jews who converted to Christianity, "so that students can learn without a magid, by oneself at home in the evening." The translation tradition of Old Yiddish was born.

Since Ashkenazi Jews continued to observe the rabbinic bans on independent translations of the Torah, they developed two printed genres of translation that evaded those prohibitions, and cleverly replicated the oral, experiential milieu in which translation had always taken place. The first genre, referred to as a word list, glossary, or concordance, took a "word for word" approach. (This method originated with Aquila, a Greek convert to Judaism who produced a Greek Bible to displace the Septuagint after its adoption by the Christian Church.) I noted that in primary education, in the *heder*, the Hebrew words or phrases were read aloud and explained by way of fixed Yiddish terms. The formulaic effect can be likened to Google Translate: because the semantic unit was often not a complete verse, but a word or phrase, these translations followed Hebrew word order rather than proper Yiddish syntax.[19] Scholars point to the awkward results of this technique, such as the "double subject" of verbs. Hebrew verbs include the pronomial subject as part of the word itself. Yiddish translators retained the pronoun even in cases where a substantive subject followed. Aptroot gives the example whereby *v'yavdel Elokim*, "and God separated," would be translated as "and *he* separated *God*" (*und er schied Got*). Another example: Hebrew adjectives follow nouns and repeat the definite article when there is one. Old Yiddish translators preserved these Hebraic traits, translating the Hebrew *ha-taninim ha-gedolim* (the large fish) as "the fish the large" (*di visch di grossen*).[20] The most famous of these glossaries, also the very first known printed book in Yiddish, is the *Sefer Mirkevet Hamishneh* (Cracow 1534); its title "the second chariot" alludes to the chariot in which Joseph rode when he rose to be second to the King of Egypt (Gen 41: 43). By implication, two chariots, Hebrew and Yiddish, could convey one to the Torah.[21] The book included 13,000 entries. Each page contains three columns, with the biblical word in Hebrew square font, reference to the sources, and the Yiddish terms in a semicursive font called *vaybertaytsh* (women's Yiddish). In the preface, the author laments that young boys confuse masculine and feminine, second person and third, singular and plural, as they have no knowledge of grammar.[22] He writes that his "little book" will enable anyone to "translate every word correctly and grammatically . . . [and] study the twenty-four books of the Bible as a whole, with a Yiddish translation of every word," and he envisions three scenarios: a father lives alone with no one to teach his son; a person who knows only Yiddish; one who has no time to teach his son, but has a wife or daughter who can read only Yiddish, who with the help of this volume, would manage to teach the boy to translate the entire Bible.[23] The second genre of Old Yiddish translation was more popular: so-called narrative Bibles, "works of homiletic prose" which included *tsusatz* or *oysred* or *oysredenish*.[24] Here, Hebrew verses and their Yiddish renderings were followed by "a paraphrased exposition of an array of additional explanations drawn from various sources, primarily Rashi."[25] Selected verses were interwoven with homilies, fables, midrashim, and traditional commentaries. Among such works, which included *Sefer shir-hashirim, Seyfer ha-magid, Seyfer Magishey Minha,* and *Khumesh mit ivri-taytsh* (1840s) the most famous was the *Tsene-Rene,* known as the "Yiddish women's Bible," which went on to become the most printed book in the Yiddish language, with over three hundred printings.

Both of these genres were acceptable, because they precluded the impression of a stand-alone Torah in a language other than Hebrew, and they preserved the link between the translated Scripture and the living milieux of teaching and learning. The first type, the word lists or glossaries, replicates the back and forth of Hebrew and Yiddish, teacher and student. The second type, the narrative Bibles designed for use where no teacher is present, integrates the teacher's voice and the supplementary sources that a preacher or teacher would have added to fill in the gaps in meaning and bring the text to life. Another way to look at it is that the first genre privileged individual words over sense; the second, sense at the expense of words. Neither presumed to bring both together. I believe this is what Leibowitz means when she writes that the basic premise of the premodern tradition of Bible translation was that the Torah is *not* a comprehensible text, and any translation had to be just as incomprehensible as the original. A word list made less sense than the original Hebrew; a paraphrase made more sense than the original; neither would give the impression of equivalence between the two.

The two medieval approaches to translation also parallel the two famous opposing hermeneutic stances, those of Rabbi Akiva and Rabbi Ishmael. Rabbi Akiva interpreted every single word in the Torah, even the direct object particle *et*. Rabbi Ishmael believed that "Torah spoke in human language," which was a way to justify idiomatic renderings that strayed from Hebrew syntax and individual words. This latter approach to the language of Torah gave rise to the concept of the exegetical translation in the first place, and also to Saadia Gaon's Arabic translation in the ninth century. Saadia called his translation *Tafsir*, meaning exegesis (usually of the Qur'an), rather than "*tarjamam*."[26] Again, underlying these two interpretive methods is the undesirability, or futility, of any method that claims to do justice to both language and sense—because only a second Torah could do such a thing.

A few points are essential for distinguishing premodern from modern Bibles. In stark contrast to the prefaces of the modern translations, the Old Yiddish paratexts—prefaces and title pages—conceal or downplay the complicated challenges the translators faced.[27] "The only issues on which some authors insist concern the use of popular literature and the obligation to pass on the tradition."[28] Second: religious literature in Yiddish translation was usually justified for girls, women, and "men who were like women." In Cremona in 1560, a translator addressed his work to "women who will no longer waste their time with other Yiddish books that are foolishness. They will be worthy to have children lovingly who will study holy books other than *khumesh teutsch*."[29] The scholar and translator Elijah Levita, in his preface to his Yiddish translation of Psalms (Venice 1545), directed the book "for pious and devout women and householders who did not have time to study in their youth."[30] Such phrases used to designate the readership, above all "women and uneducated men," have been interrogated by Yiddish scholars Chava Weissler, Naomi Seidman (quoting Chone Shmeruk), and Shlomo Berger. As Berger notes, "Indeed, it is now generally accepted that, in addition to writing intentionally for women, addressing them was also a smokescreen authors and publishers used to justify writing in Yiddish. Hebrew was considered the language in which men read, Yiddish the women's vernacular."[31] In reality, scholarly literature was in Hebrew, popular literature in Yiddish. But as many title pages reveal, this division was already in flux—a fact of which the modern German translators were keenly aware. The Bibles I discuss in upcoming chapters used a different set of codes and smokescreens to indicate whether they were designed for a popular or scholarly readership, for men or women or both. Third: the Yiddish translation tradition was very conservative in terms of vocabulary, method, and syntax. Yiddish authors of glossaries typically claimed that they learned the vocabulary from their teachers, and that they were producing these works for the instruction of children—two inviolable credentials. The methods were, in fact, consistent: later translators largely borrowed from earlier ones with minor alterations. Aptroot speaks of a canonical language of translation, an archaic vocabulary used in schools and vernacular works, as well as in rabbinical responsa, that remained fixed, even as the language evolved. Dictionaries and concordances for teachers helped to establish this standard lexicon of *humesh taytsh* (in German, "*Bibelübersetzungssprache*"), which led in turn to the "stabilization" and "standardization" of a literary Yiddish.[32] The fixed vocabulary used in these translations created the ideal conditions for an authoritative linguistic tradition, which has been of tremendous value for linguists and historians. Erika Timm mines this corpus of texts to understand how Yiddish words and phrases migrated into German Bibles and into the German language as such. In a series of fascinating lexical comparisons among Jewish and Christian Bibles in medieval Germany, Timm points out that Luther might have consulted these Yiddish texts when producing his translation of the Old Testament, but in most cases, he broke with Yiddish vocabulary and drew instead from the Latin Vulgate.

These points substantiate Jean Baumgarten's call for a "comparativist perspective" on the emergence of Old Yiddish Bibles. Baumgarten demonstrates that in many respects, the development of vernacular literature in sixteenth-century Europe, the steps taken to transmit the biblical text to the masses, and the ambivalence towards vernacular Bibles were the same in Jewish and Christian societies. The facts speak most loudly: "a number of the sixteenth-century Yiddish Bibles were printed in several of the great European publishing centres where the Reformation had triumphed and thus where a tradition of edifying books, liturgical booklets, and devotional texts developed, for example Augsburg, Constance, Basel, and Zurich."[33] Within German-speaking lands, there were 430 partial or complete editions of the Luther Bible produced between 1522 and 1546. In this same period, a vast and diverse corpus of Yiddish texts related to the Bible were printed and distributed to Jewish communities in Europe. It is not just the numbers that line up, but also the "meaning" of translation in both societies. Baumgarten concludes:

> With respect to the issue of the progressive intrusion of the vernacular into the domain of knowledge, Jews were confronted with questions that were often identical to those faced by their Christian neighbours. They worked out strategies of transmission which, while they responded to the internal needs of Jewish society and were consistent with the continuity of the Hebrew tradition, nonetheless had an obvious affinity with the models of neighbouring cultures, especially in the German-speaking lands.[34]

Cross-cultural affinities continued to shape the forms and methods of translation in the modern period, as they did at the close of the premodern phase. The translations of Martin Luther (New Testament, 1522; Old and New Testaments and Apocrypha, 1534) made the Bible into a German book. Luther not only invented the German religion, but also the German literary idiom.[35] Luther was an extremely important figure for German Jewish translators, above all in the first and fourth waves; but in Christian society, it was rejection of Luther's idiom that exemplified the modern translations. In 1800, Germany celebrated the Reformation Jubilee. Luther was honored as the exemplary religious translator, credited with infusing and enriching the national language; yet Christian scholars had long since revised and replaced Luther's translation. Not only had the language changed. Many developments in religious society, including Pietism, source criticism, and Enlightenment, rendered Luther's priorities of *sola scriptura* and a natural German idiom obsolete. The eighteenth century witnessed the "death of Scripture" and the concomitant rise of the academic and cultural Bible.[36] Most pertinent in this context is that religion renewed itself by absorbing culture as such—a negotiation that continues in the present. "The integration of religion and culture was the key to larger renewal of religion that preoccupied so many German figures in the late 18th and early 19th centuries."[37] The translated Bible was not so much "the literal word of God" as it was "divinely inspired culture," "a cultural treasure chest containing poetry, lessons, stories, ideas, ethics, outlooks, attitudes and so on."[38] With the awareness that the content of the Bible draws from many sources, the Bible became a work that could tolerate various translations and types of commentary, suitable for different audiences. Sheehan groups a number of different forms under the archetype of "the Enlightenment Bible." A question I address in the coming pages is the extent to which the Jewish *Haskalah* Bible resembles the Christian Enlightenment Bible.

THE MODERN PROJECT: RESTORING TORAH TO THE HEBREW BIBLE

In *The Hebrew Bible Reborn*, Yaakov Shavit and Mordechai Eran argue that the turn to the Bible in the eighteenth century was not a return to the ancient, but rather a turn to something modern: "neo-Orthodox Jews and liberal Jews shared the belief that the Bible was a spiritual-cultural asset common to Jews and to (Protestant) Germans."[39] The translation revolution began when new forms of translation, and new motives for translation, having become popular in Christian society, started to appeal to Jews. The phenomenon was intensified within Germany, a society whose foremost intellectuals and poets not only practiced and theorized about translation, but also valued translation philosophically, as a cultural practice that since Luther had been constitutive of language and national identity. Moreover, German Jews needed a platform from which to break with their Ashkenazi origins and still remain traditional Jews. In the age of emancipation, German-speaking Jewry "gradually unhinged itself from the house of Ashkenazic Judaism"; translation of the Hebrew Bible played an important role in this unhinging.[40]

As we shall see, translators in the seventeenth and eighteenth centuries emphasized one factor above all as the impetus for a new approach: the inadequacies of the Old Yiddish Bibles.

In point of fact, there were direct and unspoken continuities, despite the linguistic and stylistic differences, with Old Yiddish Bibles such as the *Tsene-Rene*. Chava Turniansky refers to this type of Yiddish Bible as an "open source," which selected verses and followed them with stories and homilies that related to them in an associative manner. Tremendous creativity and intellectual rigor went into the production of such a book; "the door was open to many possibilities of choices of verses, to expand or contract a topic, to choose among the commentaries and draw whatever conclusions."[41] In fact, this is exactly what Mendelssohn, Philippson, and Hirsch accomplished in their commentaries. The similarity extends from the fact that the educational mission of the medieval translators remained in force in the modern period—even when the "contents" of that education had changed dramatically. Above all, the modern translators—Mendelssohn, Zunz, Hirsch, Buber, Rosenzweig, Pappenheim—continued to operate within a religious framework. What this meant was that they continued to care more about Torah than about the Bible. Translation was a way to provide access to the Torah within the Bible, where Torah referred to the core stories, ideas, values, and historical narrative to which the translators strove to provide access in their own generation. It was their understanding of Torah that shaped the form and substance of the translation. They went further than earlier translators to show that translation was not only remedial, but positively beneficial, containing further uses and advantages that were strictly speaking extrinsic to Torah or even Judaism.

The tension facing the religious translator in every age had to do with making sure that the Bible translation remained subordinate to the Torah, or at the very least, that the two remained in careful balance. This was especially important once the two-to-one ratio of Torah to targum gave way to a new prototype that demanded a one-to-one correspondence of Hebrew to German. This rivalry is the subtext of one of the first midrashim on Genesis 1:1, also quoted in the *Tsene-Rene*, that supplies an apt starting point for the history of German Jewish Bible translation. The midrash asks why, for the first word of Hebrew Scripture, *Bereshit* (in the beginning), God chose a word beginning with the second letter of the Hebrew alphabet, the *bet*. Was this not an offense against the *alef*—the very first letter of the Hebrew alphabet? To appease the *alef*, God assigns that letter a different honor: it will inaugurate *Anokhi*, the first word of the Ten Commandments.[42] Margarete Susman observed that the little fable stands in for a serious debate over what was more important: the needs of the created world, or the Torah. One answer uses a prooftext from the book of Proverbs to establish that, in fact, Torah has priority over Creation, thereby affirming the primacy of the *alef* over the *bet*. The created world, including the Bible beginning with *bet*, must remain subordinate to the revealed Torah within.

In the modern age of Jewish translation, we see the *bet*—bearer of the created world, of history, writing, and interpretation—strive to regain the upper hand.

The revolutionary move of the Haskalah, and really of the first three waves of translation, was to demonstrate that the sense of Torah resided in the language of Torah, and that, moreover, both could be understood and illuminated by grammar and other forms of knowledge external to the Torah proper. Premodern translations explained to the uneducated reader what the Bible said and why it was important and filtered out that which was unimportant. Modern translations went further by showing the reader *how* the Bible means, above all by explaining (*be'ur*) the language of the text and language as such. Once the meaning of Torah became located within the language of the Bible, the translator assumed a new authority as author, language expert, and arbiter of sense. In order to secure legitimacy, translators had to shift the "discursive affiliations" of their enterprise (in Rita Copeland's phrase), and they began to associate the new practice with the venerated discourses of transmission and hermeneutics.[43] By this logic, the translators turned not to prior translators for legitimacy, but instead, invoked Moses, the scribes, and the rabbis.

Premodern Jewish translators had boasted that they were repeating the vocabulary of their teachers.[44] But the modern Jewish translator was an author; he or she had to present his or her project as an improvement over past ones and unique in some important respect. Put most simply, the modern translators faced inordinate pressure to frame their contributions as both new and old. The translated Torah was the same in every respect; but a new translation into German was a historical necessity. A break with the past was justified as a corrective or remedy of some kind, and above all, in light of contemporary conditions; Martin Buber argued vociferously that a new Bible was needed for "people today" (1926), but all the translators expressed that sentiment in one form or another.[45] But they also knew that their authority, their legitimacy, hinged upon stressing continuity between what they were doing and the Jewish past. The translations were conceived within the vibrant and powerful tradition of translating the Torah going back to Ezra, the Greek Septuagint, and the Aramaic targumim. For centuries, translation was an integral part of every Jew's most important commandment of "teaching the Torah to one's children" and the religious mission of teaching and transmitting sacred scripture to the community, in the confines of the synagogue and beyond. This tradition was, they believed, continuous from ancient to modern times; they insisted that there was no fundamental break. Establishing their role as the next link in that chain was the ultimate litmus test of the Jewish Bible translator's authority. The translators portrayed the tradition as a kind of torch relay, where the Scripture is passed into their hands for them to protect and carry a short distance in their day and age. The fear was that the torch relay was actually more like a children's game of telephone, where the message whispered into your ear changes just a little bit with each new transmission.

The stakes remained very high for German Jews translating the Hebrew Bible. One had to keep one eye on Jewish readers while looking over one's shoulder at past translators and at the Bibles of Christian counterparts. Their prefaces testify to these competing motives, even as their rhetoric exaggerated one goal alone: to make the Torah accessible to a new generation.

A favorite design element of early Jewish religious texts was a frontispiece featuring Moses and Aaron gracing the portico of the Temple.[46] The German Jewish translator was at once the prophet-lawgiver Moses, speaking face to face with God, and the priest-interpreter Aaron, who did whatever was necessary to sustain the community, even enable idolatry. She was also David the Psalmist, whose words of Torah provided endless delight. The German Jewish translated Bible was a new Ten Commandments, a new tabernacle, a new golden calf, a new song, and a book of the world, all in one.

CHAPTER ONE

The First Wave: Jewish Enlightenment Bibles in Yiddish and German

WORKS DISCUSSED

Jekuthiel ben Isaac Blitz. *Torah Nevi'im u'Khtuvim: Bilshon Ashkenaz* (Bible: in the Yiddish language). Amsterdam: Uri Phoebus Ben-Aharon Halevi, 1678.

Joseph ben Alexander Witzenhausen. *Torah Nevi'im u'Khtuvim* (Bible). Amsterdam: Joseph Athias, 1679.

Moses Mendelssohn. *Sefer Netivot HaShalom . . . im Targum Ashkenazi* (The book of the paths of peace, including the Five Books of Moses with Scribal Corrections and German translation). Berlin: George Friedrich Starcke, 1783.

The Bible is an antique Volume—
Written by faded men
. . .
Had but the Tale a warbling Teller—
All the Boys would come—
Orpheus' Sermon captivated—
It did not condemn—
—Emily Dickinson

INTRODUCTION: TRANSLATION REVOLUTION

The main innovation of the first wave of modern Bible translation is precisely that which we take for granted when we pick up a translated book: a one-to-one rendering of a source text in stylistically and syntactically correct prose. The new translations aspired to be an improvement over the old in every respect, and improvement was also what they promised the reader. These translators aspired to "make the crooked straight" through clearly formatted pages and "clear, correct, and beautiful" language.[1] Their priority was to convey the plain sense of Torah, unmediated *pshat,* in a way that also did justice to the form and structure of the target language. They insisted that their approach was consonant with the Jewish exegetical tradition; they concealed the extent to which they had been influenced by Christian translations and other trends that had little to do with Judaism. They had one further aspiration: to become the Bible's "warbling Teller," in Emily Dickinson's phrase, or in the words of Jehuda Halevi, "a harp to the songs" of Scripture: to enhance the Bible through translation. In short, translation in the Haskalah rose to the status of an art form. This was the groundwork, the genetic makeup, of the three Bible translations of the first wave: the two Yiddish Bibles published in Amsterdam, and Mendelssohn's Pentateuch, commonly known as the *Be'ur*.

The new approach to translation was motivated by developments internal and external to Jewish society, by religious needs and cultural desiderata. If one were to pinpoint the central cause, it would be dissatisfaction with extant translations which had become linguistically anachronistic. Aptroot summarizes the view of the Amsterdam translators and their publishers:

> The *taytsh* vocabulary had become ossified. Many words which were part of the special *taytsh* vocabulary had become not only archaic, but incomprehensible. Moreover, the teachers in primary education, the *melamdim*, and the translators of the earlier printed translations of parts of the Old Testament did not always understand the Hebrew and thus made many mistakes. Blitz and Witzenhausen proposed to produce translations which would not suffer from these shortcomings.[2]

This critique re-emerged one hundred years hence in the promotional material for Mendelssohn's *Be'ur*.

> Because even if the teacher understands the literal meaning of the verse, he cannot explain it to his pupil, because he lacks the eloquence to make the thoughts of his heart pleasing to the pupil's ear. . . . Because whenever one explains something to another, both have to know a language thoroughly and use it to express the same things. But in these regions, our language is mixed in with the languages of other peoples, and what is more, there are words and idioms that the common people invented which are repulsive—mindless words.[3]

Both generations of translators believed they were living in a neo-Babelian world, and both cited the oldest available rationale for a new and improved translation: education. But there was more to the revolution. They sought to advance Jewish civilization, to make Jewish Bibles look more like Christian Bibles, and to define the persona of the modern Jewish translator.

Scholars of Mendelssohn's Pentateuch translation and commentary often focus on the relevance of these efforts to his philosophy and aesthetic thought, and to the Enlightenment, Christian Bible scholarship, rabbinic exegesis, and language politics.[4] In lieu of the long-held myth that Mendelssohn "created" German Jewry, they situate Mendelssohn within intellectual, religious, and aesthetic trends that preceded him.[5] What has not changed is the fundamental identification of Mendelssohn with the *Be'ur*, and of the *Be'ur* with the Haskalah. But it seems to me that, with the exception of Werner Weinberg and David Sorkin, scholars have not paid adequate attention to Mendelssohn's art of translation, especially when juxtaposed with the relevant German and Judeo-German translations.[6] Beginning in the 1750s, Mendelssohn was translating philosophical texts from French, English, Greek, and Hebrew into German. Comments reveal that he viewed translation as a laborious task; that he was exceedingly attuned to the literary style; and that he understood his task as capturing or "clothing" the original style in German garb. His translations of Hebrew poetry certainly shaped his technique. No less influential were his Yiddish and Christian predecessors: Blitz and Witzenhausen, Martin Luther, Johann David Michaelis, and Johann Lorenz Schmidt all illuminate Mendelssohn's poetics. What distinguishes these first-wave translations is their literary texture. It was a priority elaborated in prefaces and other paratextual elements, and in Mendelssohn's case, in his expansive commentary (the *Be'ur* proper): a rich composite of grammar, literary criticism, working notes, and translation history. Mendelssohn aspired to turn the Jewish Bible into a great book of the world. He approached the Bible as a work of literature and Hebrew as a literary language, favoring above all the poetic passages.

In each part of this study, I compare translations that shared a fundamental agenda, despite their conspicuous differences. In the first wave, two differences have been definitive: the languages of the translations, Yiddish versus German, and the usual periodization of the Haskalah.[7] On the basis of language, the Yiddish Bibles belong in the previous wave. With regard to periodization, one cannot deny that the century between the 1670s and the 1780s was a watershed period for European Jewry, or that Mendelssohn's resources and milieu in Berlin were dramatically different from those in the seventeenth-century Dutch Republic. Yet, as Mendelssohn's Hebrew typeface demonstrates, the Haskalah was a time of intense transition, linguistic and otherwise. In fact, for most of the eighteenth century and even into the nineteenth, there was only one Hebrew phrase—*targum ashkenazi*—to designate both a Yiddish and a German translation. I place these Yiddish and German translations side by side to show that translation did more than promote German at the expense of Yiddish; it sought to educate Jewish readers about how language means, in the Bible and beyond. The Amsterdam Yiddish Bibles provided the blueprint for what was to come, as scholars of Old Yiddish have long known. They are the prehistory of the Jewish Bibles in German, but also a part of that history. A comparison of their prefaces, techniques, and sample verses reveals that it took three Bibles to launch a translation revolution

FIRST STEPS TO CULTURE: TITLE PAGES OF BLITZ AND WITZENHAUSEN BIBLES

Everything about their physical appearance, and above all their ornamental title pages, lent the Bibles printed by Uri Phoebus (with the translation by Jekuthiel Blitz, 1678) and Joseph Athias (with the translation of Joseph Witzenhausen, 1679) an aura of beauty and prominence. Old Yiddish Bibles had often incorporated small wood-engraved illustrations in their pages, but no prior translation had included artwork of this kind.[8] These title pages provided the visual entry point into a whole new kind of Bible, and they shall serve as our gateway to the story of the translation revolution.

In the German-speaking world, it had become customary to adorn theological works with ornamental title pages even before the Protestant Reformation. This tradition peaked with the Luther Bibles in the sixteenth century and continued well into the nineteenth.[9] Such pages included a predictable array of biblical characters, typological motifs, and architectural imagery. Early Haskalah Bibles followed suit. Richard Cohen explains: "Jewish and Christian publishers were following local trends in publishing that had witnessed the economic value in publishing illustrated popular books since the late fifteenth century."[10] Illustrated books were expensive, and were marketed to a financially successful segment within Jewish society that also had the good taste to appreciate the publishers' efforts. The increasing use of illumination techniques in books that were *not* required for Jewish learning—above all, in the Passover Haggadah—served as a "bridge between an emerging appreciation of objects of art, their collection, and a sense of self-elitism in Jewish society."[11] Eventually, even the Hebrew Bible became reconfigured as an *objet d'art*, appealing to an emergent social status and to "elitism in book ownership."[12]

There was no precedent for printing a translated Bible in folio format and with such extravagant design. As Aptroot explains, the Bibles produced by Phoebus and Athias stood out "at first sight . . . from all previous books in Yiddish."

> The insertion of engraved title pages is highly unusual in Yiddish prints; I know of no other examples in the period. Copper engravings were costly and intaglio plates could not be printed with the same presses as were used for type and woodcuts, which have raised surfaces. Only very few leading printing houses had rolling presses for the printing of engravings but they were usually printed by specialist plate printers. This all added to the cost of the books. Such plates were therefore not often used (Gaskell 1985: 156–158). The presence of engraved title pages in the Amsterdam Yiddish Bibles serves to demonstrate that the books were printed with the idea that they were important works, not second class popular books.[13]

The title page of Uri Phoebus and Jekuthiel Blitz's *Torah Nevi'im u'Khetuvim* of 1678 was designed by a Jewish convert from Protestantism, Abraham bar Jacob (fig. 1.1). Moses and Aaron flank the opening of the temple, whose centerpiece is the Holy of Holies with its altar and cherubim. The pairing of Moses and Aaron became iconic in Jewish print history. Perhaps Abraham bar Jacob was inspired by the title page of the 1648 Dutch translation of the Luther Bible, which featured Moses on the left, Jesus on the right, and a round framed portrait of Luther in the center below.[14] As Falk Wiesemann phrases it, Moses and Aaron represent the two "pillars" of the edifice of biblical religion: the law (tablets and staff) and the sacrificial cult.[15] At the same time, many of the motifs surrounding this sacred space come from Western secular art—fluted columns, ivy wreaths, thick theatrical curtains crowning the image, and the angel peering gargoyle-like from the altar.

Abraham bar Jacob's title page illustration, with its pairing of Moses and Aaron, had a rich afterlife beyond the Blitz Bible. It became iconic after it was reused as the background to the title page of the famous Amsterdam Haggadah (1695).[16] For that Haggadah, he also borrowed the copper engravings from *Icones Biblicae* (Basel, 1625), the author of which was the most famous German illustrator of the seventeenth century, Mathaeus Merian (1593–1650); for the first time, a copper engraving, already widely used in Christian books, was used in a Haggadah. Moses and Aaron also reappear (albeit on opposite sides) on the title page to the famous Sulzbach Haggadah (1755).[17] On other such title pages, Moses and Aaron might be joined by David and Solomon (see the title page, also by Abraham bar Jacob, for the 1698 book *Shnei luchot habrit* [*Two Tables of the Covenant*], published by Joseph Athias's son Immanuel Athias). A Christian variation of the image shows a threesome, with David kneeling in the center.

Fig. 1.1. Blitz Bible, title page (1678). Judaica Collection, Goethe University, Frankfurt am Main. Photograph: University of Frankfurt Library.

The title page of the second (Athias/Witzenhausen) Bible depicts a more complex vertical tryptich featuring Moses and David, the exemplary biblical poet (fig. 1.2). Moses points his rod toward the scenario above, where a miniature Moses is receiving the tablets at Sinai. David plays his harp, also peering upward. The columns and curtains reappear, but this time, curtains are held up by two putti holding olive branches—perhaps an allusion to the prophecy of Zachariah. Most striking is the replacement of Bar Jacob's altar with the imposing seal of the Dutch Republic with the Latin motto, *Concordia res parvae crescunt*, squarely in the center. This seal had also appeared on the Athias's *Biblia Hebraica* (1661 and 1667), a Hebrew Bible for non-Jews edited by the Hebrew professor Johannes Leusden. But it first originated on the title page of the Dutch States Bible of 1637, with the corresponding Dutch phrase, *Eendracht maeckt Macht*.[18] There was no mistaking the meaning of a lion holding seven arrows that appears on the Witzenhausen title page, but in light of the inclusion of David, the lion may have doubled as an emblem of the Israelite tribe of Judah. The crown motif in fact connects David, the lion, and the seal as a whole. Both upper and lower segments displayed scenes that had already appeared on other Athias books. In the lower panel, the biblical Joseph reunites with his father and brothers (Genesis 46) after a twenty-year sojourn in Egypt, with Egyptian couriers to the left encountering Joseph's father and brothers on the right. These embracing figures were copied from Merian's engraving *Jacob's Reconciliation with Esau*, and the horse-drawn wagon came from another Merian scene, *Jesebel's Death* (II Kings 9:1–37). The inclusion of this scenario is interpreted as a covert allusion to Athias's own father, who had died in the Inquisition in Cordoba in 1665. Might the reunion scene not also encode an allegory of the power of translation in a new age?

To summarize: the narrative of the triptych leads the eye from divinely revealed law, received with fear and trembling; to the nation—carefully balanced by Mosaic law and instruction on the left, Davidic culture/song and royalty on the right, and the Dutch Republic, the political guarantor, front and center; to a scene of reconciliation below. The embrace, an apt figure for the title page as a whole, conveys the same hopeful message as the title of Mendelssohn's translation one century later, *The Book of the Paths of Peace*.

The story of these two title pages, and the small but meaningful differences between them, gives pictorial evidence of a new tradition in formation. We will see the same types of minor differences in the actual translations of biblical verses contained inside these volumes, and also when we contrast Blitz's and Witzenhausen's choices with those of Mendelssohn and his Christian counterparts. Richard Cohen emphasizes that what is striking

Fig. 1.2. Witzenhausen Bible, title page (1679). Judaica Collection, Goethe University, Frankfurt am Main. Photograph: University of Frankfurt Library.

about illustrations in Jewish books of this period is precisely the "lack of innovation" and "redundancy in their iconography."[19] Redundancy guaranteed marketability; it identified these select works as part of a trend. The Luther Bible and the Dutch States Bible had permanently changed people's expectations of what a vernacular Bible looked like and how it sounded. Would the trend also take off among traditional Ashkenazi Jews? These two Yiddish Bibles, with their fine paper, ornate title pages, and iconic-innovative imagery, exuded that ambition. Uri Phoebus, Joseph Athias, and their translators did more than adapt a Christian prototype for a Jewish readership. They aspired to provide the Jewish nation with what Moses Mendelssohn, one hundred years later, would call "the first step toward culture"—a religious and aesthetic project.

THE STORY OF THE BLITZ AND WITZENHAUSEN BIBLES

In the city of Amsterdam, a thriving center of Jewish life and the heart of Hebrew and Yiddish book production, 318 Jewish printers were in operation between 1626 and 1732. All order of religious books—Talmud, Hebrew Bible (Tanach), and the beloved women's Bible, the *Tsene-Rene*—were in high demand, not only for the local community but for Yiddish-speaking Jews across Western and Eastern Europe. Because of the wide freedom enjoyed by Dutch Jews to write and publish, authors obtained rabbinic approbations or endorsements (Hebrew *haskamot*, Yiddish *haskomes*) to protect their words and safeguard the market; Portuguese (Sephardic) Jews sought *haskamot* from their authorities. So desirable was the imprimatur "printed in (*be-*) Amsterdam" that Jewish printers in other countries invented the phrase "printed in the manner of (*ke-*) Amsterdam," hoping that readers would not notice the subterfuge.[20] A book published in Poland in 1763 boasts of the use of "AMSTERDAM fonts," printing the actual city of publication in tiny font.[21] When Moses Mendelssohn sought a publisher for the prospectus for his Bible translation in the 1770s, he set his eyes on a famous printer in Amsterdam. A further factor was the Sephardic presence in Amsterdam.

> The example of Sephardic education in Amsterdam, in which translations the Old Testament were used, set an example for Ashkenazic education. Publishers of both Amsterdam Yiddish Bibles had close ties with the Sephardic community. Athias, who hailed from Spain, was a Sephardic Jew himself. Uri Faybush [Phoebus] was an honorary member of the Sephardic community because his father and grandfather had served there.[22]

In seventeenth-century Amsterdam (no less than in nineteenth-century Germany) Ashkenazi Jews adopted Sephardic ways when inventing new cultural forms.

It was in this context that, one hundred years before Mendelssohn's initiative, two different print shops published the first two complete translations of the Hebrew Bible into Yiddish.[23] The overarching ambition of both Yiddish Bibles was to "reform" the *taytsh* tradition inside and out. In each case, a full print run of 6,000 Bibles was produced, intended for sale above all to Polish Jews in Central and Eastern Europe. The printers not only competed for the same market, but one actually tried to shut down the other by stealing his proofreader, his funding, and ultimately, a large chunk of the Pentateuch translation, comprising a core section of 53 ½ chapters (Exodus 21:2 through Numbers 7:45). In an article that reads like a detective story, Yiddish scholar Erika Timm explains that this was not typical plagiarism; rather, sixteen folios that had been printed in one press were physically appropriated and transplanted into the second Bible, in a more or less legal manner. The "saga" of these two translations came to light only in the 1980s through the meticulous research of Erika Timm and Marion Aptroot, and I will summarize their accounts and insights.[24]

Printer One was Uri Phoebus ben Aharon Halevi (1625–1715). A native of Amsterdam, Phoebus was a well-known Ashkenazi publisher who also published many editions of the *Tsene-Rene* (1669). He worked as a printer from 1658 to 1689 and became a member (under the name Phylips Levi) of the city's guild of booksellers, printers, and bookbinders. In the 1680s, Phoebus's business activities became focused increasingly on Eastern Europe and especially Poland. With the help of a Christian financial backer, he undertook to print a complete Yiddish Bible for the Polish market. He obtained *haskomes* from the Council of the Four Lands, the central governing body of Polish Jews, which authorized Jekuthiel Blitz, a rabbi from Wittmund, Germany, as the translator, and Joseph Witzenhausen, from Hessen, Germany, as the proofreader. Witzenhausen was a well-known Hebrew typesetter and a poet, author of the popular epic poetic adaptation *A Fine Tale of King Arthur's Court* (1671).[25]

With the outbreak of the Dutch War (1672–78), Uri Phoebus went broke, and work on the translation ceased. Eventually, Phoebus found a new Christian backer. At this point, he hired a new proofreader, Joseph Athias, a Spanish-born rabbi and expert in Bible printing. As the official proofreader, Athias kept the folios in his possession. However, Athias became dissatisfied with Blitz's translation. This led to the suspension of payments and a break with the project in February 1676, at the point of Exodus chapter 21. After this break, Joseph Athias "considered himself, jointly with [Christian financier] van Halmael, as the rightful owner of the more than 50,000 sheets [= more than 200,000 pages]."[26] He took those folios to the Dutch authorities a few weeks thereafter, and, using them as evidence that he was far along in "his" translation, was able to obtain a fifteen-year privilege from the Dutch authorities, authorizing him to print a "new" Bible translation. He hired Joseph Witzenhausen, the original proofreader, away from Phoebus's project to complete the translating. Although Uri Phoebus contested Joseph Athias's privilege through litigation, it was not revoked. Meanwhile, in 1676, with further assistance from Christians, Uri Phoebus was able to resume printing Blitz's translation; his complete Bible (the Pentateuch was the last part printed) appeared in 1678. Joseph Athias's version—a composite of stolen folios translated by Blitz, plus Witzenhausen's new translations—was published the following year in 1679. Both Bibles can be downloaded in their entirety.[27]

The overarching ambition of both Yiddish Bibles was to "reform" the *taytsh* tradition, inside and out; to design an utterly new type of Jewish Bible translation. The first important innovation was that these Bibles were translations of the complete Tanach.

> This is without precedent in Yiddish literature and an important innovation in Ashkenazic culture in general. By not restricting the translation to the Pentateuch, the Scrolls, and the texts from the Prophets which are read in synagogue, Blitz and Witzenhausen depart from the path of the traditional Yiddish Bible translation which had followed the study of the Bible in *kheyder* [*heder*] and adhered to the methods set by the traditional Ashkenazic educational system.[28]

The second innovation, as Chava Turniansky elaborates, was their clear and correct language:

> [T]wo characteristics distinguished these from their predecessors: they were translations of the whole Bible, not just the sections read in synagogue; and crucially, their language was clear and comprehensible. It seems that the criticisms of rabbis and scholars of the strict word for word translations, which failed to link the words into sensible, intelligible sentences, had finally been addressed.[29]

Jerold Frakes adds: "Compared with the existing printed versions at the time, they are vastly superior in design and typography. In method they already anticipate the translations of coming centuries, for both their prefaces criticize the existing tradition of including rabbinical and Talmudic exegesis in the text itself."[30] Not only did these Bibles make history, but they boasted about doing so; formerly, one boasted mainly about reproducing the old. In addition to these novel features—complete Bible, clear language, superior design, and copper-engraved title pages—there were two others. Several pages of *haskomes*, previously reserved for Hebrew and Aramaic books, added "glory" and "unprecedented prestige."[31] Another revolutionary aspect was that the publishers and the translators relied on Christian funding and Christian translations. Developments in Christian society gave rise to the first wave of German Jewish Bibles, with regard both to the larger factors and forces that led to their production, and to the translators' models and practices: in the case of the Yiddish Bibles, the Protestant Reformation; in Mendelssohn's case, the Enlightenment Bibles.

The main impetus for Uri Phoebus's project was most likely the popularity of the Dutch States Bible (*Statenbibel, statenvertaling*), the first Dutch translation of the Old Testament done from the original Hebrew, published in 1637.[32] The Dutch Reformed Church commissioned it in 1618, and the States General, or the Parliament of the Dutch Republic, sponsored it.[33] The Dutch States Bible was a great success, which meant that there was a large market for vernacular Protestant Bibles in Amsterdam. Perhaps this is why Christians agreed to fund Uri Phoebus's project from the first. Recall that he began with one Christian partner and found a new financer in 1674 and others in 1676. By October 1676, Phoebus had to turn over his printing shop to Blaeu and Bake, along with the rights to the translation, which meant that in essence the project as a whole was turned over to Christians.[34] Interactions with Christian Bibles took still other forms. Timm notes that Blitz inserted anti-Christological comments in his translations of the Latter Prophets, and she concludes that this must have made it difficult to sell.[35] Some copies still include an insert with a statement from a rabbi declaring that those anti-Christological passages had been deleted from the entire Christian edition, even though there is no evidence of the deletion.[36] Witzenhausen's translation was later included in Otto Glüsing's *Biblia Pentapla* of 1710—an edition of five Germanic translations set in parallel format—signaling its acceptance as a classic translation of the Christian Old Testament (discussed in chapter 2).

But the Christian translations also shaped style and vocabulary, as will become clear later in this chapter. Perhaps it goes without saying that all translators steal from their predecessors, and Yiddish translators in seventeenth-century Amsterdam naturally borrowed from recent translations into Yiddish,

Dutch, and German. Blitz and Witzenhausen were not specialists in Hebrew. They did not have access to Hebrew grammars and Hebrew-Yiddish dictionaries. (Nor did they engage a Hebrew grammarian to assist them, as Mendelssohn did.) As a result, both translators, but especially Witzenhausen, drew heavily on the language of the existing Old Yiddish translations, the *taytsh* tradition, above all, for Jewish keywords, straightforward verses, and unproblematic passages. However, both Blitz and Witzenhausen could read Dutch and German, and both consulted the Luther Bible and the Dutch States Bible, as well as Low German and Dutch retranslations of those authoritative works. In their day, "no translator or publisher would wish to risk the accusation of having imitated Christian examples."[37] And yet, as I mentioned above, the fundamental premise and approach of the Amsterdam Yiddish Bibles was Lutheran. Their emphases on clear language, and on literal as opposed to the historical sense, echo Luther's priority of *sola scriptura*. They stated, as Luther had written in his famous *Circular Letter on Translating*, that biblical language should resemble the natural, spoken language of the everyday people. Luther's stylistic fluency and expressivity had enormous appeal for these Jewish translators who aspired to produce (as Luther had) an idiomatic rendering that was both clear and literary.

Timm and Aptroot go further in identifying patterns of borrowing in both of these translations. When it came to word choice, Blitz clearly wavered between the "stylistically superior" Luther and the "philologically superior" Dutch States Bible; it was well known at the time that an enormous amount of philological research had gone into the States Bible, and this fact naturally recommended it to Jewish translators. Since "the Dutch text automatically shares many literal interpretations with Jewish tradition, against Luther," these translators regarded it as more consonant with Jewish tradition, despite the fact that Dutch is linguistically farther from Yiddish than German is.[38] With regard to vocabulary, morphology, phonology, and morphosyntax, Blitz's Yiddish offers evidence of Christian influence, alongside archaic traits (i.e., Old Yiddish formulations). Aptroot uncovers evidence of copying and paraphrasing from Luther, in particular in Genesis 1, Psalm 33, and the Song of Songs. In other places, Blitz's similarity to Luther owes to his borrowing from the Dutch. Timm concludes that Blitz borrowed syntax and ideologically neutral vocabulary from the Christian Bibles, but retained most of the key words of *ivri-taytsch*.[39] Aptroot concludes her historical and linguistic analyses by noting that even as Blitz and Witzenhausen made "syntactic improvements," especially by avoiding the awkward repetition of the subject, which was a marker of the word-for-word approach, the fact that many innovations could be traced to Christian translations—that is, to Luther and adaptations of Luther—means that they cannot be said to have "significantly reform[ed] the Yiddish translation tradition."[40] What they did do, in my understanding, is exactly what Mendelssohn did, one century later: create a new prototype of Jewish translation that incorporated Christian elements to the extent possible without alienating its readership. Aptroot also concludes that Blitz's "uncritical" use of Christian sources "indicates that the mistrust of the surrounding Christian culture may not have been as great as has often been assumed."[41]

Blitz's and Witzenhausen's translations—two quite different versions that are also intricately interrelated—were commercially *unsuccessful* translations. Each had only one printing—an embarrassing fact that the publishers attempted to cover up—and the Bibles were sold mainly at auctions.[42] But they were successful in other respects. Baumgarten summarizes:

> They play[ed] a fundamental role both in moving away from the earlier versions, which were now considered obsolete, and in transforming the methods of biblical translation. In this sense, they already foreshadowed modern literary forms, such as those of the Haskalah. They also had another, albeit negative, influence: for it was in reaction to these two translations of the Bible that Moses Mendelssohn undertook his own translation into New High German. While, due to the ever expanding importance of the *Tsene-rene*, the translations by Blitz and Witzenhausen had scarcely any impact on their own era, they nonetheless proved that vernacular translation was a territory favourable to experimentation and renewal of earlier modes in the transmission of the sacred traditions.[43]

That Mendelssohn considered using them for his children testifies to the fact that they were still circulating in Germany one hundred years after publication. That he acknowledged them also testifies to their significance. Above all, his critique teaches us that they inspired him to build on their example, to improve them, to do what they did, only better. As Erika Timm told me, "Mendelssohn would have had a much harder time of it without those precedents."

FROM YIDDISH TO GERMAN: A NEW GENEALOGY

Moses Mendelssohn's critical comments about the Blitz translation are included in the lengthy Hebrew preface to his own translation titled "Light for the Path" (Or LaNetivah). The passage is often cited as evidence that Mendelssohn devalued the Yiddish language for cultural and intellectual matters, as Sorkin notes, "because of its grammatical imprecision."[44] The assumption is that if his German translation was the "first step to Culture," it was because Yiddish-language translations were not adequate to that task. I have already shown that the latter was not true in the seventeenth century, as Mendelssohn well knew. With the hindsight of one hundred years, when writing this preface, he also appreciated that Blitz's and Witzenhausen's Bibles were transitional works—revisions of the Old Yiddish translation tradition *and* early attempts at Haskalah vernacular Bibles—that had by and large not succeeded in replacing the older models. That Mendelssohn's project was analogous to that of Blitz and Witzenhausen will be demonstrated by a side-by-side analysis of sample verses and also prefaces. Perhaps the biggest surprise that emerges by the end of this chapter is that, although written in a Jewish language, the Amsterdam Yiddish Bibles were in certain ways less traditional than Mendelssohn's: they were produced for profit; they were more closely connected to Christian models of translation; and they removed commentary from the page. Keeping those Bibles in the picture teaches us that even as Mendelssohn replaced a Jewish language with a Christian one, in other ways he retraditionalized the format and appearance of the modern Jewish vernacular Bible.

But first, his comments about the Yiddish Bibles from the preface:

> The great grammarian Rabbi Elijah Bahur [Elija Levita] translated the Torah and the scrolls into Judeo-German in a painstakingly literal fashion. His translation was published in Konstanz, Switzerland [really Germany], in 5304 [1544]. Later, the books of the Bible were published in Judeo-German with Hebrew letters by the translator R. Yosel Witzenhausen in Amsterdam in 5439 [1679] and were republished in the same place in 5447 [1687].[45] Another Judeo-German translation, by the translator Rabbi Yekutiel Blitz from Wittmund, was also published in Amsterdam in 5439 [1679] with approbations and [threats of] excommunication from many eminent rabbis of that generation. Rabbi Yekutiel noted in his introduction that he had seen the Judeo-German translation of the Torah published in Konstanz, and he did much to denounce it and undermine its legitimacy, ultimately deciding that the German grammarian [Rabbi Elijah] could not have authored that translation. Admittedly, I have never seen the translation attributed to R. Elijah, for it has not spread into this land at all. However, I have seen the aforementioned translation of Rabbi Yekutiel, and I discovered that he condemns the very deficiencies that he himself exhibits. Although his intention may have been acceptable,

> which is why the sages of his generation approved of his work, his deeds were nevertheless entirely unacceptable, for he neither understood the nature of the holy language nor grasped the depth of its rhetoric. Moreover, whatever he did comprehend, he translated into a most corrupt and deformed language of stammering. The soul of the reader who knows how to speak elegantly will abhor this [translation].
>
> From then until now, no one has taken it upon himself to fix the crooked and translate the holy Torah into the language that is proper, standard, and customary in our generation.[46]

The main point, as Aptroot notes, is that Mendelssohn "placed himself in the same tradition. Like Blitz and Witzenhausen before him, he criticized earlier translations to justify his own."[47] He deconstructs Blitz's criticisim of Rabbi Elijah: "I have seen the aforementioned translation of Rabbi Yekutiel, and I discovered that he condemns the very deficiencies that he himself exhibits." Blitz was not a Hebraist. But Blitz had made the exact same criticism of the Old Yiddish Bibles, both the mechanical glossaries and the narrative Bibles, lamenting that there was no literal, clear rendering of Scripture that did justice to *leshon Ashkenaz* that could be used to educate young people "in a language that is proper, standard, and customary" for a new generation.[48] The fact that Mendelssohn read the preface to Blitz's translation is significant; later on in this document he repeats other arguments made by Blitz, for example, the claim that the Oral Torah justifies translation. Mendelssohn also starts off by praising the "painstakingly literal" translation of an earlier Yiddish translator of the Hebrew Bible, Elija Levita (1468–1549), also known as Elija Bahur. Levita was an extraordinary Hebraist, an expert on the Masoretic tradition, a famous Yiddish poet, and a teacher. Although admitting that he did not know Elija Levita's translation first hand, he nonetheless allies his project with Levita's; the predecessor of one's predecessor becomes a source of legitimacy. This passage illustrates the ways that Mendelssohn's preface (discussed further below) provided a counterhistory of Bible translation in Ashkenaz. Here and elsewhere, Mendelssohn takes the long view, reaching back into Jewish history to invent a genealogy for the modern Jewish translator. Yiddish is unquestionably a part of that history.

Mendelssohn's rejection of the Yiddish translations is one of three oft-repeated justifications for his own translation project that have reverberated through the centuries. The other two myths are that he translated for the sake of his children and to provide his nation with a "first step to culture."

Each of these is true, but as was the case with the first, the picture is more complex than would appear at first glance.

"I translated for my sons" was an airtight alibi, a defense that had absolute integrity. Biographers confirm that Mendelssohn did indeed begin translating the Pentateuch for his sons' education, with no intention to publish. But recall that the longstanding rationale for translation in the *taytsh* tradition had been for women, children, and men who were like them. In other words, translating "for the children" was the oldest rationale available for translation. In repeating this point, Mendelssohn downplayed the innovative and modern character of the work, and his ambition to create a Jewish Enlightenment Bible.

By contrast, "The first step to culture" was a rationale that was bound to elicit support in German intellectual circles in the late eighteenth century. If the German language lacks culture, one way to acquire it is to expand its horizons, to enter into the world of the foreign—Greek, Roman, Oriental, French, English—ancient and modern—and enlarge the national culture by means of translation. In 1781, the year that Mendelssohn's Exodus was published, the classicist Johann Heinrich Voss (1751–1826) published a German translation of *The Odyssey*. As Herder made clear, the German use of translation differed distinctly from that of the French.

> We poor Germans, on the other hand—lacking as we do a public, a native country, a tyranny of national taste—just want to see him as he is . . . . We will gladly make this journey with the translator, if only he would take us with him to Greece and show us the treasures he has found . . . he must be our tour guide, point things out to us—not as tourists interested in word thefts or tired old legends out of schoolbooks, but as pilgrims seeking the great state secrets of Greek literature.[49]

Herder's words help elucidate what Mendelssohn meant by a "culture" that could be transmitted through translation. In a certain respect, the German lacked a "tyranny of national taste" and a "native country" as much as the Jew did. Such laments were, in fact, common in the German eighteenth century (when translation was used as a way to "improve" German literature and thereby to improve the German collective self). One term for such improvement was *Bildung*. Mendelssohn tapped into this notion. When Mendelssohn suggested that translation could advance his nation's *Bildung*, he subscribed to an ideology that held that translation, when undertaken in a certain mode and method, was literally an "*Über-setzung*," a transposition of the text and its readership to another place. As Antoine

Berman explicates it in *The Experience of the Foreign: Culture and Translation in Romantic Germany*, not only is translation like education—along the model of the "Grand Tour"—"translation (as the mode of relation to the foreign) is structurally inscribed in *Bildung*."[50] *Bildung* begins with the familiar, ventures towards the foreign, then returns to the point of departure with a mediated, critical perspective. To have the desired outcome, translation must make fidelity a priority, not to the language of the original, but to its spirit. It must also be clear about its limitations—lest the process lead to a loss of the native in the foreign.[51]

But let's look at the phrase in its original context—a famous 1778 letter from Mendelssohn to his close friend and correspondent, the Danish envoy August Hennings.

> According to the first plans of my life, as I designed it in my better years, I was far removed from ever becoming an editor or translator of the Bible. I wanted to confine myself to having silken materials manufactured during the day and to being in love with philosophy in my free hours. However, it has pleased Providence to lead me toward a different path. I lost the ability to meditate [*meditieren*] and, as a result, initially, the major portion of my happiness. After some examination I found that the remainder of my strength might still be sufficient to render a useful service [*Dienst*] to my children and perhaps to a considerable part of my nation, by giving into their hands a better translation and explanation of the holy Books than they had before. This is the first step to *Kultur*, from which, alas, my nation is kept at such a distance that one might almost despair of any possibility of an improvement. However, I considered myself obliged to do the little that lies in my power, and to leave the rest to Providence, which as a rule requires more time for the execution of its plan than we can see at a glance.[52]

Mendelssohn's letter moves from reluctance to loss and despair. He begins by noting that translation was not a chosen vocation; God sent him down that path, and like Moses at the burning bush, he followed the call reluctantly. Such work lacks the eros of philosophy; to translate is to work in the lowlands, to "serve" one's children and the members of the nation that are like children; this is the kind of labor that Franz Kafka, in a skeptical parable, referred to as "our everyday cares." Notice that "translation and explanation" go hand in hand here—it was no coincidence that he called it a targum, for the same reason that Saadia, the ninth-century Arabic philosopher-translator, called his translation *Tafsir*.[53] Finally, the targum would be "the first step to culture," which is not "culture" in the loose contemporary sense, but more like what Schiller would call "aesthetic education." Translation would improve and advance his nation. Still, the letter as a whole is overly negative in tone and impression; it hardly conveys the energy of Mendelssohn's translations, and it tamps down the effusiveness of his hopes for biblical language and poetry. What this letter confirms is that Mendelssohn began by envisioning his Bible translation as *Spätstil*, late style: a kind of writing famous for being neither oppositional nor especially coherent, but rather conciliatory and dissonant at once.

In the end, Mendelssohn's accomplishment as a translator went beyond the three different motives he himself expressed: teaching his sons Torah (without relying on Christian translations), introducing Ashkenazi Jews to culture, and improving upon the efforts of Blitz and Witzenhausen. It was a religious-cultural project in the truest sense—to rejoin Torah (understood as the core set of Jewish norms, Jewish outlook, Jewish everything) with the language of the Hebrew Bible. The translator would be a "tour guide" to secret national treasures—not only laws, knowledge, and history, but language itself, its aesthetic qualities, emotive potential, rhyme, and rhythm. A brief "tour" of the very first page of his translation shows how this would be done.

FIRST IMPRESSIONS: MENDELSSOHN'S PAGE LAYOUT

Mendelssohn (and his publisher) designed a well-balanced and familiar page layout (fig. 1.3). The segmented page layout, using only Hebrew letters, could easily have been mistaken for a page of the rabbinic Bible (*Mikraot Gedolot*, 1518). The German translation, printed in Hebrew letters, was hiding in plain sight. Each section had its own heading, and each was in a different font, which added aesthetic appeal. Two modern components were placed on the left half of the page and two ancient discourses on the right. Mendelssohn explained the exact role and interdependence of these four elements in his preface. Each had subtexts.

1. The translation proper, called *Targum Ashkenazi*, occupied the upper left portion, the space normally occupied by the Aramaic Targum Onkelos. More than any other translator, it was Onkelos whom Mendelssohn wished to be mistaken for.[54] Targum means "explanation, commentary, translation, and later, specifically, translation into Aramaic."[55] The targumim were the oldest vernacular translations of the Hebrew Bible, dating back to somewhere between the first and the fifth centuries. Beginning with the rabbinic

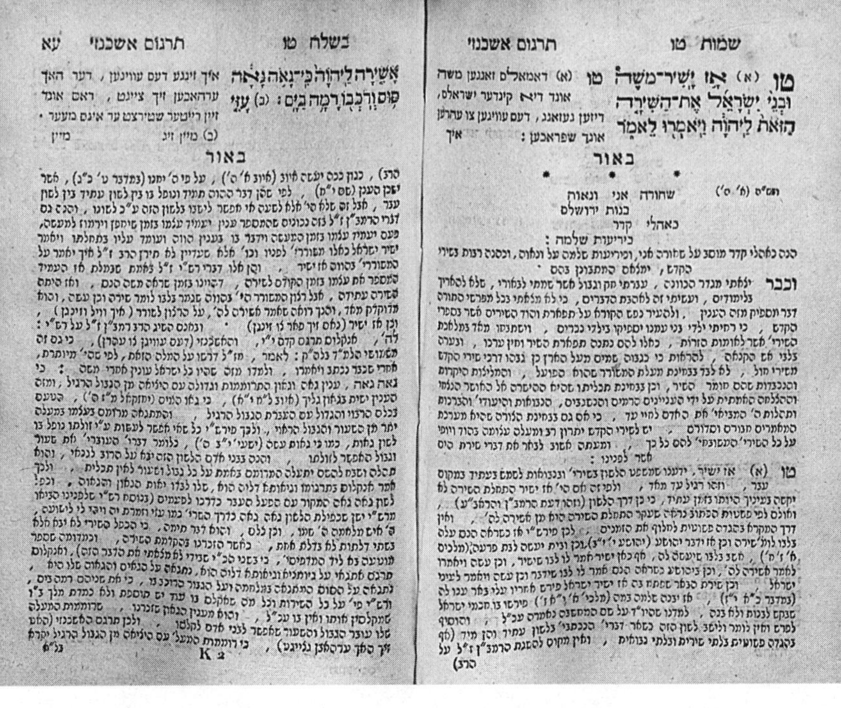

שמות טו תרגום אשכנזי

טו (א) אז ישיר־משה ובני ישראל את־השירה הזאת ליהוה ויאמרו לאמר

טו (א) דאמאלס זאנגען משה אונד דיא קינדער ישראלס, דיזען געזאנג, דעם עוויגען צו עהרען אונד שפראכען : איך

באור

שחורה אני ונאוה
בנות ירושלם
כאהלי קדר
כיריעות שלמה :

בשלח טו תרגום אשכנזי עא

אשירה ליהוה כי־גאה גאה סוס ורכבו רמה בים : (ב) עזי

איך זינגע דעם עוויגען, דער האך ערהאבען זיך צייגט, ראס אונד זיין רייטער שטירצט ער אינס מעער • (ב) מיין זיג מיין

באור

K 2

Fig. 1.3. Mendelssohn Bible, Ex 15:1 (1783). Photograph: Judaica Collection, Harvard University Library.

Bible, targumim began to be included on the page or in the back matter, because medieval commentators quoted them as the basis for their interpretations. And Mendelssohn followed suit, referring to Targum Onkelos and also Targum Yonatan Ben Uzziel in his own commentary. By placing his translation in that space, Mendelssohn tacitly coopted the sanctity and legitimacy of an ancient translation that was also a valued hermeneutic.

The printing of German in Hebrew letters, a style called *Jüdisch-deutsch*, exemplifies both the promise and the provocation of the project as a whole. Steven M. Lowenstein writes:

> In the time of Mendelssohn and his disciples, *Jüdisch-deutsch* was one of the means used by the Maskilim [followers of the Enlightenment] to spread their ideas among the Jews. The Bible translation by Mendelssohn in Hebrew letters and other works by David Friedländer, Herz Homberg and others, were intended to wean the German-Jewish masses away from

> Yiddish, their usual language of speech and reading, and to teach them German. The *Jüdisch-deutsch* of Mendelssohn's translation and similar texts was very difficult for the ordinary German Jews and one of the chief objections to it by the rabbis was that the reader would waste too much time trying to understand the difficult German.[56]

Werner Weinberg explains further:

> The status of High German among Jews was as yet fluid and wavering, their choice of alphabet, when writing it, was even more so. From the standpoint of an author and publisher it was obvious and made good sense that he would employ the German alphabet (Gothic or Latin letters) when a book was intended for a Christian readership, and the Hebrew alphabet, when the book was to be read by Jews. Thus the fact that the Pentateuch translation was printed in Hebrew letters but the Psalms translation in Gothic ones, forms a clear indication of the two different audiences Mendelssohn had in mind for either. When Christian Gottlob Meyer wanted to make the Pentateuch specimen of 1778 accessible to his newly acquired Christian brethren he transliterated the translation into the Gothic alphabet. And hardly had Mendelssohn's complete book of Genesis come off the press, when Professor Josiah Friedrich Christian Löffler published it, too, in Gothic letters.[57]

Here too Mendelssohn claimed to be following a precursor: Ezra, the first-century scribe, whom the Talmud credits with giving the Torah anew "in Aramaic language, in Ashurite script" after the return from Babylonia.[58]

Another secret in this German targum is the method Mendelssohn used to punctuate the Judeo-German script: he followed the *ta'amim*, the signs for cantillation in the Hebrew verses. A soft division or pause (akin to a comma) was represented by a backslash, whereas a stronger break, signaled by an *etnachta*, which marks a sentence break within a verse, and a *sof pasuk*, at the end of the verse, were marked with colons. Naturally, these traces of the Hebrew text could not be imported into the later versions in Gothic letters. But that he sought to preserve them in translation, indeed, to fuse them with the German language, teaches us that he regarded the apparatus of the cantillation as part of the way that biblical syntax means—in whatever language.

2. The text of Hebrew Scripture was printed in the top right quadrant, again following the format of the rabbinic Bible. This was done to allay

any doubts that the original of the translation was the Masoretic Hebrew text. But the Hebrew was very much also integrated into the translation as a whole. The *Be'ur* below consistently directs the reader upward to the Hebrew to explain how this translator and others before him reached their decisions about word choice and syntax.[59] As the preface makes clear, the overall enterprise was as much about explaining the ways of Hebrew as about modeling good German style, and the Hebrew belonged.

3. In the original edition,[60] the *Tikkun Soferim* (Scribal Corrections) occupies the lower outer quadrant. This column, compiled by Solomon Dubno, who was a specialist in masoretic studies, lists Hebrew words that scribes were thought to have corrected. The column is a kind of registry that includes "the specific words representing the presumed uncorrected, original text."[61] Scribal Corrections were first included on individual pages of Scripture in the second edition of the Rabbinic Bible published in Venice in 1525. In that edition, for the first time, the "apparatus of the Masorah"—*Masorah Parva* and *Masorah Magna*—appeared on every page, rather than in tiny script in the margins or as 5,000-word lists, alphabetized and cross-referenced, in the back of the book.[62] But why would Mendelssohn include Scribal Corrections in the translation? Altmann suggests that these were included at Dubno's insistence.[63] Perhaps they served a symbolic purpose as well. The material integrity of biblical letters and words was the anchor of a modern translation—not homilies, *drash*, and lore. In his preface, Mendelssohn explicitly affirms that the modern translator is allied with, or supported by, the ancient scribes dating back to Ezra and the Great Assembly.

4. Finally, the commentary, titled *Be'ur*, occupies the lower part of the page. Mendelssohn authored the commentary for the first six chapters of Genesis, and for most of Exodus; that he "took personal charge of the commentary on Exodus," while assigning the commentary for the remaining book of the Pentateuch to Wessely and others, bears out the argument of my book.[64] Mendelssohn claimed that commentary was the condition of publication. The Hebrew word *be'ur* means "explanation." By occupying the zone where Jews would normally find the explanations of Rashi, Ibn Ezra, or Nachmanides, translational matters rose symbolically to a form of commentary. This new/old commentary wove translational matters, exegesis, general knowledge, as well as history, into a single discourse. Translation was thus not a strange new approach but cushioned by these among many others—dependent on them, and implicitly like them. Only this time, what had to be explained was not only the *pshat*, the literal meaning of the text, but also the choices of the translator, and in this respect the *Be'ur* had a very different function than Rashi.[65] One example shows why.

Genesis 18:12 relates that when the matriarch Sarah, wife of Abraham, received the announcement that she would bear a son at the age of ninety-nine, she "laughed within herself" (KJV). Mendelssohn's "da lachte Sarah in ihrem Herzen" seems straightforward, but it was actually bold. Sarah's laughter is often understood to be mocking and derisive. The decision required an explanation—and here is only a fragment of Dubno's much longer note:

> The language of *tzahak* (laughed) can be explained in five ways (*spielen, spotten, lachen, schimpfen, freuen*) [= playing, mocking, laughing, insulting, being joyful], and each one is understood from the context. However, the Ramban demonstrates that "laughing to oneself" is derisive, as it is written, "He who enthroned in Heaven laughs; / the Lord mocks at them" (Psalms 2:4), which is not joyful, whereas joyful laughter is laughing in the mouth, like "our mouths shall be filled with laughter" (Psalms 126:2). The intent of the Rabbi of blessed memory was to show that when Scripture explicitly notes laughter in the heart, this is derisive laughter, whereas laughter in the mouth is joyful, and if it just says laughter, then one needs to interpret it in context.

The note teaches the reader about laughter in Hebrew and German, but also about translation undertaken within a Jewish interpretive framework. Dubno pays homage to the traditional approaches of Rabbi (Rashi) and Ramban (Nachmanides)—the road not taken. It sounds like what biblical exegetes do all the time, but there is something more going on: the translator has both knowledge and agency to make choices, not just among synonyms, but among hermeneutics old and new.

MENDELSSOHN'S FIRST STEPS: TRANSLATING JEHUDA HALEVI AND BIBLICAL POETRY

Jehuda Halevi

Moses Mendelssohn did not avail himself of copper engravings or an illustrated title page to announce his intention to elevate translation to an art. The endeavor that anticipated his cultural ambitions for Bible translation and shaped his method was translating Hebrew poetry. In the 1750s, Mendelssohn was intensively engaged with poetry and translation, to a degree that earned him the title "poet laureate of the Berlin Jewish community."[66] Scholars who focus on Mendelssohn's efforts to shape a Jewish aesthetic sensibility discuss the short-lived Hebrew periodical he founded, *Qohelet*

Musar (Preacher of Morals),[67] and his translation of Psalms, but do not link those projects to the Be'ur. The common view, as Rawidowicz writes, is that Mendelssohn translated the Psalms in a non-religious, creative, artistic vein, "to reveal the lyric of the early Hebrews," but the Pentateuch out of despair, during his illness, out of pedagogical motives.[68] I trace a clear path, beginning with a translation of a single hymn by Jehuda Halevi, to translations of biblical poetry and Psalms (1770–83), to the Pentateuch (1780–83).[69] For Mendelssohn—as for others in this study, but most famously Franz Rosenzweig in the 1920s—translating poetry was the first fruit of an evolving theory and practice of translation. To engage with poetry—as author, translator, or editor—was the mark of a true German intellectual; no less was the aspiration to be a "harp to [Zion's] songs," in the words of Jehuda Halevi's "Ode to Zion," the ultimate credential of the Jewish religious translator.

Mendelssohn translated the "Ode to Zion" in 1755–56 for publication in the literary periodical *Beschäftigungen des Geistes und des Herzens* (Preoccupations of the Spirit and the Heart) edited by scholar and translator Johann Georg Philipp Müchler.[70] He and Müchler had collaborated on another project, a "moral weekly journal" titled *The Chameleon*. Müchler cofounded a society for scholars and authors in Berlin including Gotthold Ephraim Lessing, Friedrich Nicolai, and the poet to whom Mendelssohn later dedicated his Psalms translation, Karl Wilhelm Ramler. Mendelssohn published two reviews of the most important scholarly work on Hebrew poetry, Bishop Robert Lowth's *De sacra poesi Hebraeorum*, in 1753 and 1757;[71] he wrote letters to Lowth praising his work and sent him his own Genesis and Exodus translations in 1781. Mendelssohn not only translated from Hebrew into German, he wrote in Hebrew, translated *into* Hebrew, and expressed a desire to write poetry. Translating poetry was perhaps just one remove from composing poetry, and when we look closely at this particular episode, we shall see why.

The "Ode to Zion" (Tzion Ha'lo Tishali), composed by the Jewish national poet Jehuda Halevi (1095–1135), may be the most illustrious and oft-imitated poem in Jewish history (outside of the Bible). Mendelssohn was of course familiar with Halevi's philosophical dialogue, the classic work *The Kuzari*, and he adopted and quoted Halevi's theories about the Hebrew language in the *Be'ur*.[72] For Ashkenazi Jews, the "Ode to Zion" was the best-known of the *qinot*, the liturgical laments recited on the fast day of the Ninth of Av, commemorating the destruction of Jerusalem. It was also known in the Ottoman period in south Asia and the Mediterranean. French-German poets imitated Halevi in dirges written after the murder of Jews in the Rhineland in the twelfth century. The most famous Jerusalem song of the twentieth century, Naomi Shemer's "Yerushalayim shel zahav" ("Jerusalem of Gold") written in the wake of the 1967 Arab-Israeli war, crafted its refrain from Halevi's lines: *ha'lo l'khol shirayich, ani kinor* (Am I not, to all your songs, a lyre?). But back in the eighteenth century, before Halevi's *Diwan* had been edited and published, the Ode was a liturgical text. It is possible that Mendelssohn also knew the Ode in Yiddish translation from Yiddish *qinot* collections.[73] But he was the first to translate it into German—not only to give it a "home" in the German language (in Franz Rosenzweig's phrase) but to launch it into German high culture, to create a first bridge between Jewish poetry and German belles-lettres. In fact, the philosopher Johann Gottfried Herder later produced his own adaptation of Mendelssohn's version, which he then shared with Goethe; Herder also mentions Halevi in *On the Spirit of Hebrew Poetry* (1785). Most significant for our story is that Mendelssohn included his German translation of the Ode, transliterated into Hebrew by Solomon Dubno and printed facing the original Hebrew, in the prospectus for the *Be'ur*.[74] That Mendelssohn chose to republish this poem as a selling point for a Bible translation, even though it was not a biblical poem, signals that poetry and Bible translation were deeply interconnected in his mind. He (or the editor of the prospectus) wrote that the poem was included for the purpose of filling in some blank pages, but other evidence suggests that including poetry as part of the Bible served the same function as a woodcut illustration or a copper-engraved title page: it increased the appeal and marketability of the religious book. I would argue further that Mendelssohn's translation of Halevi's Ode brings his agenda into clear view; it is, as it were, a first chapter in his vocation as a Jewish translator.

Mendelssohn's translation, titled "Elegie an die Burg Zion gerichtet" [Elegie dedicated to the City of Zion] is closer to what John Dryden called imitation; it is a new poem in the German language. The first eight lines of Hebrew verse expand to seventeen German lines. Among many additions—italicized in the excerpt below—perhaps the most revealing comes at line 15, where Mendelssohn renders "I" (Hebrew: *ani*) as "my joyful disposition" (German: *mein frohes Gemüth*): this rendering marks an exuberant assertion or projection of the translator's own lyric I, born through the process of translation.

Hebrew (first eight lines):[75]

צִיּוֹן הֲלֹא תִשְׁאֲלִי לִשְׁלוֹם אֲסִירָיִךְ
דּוֹרְשֵׁי שְׁלוֹמֵךְ וְהֵם יֶתֶר עֲדָרָיִךְ
מִיָּם וּמִזְרָח וּמִצָּפוֹן וְתֵימָן

שְׁלוֹם רָחוֹק וְקָרוֹב שְׂאִי מִכֹּל עֲבָרָיִךְ
וּשְׁלוֹם אֲסִיר תַּאֲוָה נוֹתֵן דְּמָעָיו כְּטַל
חֶרְמוֹן וְנִכְסַף לְרִדְתָּם עַל הֲרָרָיִךְ
לִבְכּוֹת עֱנוּתֵךְ אֲנִי תַנִּים וְעֵת אֶחֱלֹם
שִׁיבַת שְׁבוּתֵךְ אֲנִי כִנּוֹר לְשִׁירָיִךְ

Zion! wilt thou not ask if peace be with thy captives
That seek thy peace—that are the remnant of thy flocks?
From west and east, from north and south—the greeting
"Peace" from far and near, take thou from every side;
And greeting from the captive of desire, giving his tears like dew
Of Hermon, and longing to let them fall upon thine hills.
To wail for thine affliction I am [like] the jackals; but when I dream
Of the return of thy captivity, I am a harp for thy songs.

Mendelssohn, "Elegie an die Burg Zion gerichtet" (first 17 lines; italics indicate words not present in the Hebrew):

Vergißt du, Zion! der Deinen,
Die sclavisch in *Fesseln ietzt schmachten*?
Des Ueberrests jener unschuldigen Heerde,
Die vormals in deinen ruhigen Thälern geweidet?

Nimmst du den Frieden nicht an,
Mit welchem sie Dich von allen Seiten begrüßen,
Dahin sie ihr Treiber zerstreuet?

Den Gruß eines *in Fesseln noch* hoffenden Sclaven,
Dem *wimmernd* die Zähren, wie Tropfen
Des *nächtlichen* Thaues auf Hermon herabrollen.
Zufrieden. Könnte sein Thränenbad nur Deine *verlassene* Hügel
befeuchten.

O! Seine Hoffnung sinket noch nicht;
Ietzt da ich dein Elend beweine,
Gleiche ich der *nächtlichen* Eule,
Und wenn mir von deiner Erlösung geträumt,
Wird *mein frohes Gemüth*,
Die Harfe deiner *freudigen Dank*lieder Bethel.

Mendelssohn's "Elegie" in English (first 17 lines):

Do you forget, Zion! your people
Who now slavishly languish in chains?
Those remaining of the innocent herds
Which long ago grazed in your peaceful valleys?

Do you not accept the peace
With which they greet you from all the corners of the world,
To which their oppressors (herders) dispersed them?

The greeting of a slave, enchained, and yet still hoping
And wailing, whose tears—like the drops
Of the nighttime dew on Mount Hermon—roll down.
Sated. Would that his tearbath moisten your abandoned hills!

O! His hope does not yet sink;
Now, as I cry for your misery,
I resemble the night owl,
And when I dream of your redemption,
My happy disposition becomes
The harp of your joyful hymns of thanksgiving, Bethel.[76]

Mendelssohn's verse illustrates what it meant to become the "harp to the songs" of Hebrew poetry. First and foremost, Mendelssohn used free rhythms—quite innovative for his time; one thinks of the religious odes of Friedrich Klopstock—which gave him license to ignore the rigorous formal structure of the Hebrew, including rhyme scheme, uniform stanzas and verse lengths, and regular meter.[77] In keeping with this style, Mendelssohn's verse is heavily dactylic (*freudigen Danklieder*). He elaborates and amplifies the pathos of the Hebrew by adding adjectives, adverbs, and expansive images.

First, he exchanges the bold opening apostrophe "Zion!" for a more prosaic opening question. "Captives" become "those who slavishly languish in chains"; "remnant of your flock" becomes the pastoral "innocent ones who formerly grazed in your still valleys." Whereas Halevi repeats the Hebrew word *shalom* (greeting or welfare) four times—always with extensive alliteration (*tishali lishlom*; *dorshei shlomeich*; *shlom . . . se'i*), Mendelssohn clarifies by alternating between "peace" "*Frieden*" and "greeting" "*Gruß*." In lines 9–11, he amplifies the trope of "tears like dew" by adding six different "liquid" words (*Tränenbad, befeuchten, herabrollen, Zähren, Tropfen, beweinen*); tears were one of the hallmarks of German Sentimentalism (*Empfindsamkeit*).

Mendelssohn took other steps to recalibrate the original for an eighteenth-century German readership. Rather than list the four directions of the earth as Halevi (and often also the Bible) does, Mendelssohn summarizes: "from all sides." Perhaps he felt that naming all four directions was overly pedantic. Adding in an "oppressor (herder)" (*Treiber*) introduces a perpetrator of the exile, not present in Halevi's poem. Finally: Mendelssohn made numerous efforts to smooth out any abrupt or paratactic effects. He moves the word "Bethel" from the following verse up to the end of his line 17, so that the apostrophe would have a clear addressee. He also invents an entire line at the beginning of stanza 4, "*O! Seine Hoffnung sinket noch nicht*" (O! his hope does not yet sink!) (12), perhaps to anticipate the poem's turning point—the introduction of the lyric self. The words "*gleiche ich*" (I resemble) turn Halevi's metaphor into a simile. As a sign of how far he would go to improve the poem, Mendelssohn omits two entire lines of verse much later in the poem, noting later apologetically that the poet skipped around too much. The publisher Christian Gottlob Meyer filled in the ellipsis.[78]

Translating the Hebrew poem gave wings to Mendelssohn's own poetic imagination, empowering his own *frohes Gemüth* (happy disposition) to produce *freudige Danklieder* (joyful songs of thanks). What was the cause of all this happiness? It is no surprise to find good poetry in the Hebrew Bible—that, too, was cause for celebration, as we shall see. But the fact that the Jewish poetic imagination flourished in the diaspora—whether in twelfth-century Al-Andalus or eighteenth-century Berlin—is truly a reason to celebrate. Translating Halevi transformed Mendelssohn into a Jewish poet in the German language.

Mendelssohn's "Ode to Zion" was the *third* sample translation included in the prospectus for the Pentateuch, following Exodus 1–2 and Numbers 23–24 (about which I comment below). According to the editor, the poem was used only to fill up some blank pages—just by chance. But chance is frequently a code word for aesthetic experience; moreover, Mendelssohn's correspondence teaches us that in the eighteenth century, poetry was attractive to potential subscribers. This point came up regarding another of Mendelssohn's poetic compositions, the translation of *Das Deborahlied* (Song of Deborah) from Judges 5. In 1780, the publisher of the *Be'ur* in Gothic letters, Josias Friedrich Christian Löffler, opted to include the masterfully translated *Deborahlied* as a "bonus text" in Genesis, explaining that Genesis is rather short on poetry.[79]

Psalms

When the prospectus came out in 1778, Mendelssohn had been translating the Pentateuch for four years and the Psalms already for eight years. In both of these projects, he extended and expanded the method he used for Halevi's *Elegie*. Scholars normally identify his main motive for retranslating the Psalms as a wish for a non-Christological translation for Christians, and as Sorkin points out, from this angle, it was no surprise that the Psalms was not a commercial success: "In many ways it was a work without an audience"; too humanistic for Christians, too German for Jewish readers.[80] Yet a number of letters reveal that from the very start, an unmistakable artistic ambition coincided with the religious one. Michaelis was also translating the Psalms at the time. The correspondence conveys that everyone knew about this project. In an important letter to Michaelis of 12 November 1770, Mendelssohn suggests that his colleague was better suited to the task than Mendelssohn himself:

> I must admit that I am very unsatisfied with extant translations of the Psalms, even less with the poetic than the prose versions. Even when they by chance manage to capture the sense, the occidental verse structure spoils the uniqueness of Hebrew verse [*das Eigenthümliche der hebräischen Dichtkunst*]. But they only randomly manage to capture the sense, as I said. Some time ago I translated about twenty Psalms into German, some of the most difficult ones among them, in a free syllabic meter that, to my ears, comes closer to the Hebrew. I was determined to circulate these as a "sampler of the lyric poetry of the Hebrews." But as of now, that will remain uncompleted until I have seen the commentary of Your Excellence. I am certain, and what I have read by you in recent times justifies my certainty, that you will treat the Psalms as poetry, without setting great store in the prophetic and mystical [aspects], which both Christian and Jewish interpreters until now have sought in the Psalms, as if the Psalms had been composed in a monastery by a penitent monk.[81]

Mendelssohn desired a Psalms translation that did justice to the "uniqueness of Hebrew verse"—very difficult to accomplish in a European language, but potentially accomplishable by one who placed literary matters above religious ones. The Psalms are first and foremost—in the words of Franz Rosenzweig—great poems in the Hebrew language, and Hebrew does not easily align with German. Mendelssohn gives voice here to the asymetrical relations between languages, in Seidman's term, or more exactly, the asymmetry between a religious translation (of any sect) and a cultural one. In theory, a truly poetic Hebraic Psalms could supersede the prophetic and mystical mistranslations of either religious community. Mendelssohn gave voice to the sheer difficulty of translating poetry and even of understanding the Psalms on other occasions.[82] In an open letter published in a French literary gazette in 1771, Mendelssohn addressed rumors that he was preparing a Psalms commentary—a *Be'ur* to Psalms—saying that he was not likely to do so.

> Translations of Psalms have been done in numerous languages; we have explicated them, paraphrased and imitated them, in verse and in prose: but I dare say that the end result has been rather to eclipse, rather than illuminate, the true meaning of the Psalms, and I admit that many remain incomprehensible to me.[83]

Yet in the texts themselves, as well as in the paratextual comments, Mendelssohn's Romanticism, rather than his Hebraism, comes to the fore. Though he published samples in a periodical in 1781, the complete Psalms were published in Berlin in 1783, with new editions appearing in 1787 and 1788.[84] Mendelssohn dedicated the volume to Ramler, his "critical muse," and singles out "Dr. Luther" as his precursor, above all, for incorporating "hebräische Redensarten" (Hebraic idioms) at the cost of "ächtes Deutsch" (authentic German)—the very approach that had fallen out of fashion among his eighteenth-century Christian contemporaries. Identifying Luther as a precursor was unheard of for a Jewish translator, and it was, to some degree, a misrepresentation. As Dominique Bourel's verse comparisons establish, Mendelssohn's style did not clearly imitate Luther's, whose Psalms are far more prosaic. When juxtaposed with parallel verses from Luther, Georg Christian Knapp (*Die Psalmen*; 11 editions, 1778–89), Johann Andreas Cramer, Johann David Michaelis, Herder (who included many Psalms in *Vom Geist der Ebräischen Poesie*), and even Martin Buber, Mendelssohn's versions sound, above all, poetic, surpassing the others in use of images, in lyrical, dramatic, and musical features.[85] These are not literal renderings. As in the Halevi poem, he uses paraphrase; changes the word order and even verse lines; and uses parentheses for especially difficult verses. The upshot is to show that Mendelssohn translated Psalms as a poet, rather than as religious thinker—a point that comes through unmistakably in his brief preface:

> I did not translate the Psalms in order, one after the other, rather I simply picked a Psalm that appealed to me . . . My Reader, you read them as I

> have written them! Pick a Psalm that corresponds to your mood [*Gemüthszustande*] at a given moment: forget, for a brief time, everything that you have read about that Psalm by translators, interpreters, and paraphrasers. Read my translation and judge![86]

The invitation to read the Psalms impulsively, to pick and choose based on one's disposition or *Gemüthszustande,* calls to mind Mendelssohn's inclusion of that same word *Gemüth in* his version of Halevi's Ode, as well as the publisher's insistence that the poem found its way into the prospectus "by chance." In his 1770 letter to Michaelis, Mendelssohn noted that he had translated twenty Psalms "at his leisure, for pure enjoyment" (*bey müssigen Stunden zum Vergnügen*). Poems exist to commune with the moods and vagaries of the human soul. As an extension of these poetics, Mendelssohn closes the preface by asking the reader to suspend all "critical consideration. In a nutshell: I believe I have translated without critical biases, wish to be read and judged without critical biases, and promise to accept any rebuke without critical stubbornness."[87]

Biblical Poetry

Mendelssohn's excitement about poetry is no less palpable in the pages of the Pentateuch translation. He made use of typography and commentary to call attention to poetic passages. Uri Phoebus's formatting of the Blitz translation set the Song of the Sea in a different typeface with its own special heading, "The Fifteenth Chapter: *Di Shira* (The Song)," and turned each verse into a what looked like a stanza (fig. 1.4). But it is above all in the *Be'ur that* Mendelssohn did what he said he would not do: transgress the proper limits of the commentary to elaborate in detail his own ideas about Hebrew verse, *hebräische Dichtkunst,* beginning with the first "poem" in the Hebrew Bible, Lamech's speech to his wives Adah and Tzilah (Gen 4:23–24), and continuing with Exodus 15, the Song of the Sea, which extends over three full pages (see fig. 1.3).[88] Mendelssohn actually apologizes for the long digression, even as he confesses that he could have gone on and on. This was the first time a Jewish biblical commentator wrote about the formal aspects of biblical poetry.[89] In fact, Mendelssohn also wrote about translating poetry, and in particular, the "pressure and trouble" (*lachatz*) experienced by the translator of metrical verse into another language.[90] He compares poetry in translation to fine oil released from a vessel, which quickly loses its fragrance.[91] But it is crucial to note that for Mendelssohn, it was precisely the fragrance—and not the vessel—that was the heart of the matter. The many

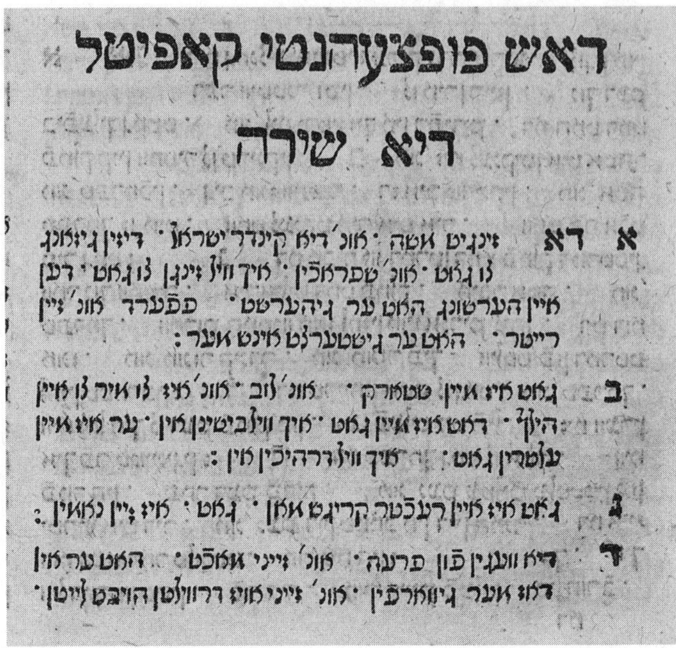

דאש פופצעהנטי קאפיטל

דיא שירה

א דא זינגט משה אונ' דיא קינדר ישראל דיזן געזאנג
צו גאט אונ' שפראכין איך וויל זינגן צו גאט דען
איין הערשונג האט ער גיהערשט פפערד אונ' זיין
רייטר האט ער גישטערצט אינש מער:

ב גאט איז מיין שטארק אונ' לוב אונ' איז צו מיר צו מיין
הייל דאס איז מיין גאט איך וויל בישיינן אין ער איז מיין
עלטרין גאט איך וויל דר היכין אין:

ג גאט איז איין רעכטר קריגש מאן גאט איז זיין נאמן:

ד דיא וועגין פון פרעה אונ' זייני מאכט האט ער אין
דאז מער גיווארפין אונ' זייני אויז דר וועלטן הויבט לייטן:

Fig. 1.4. Blitz Bible, *Di Shira* (The Song) (1678). Photograph: Judaica Collection, Harvard University Library.

examples of biblical parallelism provided in these excurses do not fundamentally provide a lesson in poetic form. That was the purview of Greek and Roman poetry, and medieval *piyyutim* with their strict meters based on Arabic verse forms, which were intended for the "ear," especially when set to music. But the biblical poet cared about *content*, not form; the words go by way of the ear to the heart, to awaken *Emotionen*. It is not the meter of poetry that matters as much as the variations, the natural irregularities, which also improve memory. Like the variations in choral arrangements, poems divided into short clauses with frequent rests "help[] considerably to awaken attention to the intended meaning and impress this intended meaning on the heart, as linguists observe."[92] The upshot is that when sacred poetry is translated into another language, "even if its flavor is weakend and its fragrance made bitter by the translation, there nevertheless remains the sweetness of the content that we have mentioned."[93]

After giving numerous examples of irregular verse lengths,[94] Mendelssohn closes with the regret that Jewish youth love only non-Jewish poetry, and his conviction that these sacred poems are superior to the poetry of the Gentiles just as "the heavens are higher than the earth" (Isaiah 55:9; KJV).

Mendelssohn's lengthy excurses on Hebrew poetry in his commentary to the Song of the Sea in Exodus 15 encodes a version of the translator's apology—a defense of the translator's approach to the Pentateuch as a whole. The essential point is just as Hebrew poets rejected strict metrical models of poesis used by other nations, the Jewish translator must reject a mechanical approach to translation, above all because that approach cannot do justice to the meaning and art of biblical poetry.

MENDELSSOHN'S CHRISTIAN CONTEXTS

Mendelssohn's vocation as a Hebrew translator began with Halevi's "Ode to Zion" and Psalms. Blitz and Witzenhausen provided a Jewish prototype and a negative impetus for a new translation. Developments in the Christian context during the century that separated the Amsterdam Yiddish Bibles and Mendelssohn's *Be'ur* played an equally important role.

First and foremost, Christian Bible scholars had rejected the Luther Bible and sought to update its methods. In the aftermath of the religious conflicts of the seventeenth century, Germany experienced an enormous wave of new Bible translations, beginning with the efforts of scholars such as August Hermann Francke and Johann David Michaelis at the University of Halle. An astonishing number of translated Bibles were published within a hundred years—over one million New Testaments and nearly two million complete Bibles.[95] "The same zeal that made the Reformation such a productive period for biblical translation in Germany, in other words, still drove the early eighteenth-century invention of what would become the Enlightenment Bible."[96] The textual focus of radical Pietism, which was also a pedagogical revolution, drove the translation explosion. Some of these developments related to Mendelssohn's project, while others are relevant to later waves.

Pietism

Contrary to its image in literary history, Pietism not only advocated a mystical and emotional relationship to Christ; it also took the forms of scholarship, pedagogy, exegesis, and translation.[97] Why would Pietists desire a new type of Bible? Many of the reasons also apply to Blitz, Witzenhausen, and Mendelssohn and anticipate factors shaping the subsequent generation of Jewish translators. Perhaps most importantly, Pietist scholars desired a more correct translation. The Luther Bible was a cultural treasure, but it was full of errors, and furthermore, Pietists opposed Lutheran orthodoxy. Scholars began studying not only biblical and rabbinic Hebrew, but also Chaldean

(Aramaic), Syriac, Ethiopian, and the Arabic vernacular, and they began to subject Scripture to philological analysis. One of the senior Michaelis's first projects as director of the new Oriental Institute in Halle was the publication of a *Biblica Hebraica* in 1720.

The use of translation to disseminate new knowledge to the unlearned was also an essential goal of the Haskalah. Mendelssohn knew it was not enough simply to include Hebrew and German on the page; modern Jews needed a new kind of tour guide to biblical language—which in turn provided the key both to (modern) translational decisions and to a (medieval and ancient) interpretive tradition. (As a testimony to its ambiguous character and transitional role, the commentary quickly became viewed as anachronistic and was removed from the *Be'ur*. Traditionalists in subsequent generations restored medieval commentaries or added updated ones.) This leads to a caveat: Mendelssohn's *Be'ur* was not really for the uneducated Jews. One had to know Hebrew to follow it, and as rabbis early on noted, the German was too difficult for the average reader—it required a guide of its own.[98] Similarly, Michaelis's "translation for *Ungelehrte*" was packed full of footnotes and information more appropriate for *Gelehrte*. Schmidt's translation also included a long preface and footnotes. This conjunction of scholarly/philological accuracy and a literalist/Hebraic style in Pietist Bibles marks the second wave even more clearly than the first. Fifty years after the *Be'ur*, Jewish translators—many of them sons and pupils of *biurists*—were in the position to advocate for, and design, foreign-sounding Hebraic translations with a scholarly basis.

The Enlightenment

Mendelssohn alludes to Christian biblical scholarship in his preface, when he claims to have assessed R. Saadia Gaon's (corrupted) translation against the list of emendations in Johann Gottlieb Eichhorn's *Introduction to the Old Testament* (1780).[99] And the statement, "From then until now, no one has taken it upon himself to fix the crooked and translate the holy Torah into the language that is proper, standard, and customary in our generation," describes the new standard to which all German translations in Mendelssohn's day were held. The translations produced by the German Enlightenment sought to modernize the Luther Bible according to eighteenth-century tastes and linguistic developments, and to produce a translation that would make religion appealing to the modern, educated German reader. The style that had been so admired in the sixteenth and seventeenth centuries became an object of derision. Luther's Hebraic euphemisms, which gave the Bible its oriental flavor, would, moreover, confuse and alienate the uneducated reader, disturb his piety (*Andacht*), and lead him to devalue religion. Such laments were, in fact, common in the German eighteenth century (when translation was used as a way to "improve" German literature as such and thereby to improve the Germans). Mendelssohn, Herder, and later the German Romantics also drew from Leibniz and valued a language's "ordinary use in speech and writing. It is here that the richness, purity, and brilliance of the German language should appear, three essential qualities of any language."[100] Mendelssohn not only participated in these trends, he borrowed vocabulary and stylistics from Christian translations.

At one extreme was the controversial Wertheim Bible of 1735, which Mendelssohn discovered in 1756 and purchased for his own library. Its unnamed author was the Christian Hebraist and rational theologian Johann Lorenz Schmidt (1702–49), who was jailed for a translation that was also banned and confiscated. The Wertheim Bible, an important text in Pietism, inspired the famous Deist critique of the Bible by Hermann Samuel Reimarus published by G. E. Lessing in the 1770s. That Mendelssohn never mentioned the Wertheim Bible is not surprising. Schmidt's was an early example of a translation that aimed at conceptual fidelity; it was an "annotated, dynamic, modern-language version of the Pentateuch, one often verging into paraphrase."[101] Schmidt took the method to an extreme, to the point where much of his translation reads like a stylized paraphrase. Genesis 1:1 reads, "All worldly bodies, and our earth too, were created at the beginning by God." For Genesis 1:2, rendered famously in the KJV as "And the earth was without form, and void" (*tohu va'vohu*), Schmidt wrote: "Concerning earth in particular, it was at the start wholly desolate" (*Was insonderheit die Erde betrift, so war dieselbe anfänglich ganz öde*). This is exactly the kind of exaggerated transition, used to reject the "ands," that we will see in Mendelssohn.[102] But what made this translation heretical was its naturalism. To take a famous example, Genesis 1:2, Schmidt rendered *der Geist Gottes* ("the Spirit of God"; KJV) as "strong winds" (*heftige Winde*).[103] Applying Leibnizian and Wolffian ideas, Schmidt used translation to challenge the typological interpretation of the Old Testament that was a cornerstone of all the Confessions. Schmidt's "minor" mistranslation of Genesis 3:15 changed "He will step on your heel" to "men will . . ." thereby erasing the very first evidence of Jesus's deliverance.[104] Mendelssohn had something further in common with Schmidt, as Sheehan eloquently notes: a "new pedantry." "Pinning down the exact meaning of words, no matter how banal, was crucial in defining the exact concepts found in Scripture."[105] Mendelssohn's translation frequently added in *Das heißt* (in other words) or *nämlich* (namely) to explain things that do not appear to need explanation.

But Mendelssohn differed from Schmidt in a critical respect. The latter not only sought to purify the Bible of typological interpretations, he wanted to purify it of "Jewish literary barbarisms." "To sanitize the Bible—to achieve the linguistic purity cherished by Locke and Wolff—one needed a 'free' translation, one aimed not at verbal but at conceptual fidelity."[106] Against this background, we can appreciate Mendelssohn's efforts to show that Hebrew was holy, beautiful, and logical—not debris blocking the meaning of Torah, but a path (*netivah*) to sense. Mendelssohn embraced conceptual translation, alluding to it as "the correct method of our time." The language had to be modern, to emphasize that the Bible was not an "antique volume" but a work of great Jewish literature with relevance to modern life. But Mendelssohn compensated for such modernizing techniques by finding ways to praise Hebrew as a poetic, even sublime language, with a proper grammar, puns, word play, and other nuances. Paul Spalding notes that Schmidt made an exception when it came to Hebrew names, using the Hebraic forms that Luther had rejected—*Mizrajim*, for example, instead of *Aegypten*—the same practice that Mendelssohn adopted. He speculates: "What except for the Wertheim Bible could have persuaded Mendelssohn that the Hebraic pronunciations of Jewish tradition could, after all, be an acceptable usage in modern German?"[107]

The most important counterpart in the Christian world was Johann David Michaelis, the nephew of the Halle Orientalist. The younger Michaelis was not as extreme as his uncle. He published his own thirteen-volume *Deutsche Uebersetzung des Alten Testaments mit Anmerkungen für Ungelehrte* (German translation of the Old Testament with notes for the uneducated; 1769–83). Was it to call attention to the Bible's literary value that Michaelis placed the book of Job in the very first volume (fig. 1.5)? In his preface to that volume, he cites not only the evolution of the language since Luther's time but also the annoyance of "*wortgetreue Übersetzungen*," literalisms and Hebraisms that led to the foreign domination of the German language.[108] Michaelis's approach was consonant with the translation theory of his day, which held that a good translation should not be lexical, or "*sclavisch-treu*" (slavishly faithful). Perhaps the most striking part of the title is "for the unlearned." First-wave translations aimed high: their sophisticated language and long-winded notes (*Be'ur* for Mendelssohn; *Anmerkungen* for Schmidt and Michaelis) were not really accessible to the layperson. The unlearned reader Michaelis had in mind was not ignorant, but

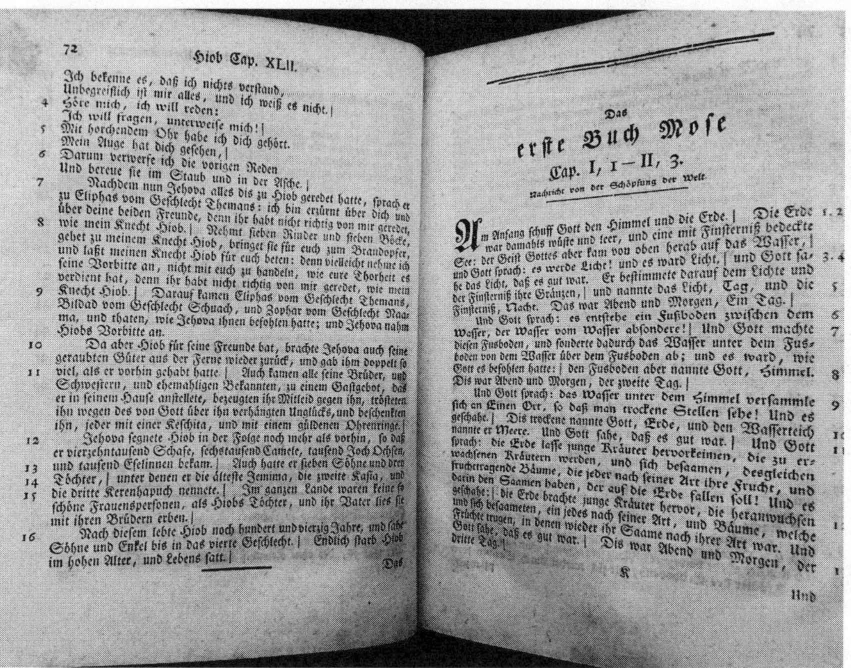
72 Hiob Cap. XLII.

Ich bekenne es, daß ich nichts verstand,
Unbegreiflich ist mir alles, und ich weiß es nicht. |
4 Höre mich, ich will reden:
Ich will fragen, unterweise mich! |
5 Mit horchendem Ohr habe ich dich gehört.
Mein Auge hat dich gesehen, |
6 Darum verwerfe ich die vorigen Reden
Und bereue sie im Staub und in der Asche. |
7 Nachdem nun Jehova alles dis zu Hiob geredet hatte, sprach er
zu Eliphas vom Geschlecht Themans: ich bin erzürnt über dich und
über deine beiden Freunde, denn ihr habt nicht richtig von mir geredet,
8 wie mein Knecht Hiob. | Nehmt sieben Rinder und sieben Böcke,
gehet zu meinem Knecht Hiob, bringet sie für euch zum Brandopfer,
und laßt meinen Knecht Hiob für euch beten: denn vielleicht nehme ich
seine Vorbitte an, nicht mit euch zu handeln, wie eure Thorheit es
verdient hat, denn ihr habt nicht richtig von mir geredet, wie mein
9 Knecht Hiob. | Darauf kamen Eliphas vom Geschlecht Themans,
Bildad vom Geschlecht Schuach, und Zophar vom Geschlecht Naa-
ma, und thaten, wie Jehova ihnen befohlen hatte; und Jehova nahm
Hiobs Vorbitte an.
10 Da aber Hiob für seine Freunde bat, brachte Jehova auch seine
geraubten Güter aus der Ferne wieder zurück, und gab ihm doppelt so
11 viel, als er vorhin gehabt hatte. | Auch kamen alle seine Brüder, und
Schwestern, und ehemahligen Bekannten, zu einem Gastgebot, das
er in seinem Hause anstellete, bezeugten ihr Mitleid gegen ihn, trösteten
ihn wegen des von Gott über ihn verhängten Unglücks, und beschenkten
ihn, jeder mit einer Keschita, und mit einem güldenen Ohrenringe. |
12 Jehova segnete Hiob in der Folge noch mehr als vorhin, so daß
er vierzehntausend Schafe, sechstausend Camele, tausend Joch Ochsen,
13 und tausend Eselinnen bekam. | Auch hatte er sieben Söhne und drey
14 Töchter, | unter denen er die älteste Jemima, die zweite Kasia, und
15 die dritte Kerenhapuch nennete. | Im ganzen Lande waren keine so
schöne Frauenspersonen, als Hiobs Töchter, und ihr Vater lies sie
mit ihren Brüdern erben. |
16 Nach diesem lebte Hiob noch hundert und vierzig Jahre, und sahe
Söhne und Enkel bis in das vierte Geschlecht. | Endlich starb Hiob
im hohen Alter, und Lebens satt. |
Das

Das
erste Buch Mose
Cap. I, 1 – II, 3.
Nachricht von der Schöpfung der Welt.

Am Anfang schuff Gott den Himmel und die Erde. | Die Erde 1. 2
war damahls wüste und leer, und eine mit Finsterniß bedeckte
See: der Geist Gottes aber kam von oben herab auf das Wasser, |
und Gott sprach: es werde Licht! und es ward Licht. | und Gott sa- 3. 4
he das Licht, daß es gut war. Er bestimmete darauf dem Lichte und
der Finsterniß ihre Gränzen, | und nannte das Licht, Tag, und die 5
Finsterniß, Nacht. Das war Abend und Morgen, Ein Tag. |
Und Gott sprach: es entstehe ein Fußboden zwischen dem 6
Wasser, der Wasser vom Wasser absondere! | Und Gott machte 7
diesen Fusboden, und sonderte dadurch das Wasser unter dem Fusboden von dem Wasser über dem Fusboden ab; und es ward, wie
Gott es befohlen hatte: | den Fusboden aber nannte Gott, Himmel. 8
Dis war Abend und Morgen, der zweite Tag. |
Und Gott sprach: das Wasser unter dem Himmel versammle
sich an Einen Ort, so daß man trockene Stellen sehe! Und es 9
geschahe. | Dis trockene nannte Gott, Erde, und den Wasserteich
nannte er Meere. Und Gott sahe, daß es gut war. | Und Gott 1
sprach: die Erde lasse junge Kräuter hervorkeimen, die zu er- 1
wachsenen Kräutern werden, und sich besaamen, desgleichen
fruchttragende Bäume, die jeder nach seiner Art ihre Frucht, und
darin den Saamen haben, der auf die Erde fallen soll! Und es
geschahe: | die Erde brachte junge Kräuter hervor, die heranwuchsen
und sich besaameten, ein jedes nach seiner Art, und Bäume, welche 1
Früchte trugen, in denen wieder ihr Saame nach ihrer Art war. Und
Gott sahe, daß es gut war. | Dis war Abend und Morgen, der 1
dritte Tag. |
K
Und

Fig. 1.5. Michaelis Bible. The end of Job precedes the beginning of Genesis (1789). Photograph: Harvard Divinity School, Andover-Harvard Theological Library (SCR 357 Ger 1789).

rather enlightened and skeptical of the notion that the Bible is a tasteful work of literature, worthy of admiration.

The remaining sections in this chapter discuss Blitz, Witzenhausen, and Mendelssohn comparatively.

VERSE COMPARISONS: AN IDIOM IN FORMATION

As punishment for killing his brother Abel, God branded Cain a "fugitive and a vagabond" (Gen 4:12; KJV) or a "restless wanderer" (Alter). Neither English version matches the eloquence of the punishment in Hebrew: *na vanad*, a phrase as euphonious as *tohu va'vohu*. The Yiddish and German translators of the seventeenth and eighteenth centuries did not care to capture alliteration or euphony (as Buber and Rosenzweig did with "Schwank und schweifend"). They were more or less consistent in their approaches, spanning 250 years. Two of them copied directly from Luther:

Luther: unstet und flüchtig (wandering and fugitive)
Blitz: umshtetik un flikhtik
Mendelssohn: unstet und flüchtig

Two others, Witzenhausen and Michaelis, chose to innovate:

Witzenhausen: unruing un farvoglt (restless and drifting)
Michaelis: zitternd und flüchtig (trembling and fugitive)

These small differences don't appear revolutionary, but together, they convey a biblical idiom in formation. In another example, notice the dramatic shift from simple to complex in translations of Genesis 2:4a. Mendelssohn rejects the simple terms of three precursors in favor of a fancy multisyllabic word and makes use of the genitive case in lieu of the prepositions *fun/von* (of).

KJV: These *are* the generations of the heavens and of the earth
Anchor: Such is the story of heaven and earth
Luther: Also ist Himmel und Erde worden
Blitz: Dis zayn **di gishikhtn** (= history) fun himl un erd
Witzenhausen: Dos doziki zaynen **di gebirt** [= birth] fun dem himl un di erd
Michaelis: Dies war der **Anfang** (= beginning) von Himmel und Erde
Mendelssohn: Dies ist die **Enstehungsgeschichte** (= history of the origins) **des** Himmels und **der** Erde

In the comparisons that follow, we observe continuities and discrepancies among a "pentapla" of first-wave translations and their precursors: Luther (1534), Blitz (1678), Witzenhausen (1679), Michaelis (1770), and Mendelssohn (1783). Each set tells a story of its own.

My purpose is not to determine who borrowed from whom, but rather to illustrate patterns and shared practices among translators with similar priorities. As we shall see in their prefaces, Blitz, Witzenhausen, and Mendelssohn made much of the challenge of choosing between *pshat* and *drash*—plain sense or received sense. But they also strove to meet the criteria of any good story: clarity, correctness, and beauty. In the interest of clarity and accuracy, they smoothed out biblical syntax by adding conjunctions, connecting words within and between verses, and adjusting tense when necessary. To clarify cryptic phrases or even minimally confusing verses, they used parentheses. Finally, by varying vocabulary, experimenting with word order, formatting, and punctuation, they sought to amplify the literary character of the Hebrew Bible. Beyond these common goals, three notable trends become apparent. First: as in the first example used above, Mendelssohn and the Yiddish translators before him (especially Blitz) often followed Luther. Second: on key stylistic issues, the later translators Michaelis and Mendelssohn departed from the earlier ones, Luther, Blitz, and Witzenhausen. Third: Mendelssohn generally followed the original Hebrew *more closely* than did his Yiddish or Christian counterparts. Though the *Be'ur* was later criticized for being a paraphrase, too German, in this group Mendelssohn actually sounds like a Hebraist.

Beauty

When Laban says to Jacob, "thou art my bone and my flesh" (Gen 29:14; KJV), Mendelssohn added "my close relative" (*mein näher Anverwandter*) in parentheses. But as a rule, these translators hardly needed parentheses to elevate (in their eyes) biblical diction.

The Hebrew Bible boasts of Noah's legendary righteousness using three separate attributes, the most famous being "Noah walked with God" (Gen 6:9; JPS).

> KJV: These *are* the generations of Noah: Noah was a just man *and* perfect in his generations, and Noah walked with God.
>
> Anchor: This is the line of Noah.—Noah was a righteous man; he was without blame in that age; Noah walked with God.

None of the first-wave translators, not even Luther, wrote "walked with God." Luther and Blitz both rendered that phrase "led a godly life in his time(s)":

> Luther: Dies ist das Geschlecht Noahs. Noah war ein frommer Mann und ohne Tadel, und **führte ein göttlich Leben zu seinen Zeiten**;
>
> Blitz: dos iz dos geshlekht noyekh. noyekh vor eyn frumer man, shtil un aynfeltik un **firet eyn getlekh lebn in zayner tsayt**

Blitz, as we see, elaborated Noah's virtues, and Witzenhausen chose to be more elaborate still; Mendelssohn mostly followed Witzenhausen:

> Witzenhausen: Dos dozik zaynen di gibirt fun (noyekh. noyekh) vor eyn gerekhter oyfrikhtiker man in zaynen geshlekhter. (noyekh) vor zikh dermayen mit Got.

Mendelssohn: Folgendes ist die Geschlechtsfolge des Noach. Noach war eine gerechter aufrichtiger Mann in seinen Zeiten, und wandelte mit Got.

Why tamper with "walked with God"? The Hebrew *hithalech* is after all a reflexive verb, suggesting something more complicated than normal walking. Witzenhausen and Mendelssohn each took imaginative approaches. The former used an old German verb, "der mayen sich," meaning "rejoiced with" or "delighted with" God. The latter chose *wandeln*, a Romantic word that evokes a stroll or promenade.[109] He may have gotten the idea from Schmidt, who used the same term but in the noun form: "About this man Noach, it is important to note that contrary to the habits of his age he was a pious man, who led a faultless and holy **way of life** (***Wandel***)."[110] With respect to other parts of the verse, Witzenhausen innovated using *Geburt* for *toldot* and later "Geschlecht" for *bedorotav*. Mendelssohn opened with "The following," and expanded Luther's and Blitz's *Geschlecht* into *Geschlechts-folge* (today: *Geschlechterfolge*), genealogy.[111] Understandably, for the phrase *bedorotav* (in his generations, age),[112] Mendelssohn preferred Luther's and Blitz's poetic "in his age."

Many may not be aware of the fact that Noah's ark had a skylight (*tzohar*). The older translators called it a window. Mendelssohn went for "light source," and he also chose a foreign word *Arche*, rather than *Kasten* (box) or *Lod, Lade* like (*Bundeslade*, the ark of the covenant), in Genesis 6:18:

KJV: A window shalt thou make to the ark.
Luther: Ein Fenster sollst du dran machen
Blitz: eyn fenster zolstu deron makhn
Witzenhausen: eyn fenster zolstu makhn tsu der lod
Mendelssohn: Du sollst auch an der **Arche eine Beleuchtung** machen

Another opportunity for expanding biblical vocabulary was presented by what one might call Jewish keywords—Hebrew terms that were well known in Jewish society, which some retained as *Fremdwörter*. Mendelssohn invented sophisticated neologisms for Passover/*Pessach* (*Überschreitungsopfer* = stepping-over-sacrifice, Ex 12:27); and for *totafot/tefillin* (*Stirnbunde* = headband, frontlet Ex 13:16). In the latter example, Witzenhausen and Blitz retain the Hebrew (originally Aramaic term). Notice Blitz's interpolation of "the *left* hand" (linke hand)!:

KJV: And it shall be for a **token** upon thine hand, and for **frontlets** between thine eyes:
Witzenhausen: un es zol tsu eynem **tseykhn** zayn oyf dayner hant un tsu **(tfiln)** tsvishn dayne oygn
Blitz: un dos zol dir tsu eyn **tseykhn** zayn oyf dayner **linke** hand un tsu **(tfiln)** tsvishn dayne oygn
Luther: Und das soll dir ein **Zeichen** in deiner Hand sein und ein **Denkmal** vor deinen Augen;
Mendelssohn: Dises soll dir zum **Merkzeichen** auf deiner Hand, und zur **Stirnbunde** zwischen deinen Augen dihnen.

Is it conceivable that Mendelssohn chose words solely because they were evocative in the German cultural context? One of the most dramatic examples is surely the first line of the Song of the Sea (Ex 15:1): "Ich singe, dem Ewigen, der hoch **erhaben** sich zeigt" (= I sing to the Lord, who shows himself highly **sublime**). With this line, Mendelssohn introduces sublimity into the Pentateuch. He had written about the sublime, *das Erhabene*, in his philosophical writings (see chapter 2), and regarded the Psalms as a sublime work.[113] But no previous translator to my knowledge used the word *erhaben* in this context. Translations of the highly poetic, virtually untranslatable phrase *ga'oh ga'ah* vary widely. In contrast to Luther and Michaelis, Blitz and Witzenhausen both found a way to convey the repetition in the Hebrew, and its poetic character, in their Yiddish.

KJV: I will sing unto the LORD, for he hath triumphed gloriously: the horse and his rider hath he thrown into the sea.
Luther: Ich will dem HERRN singen; **denn er hat eine herrliche Tat getan**;
Blitz: ikh vil zingen tsu got **den ayn hershung hot er gehersht**
Witzenhausen: ikh vil tsu [far] got zingen **den er iz hoykh der heykht**
Michaelis: Ich will Gotte singen, **denn er war höher als die Stolzen**:

Perhaps Mendelssohn also wanted to refute Michaelis's *die Stolzen*, meaning lofty or proud ones. It was not only the biblical God who would be associated with the heights of sublimity, but by extension, the Bible of German Jewry.

Among the biblical stories that cry out for a literary treatment, there is nothing quite like the Joseph saga (Gen 37–50). The climactic scene, when Joseph finally reveals his identity to his brothers, may be the Hebrew Bible's most dramatic reunion. Even slight changes in vocabulary and punctuation, such as the addition of an exclamation point, heighten the drama (Gen 45:3):

KJV: And Joseph said unto his brethren, "I *am* Joseph; doth my father yet live?" And his brethren could not answer him; for they were troubled at his presence.

Anchor: Joseph said to his brothers, "I am Joseph! Is Father still in good health?" But his brothers were unable to reply, so dumfounded were they at him.

Luther: Und sprach zu seinen Brüdern: **Ich bin Joseph. Lebet mein Vater noch**? Und seine Brüder konnten ihm nicht antworten, so **erschraken sie vor seinem Angesicht** [= before his face/presence]

Blitz: **un** shprokh tsu zayne brider / **ikh bin yoysef** / **lebet mayn foter nokh**. un zayne brider kontn im nit entfern zoy **dershrokn zi far zaynem ongezikht**.

Michaelis: **Ich bin Joseph**, sagte er zu seinen Brüdern, **lebt mein Vater noch**? Sie konnten ihm **vor Schrecken** nicht antworten.

Mendelssohn: **Josef** sprach **nämlich** zu seinen Brüdern. **ich bin Josef! Mein Vater, lebt er noch?** Die Brüder **aber** konnten ihm nicht antworten / denn sie waren **vor ihm erschrocken**.

Blitz copied Luther almost verbatim, and both retained the word "face," as in the original Hebrew, at the end of the verse. Michaelis eliminated the Hebraism "before his face," and brought the word order of both clauses in line with German grammar. Mendelssohn also took out "face," and made other changes to heighten the drama. He added exclamation points and question marks. He inserted proper names or pronouns, and rearranged words to create a more naturalistic narrative and, above all, to raise the emotional tenor of the moment. By breaking up Joseph's utterance, Mendelssohn has him almost stuttering with emotion: "I am Joseph! My father—does he still live?" He also added two flavoring words, *aber* (however) and *nämlich* (you see; that is to say). The small differences between Blitz, Mendelssohn, and Michaelis provide a picture of translators striving for a similar overall effect, borrowing from one another and yet trying to refine and to innovate.

Some time ago sounds like the beginning of a Grimms fairy tale. Mendelssohn used the phrase to set up the saga of Moses's birth in Exodus 2—an important biblical chapter with a very infelicitous opening. He added numerous words to vivify the drama of Moses' concealment and discovery by a "princess" and her "chambermaids." Here Exodus 2:1–6, as translated in the KJV and by Mendelssohn:

KJV: And there went a man of the house of Levi, and took *to wife* a daughter of Levi. And the woman conceived, and bare a son: and when she saw him that he *was a* goodly *child*, she hid him three months. And when she could no longer hide him, she took for him an ark of bulrushes, and daubed it with slime and with pitch, and put the child therein; and she laid *it* in the flags by the river's brink. And his sister stood afar off, to wit what would be done to him. And the daughter of Pharaoh came down to wash *herself* at the river; and her maidens walked along by the river's side; and when she saw the ark among the flags, she sent her maid to fetch it. And when she had opened *it*, she saw the child: and, behold, the babe wept. And she had compassion on him, and said, This *is one* of the Hebrews' children.

Mendelssohn: **Vor einiger Zeit** ging ein Man aus dem Hause Lewi. Und nahm eine Tochter Lewis. Die Frau ward jetzt schwanger, gebahr einen Sohn. Als sie ihn sahe, dass er **wohlgebildet** war, verbarg sie ihn drei Monate. Länger aber konnte sie ihn nicht verbergen, da nahm sie für ihn **ein Kästchen aus Binsen**; beklebte es mit Leim und Pech. Legte das Kind hinein und setzte es in das Röhricht, am Ufer des Flusses. Seine Schwester stellte sich von ferne. Um zu wissen, was ihm **widerfahren** wird. Da ging die Tochter Pharaos hinab in den Fluß, sich zu baden, und ihre **Kammer Mägde**, gingen herum am Ufer des Flusses. **Die Prinzessin** erblickte das Kästchen im Röhricht, Da schickte sie ihre Sklawin, und liess es holen.

- *Vor einiger Zeit*: some time ago. The phrase, likely borrowed from Schmidt, not only adds a literary touch, it also solves a notorious difficulty. Moses was not the firstborn child of this couple. Since his siblings Miriam and Aaron were already born, the marriage announced in chapter 2 must have occurred earlier. A famous midrash solves the problem by suggesting that this was a remarriage urged by Miriam in defiance of Pharaoh's decree, thus adding to the wonder of Moses's conception. Mendelssohn's adverbial phrase, like his translation of Sarah's laughter, pushes back against that midrash.
- *wohlgebildet*: well-formed. Mendelssohn must have chosen this descriptive of Moses because it has four syllables. Luther, Blitz, and Witzenhausen use the simpler words *fein*, *sheyn*, *gut fayn*. Perhaps by emphasizing that Moses was a good-looking or well-formed baby (as Ibn Ezra interpreted), Mendelssohn also closes out Rashi's midrash to the effect that when Moses was born, the house was filled with light.

- *Kästchen aus Binsen*: box of rushes/sea grass. Spalding argues that *Binsen*, here and with regard to the Reed Sea (*Binsenmeer*), proves that Mendelssohn borrowed from Schmidt.[114]
- *widerfahren*: befell him. Sophisticated language (to befall him vs. Hebrew "to happen to him").
- *Die Prinzessin*: "the princess" is inserted in lieu of "she." The Bible never refers to Pharaoh's daughter as a princess. Mendelssohn likely borrowed the phrase from Schmidt (who also used "*Die königliche Prinzessin*" (the royal princess) for "Pharaoh's daughter" in 2:5).[115] Mendelssohn also introduces "*Kammer Mägde*," chambermaids, where Schmidt has "*Sklavinnen*." These words lend the narrative the aura of a courtly romance.

Mendelssohn's enhancement continues apace. A few verses later (Ex 2:10),

> KJV: And the child grew, and she brought him unto Pharaoh's daughter, and he became her son. And she called his name Moses: and she said, Because I drew him out of the water.
>
> Mendelssohn: **Als der Jüngling heran wuchs**, brachte sie ihn der Tochter Pharaohs, **er war ihr wie ein Sohn**: **Diese nennte** ihn Mosche, und sprach, weil ich ihn aus dem Wasser **heraus gezogen** habe

Blitz and Witzenhausen had also elevated the diction of these passages in different ways, compared to Luther. Luther writes, "und es ward ihr Sohn" [= and it became her son]. Blitz writes, "She regarded it as her son"; Witzenhausen, "And it became for her as a son"; and Mendelssohn, "he was to her like a son." Mendelssohn also changes *Kind* (child) to *Jüngling*, a lad who might be found in a German folk ballad. He appends directional prefixes to lengthen verbs, *heranwuchs* and *herausgezogen*. Instead of "heißen," to call, he uses "nennen," to name. Most notably, Mendelssohn put in "diese," meaning "the former one," rather than "she," hinting at a controversial interpretation that he spells out in his commentary (see below)—that it was not in fact not the royal princess who named Moses, but his mother or sister.[116]

Clarity and Continuity

Improving biblical syntax involved omissions as well as additions. For Mendelssohn and Michaelis, the first thing that had to go was the slavish "and"/*und*. Here we see a clear departure from Luther, Blitz, and Witzenhausen.

Luther used "*und*" (as the KJV used "and") for Hebrew's connective or consecutive vav, which was for centuries misconstrued to connote "and," and is responsible for the distinctive paratactic rhythm of the Hebrew Bible. Biblical verbs are most commonly encountered in their imperfect, "converted forms," especially in the case of a chain of verbs describing "a consecutive set of actions transpiring in the past."[117] Bible scholars today agree that the vav is part of the narrative structure and does not mean "and." On this issue, the one-hundred-year gap between the Amsterdam Yiddish Bibles and the *Be'ur* made a definitive difference. Compare the approaches to Esau's actions after he bargains away his birthright, first with the "ands" and then without them. Genesis 25:34:

KJV: and he did eat and drink, and rose up, and went his way: thus Esau despised *his* birthright.

Blitz: un er eset un trinket un stund oyf un ging derfun alzoy farakhtet (eysev) zayn ershtgeburt.

Michaelis: Esau aß, trank, stand auf, ging davon, und verachtete seine Erstgeburt.

Mendelssohn: Dieser ass, trank, stund auf, und ging davon. So verachtete Esav die Erstgeburt.

Here as elsewhere, Michaelis's rendering is freer than Mendelssohn's: he moves the subject (Esau) up to the beginning of the clause for a more natural effect, whereas Mendelssohn places Esau's name very late in the verse—following the Hebrew. In other instances as well, Michaelis substitutes a name for a pronoun or vice versa.

The Bible's relentless parataxis would hardly appeal to an eighteenth-century reader. Mendelssohn added transitional phrases and adverbs throughout the text, such as *ferner* (furthermore) and *nämlich* (that is, i.e.), which enabled him to weave a continuous narrative. Comically, he even inserted these in the genealogies or "begats," linked only by "ands" or by nothing at all. (Michaelis simply used commas.)

Compare the list of Yoktan's offspring in Genesis 10: 26–28 in the Anchor Bible and in the *Be'ur*:

Anchor Bible: Joktan begot Almodad, Sheleph, Hazarmaveth, Jerah, Hadoram, Uzal, Diklah, Obal, Abimael, Sheba . . . .

Michaelis: Von diesem Joktan stammen ab, Almodad, Schalef, Hadramauth, Terach, | Hadoram, Sanaa, Diklah, | Obal, Abimael, Saba, | . . .

Mendelssohn: Joktan zeugte Almodad, Schalef, Chazarmawet **und** Jarach.

Wie auch (= as well as) Hadoram, Usal und Diklah. **Ferner** (= furthermore) Owal, Awimaél und Schewa.

In cases where the Bible lacked transitional words, Mendelssohn added them. In Genesis 18:1, Mendelssohn added the German word "*ferner*" (furthermore) to soften an abrupt transition when a new chapter refers to Abraham only as "him" (*elav*). The rabbis had also wrestled with this verse, and their explanation, cited in Dubno's commentary, gave legs to Mendelssohn's addition.

KJV: And the Lord appeared unto him in the plains of Mamre;
Mendelssohn. Der Ewige erschin ihm **ferner**, in dem Haine des Mamre

Comment: In the view of Nachmanides (may his memory be a blessing), the verse "Adonai appeared to him" is connected to the preceding chapter. Because he was circumcised and fulfilled God's commandment, God appeared to him to honor him.

Michaelis went further, adding in adverbs of time:

Michaelis: **Bald nachher** erschien ihm Jehova **von neuen** unter den **Terebinthen** Mamre[118] (= **Shortly thereafter** Jehova appeared to him **again/anew** under the Terebinths of Mamre).

Michaelis's "Terebinths" sends us back to inquire about Mendelssohn's choice of *Haine* for "grove." *Hain* was a word with cultural currency at the time. Perhaps Mendelssohn implanted in the Hebrew Bible an allusion to Klopstock's ode "Der Hügel und der Hain" (The Hill and the Grove, 1767), or to the *Sturm und Drang* poets' society founded in Göttingen in 1772, Göttinger Hainbund (Grove League of Göttingen)?

One final example: the Hebrew Bible, like other ancient documents without punctuation, has a particular way of introducing direct speech:

Exodus 13:1 וַיְדַבֵּר יְהוָה אֶל-מֹשֶׁה לֵּאמֹר.
KJV: And the Lord spake unto Moses, **saying**,

Every translator from Luther through Buber and Rosenzweig who aspired to capture the rhythm of Biblical Hebrew preserves some form of that second "saying,"

Luther: Und der Herr redete mit Mose **und sprach**:
Blitz: un got redet mit moyshe **und sprokh**

Witzenhausen: un got redet tsu (moyshe) **tsu zogn**
BR: Er redete zu Mosche, **sprechend**:

But to eighteenth century ears, this formulation would have sounded antiquated. Michaelis eliminated "saying" altogether ("Und Gott sprach zu Mose"). But Mendelssohn devised a fancy alternative:

Der Ewige sprach zu Moscheh, **wie folgt** (= as follows):
Der Ewige sprach zu Moscheh und Aharon im Lande Mizrajim, **wie folgt**. (Ex 12:1)
Soden redete der Ewige alle dise Worte, **wie folgt**. (Ex 20:1)

Parentheses

On some occasions, rearranging word order, paraphrasing, and eliminating Hebraic euphemisms did not sufficiently clarify the meaning of the text. Parentheses and square brackets enabled the translators of the first wave to cheat a little bit. These internal additions were anachronisms, holdovers from the *taytsh* translations. The translators could not resist inserting an explanation and still maintaining a visible boundary between Scripture and translation. A clear example is the vexing final clause of Exodus 2:25.

KJV: And God looked upon the children of Israel, and God had respect unto *them*.
Anchor: And Deity saw Israel's sons, and he made himself known to them.
Luther: Und er sah darein, und nahm sich ihrer an.
Witzenhausen: Un got zakh die Kinder **(Yisroel)** an. Un got kenit **[zi]**.
Mendelssohn (German): Gott sahe die Kinder Yisrael (**in welchen Zustand sie sichbefanden**): Gott kannte sie, **(das heißt, beschloss sich ihrer anzunehmen)**
Mendelssohn (English): God saw the children of Israel (the condition in which they found themselves): God knew them (which means, decided to adopt them).

Luther translated, "and took note of them" (*und nahm sich ihrer an*) and Blitz replicated Luther exactly. But Witzenhausen's approach required both round and square brackets—round ones for the Hebrew word "Israel," and square ones to add a direct object pronoun "them," a word not present in the Hebrew and thus italicized in KJV (fig. 1.6). Mendelssohn followed

(מצרים) שטארב · אונ' דיא קינדר (ישראל) זיפֿצטן אונ' שריאן פֿון
וועגין דעם דינשט · אונ' איר גישרייא פֿון וועגין דען דינשט גינג אויף
צו גאט : כד אונ' גאט הערטי איר גישרייא · אונ' גאט גידאכֿט
זיין פֿאר בונד מיט (אברהם · מיט יצחק · אונ' מיט יעקב) : כה
אונ' גאט זאך דיא קינדר (ישראל) אן · אונ' גאט קענט [זיא]:

דאש דריטי קאפיטול ג

א אונ' (משה) האט דיא שאף גיווייידט פֿון זיינם שוועהר
(יתרו) · דער הער פֿון (מדין) · אונ' ער פֿירט דיא
שאף הינטר דיא וויסטינייא · אונ' ער קאם צו דעם געטליכן בערג
קען (חורב) : ב אונ' איין ענגיל פֿון גאט ביוויז זיך צו אים · אין
איינר פֿלאם פֿייאר פֿון צווישן דער דארן העק · אונ' ער זאך · אונ' נון
דיא דארן העק ברענט אין דעם פֿייאר · אונ' דיא דארן העק פֿאר
ברענט ניט : ג דא שפראך (משה) · איך וויל איך אילונדרט דא

Fig. 1.6. Witzenhausen Bible, Ex 2:25 (1679).

Witzenhausen and went even further. To be more faithful to the Torah, he chose "saw" instead of "looked at" (*sehen* rather than *ansehen*). He retained a form of Witzenhausen's "*kenit*." But he added expansive parentheses to both clauses in which he introduced sophisticated vocabulary and also the verb *annehmen* found in Luther and Blitz.

Blitz and Witzenhausen, but especially Witzenhausen, used round parentheses to demarcate Hebrew personal names, place names, and Jewish keywords within the Yiddish translation; "also, generally, words of Hebrew-Aramaic origin that are part of Yiddish and that, by conventions of Yiddish spelling from its very earliest days to the present, are spelled as in the source language and *not* in the more phonetically-oriented spelling system."[119] But in the first words below (Genesis 28:8–9), he also added a phrase in square brackets to smooth the transition:

> KJV: And Esau seeing that the daughters of Canaan pleased not Isaac his father; Then went Esau unto Ishmael and took unto the wives which he had Mahalath, the daughter of Ishmael, Abraham's son, the sister of Nevajoth, to be his wife.

Witzenhausen (Yiddish): un [do nun] (eysev) za dos di tekhter fun (knaan) ibl gefiln in den oygn fun (yitskhok) zaynem foter. do ging (eysev tsu yishmoel) un er nam (makhles) di tokhter fun (yishmoel) der zun fun (avrom) di shvester fun (nevoyes) bay zayne vayber tsu eyner froy

Witzenhausen (English): And **[when]** (Esau) saw that the daughters of (Canaan) were displeasing in the eyes of (Isaac) his father, then went (Esau to Ishmael) and took (Mahalath) daughter of (Ishmael), son of (Abraham) the sister of (Nevaioth) by his wives for a wife.

Two more examples: Rebekah's cryptic reaction to her difficult pregnancy, "if *it* be so, why *am* I thus?" (Gen 25:22; KJV), has an existential tone that challenged the first-wave translators and required paraphrase. Witzenhausen, who starts off following Luther (*Und die Kinder stießen sich miteinander in ihrem Leib*), required four sets of brackets to produce a fluid rendering of the Hebrew. Mendelssohn improvised only the second half of Rebekah's questions, but without parentheses.

Witzenhausen (Yiddish): un di kinder shtisn zikh mit an ander in irem layb. do shprokh zi. **ven es aza (eyn tsar) iz [um dos trogn] vorum hob ikh den [gebetn um] dos dozik**. un zi ging hin tsu forshtn [di lerner] fun got.

Witzenhausen (English): And the children collided together in her body. And she said, **if it is (a grief) [to bear], why then [did] I [ask for] it**? And she went hither to investigate [the authorities; students] of God.

Mendelssohn (German): Nun bewegten sich die Kinder heftig in ihr, da sprach sie, **wenn dem also ist, warum habe ich es den gewünscht**? Und ging, den Ewigen zu befragen.

Mendelssohn (English): Now the children moved vigorously in her, and she said, **if that is the way it is, why then did I wish for it**? And went to inquire of the Eternal One.

But on another occasion, Witzenhausen used parenthesis to insert a well-known midrash—in the manner of the *Tsene-Rene*—to explain young Jacob's tendency to "dwell in tents" (Gen 25:27). Mendelssohn, by contrast, stuck with the literal meaning.

KJV: and Jacob *was* a plain man, dwelling in tents.

Blitz (Yiddish): (yankev) ober vor eyn frumer man un voynet in der hitn.

Witzenhausen (Yiddish): ober (yankev) vor eyn oyfrikhtiker man er zas in den getseltn **[un lernt toyre]**.

Witzenhausen (English): (Jacob) was an upright man. He sat in the tents **[and studied Torah]**.

Mendelssohn (German): Jaakow aber ward ein frommer Mann, der in Zelten wohnt.

Mendelssohn (English): But Jacob was a pious man who dwells in tents

The Bible often uses the same root for "sit" and "dwell." The midrashic interpretation cited by Rashi that Jacob studied in the yeshiva of Shem and Eber was widely accepted. Witzenhausen retained it, despite his principles. Witzenhausen did the same with regard to Jewish keywords in Hebrew that he retained whether for pedagogical purposes or because he did not know a German term and did not see fit to translate as the Christians had done. This applies to the case of Esau's spurned birthright, his *bechora* (Gen 25:34):

KJV: Thus Esau despised *his* birthright.

Witzenhausen: un (eysev) farshmeyt di (bkhoyre)

By contrast, Luther and the *Statenvertaling* wrote, "also verachtete Esau seine Erstgeburt." Mendelssohn retained the formulation almost exactly: "so verachtete Esaw die Erstgeburt."

But Michaelis devised a new usage for parentheses: he rendered the etymology of Jacob's and Esau's names accessible in translation, and added boldface inside those brackets for further emphasis. These techniques became common among the *second wave* of Jewish German translations. See Gen 25:25–26:

KJV: And the first came out red, all over like an hairy garment; and they called his name Esau. And after that came his brother out, and his hand took hold on Esau's heel; and his name was called Jacob: and Isaac *was* threescore years old when she bare them.

Michaelis: der erste, der heraus kam, war ganz mit rothem Haren, als mit einem rauhen Pelz überdecket [= overlaid], daher nannten sie ihn Esau, (d.i **bedecket** [= covered]) | nach ihm kam sein Bruder, und hatte Esaus Fersen [= heels] in der Hand. Davon bekam er den Nahmen, Jacob, (das ist, **Er hält Fersen** [= he holds heels]). (boldface in the original)

Michaelis also used parentheses to explain the odd notice about the sons of God (*bnei elohim*) marrying the daughters of man (Gen 6:2). He could not do much about "sons of God" and "daughters of men," but he could use parentheses to naturalize these odd phrases.

Michaelis: sahen die Söhne Gottes, (die Gott für Vater und Schöpfer erkannten) auf die Töchter der Menschen, (d.i. auf die, welche weiter nichts als Töchter der Menschen zu seyn glaubten) weil sie schön waren, und nahmen sich Frauen unter allen, die ihnen gefielen.)

Blitz and Mendelssohn borrowed *bnei rabrebaia* ("sons of the great men" or "sons of the rulers") from the Aramaic targum in order to translate "sons of God" as godfearing, important, or godly people.

Michaelis even went so far as to place a biblical phrase or even a complete verse in parentheses if he believed it was rightfully a parenthetical comment. In Exodus 7:7 he uses a single parenthesis:

Michaelis (German): (Mose war achtzig, und Aharon drey und achtzig Jahr alt, da sie mit Farao redeten.)

Michaelis (English): (Moses was eighty and Aaron eighty-three years old when they spoke with Pharaoh.)

Mendelssohn occasionally did the same, as in Genesis 16:3:

Mendelssohn (English): Sarai, Abram's wife, took her Egyptian maid Hagar (after Abram had lived in the land of Canaan for ten years) and gave her to her husband Abram for a wife.

Typically, Mendelssohn uses parentheses to explain anything vaguely corporeal—anthropomorphic, or figures of speech involving the body. In doing so, he followed in the footsteps of the Targum Onkelos, though he also borrowed terms from a contemporary Christian translation, the Wertheim Bible. Examples of rationalist language include the words *erscheinen* (to appear) and *Erscheinung* (appearance, epiphany) to describe the theophanies at Sinai and also at Genesis 28:17, following Jacob's dream:

KJV: this *is* none other but the house of God, and this *is* the gate of heaven.

Mendelssohn: Hier ist Gottes Haus, und hier das Tor des Himmels (aus welchem nämlich die Erscheinungen Gottes auf Erden kommen) (= namely, from which God's epiphanies come to earth).

Neither Blitz nor Michaelis had problems with "God's House" or "Gate of Heaven." Blitz introduced the term "Pfort" (gate) and Michaelis added expressions and details to dramatize Jacob's discovery.

Blitz: hi iz niks andersht den gots hoyz un hi iz di pfort des himls.

Michaelis: Als nun Jacob von seinem Traum erwachete, **brach er in die Worte aus: wahrhaftig! Jehova ist an diesem Orte! Und ich wußte es nicht!** | und mit einem Grausen sagte er: **wie fürchterlich ist dieser Ort! Er ist nichts anders als Gottes Haus! er ist das Thor des Himmels.** | . . . . und bennenete den Ort, Bethel, (oder Gottes Haus,) . . .

Michaelis (English): Now, when Jacob awoke from his dream, **he broke into these words: Truly! Jehova is at this place! And I didn't know it!** | And with dread, he said: **how fearsome is this place! It is nothing less than God's house! It is the gate of heaven**! . . . And he named the place Bethel (or God's house).

Looking at the Hebrew Bible through the lenses of these translations highlights the fact that even simple phrases are, as Erich Auerbach wrote, "fraught with background." The first-wave translators used myriad techniques to do justice both to language as such and to the "promise" within it. They were the heirs of Rebekah, determined to find an answer; Jacob, wrestling for the blessing; and Moses, striking the rock to produce water for a thirsty nation.

EXCURSUS ON MENDELSSOHN'S COMMENTARY: EXPLAINING THE WAYS OF LANGUAGE

Bible translations of the first wave tell the reader what Scripture means; commentary explains *how* it means. A typical comment in the *Be'ur* begins with elementary observations about definition, part of speech, or syntax. It seems that even basic knowledge could not be taken for granted, as when Mendelssohn explains that "garments of skins" meant "garments *made* of skins," or that "they knew they were naked" means that "they felt the feeling of shame that humans feel when they are naked," or that the word "month" refers to the 29 days 12 hours and 43.93 parts of an hour it takes for the moon to rotate, or that a solar year is twelve or thirteen lunar months and 365 days long.[120] Like every Jewish commentary, the *Be'ur* free-associates to cognate verses throughout the Tanach and opens up the history of hermeneutics by citing earlier translators and exegetes. The past had a vote, but not a veto. Into that mix, it added grammar rules and axioms of interpretation. The notes vary in length. The longest excursus comes before the Song of the Sea in Exodus 15; other long comments are found before the Decalogue in Exodus 20; the "frontlets" worn as a sign between the eyes in Exodus 13:15; and the problem of translating names. When reading, one senses a narrator addressing a reader; many notes conclude, "and so it is translated in L.A." (*leshon Ashkenaz*) or "the German translator writes." But the normal texture (or tenor) of Mendelssohn and Dubno's commentary is workman-like, with the goal of portraying translation as a process of trial and error. The *Be'ur* was a site of experimentation as well as explanation, and it opens a window onto the pressure points of the translation, and also to the untranslatable. At times it includes an alternate rendering that Mendelssohn would not have dared to use above the line.

The first two verses of Genesis show the many uses that Mendelssohn and Dubno found for commentary. In the KJV, Genesis 1:1 reads "In the beginning God created the heaven and the earth." Mendelssohn's first note is, "**Bereshit**—like in the beginning. And Onkelos translated " *b'kadmon*," "at first." And it is not as much dependent on [something else] (in the manner of an adjective)."

The very first note about the very first word of the Bible seems only to state the obvious. To explain that *Bereshit* means "in the beginning" was to part company with Rashi's famous comment that the first word is not a stand-alone phrase but a reliant or connecting word meaning "In the beginning of" rather than "At first," effectively turning the first clause into a subordinate clause. (Hirsch insists on this latter nuance and translates *Vom Anfang* [= from the beginning]).

Mendelssohn's second point pertains to the definite direct object marker 'et', the fourth and sixth words of the Hebrew Torah, which spawned numerous midrashic interpretations. This particle is hard to describe, because it has no equivalent in English or German. Knowing that fact, Mendelssohn opens with a grammar lesson designed to show that Hebrew has the same grammatical structure as the "languages of the nations." In the quotations that follow I retain Mendelssohn and Dubno's original parentheses, used to demarcate all German words:

> ***Et***. *Et* is the sign of the verb in all cases, so sometimes the sign of (accusative) and sometimes the sign of (nominative). Because in all basic rules about what in German are called active verbs (handelne Zeit Wörter), the subject of the sentence is active and is marked nominative, and the object of the act is connected to it by accusative. As in this statement, God is the subject and is marked nominative, and the heavens and earth are objects of the act and come in the sign of accusative. In the case of passive verbs (leidende Zeit Wörter) the object is itself the subject, as in "The skies are created" (German). The languages of the nations chose

to mark the subject with a nominative, as the subject of this statement, even if it is also the object. So the speaker of the Holy Tongue will mark it with an *et* as in Exodus 21:28, Exodus 10:8, Numbers 32:5.

The translation and comment to Genesis 1:2 announce a bold break with both premodern and contemporary renderings. First, compare Mendelssohn's version with others:

Mendelssohn: Die Erde aber war **unförmlich und vermischt**.
Luther: Und die Erde war **wüst und leer (= desolate and empty)**.
Blitz: un di erd var **vist un leer**
Witzenhausen: un di erd ist gevesen **vist un leer**.
Michaelis: Die Erde war damahls **wüste und leer**

Mendelssohn's comment addresses two big topics. First, he explains his omission of the famous slavish "and"/*und* introduced by Luther (and KJV) to approximate the role of the conjunctive vav—the letter with which this verse and so many others begin. Mendelssohn chose to replace this *und* with *aber* (but), basing the decision in Hebrew grammar.

aber: The purpose of this vav is not to connect. Because the vav has many purposes, as I noted in my preface. Here, the purpose is to continue the clause.

The introduction of coordinating and subordinating conjunctions to mitigate the paratactic rhythm of the Hebrew Bible, to impose syntax, is a central stylistic feature of his translation. With regard to the famous *tohu va'vohu*, both Yiddish translators and Michaelis followed Luther's *wüst und leer*. But Mendelssohn chose to do something daring. Mendelssohn's rendering of the uncreated universe wanted to emphasize, not emptiness and desolation but the lack of form and order. The comment quotes Rashi's use of the Old French *estordison* (dizzying), which he translates as *betäubend*, as a way into his own idea—because what inspires such feelings if not a lack of order? With *vermischt*, Mendelssohn sees *vohu* as a composite of two words *vo hu*, "it is inside of it." What was inside? "The foundations of all material created things." *Tohu va'vohu* is the mind of the unenlightened reader. The next generation following Mendelssohn quickly rejected this innovative rendering; Zunz translated it "öd und wust."

To sum up: the very first set of comments in the famous *Be'ur* challenges the medieval exegetes; teaches German and Hebrew grammar; defends an innovative translation (new to German, but vaguely tied to Rashi's translation into the Old French); and establishes for the modern Jewish Bible a signature feature of the Enlightenment Bible, namely the rejection of the slavish German *und* or Yiddish *un*.

We have seen that Mendelssohn used translation to illuminate and improve upon biblical Hebrew; the comments show how and why such improvements were needed. Mendelssohn made sure to clarify any confusion or inconsistency regarding subject-verb agreement. When Adam and Eve hide from God's voice in 3:8 after eating the forbidden fruit, the Hebrew reads, in effect, "And **he** hid himself, Adam and his wife, before God."[121] Mendelssohn took the occasion to explain that in Hebrew, a singular verb may precede a plural subject.

> **V'yitchabeh** (and he hid himself): [The verb is] in the singular form applied to Adam and his wife as we discussed above in the preface. When the verb precedes the subject there is no need to preserve the number. In the view of the grammarians, this word draws itself and another with it.

Another famous inconsistency involves the Hebrew midwives and their houses in Exodus 1:21. Here, a masculine plural pronoun (them) fails to agree with its female referent (midwives). (This difficulty becomes irrelevant in German and in English, where "them" is always gender neutral.)

> JPS: And because the midwives feared God, He established households for **them**

But Mendelssohn translated the verse in a way that suggests that the referent might not have been female after all:

> Mendelssohn: Als nun die Hebammen Got fürchteten: **Und Gott neue Häuser in der Nation entstehen**[122] **ließ** (= Now when the midwives feared God, God allowed new homes to arise in the nation).

The translator could have elided the problem entirely (as Luther, Blitz, and Witzenhausen did)[123] but chose not to. The comment offers a series of traditional interpretations, with which it disagrees on the basis of grammar;[124] because there is no getting around the fact that "the word *lahem* [them] goes against all of these interpretations, because it is masculine." His creative solution is to link the phrase about the houses back to verse 20, whose subject was not the midwives but the people of Israel, "Nation."

Sometimes, the commentary made a strong statement by saying nothing at all (Gen 4:8):

> JPS: Cain said to his brother Abel. And when they were in the field, Cain rose up on his brother Abel and killed him.

What did Cain say to Abel before he killed him? Words were spoken, but the Hebrew Bible does not record them. Still, the odd verb "rose up" (*va'yakom*) gave commentators a clue: Cain must have approached Abel from below, perhaps feigning weakness, looking for a pretext to take action. The brothers quarreled about property and about women (!), according to the *Tsene-Rene*. Abel threw Cain to the ground in anger. Cain then tricked Abel into allowing him to "get up," whereupon he killed him. In this context, Mendelssohn's comment about those missing words shows notable restraint:

> And it doesn't tell us what he said to him. Although the custom of the Holy Tongue is to explain the word "said" by giving us what was spoken, whenever possible. It could be that he said to him, "Let us go out to the field," as it is written in Targum Yonatan and also in the Greek translation we have in our hands, attributed to the seventy elders.

Mendelssohn stuck with *pshat*, even at the cost of admitting that the text does not make sense. But he goes on to mention that ancient translations, Targum Yonatan and the Septuagint, do fill in the missing comment—thus making a subtle statement about the power of translation to make sense of Scripture. The comment exemplifies Mendelssohn's commitment to showing that the sense of any biblical verse, even one so blatantly incomplete, had to be found within the words themselves.

The *Be'ur*'s most important function, also spelled out in the preface, was to bridge any discrepancies whatsoever between the literal sense of the Hebrew and the German rendering or "L.A." (*leshon Ashkenaz*). Figures of speech, many involving body parts, generally gave Mendelssohn trouble; already in Genesis 1:2, he crafted a note to explain that the figurative "face of the deep" was only "borrowed" from the human body and referred only to the outermost piece. But he consistently departed from the literal sense with regard to the "Bodies of God," in Benjamin Sommer's phrase—anthropomorphisms and figurative language related to divinity. When these came together, as in "the hand of God," he had to make account. In the case of Moses's "heavy mouth and heavy lips," he used parentheses to explain the figure meant that

Moses "cannot use mouth and lips as he would want to." But with the hand of God in Exodus. 14:31, the euphemism was simply mistranslated, as it still is in JPS:

> Mendelssohn: Als nun Jisrael **die große Macht** sahen, welche der Ewige an Mizrajim aus geübt, da fürchtete das Volk den Ewigen . . . (= Now when Israel saw **the great power** that the Eternal One wielded in Egypt, the people feared the Eternal One . . .)
>
> JPS: And when Israel saw **the wondrous power** which the LORD had wielded against the Egyptians, the people feared the LORD . . .

Long before the JPS, the targumim doctored the verse to read "the **strength of the** great hand," and even the KJV has "that great work" in lieu of "hand."[125] And in fact, it was not really the hand that they saw, but its might! Mendelsohn was in very good company, but his comment still had to defend that decision—here, using the logic of synecdoche—and highlight the translator's authority to decide.

> He translates "the great hand" as "the great power that God's hand wrought," and many languages have different meanings for hand, and all of them mean hand, and the interpreter will adjust the meaning according to the context (Rashi). Onkelos translated "yat gevurat yada rabata," and that's how it is in the German translation.

Finally: Does an Egyptian princess know Hebrew? Mendelssohn took a special interest in the problem of translating foreign names—a *Grenzfall* (a limit case) in any translation, but especially in the Tanach. The naming of Moses presented a particular problem. Mendelssohn knew that that Bible included many *Fremdwörter*, but he was unwilling to take Moses's naming at face value. The Bible seems to say that Moses is named by Pharaoh's daughter. But how could she have provided a Hebrew name, based on "because I drew him out [*mishitihu*] of the water"? Did Pharaoh's daughter—whom Mendelssohn called the princess—know Hebrew? Even more confusing—is it possible that the Hebrew name Moshe is actually a translation of the original non-Hebrew name? The mistake made by Ibn Ezra and by other commentators is that they attributed "and she called his name Moshe" to Pharaoh's daughter.[126]

After introducing the problem, Mendelssohn confronts Ibn Ezra, who wrote that Pharaoh's daughter gave Moses the Egyptian name "Munius," which the Torah translated into Hebrew as Moshe. After rejecting Ibn Ezra, he suggests another possibility (given by the thirteenth-century commentator Chizkuni): it was Moses's mother who named him, and not the princess. The grammatical form of *mishitihu* (I drew him out) is irregular; it could also mean, "*you* drew him out." Mendelssohn crafted a translation that supported the idea that Moses's mother—who is any case the subject of the first verb in the verse—gave him his (Hebrew) name.[127] Proper names, like foreign words, prompted intriguing comments.[128]

On one occasion, Mendelssohn concludes his survey of previous translations by noting that previous approaches are so laden with errors that no precedent can be found, and since "silence is better than speech that is invalid," it was best not to attempt translation: such was his approach to the names of the twelve precious stones on the breastplate of the High Priest, mentioned in Exodus 28:17–24 and again in 39:10–13.[129] However, he did have a strong precedent here: Ibn Ezra. In the words of modern translator William H. C. Propp: "When it comes to identifying the gemstones, 'we all grope at the wall, as if blind' (ibn Ezra [shorter commentary quoting Is 59:10]). When completely at a loss, I simply transliterate the Hebrew. For the rest, we have educated guesses."[130] Unwilling to make an educated guess, Mendelssohn retains the Hebrew for ten of the gems, translating only the two that were known in his day, sapphire and jasper. But his decision to retain the Hebrew names was also a repudiation of two distinct approaches to the gems used in recent history: the Yiddish translation tradition and Luther. Luther, as Erika Timm demonstrates, might have looked to Old Yiddish translations, but he rejected those and instead followed the Vulgate in all but two cases, one of which was his (imaginative) invention of *Demand* (diamond) for *yahalom* because it seemed only proper in a list of this sort.[131] Witzenhausen and Blitz stuck with the Old Yiddish names for the gems, with one exception: they incorporated Luther's "diamond," which must have appealed to them.

Mendelssohn's commentary was an integral part of the translation. In addition to performing some of the functions of Rashi and Ibn Ezra (citing and taking issue with other commentators and opening up interpretive history), the notes addressed translational challenges by discussing grammar and style, as well as the history of translation, with an overwhelming focus on the ancient translators: Aramaic targumim, the Septuagint, and Saadia. For these reasons, the *Be'ur* records Jewish translation history. Most importantly perhaps, the *Be'ur* externalized, pointed to, the essential character and multifaceted texture of Mendelssohn's approach to translation—this is the deeper meaning of the words *Targum Ashkenazi*.

APOLOGIAS: THE RELIGIOUS MANDATE OF THE MODERN TRANSLATOR

Even more than later translators, these first three modern Jewish translators of Scripture strove to counterbalance innovation, which they knew would give the impression of "tampering with the sacred language," with traditionalism.[132] An enterprise undertaken in the name of *language as such* had to be justified in the name of *Torah as such* and projected back into Jewish history and memory. Fortunately, Judaism's concept of the Oral Torah, better translated "Torah that is spoken," communicated to Moses on Mount Sinai together with the Written Torah, provided the ideal rubric. Blitz, Witzenhausen, and Mendelssohn composed prefaces that aspired to justify, defend, and promote the task of translation in Jewish society, but also to persuade their readership that the translated book they held in their hands was the very same Torah transmitted to Moses on Sinai. In the manner of medieval religious writing, these three prefaces, two in Hebrew and one in Yiddish, were woven out of biblical and liturgical allusions.

Jekuthiel Blitz's Hebrew preface, the shortest of the three, was called "Introduction in the Holy Tongue." Joseph Witzenhausen called his slightly longer Yiddish introduction "Translator's Apology." Moses Mendelssohn gave his lengthy, three-part essay a symbolic title linking it to the Pentateuch: the latter was *Book of the Paths of Peace* (*Sefer Netivot HaShalom*), and the preface, accordingly, was called "Light for the Path" (Or Lanetiva). Both of these titles, taken from traditional sources, reflected wishful thinking. In Jewish liturgy, the paths are those of Torah ("all its paths are peace").[133] The "path" appears in another crucial line in Mendelssohn's preface: "It is impossible to understand Scripture without understanding the ways of language." Blitz likened translating to splitting the seas of language to expose the road upon which the Israelite nation could journey from bondage to liberation.[134]

The notion of an Oral Torah revealed to Moses alongside the written Torah originated in the third or fourth century CE, ostensibly to solve a critical problem: how to endow the earliest postbiblical, canonical work of Jewish law, the Mishnah, with normative authority. Affiliating the art of translation with what Jacob Neusner calls "the myth of the dual Torah" was a defining feature of the first-wave translation; it would eventually play a role in Samson Raphael Hirsch's theory of translation.[135] Each translator elevated the "ways of language" to become part of the Oral Torah.

Blitz's one-page Hebrew "introduction in the holy tongue" is a heavily rabbinic discourse. It begins with a long quotation from the *Book of Principles* by Spanish Jewish philosopher Rabbi Joseph Albo, praising the Torah and lamenting the decline of wisdom, as his inspiration to translate (*l'ha'atik*) the three parts of the Hebrew Bible into the language of the exile. Blitz first justifies translation as a way to recover lost knowledge. The next section quotes talmudic passages about translation and the question of which script can be written—a direct response to the prohibitions against writing down translations of sacred literature discussed in the introduction. Finally, after emphasizing that he wishes to translate "for the purpose of his generation, to guide them on a path paved and trodden by the world" (*l'toelet hador l'hadricham b'derech slulah ukhvushah me'avot ha-olam*), Blitz turns to Moses and the Oral Torah, offering a long defense. He goes so far as to say that if the purpose of revelation on Mount Sinai had only been to give Moses the two tablets, God could have managed it in "one brief hour"—He would not have needed forty days and nights! Instead, Moses spent that time studying the Torah's "interpretations and grammar" (*perusheha v'dikdukeha*), because without the "interpretation of the Oral Torah (*perush ha-torah b'al peh*) the Torah is like a sealed book . . . because the verses break and contradict each other." Blitz then lists examples of problematic biblical verses, illustrating many of the things that would not be understandable without the Oral Torah. "Thus God wrote remembrances of the commandments in shorthand in the written Torah, their explanations and grammar in the Oral Torah." It's a kind of Jewish grammatology. Blitz then quotes Pirkei d'Rabbi Eliezer.

> Since God foresaw that the nations of the world were destined to write the twenty-four books of the Torah, Prophets, and Writings and to turn them over to evil, God gave oral signs [*simanim*] to Moshe. Since God gave the *perush* (explanation) of Torah and *ikarah* (its principle) to Moshe orally, and they were passed down from person to person in every generation, God warned Israel not to veer from the words of the elders, neither right nor left. And it is written, You shall come to the priests and the Levites and the judge who will be with you in times to come . . .

By association with the *simanim*, explanations, and principles revealed as part of the Oral Torah, a translation becomes a means of guarding and protecting the Torah and Israel as well.

Blitz concludes with an empowering quotation from the Scroll of Esther, describing how the dispatches of the Persian king "were sent to all the provinces of the king, to every province in its own script and to every nation in its own language, that every man should wield authority in his home and speak the language of his own people" (JPS, Esther 1:22). The preface as a whole, like those royal messengers—and much like the ornate title pages—

travels a great distance: it begins with a lament over the decline of knowledge and the fallen state of the Jews, and concludes with an empowering model of translation associated with the dissemination of knowledge and the restoration of patriarchal authority in the diaspora. Blitz's brilliant move is to evoke the *simanim* (signs) which in rabbinic usage refer to vowels, accents, verse breaks—the marks necessary to decode written Scripture—and other schemes by which Torah is learned,[136] and to frame translation of the text as one of these *simanim*, extratextual signs or mnemonics given to Moses. On the one hand, translation is part of the Oral Torah, a form of *perush* or a key to unlocking its meaning. On the other hand, in such a scenario, the Written Torah becomes just slightly *less* important than the Oral Torah, which in turn makes it immanently translatable.

Mendelssohn's Mosaic Origins

The importance of Moses in the genealogy of the modern Bible translator cannot be overstated; yet the most playful treatment occurs in Mendelssohn's prospectus and preface. The prospectus includes three sample translations: Exodus 1, Numbers 23–24, and the "Ode to Zion" by Jehuda Halevi. Why these excerpts, and why not Genesis? Genesis 1 was highly contested among Christians and Jews alike; but Exodus 1 sets the stage for the Jewish national story.[137] Translation becomes a national necessity, even a condition of Jewish survival—perhaps even an act of defiance, akin to the midwives' response to Pharaoh in Exodus 1.[138] This passage hints at Mendelssohn's status as a new Moses—an image popular in his lifetime, also evoked in Naphtali Herz Wessely's tribute poem also included in the front matter. Moses reappears in the very first line of "Light for the Path": "This is the Torah [teaching] that Moses set before the Israelites at the Lord's word by the hand of Moses." All synagogue-attending Jews would have recognized these words in Hebrew—not so much from their biblical context,[139] but because they are sung every Sabbath morning, following the reading from the Torah scroll, after the scroll is unrolled and raised up high to face the congregation, who in turn rise up and sing as if to reenact the biblical scene. In co-opting the liturgical verse into the preface, the modern author announces that "this" translated Torah *is that same book* that Moses brought us at the bidding of God. In an age of Bible criticism, when the authorship of Scripture was up for grabs, it is a clear declaration of his convictions. It also adds a new twist to Richard Cohen's assertion that the modern Bible became the new synagogue. Mendelssohn cleverly reinscribes this "look and see" moment in his preface, both for its performative value and its content.

But Mendelssohn's preface goes much further than that of Blitz: he opens up an inquiry into the materiality of Scripture—not the narrative, laws, and stories, but the material texture of the written book. Moses, God's first secretary, again plays a crucial role. Mendelssohn cites many debates about Moses's authorship of Scripture from the Talmud and commentaries. How did he pen the final eight verses of Deuteronomy describing his own death?[140] He makes reference to the prophet Jeremiah and his scribe, Baruch ben Neriah, another "invisible translator" who referred to himself in the third person. The subtext here is that even when we insist that the text comes straight from God to Moses, transmission requires intermediaries. Scripture had to enter the human domain; human ears heard the words and human hands recorded them. All forms of transmission of Torah—vocalizing, writing, copying, editing, annotating, correcting, and translating—require a human component. Switching registers, Mendelssohn concludes that section of the introduction by noting that even with all these disagreements, the concept of Mosaic authorship is a tenet of faith; it is not known for a fact but is "believed" to be true. In closing: "As long as the heavens are above the earth, [our holy Torah] lies guarded and ordered in our hands, and will not be forgotten from the mouths of our heirs."[141]

But Mendelssohn went still further. Whereas Ludwig Philippson, about fifty years later, took the opportunity to explicate biblical contents, ideas, tendencies, characters, and plot, Mendelssohn opens up an inquiry that is in some ways far more tendentious: how has the written book you are holding in your hands today come to be what it is? The material history of Scripture has never been a part of a traditional Jewish religious education, which focuses instead on commandments, stories, and morals. What Mendelssohn goes on to recount are numerous instances of writing, translating, vocalizing, and copying, which all add up to a dialectic of change and preservation. The narrative with which he introduces his translation plays out diachronically, over and through time, and synchronically, along the divine-human axis. The unstated theme is the essential unchanging nature of the Torah. Rhetorically, the preface is not unlike those of the Yiddish translators, as interweaves biblical and rabbinic quotations. In stark contrast to his reverent rhetoric and the verses with which he punctuates the narrative ("our life and the length of our days"), all the data demonstrate, again and again, *lo ba'shamayim hi* ([Torah] is not in the heavens): that is, once transmission of Torah relies on human beings, it is hardly foolproof. To some degree, the preface projects back in time, or sublimates, pending controversies among Bible critics about the origins and integrity of Scripture that he dared not mention. But the relish with which he describes the various arguments and controversies suggests that his longwinded narrative functions somehow to consolidate his own authority. Among many topics raised, the leitmotif most pertinent in this context is the idea that, at each step, human intervention was, and is, needed to secure and safeguard scripture. The lineage reaches from Moses, to Ezra, to the scribes (*sofrim*), the Targum Onkelos, to the Rabbis of the Talmud, the Masoretes in the tenth century, to Elija Levita in the sixteenth century, to Mendelssohn himself. Ultimately, he tries to reassure the reader that those human beings entrusted with mediating the Torah to the "Nation"—he himself, Moses, and other precursors—are its guardians, custodians of the "living word," and that to translate is to place a fence around the "fountain of living waters" (Jeremiah 2:13).

In sum, Mendelssohn argues from within Jewish history and memory that Torah is not an antique volume, not a Platonic form, but a linguistic entity, written and spoken, copied and sung, vulnerable to the exigencies of temporality and the contingencies of human transmission. He uses liturgy, scriptural verses, and rabbinic maxims to reiterate that although the scriptural text has been subjected to a long tradition of change, the heart has remained the same. He describes a dialectic of change and preservation: he does justice, in other words, to the tension between the Torah and the Bible; between the eternal, unchanging nature of Scripture and the history of its transmission. His decision to render of the name of God, "the Lord" or *Adonai*, as *der Ewige*, "The Eternal One," can also be seen as the ultimate trace of the eternal essence of Torah itself. In a Platonic sense—and Plato does receive mention in the preface for having read the Torah in Greek translation—*der Ewige* represents the pure form of Torah as distinct from the physical, tangible, visible Torah. *Der Ewige* is the only true *Leitwort* of the Mendelssohn Bible—and, perhaps for this reason, *ewig* is a word that Buber and Rosenzweig avoid at all costs in their translation.

MANIFESTOS: THE JEWISH TRANSLATOR AS MODERN AUTHOR

What was most *modern* about Blitz and Witzenhausen, according to Erika Timm, was their ambivalence: at each step, they had to decide whether to draw from the standardized Yiddish translation vocabulary or to borrow from a Christian translation. Their choices were not made consistently, for a variety of reasons—above all, because the translators lacked knowledge of biblical Hebrew, were not specialists in Hebrew, and did not have access to Hebrew grammars and Hebrew-Yiddish dictionaries, or because certain verses had unshakeable significance for Jewish readers.[142] By Mendelssohn's time, when there were many more options, the ambivalence was amplified many times over. This dilemma had an important parallel in Christian society.

In his study of German translation practices in Romantic Germany, Antoine Berman illuminates the problem of methodology in Luther (drawing upon Franz Rosenzweig's essay *Scripture and Luther* in the process). The precedent set by Luther is not only that a translated Bible becomes the foundation of national identity, creating a rupture, a before and after. Nor is it only the translator's determination to "give room to Hebrew" at the expense of German. Berman highlights Luther's rejection of method. Whereas Jerome comes right out and says, in his letter to Pammachius, "I have not translated word for word but meaning for meaning," Luther "seems to oscillate between several modes of translation."[143]

> Not to choose between literalness and freedom, between the "meaning" and the "letter," between Latin and Hebrew, does not signify a methodological wavering but a perception of the fundamental aporias of translation and an intuition of what can and must be done at a given historical moment.[144]

Many aporias structure the tradition of German Jewish Bible translation: sense vs. word; cultural vs. religious goals; German vs. Jewish; oral vs. written ancient and modern; ambiguity vs. certainty; author vs. copyist; Torah vs. Bible.[145] As important as the choices themselves was the translators' public self-presentation as individuals empowered to make those difficult choices, whether on religious, aesthetic, linguistic, perhaps even subjective grounds (i.e., personal taste).

In a powerful expression of how novel they knew their roles to be, the translators of the first wave invoked the impossibility of translation, then established that they had the knowledge and skills to realize the impossible. Joseph Witzenhausen's "translator's apology" of 1679 begins as follows:

> The Translator says: Because every knowledgeable person knows that when one wants to translate something from one language to another, one cannot translate it word for word—it is absolutely impossible (*i efshor meyoylom*).
>
> It is not appropriate, as when one daily encounters a stranger who does not know *taytsh*, and wants to begin to speak *taytsh*, he speaks always placing the last word first, because his language, whatever that language is, does it that way, and he thinks that because that is correct in his language, it would be correct in *taytsh*. In reality, it is the reverse in *taytsh*.

The problem laid out here, in Berman's words, is that "different languages are translatable, but they are also different, hence to a certain extent untranslatable."[146] Witzenhausen found a clever way to make this abstract idea relatable by appealing to the everyday interactions between Jews and Gentiles: the experience of hearing a Dutch or German speaker garble Yiddish, would mirror back (in Goethe's phrase) to Jewish readers the deficits of the *taytsh* tradition, the extant Yiddish translations of the Torah. An intriguing rhetorical strategy! What is more, in invoking the unnatural flow of language in spoken conversation, Witzenhausen echoes Luther's rationale in the famous passage from his *Circular Letter on Translating* (1530):

> Only an idiot would go and ask the letters of the Latin alphabet how to speak German. . . . You've got to go out and ask the mother in her house, the children in the street, the ordinary man at the market. Watch their mouths move when talk [*sic*], and translate that way. Then they'll understand you and realize that you are speaking *German* to them.[147]

This axiomatic impossibility of translation, once stated openly, provided the impetus for something new and better. Witzenhausen continues, stating his own method:

> Thus, when one wants to translate something, one has to be careful to understand the matter [first], and then one can translate into whatever language one chooses, in a pure, clear, beautiful language, as a story or narrative [*sipur dvarim*], just as when one recounts a story in good order. But [one] does not reverse the words or place the last word first, as [one does] when a foreigner wants to speak *taytsh* and can't do it properly. Now otherwise, in another book, one can add a few words in order to decorate the language, in order to help one to understand it properly, which cannot be in that book [the Bible], because it should not be more than the *pshat* of the *taytsh* of the verse, and by no means through the *drash*, so as not to give an excuse to the other nations to say that you are falsifying the Torah, God forbid, and writing more or less than is in truth in the holy Torah.

The translator with understanding, who is no "stranger" to the text, is qualified to produce a new kind of translation, one that is pure, clear, and beautiful; one that resembles a pleasurable real-life experience, that of telling and hearing a good story. To advance the Jewish translated Bible from an awkward, garbled text into a good story: this captures the mission of the first wave. However, to the religious mindset, this division of Scripture into form and content was not without pitfalls: "One must not give a justification to the other nations to say that you are falsifying the Torah, Heaven forbid, and writing more or less than is in truth in the Holy Torah." A free rendering, by nature, is no longer tethered to the actual words in the Hebrew verse, let alone to syntax and word order. The translator will invariably be accused of adding and omitting words from Scripture. This was of course the case with Martin Luther, who got in to trouble for "adding" a single word to Paul's sermon in Romans 3:28—an accusation which prompted him to write the *Circular Letter* in his own defense. A Jewish translator had to obey the biblical proscription, "You shall not add anything to what I command you or take anything away from it" (Deut 4:2; JPS), and even more seriously, he had to avoid even the appearance of tampering with the Masoretic text of Scripture. Ultimately, the translator who veered from the word-for-word method had to defend his integrity:

> Thus, I made the effort with all my strength and might, day and night and under extreme pressure, to proofread this translation many times, so that it is translated correctly just the way it is in the verse, without additions or subtractions, and so that no word in the verse is omitted. But at times, one had to put a word in the middle in the verse so that it is appropriate in *taytsh*, just as the practice of all translators is, and where it is needed, one must add one word or sometimes more, either to make the language more decorative, or so that can properly understand the meaning of the verse. Those words that one had to add are placed with this sign [ ] whereby one can recognize that the word or those words are not in the holy tongue. Rather, these words are added for the reasons I listed above. Only the word [*fun*], which often does not appear in the verse, one often does not pay careful attention to place it in the brackets, because other translators in other languages also were not careful about the word [*fun*].[148]

Witzenhausen asserts that his heroic efforts, cautiousness, exertions in proofreading, and piety prevented him from tampering with the original. Nonetheless, he saw fit to include a visible sign, *siman*—square brackets around any added words—to guarantee that the scriptural verse remained intact even in translation.

The impossibility of translation resurfaced one hundred years later, in a preface that was many pages longer than Witzenhausen's but made the same fundamental point: "It is impossible to understand Scripture without knowing the ways of language." Mendelssohn needed more than personal integrity to persuade Jewish society that a clear, correct literary translation of the Bible was an idea whose time had come; it was not enough to tell a good story. He inserted an entire chapter on the "ways of language" in his preface, and added many lessons to the page of Scripture in the form of commentary. These language lessons were truly a well-lit path from ignorance and distortion to knowledge and to "peace."

When facing the dilemma of whether to follow a Jewish precursor or to borrow from one of the many German Christian translations available to him, Mendelssohn considered all options. But in his preface, he emphasized one, traditional choice: *pshat* or *drash*—the literal meaning or the exegetical Jewish rendering. The formulation "sometimes A, sometimes B" appears first in Mendelssohn's personal account of how he came to translate to "*die reine und regelrechte deutsche Sprache*" for his sons:

> I placed the translation in their mouth, together with the learning of the text, *sometimes word for word and sometimes according to the meaning and context of the subject matter*, in order to accustom them to the meaning of the verse, the subtleties of the language and clarity of its teaching, until they would grow up and understand it themselves.[149]

The personal anecdote heightens Mendelssohn's religious authority as a pedagogical translator; the new model is explicitly linked to what Christians do.

> Because the Christians translate the Torah in each generation in the languages of their nations, according to the needs of the age, into correct language and pleasing style, sometimes following words and sometimes sense, sometimes word for word and sometimes expansively and with the addition of explanations, so that it doesn't lack the proper mixture (*Mischung*) to satisfy the thirst of the learner based on his wishes and needs.[150]

A few pages later:

> Everywhere, where the ways [*Wege*] of *pshat* and *drash* deviated from one another, I chose in my translation sometimes only those of *pshat*, at other times only those of *drash*, and he (Dubno) explained in his *Be'ur* why I proceeded that way.[151]

Mendelssohn announces this dilemma as a philosophical one that goes with the territory of translation.

What I have called first-wave manifestos are the various assertions that the modern translator, despite his protestations to the contrary, was an author, an artist, an agent. There are decisions to be made based on human knowledge and "intuition" rather than divine authority, which might very well be wrong. They are historically contingent, and thus contestable. In the following passage, Mendelssohn uses religious language and faith in God to sublimate the tension, repeating the additional assurance that "both are true."

> In order that our life does not hang down on the hair of opinion and the thread of observation, our Sages, of blessed memory, erected the Masorah and built a fence around the Torah, the commandments [*Gebot*], the statutes [*Satzung*], and the law [*Recht*], so that we are not tapping like blind men in the darkness. Since then, we are not permitted to diverge from their paved path, or prepare our own life's path, without the scales of justice . . . we do not live by the mouth [of the grammarian or editor] but rather by that which our Masoretes transmitted. According to their teaching *we understand Scripture . . . sometimes according to the simple, literal sense, and sometimes according to the explanation of our Sages, of blessed memory, because both types* [Arten] *together are true*, as I—with God's help—will explain further below.[152] (emphasis added)

Mendelssohn goes on to speak of "cutting a covenant [*brit*] for our *Be'ur*."[153]

> But we have not forgotten the rule (*klal*) we set out in our introduction regarding the difference between that which contradicts (*soter*) and that which is interchangeable (*mitchalef*), namely that the *pshat* may be interchangeable with the received tradition of our rabbis in the ways of explanation, but is impossible to contradict them in laws and statutes. Because things that are interchangeable may in fact both be true, but those things that are contradictory—if one is true, the other is of necessity false. Therefore, in every place where what seems to be disclosing the simple meaning of Scripture contradicts the received tradition of our rabbis in [matters of] laws and judgments (*halachot v'dinim*), the commentator is obligated to leave the path of *pshat* altogether and walk in the way of the true received tradition, *or make a compromise between them*, if he can succeed. *And we have cut this covenant for our* Be'ur (*et ha-brit ha-zeh karatnu l'be'urenu*) and we will preserve it as the good hand of God is upon us.[154] (emphasis added)

The terms of this covenant guarantee that the translator will choose judiciously between the simple sense and the received sense when they are "interchangeable," but that in consequential legal matters, he will adhere to tradition or "compromise." A translator's covenant is needed in light of the impossible task of doing justice to Torah by translating the Bible.

Above all, translation is no longer the manifestation of a fallen state of affairs; *translation is an art form, and the translator is an authorial subject*. The point crystallizes in the middle section of his preface, where Mendelssohn traces the lineage of the modern Jewish translator up to the passage on Yiddish translators Levita and Blitz discussed above. He assesses each translator in turn, working hard to embed himself in an illustrious genealogy. The consumers of translations are also endowed with agency; Mendelssohn calls attention to objective standards of taste for determining whether a language, a translation, or a book is good or bad, based on the correct quality of its language and aesthetic appeal. He is an arbiter of the good and bad, but he is also very much a scholar, sifting through sources of different generations, relying not only on his own eyes but also on those of others, the most important being Elija Levita (Yiddish) and Azariah de Rossi (Hebrew). This narrative has been called the first history of Jewish Bible translation.

Mendelssohn's inclusion of the excerpt from Numbers about the non-Jewish prophet Balaam alongside Moses and Halevi begins to make sense. Balaam's identity, like that of Job and Jonah, is ambiguous. God can't seem to decide how to deal with him, communicating in the end through a talking donkey. Biblical and postbiblical literature is "divided as well in evaluations of Balaam," who may or may not have been a real person.[155] The rabbis don't like the prophet Balaam. Talmud refers to him as "Balaam the Wicked," "the prophet for hire who was only interested in his own material gain and self-aggrandizement."[156] In his commentary on the passage, Samson Raphael Hirsch piles criticism upon criticism. Why then use Numbers 23–24 in the prospectus for the *Be'ur*?

The story of Balaam offers an apt parable for the German Jewish translator of the first wave. Balaam is suspected by the community but favored by God.[157] He deploys language to elevate the Israelite nation in the eyes of their foes. At one point, the only thing that stands between the Israelites and the Moabites are the beautiful poems of Balaam. Balaam is a mistranslator who saved Israel by converting the language of curse into the language of blessing.

CONCLUSION: REFRAMING THE LEGACY

By sales alone, the Amsterdam Yiddish Bibles were unsuccessful. Chava Turniansky explains: They "failed to meet the needs and wishes, habits and taste of their intended readers. Enthused by the potential of printing, were these translators and printers offering the public something no one either wanted or needed?"[158]

Israel Zinberg sums it up:

> The homiletical style of Tze'enah U'Re'enah was more congenial to the contemporary reading public. For the old-fashioned system of education which even such an authority as the Maharal of Prague could not destroy, the traditional style, was far more suitable than Blitz's and Witzenhausen's new accomplishments. Tze'enah U-Re'enah won the battle and displaced both new translations . . . Tze'enah U-Re'enah was triumphantly disseminated in scores of editions throughout all the dispersions of Israel and ruled boundlessly for generations over the minds and hearts of Jewish women.[159]

Blitz's and Witzenhausen's innovation "remained a singular experiment for more than a century," until Mendelssohn again reached out to Yiddish-speaking Jewry. In the interim, "even in the late eighteenth century, it was the *Tsene-rene* that was still being printed in Amsterdam."[160] Early twentieth-century America gave rise to another pair of Yiddish enlightenment Bible translations, both with Hebrew text on the page: the first one based on the edition of scholar Rabbi Meir Letteris (1800–1872), and the second, the classic, much-admired translation by the Yiddish poet and writer known as Yehoash (1872–1927).

Moses Mendelssohn died in 1786, but his translation had an incredible afterlife with over two hundred subsequent printings. The *Be'ur* was reprinted, reformatted, adapted, and imitated by those who came to be known as biurists.[161] The carefully balanced original design, with Hebrew, German, commentary, and Scribal Corrections quickly became obsolete. Some traditionalized the page by restoring Rashi and Targum Onkelos, whereas others modernized it by removing any vestige of Hebrew and printing just the German translation and an abridged (or updated) commentary in Gothic letters.

In the 1927 *Jewish Lexicon*, under "Bible translations," Hugo Fuchs calls the *Be'ur* the gravedigger of Yiddish. "The hegemony of the Judeo-German was concluded for German Jews by Moses Mendelssohn though his 1783 published translation of the Pentateuch."[162] Ben-Chorin writes, "Mendelssohn did not want . . . to transmit to his people, the Jews in Germany, the biblical word in a new idiom; rather, he wanted, through the medium of the biblical word, to bring the Jews in Germany closer to the German language, to prepare their intellectual emancipation and make them into German Jews."[163] What some rabbinic contemporaries found problematic was an idiom that, from their perspective, was just a paraphrase. Ezekiel Landau noted, "He did not translate the words, but rather the connection on the level of sentence and themes. . . . such a translation is only suitable to those who are experts, but has no value for education and should be rejected."[164]

Scholars of Old Yiddish understand that Mendelssohn did not produce the first modern Jewish Bible translation; he did design a new prototype for a Jewish vernacular Bible. This was not a one-way street: Joshua Fishman writes that the "father of the Galician *haskole,*" Menahem Mendel Lefin-Satanover (1749–1826), visited Mendelssohn in the 1770s and 1780s (Mendelssohn regarded him as his best Polish student) and was inspired to produce a new Yiddish translation of the Hebrew Bible—a Yiddish language *Be'ur.*[165] Chava Turniansky writes of an unpublished maskilic *Tsene-Rene* by biurist Herz Homberg, meaning that Homberg experimented with inserting modern content into the open-source format. These two borderline cases confirm that although Mendelssohn "rejected" the two modern Yiddish Bibles, he reclaimed the pedagogical-religious mandate of the Old Yiddish translation tradition by anchoring a modern translation to Hebrew, commentary, and the Scribal Corrections.

Was the *Be'ur* a Jewish version of the Christian Enlightenment Bible? In Jonathan Sheehan's schema, the Mendelssohn Pentateuch qualifies as a hybrid poetic-pedagogical Bible. But it was hardly a "post-theological" Bible, as it implicitly and explicitly bore the seal of approval of both Moses and the rabbis, as signaled by the six *haskamot* that opened its pages. Can it be called a belated vernacular bible, as Olga Litvak has argued? Was the approach in the end too Hebraic to incite a true religious or intellectual revolution? Goldschmidt asks,

> Does the fact that Mendelssohn's German translation was printed in Hebrew characters explain the immediate acceptance and acclaim that transformed it into the sign that a new historical hour was at hand? Or on the other hand, did those same Hebrew letters impede the reception of the translation?[166]

However one understands the legacy, it cannot be denied that he who was the "first" German Jewish translator of the Hebrew Bible was also the third to produce a Jewish Enlightenment Bible. Mendelssohn was not wrong in imagining his *Be'ur* to be "the first step to culture" for Ashkenazi Jewry; the publishers and translators of the Amsterdam Yiddish Bibles had taken the leap that made the first step possible.

CHAPTER TWO

The Second Wave: Emergence of a Bible Industry

WORKS DISCUSSED

Joseph Johlson. *Die heiligen Schriften der Israeliten, erster Theil: Die fünf Bücher Mose, nach dem masoretischen Texte worttreu übersetzt, mit Anmerkungen* (The Holy Scripture of the Israelites, part one: The Five Books of Moses according to the Masoretic text literally translated, with notes). Frankfurt am Main: Andreäische Buchhandlung, 1831.

Gotthold Salomon. *Die deutsche Volks- und Schulbibel für Israeliten. Aufs Neue aus dem massoretischen Text übersetzt* (The German people's and school Bible for Israelites). Altona: Hammerich, 1837.

Leopold Zunz, ed. *Torah Neviim Ketuvim. Die vier und zwanzig Bücher der heiligen Schrift: Nach dem masoretischen Texte* (Torah, Prophets, Writings: The twenty-four books of the Holy Scripture, according to the Masoretic text). Translated by Heymann Arnheim, Julius Fürst, and Michael Sachs. Prague: Veit & Comp., 1838.

Salomon Herxheimer. *Die vierundzwanzig Bücher der Bibel im hebräischen Texte: Mit worttreuer Uebersetzung, fortlaufender Erklärung und homiletisch benutzbaren Anmerkungen* (The twenty-four books of the Bible in Hebrew text, with literal translation, running explanation, and homiletically suitable notes). 4 vols. Berlin: J. Lewent, 1841–48.

INTRODUCTION: THAT RED, RED STUFF

The Bible translations of the second wave appeared in rapid succession in 1831, 1837, 1838, and 1841. They shared an underlying purpose: to provide an alternative to Mendelssohn's idiomatic German translation; to be *worttreu*, literal. One verse demonstrates how the second wave aspired to improve on the first. Genesis 25:30 recounts how Esau, tired from a long day of hunting, begs his brother for some lentil stew:

וַיֹּאמֶר עֵשָׂו אֶל-יַעֲקֹב הַלְעִיטֵנִי נָא מִן-הָאָדֹם הָאָדֹם הַזֶּה

JPS: And Esau said to Jacob, "Give me some of **that red stuff** to gulp down, for I am famished"
Alter: And Esau said to Jacob, "Let me gulp down some of **this red red stuff**, for I am famished."

In the Hebrew, as in Alter's translation, "red" appears twice. Does it matter if Esau says "red red stuff" or "red stuff"? First-wave translators paraphrased:

Luther: Laß mich kosten das **rote** Gericht;
Blitz: shut mir ein fun disem **rote** girikht
Witzenhausen: shut mir nun ayn fun **dem dozigen roten**
Mendelssohn: laß mich doch von disem **rohten** Gerichte kosten,

But the second-wave translators included *red red* (as well as Mendelssohn's *doch*):

Johlson: Lass mich doch kosten von dem rothen—von diesem rothen da!
Salomon: Laß mich doch kosten von diesem Rothen, Rothen da!
Zunz: Laß mich doch schlingen von dem Roten, dem Roten da
Herxheimer: Laß mich doch schlingen von dem Rothen, dem Rothen da

When we hear Esau exclaim, "Give me some of that red stuff—that red stuff over there!" the desperation of a very hungry man who doesn't even know what he's asking for becomes palpable. Redness is Esau's epithet from birth. A literal translation had to take repetition seriously. In this respect, second-wave translators pioneered the method associated with Buber and Rosenzweig in the 1920s:

BR: Laß mich doch schlingen von dem Roten, dem Roten da

Throughout the nineteenth century, Mendelssohn's *Be'ur* continued to be reprinted, revised, and disseminated. It was widely used by Orthodox Jews in Western Europe and increasingly in Eastern Europe.[1] Johlson, Salomon, Zunz, and Herxheimer had a different audience in mind: Jews, proficient in German, for whom traditional Judaism had lost its innate appeal. Acculturation had occurred so rapidly that knowledge of Hebrew and Judaism as such was at a low. In addition to the new and growing demand for prayer books and synagogue Bibles with German translation, two phenomena led to the plethora of new translations: new forms of scholarly production, and new methods of education. Rabbis and intellectuals who promoted a return to Torah, whether through scholarship, education, or in the synagogue, required a German translation that was modern in appearance, current with regard to advances in biblical scholarship, and—for a variety of reasons—more Hebraic in style. These four translators were more than up to the task. They had been educated by Maskilim and trained in German gymnasia and universities. They had the knowledge, skills, and the sense of urgency that led them to produce translations of all manner of Jewish texts—biblical, liturgical, rabbinic, literary. Even as their common motive was to replace the *Be'ur* with an up-to-date German Bible for Jews, each had his own vision of what that entailed. The differences among them illuminate the paths that emerged from the Haskalah—education and philology, culture and *Wissenschaft* (scientific scholarship), homiletics, popular and middlebrow culture—during the confusing early decades of the nineteenth century, when the first generation of Jewish writers in German emerged on the scene.

The result was a veritable Bible industry, with translators competing for subscribers. "I'm sorry that [the Bible of] Dr. Salomon appeared everywhere before yours," wrote Samuel M. Ehrenberg to his former pupil Leopold Zunz:

> Yesterday I tried to get Dr. Herzfeld in Braunschweig to garner subscribers for you, but he had already gotten a contract to do this for Dr. Salomon. He has already publicized the translation in the local [Jewish] national paper. In Frankfurt am Main the Johlson translation is of course in the way, but even there he has managed to find subscribers.[2]

The German Jewish Bible industry replicated, to some degree, conditions in mainstream society for much of the eighteenth century, when publishers brought forth a plurality of styles of Bible translation with the tacit understanding that no vulgate, no single authorized translation, would suffice. Leaders of various communities designed different translations, commentaries, and supplements for different constituencies. Still, "the battle over the Bible was intense," as new translations and commentaries competed to become the next *Be'ur*, the next authoritative German Jewish Bible.[3] In all this, the Hebrew Torah in the Masoretic text remained sacred and uncontested. What changed, as it had one hundred years before, was the relationship between the Hebrew Torah and its German garb.

I begin by comparing the translations of Joseph Johlson (1831) and Leopold Zunz (1838), which exemplify the Hebraic turn of the second wave.

Two other contemporary translations fall to the left and right, both ideologically and methodologically: Gotthold Salomon's *People's and School Bible* (1837), as its title indicates, was designed to appeal to a popular audience; Salomon Herxheimer's *Twenty-four Books . . . with . . . Explanation and Homiletically Suitable Notes* (1841–48), as its title suggests, restored supplementary information to the pages of a literal, critical translation, anticipating the third-wave Bibles of Philippson and Hirsch.

SOCIAL CONTEXTS OF THE SECOND WAVE

The early decades of the nineteenth century were confusing times. On 11 March 1812, Prussia had granted its 32,000 Jews citizenship and full civil rights. Yet the Congress of Vienna in 1815 refused to universalize emancipation, and a reactionary spirit and outright anti-Semitism revived in its aftermath. There were riots against Jews and Jewish property in 1818 and 1819. In 1822 and 1823, the Prussian government passed new restrictive edicts, revoking freedoms and emancipatory measures. The age of idealism inspired by the French Revolution and the Napoleonic Wars had ended in 1815; but the dynamic age of Jewish cultural and religious regeneration, when second-generation reformers became active in the wake of the Geiger-Tiktin controversy, had not yet begun. David Philipson refers to a twelve-year period of "apathy" stretching from 1823 to 1835; Gunther Plaut dates this period 1817–38.[4] Plaut sums up this transitional time in German Jewish religious and cultural life:

> The second period seemed to gather up the pent-up political and social emotions of the age and yielded some fruits in England and France, where more liberal laws made their appearance. In Jewish life, too, it was as if all were preparing for the great outburst. In this time, Zunz published his path-breaking work on the history of the Jewish service, Mannheimer instituted reforms in Vienna, and Creizenach prepared a new generation at the Frankfort Philanthropin.[5]

In the late 1830s and 1840s, religious reform reached its peak. By the 1850s, orthodoxy had begun to reassert itself among German Jews.[6]

But in these early decades, the religious sphere was no less confusing than the political. Jews had begun to achieve social and cultural integration, but religious reform was proceeding slowly. The rabbinic leaders were locked in extreme positions, with no middle ground anywhere on the horizon. Because there was only one official Jewish community (*Gemeinde*), new, liberal synagogues had to be privately arranged and funded, and the opposition of observant rabbis and government regulation of religious life were major impediments. The first period of reform following the Prussian edict of 1812 had led to the creation of the Reform Temple in Berlin in 1815, against the wishes of the rabbinate. In 1817, heeding the rabbis' wishes, the government closed the two "private" temples in that city. By 1823, the Prussian state, also at the bidding of traditional rabbis, forbade worship in German. The famous Hamburg Temple had been founded in 1818, and instituted an organ, a chorus, a sermon in the vernacular German, and a new prayer book that opened from left to right, like a German book; even more controversial within Jewish circles, it replaced Ashkenazi *piyyutim* (hymns) with Sephardi ones and Ashkenazi Hebrew pronunciation with Sephardic.[7] Observant rabbis denounced the Temple as heretical; liberal scholar Abraham Geiger criticized it as not radical enough. These initial efforts to adapt Jewish religious practice to German ways were inspired by reforms within the Protestant community, rather than by philosophical or theological principles; they sought mainly to improve the image of the Jew, Judaism, and Jewish space in Christian eyes, but without appearing to have yielded to long-held prejudices against Judaism. An editorial in a Jewish newspaper in 1837 expresses the lack of a new direction: "The number of those who withdraw themselves completely from all participation in the religious services grows considerably from year to year, not because they do not experience the need of true religious edification, but because the services in the synagogue, as conducted at present, are not such as to meet this need."[8] Meanwhile, outside the hubs of reform, as Michael Meyer writes, the majority of Jews, especially in the countryside, retained a traditional way of life, observing Sabbath and holidays, laws of family purity and local customs such as the centuries-old Frankfurt Synagogue rite. Jews continued to speak Yiddish in the private sphere; Hebrew remained the language of worship in most synagogues. Alongside the creation of new schools, both by the German government and by Maskilim, old-style teachers (*melamdim*) and rabbis held to the old ways.[9]

Gotthold Salomon, the preacher of the Hamburg Temple, captures the confusion in an 1830 letter to Rabbi Isaak Noa Mannheimer of Vienna:

> [T]here is no unity even in this fragmented group; some have their children confirmed, others are against it; marriage ceremonies occur rarely in our group; the *b'rith* for newly born boys is not the most alluring. Funeral sermons are still taboo. There is a wide divergence of views amongst the trustees; one member is for advancement, the other thinks we have

> already advanced so much that no congregation can follow us and that, therefore, we are standing alone.[10]

The sign of a transitional time was that when it came to important life-cycle events, birth, death, and marriage, Temple-going Jews were not prepared to relinquish traditional rites and liturgy. Even some liberally minded rabbis, now called preachers (*Prediger*), were rethinking their positions, as excerpts from Rabbi Mannheimer's letters over a three-year period (1826–29) convey:

> To restore the divine service in its purity, to win over the members of the community—all the people, women and youth—is the one goal we wish to realize. . . . The basic *Tefillah* (prayer) as a ritual act can still remain in Hebrew. Not much will be gained by modifying the *Tefillah*; in fact, a great deal may be lost in respect to popular appeal. . . . I have found out long ago that nothing is gained with superimposed reforms. Young people reject the new because only after a few years it becomes as old to them as antiquity. There has to be an inner strengthening, a strengthening of faith.
>
> I would never figure on an organ, even if all outward objections against it were to cease. I admit that the sound of the organ, like the sound of bells, has become too much a characteristic of the Christian church, and it is, therefore, offensive to the Jew. Honestly, in the five years since I have become unaccustomed to the sound of the organ, it would no longer quite suit my own feelings.[11]

These comments suggest that even for a committed reformer, a series of reality principles had begun to weigh in. What is the proper balance of German and Hebrew in the synagogue liturgy? Why change things when anything new was quickly deemed old? Perhaps less is more when it comes to liturgical reform? How do we implement reforms without setting ourselves apart? How do I deal with my own nostalgia for the past? Such doubts revitalized the efforts to create an "inner strengthening, a strengthening of faith," a call that resounded in each of the four waves discussed here. Franz Rosenzweig in his day called for "a new thinking" about teaching, learning, liturgy, scholarship, and above all, about how to remain authentic Jews in an age of reform.

On 7 November 1819, in Berlin, Leopold Zunz and other young intellectuals formed Der Verein für Cultur und Wissenschaft der Juden (The society for culture and science/scholarship among/of the Jews). Ismar Schorsch argues that it was "the recent outbreak of popular antisemitism," referred to as the Hep-Hep riots, that inspired the formation of a specifically Jewish academic association.[12] The central personalities were Eduard Gans, Isaak Markus Jost, Moses Moser, Ludwig Marcus, Joel List, and Joseph Hillmar. These young men were tied to their Jewishness by biography, friendships, and upbringing, but they were alienated from it spiritually. They held meetings and published scholarly articles, as well as a widely respected periodical edited by Zunz, the *Zeitschrift für die Wissenschaft des Judentums*, of which they published only three numbers. Heinrich Heine was involved for a brief time, as were Jewish intellectuals David Friedländer, Israel Jacobson, and Lazarus Bendavid. Schorsch gives the reasons for the disintegration of the Verein in February 1824. "A dwindling membership, the utter indifference of the Berlin Jewish plutocracy, and the rising tide of political reaction had crushed the sense of fervor, mission, and elitism which sustained its frenetic activity."[13]

In 1822, ten years after the emancipation, a Prussian decree prohibited Jews from teaching at universities and secondary schools. Jewish scholars taught in secondary schools, took positions as rabbis/preachers, became independent scholars and translators. Heinrich Heine, upon completion of his legal studies, underwent conversion—the Jew's passport to a career. Eduard Gans, a famous scholar of jurisprudence, agreed to be baptized in 1825 in order to become the colleague of his mentor, G. W. F. Hegel, at the University of Berlin. Zunz fought for the right to obtain a university position, twice proposing the "establishment of a tenured Chair for Jewish History and Literature" in Berlin in 1843 and again in 1848.[14]

The German Jewish intellectuals of the second wave felt a mandate to translate the philosophical principles and universalistic ideals of the Haskalah into a social and educational program. Most of them remained observant Jews who sought to improve traditional Jewish life. They privileged knowledge of Hebrew and German. Yet they also became modern educators. "They opposed the system of education steeped in rabbinic literature, the consequently narrow occupational base of the Jewish community, and the continuing power of the rabbis to control the very thoughts of their constituents."[15] Adding to the momentum was the institution of compulsory education for all German children.[16] Moreover, German states made *religious* education compulsory for Jewish children, no matter what type of school they attended, creating a market for new curricula in German, textbooks, readers, and catechisms.

What did educational reform look like at the turn of the nineteenth century? Jewish communities had for centuries supported schools that were singularly focused on talmudic study. The new Jewish schools founded by Maskilim provided "an institutional framework for influencing a generation of children inculcated with secularized values"; the beneficiaries of these innovations were mainly poor children, such as Leopold Zunz himself.[17] At these schools—in Berlin (founded 1778), Breslau (1791), Dessau (1799), Seesen (1801), Frankfurt (1804), and Wolfenbüttel (1807)—students were exposed to secular society and values in a Jewish context.[18] They experienced a new kind of worship service—devotional prayer services (*Andachtsstunden*) held on Sundays—and they imbibed a new religious worldview that made it difficult for them to feel at home in the traditional synagogue. The case of Frankfurt am Main bears special mention. Frankfurt's Jews had been permitted to attend secular schools as early as 1800.[19] Between 1800 and 1803, twenty-nine Jewish students attended the city's gymnasium. When the first Bürgerschule (modern public school) opened in 1803, twenty-two Jewish children applied, comprising one quarter of the student body. But such a school was still affordable only for upper-class Jews.[20] In 1804, Siegmund Geisenheimer and 260 families in the *Israelitische Gemeinde* in Frankfurt founded the Jüdisches Philanthropin, and they agreed to support it for the first three years. Its founders drew on the new pedagogies of Rousseau, Basedow, and Pestalozzi. The Philanthropin, where Joseph Johlson, Michael Creizenach, and Isaak Markus Jost taught, sought to integrate Jewish and secular education, knowledge, and skills.[21] Its students had 53 hours of instruction per week: 21 hours were devoted to German (language study, reading, and writing), 14 to Hebrew instruction, and 10 to religion, taught (in German) by way of the Mendelssohn *Be'ur*; they devoted the remaining hours to math, drawing, natural history, music, and exercises for improving the memory. The school became a "seedbed for radical Reform in Germany."[22] The Nazis closed it down in 1942; the Frankfurt Jewish community reopened it in 1966.[23]

> [W]ith the notable exception of the Jewish Philanthropin in Frankfurt am Main, the early schools established by the maskilim . . . did not survive more than a generation or lost their Jewish character. Increasingly, Jewish parents preferred to send their children to the Christian schools.[24]

Though the schools may no longer have been viable, the educational mandate they embodied only intensified over time. Future translators Philippson, Hirsch, Buber, Rosenzweig, and Pappenheim each founded educational institutions "in their image," reflecting their values and principles.

Christian Contexts

Christian society had recently experienced two surges of Bible translations, in the sixteenth and eighteenth centuries. Though not a contemporaneous context, events in the early 1700s anticipate, or perhaps are merely analogous to, the early nineteenth-century Jewish Bible industry. I refer above all to the Pietists' double emphasis on biblical scholarship and literalism as the criteria of a good translation, based on the idea that both together would produce better access to the true scriptural text. Extreme literalism, inspired by increasingly accurate knowledge of Hebrew and its Semitic sister languages, came to be justified in the name of extreme fidelity to God's Word; incorrect German was almost a theological virtue. Pietists broke with Luther, whose priority had been to disambiguate Scripture and translate Hebrew into a natural German prose style; by contrast, these early foreignizing translations would make clear on the page what scholars had long known—namely, that the Bible often does not make sense. They included a scholarly apparatus, including parentheses, footnotes, and alternative translations, to counterbalance for the problems and stumbling blocks inevitably found in a literal translation. These developments anticipated the goals and methods of the second-generation German Jewish translators as they forged a path that diverged from the Mendelssohnian. In fact, the particular conjunction of scholarly/philological foundation and a literalist/Hebraic style was unique to the second wave. One hundred years after the Pietist surge in translation, and fifty years after the *Be'ur*, Jewish translators—many of them sons of Maskilim and pupils of biurists—were in the position to design foreign-sounding Hebraic translations with a scholarly basis.

A unique episode in the history of the German Bible, the polyglot *Biblia Pentapla* edited and compiled by Johann Otto Glüsing, is also relevant here, as a form of what Jonathan Sheehan calls the "post-theological Bible."[25] In an extraordinary demonstration of parity, Glüsing printed five translations in the German dialects side by side, those of Luther (Protestant, 1520), Ulenberg (Catholic, 1630), Piscator (1602), the Dutch States Bible (1632), and Witzenhausen (Jewish, 1679); in the New Testament, the fifth column was occupied by a new translation by the radical Pietist Johann Heinrich Reitz. What motivated Glüsing to provide the average reader simultaneous access to multiple translations from different faith communities? As Sheehan explains, his motive had little to do with cultural relativism or ecumenicalism. While readers were given agency to compare and contrast translations, the ultimate goal was not to demonstrate that all translations are valid, but rather that none qualifies as a "perfect replacement," and in that case, a spectrum of translations may enable the reader to understand the true Original Text, the Holy Spirit.[26] The ideal Original corresponds in the Jewish context to the Torah within the Bible. A plural translation like the *Biblia Pentapla* replaced the Greek and Hebrew originals in order to highlight the impossibility of doing justice to Scripture through translation in a posttheological context. A plural translation, like a Bible industry, tacitly admits that a one-to-one correspondence between Scripture and translation—the illusion promulgated by the first wave—is no longer possible. A similar condition arose with the proliferation of German Jewish Bible translations in the 1830s and 1840s, whose prefaces and reviews left no doubt that none could replace the *Be'ur*, none was authorized or canonized, and that all were fighting an uphill battle for sense. What bound them together was the ambition to improve Jewish society through translation—another uphill battle—and to improve translation itself, by forging a literal, critical path to the Torah.

In the world of Bible scholarship, important developments in the discipline of Oriental studies in German universities had a critical impact. Back in the eighteenth century, Johann David Michaelis, Bishop Robert Lowth, and Johann Gottfried Herder had turned to the Old Testament as part of a theological agenda. These enlightened Christians had sought to better understand the Old Testament as part of the New; to reinterpret Hebrew Scripture in light of Enlightenment critiques, rationalism, Deism, and attacks on the Masoretic text. German scholars defended the Masoretic text, under attack in what was called the "vowel points debate," longer than scholars in England and elsewhere. But after 1820, as Suzanne Marchand explains, Orientalism and historicism became especially influential. German Orientalism's focus was still on "religion in general and on the Old Testament in particular," but "historicist study came to the fore."[27] Jewish history became integrated into the study of the ancient world. Historical approaches to the Bible reached an apotheosis with David Strauss's groundbreaking *Das Leben Jesu* (1835), which Michael Sachs, one of Zunz's fellow translators, read with astonishment and fascination. These new conditions shaped the education and training of the translators in this period. The notion that knowledge of the ancient world and its languages—Syriac, Egyptian, Arabic—and other "'oriental' cultures and languages might be used to explain the scriptures" was not in itself new;

> Michaelis and Herder showed how this might be done in detail, and showed too that it could be done without being persecuted for heresy.

> Their descendants, among whom one can count W. M. L. de Wette, Johann Eichhorn, Wilhelm Gesenius, and Heinrich Ewald—all trained as Christian Hebraists—followed very much in this tradition. None of these men wanted to throw out the Old Testament, and thanks to their scholarly efforts . . . the Old Testament after 1820 was rehabilitated as a truth-containing text. Even more than in Michaelis' day, however, the truths it contained increasingly became historical, not theological ones, and truths specific to the Jewish people, not to all peoples.[28]

These developments in the academy shaped the careers of nineteenth-century translators, and it laid the ideological groundwork for their enterprise. New translations had to allow one to read the Hebrew Bible as an ancient Hebrew document, accessible through modern methods that were no longer the province only of Christian scholars.

In these decades, the Age of Goethe and twilight of German Romanticism, Jews participated in, imitated, and became knowledgeable about all forms of literary and cultural production.[29] In 1831, Heinrich Heine declared, without exaggeration, "Goethe is dead; God is dead," ushering in an epigonal age. Second-wave translators were epigones of a different sort.

All of these developments in the first four decades of the nineteenth century led to a proliferation of Bible translations. "The battle over the Bible was intense. By the middle of the nineteenth century, six other German versions [besides Mendelssohn's] were on the market, three in Hebrew script and three in German script."[30] The new translators were young scholars, rabbis, and teachers who were translating independently and in full awareness of cultural and intellectual trends. The prominent Orientalist G. H. A. Ewald and his Jewish student Michael Sachs were both translating the Psalms in the 1830s. Ewald wrote to Sachs: "It is truly an unusual case that this summer, 5–6 works on the Psalms have come out, without any of the workers knowing about the others. It's an encouraging lesson—how these studies are beginning to develop."[31]

MOVING BEYOND MENDELSSOHN

> The guys are furious with me, I hear, probably because I sometimes go to pray the afternoon service by Rabbi Yaakov Yosef, and because I dare to write a book and challenge Mendelssohn, because to translate something that Mendelssohn already translated means to rebel against him and annihilate him.
>
> —Michael Sachs, 1835[32]

The second wave of German Jewish Bible translation responded to the uncomfortable but undeniable reality that the *Be'ur* was no longer adequate for German-speaking Jews. The unwieldy Hebrew commentary looked more and more medieval with the passage of time; the fields of exegesis, Hebrew grammar, and lexicography had advanced considerably in fifty years. When printed in Latin (rather than Hebrew) script, without the Hebrew original and the notes, the translation itself sounded outdated. Moreover, Mendelssohn had only translated the Pentateuch, Psalms, and Song of Songs; biurists such as Moses Philippson (father of Ludwig Philippson) combined his translation and their own commentary, or sought to imitate his method and translate the remaining biblical books. Second-wave translators were not biurists;[33] they were Mendelssohn's epigones. However defensible their efforts, the fact remained that *to translate something that Mendelssohn already translated was to annihilate him*.

In an 1894 essay dedicated to "Zunz's Bible," Leopold Zunz's student David Rosin conveys the epigonal mood. He repeats the axiom that every historical upsurge in Jewish life requires a reworking of Scripture to "safeguard" this most important treasure in a new age—the motive of Ezra and Nehemia, the targumim and Septuagint, Saadia's *Tafsir*, and Mendelssohn's High German translation of the Pentateuch, completed by his younger contemporaries in a "more or less flawed" effort.

> However, as great and unexpected as the edifying (*geistbildend*) impact of the Mendelssohn translation upon the Jews of that time is, and as valuable and appealing as we find this work even today, executed with such skill and elegance, and as formidable the correct understanding of the Hebrew text, made possible through this translation accompanied by a modern Hebrew commentary—in the wake of two extremely fertile scholarly generations, it could no longer be widely satisfactory, especially considering that, in addition to the Pentateuch, Mendelssohn only translated the Psalms and the Song of Songs, and, also, as I already noted, all the other biblical books fell prey to different continuators who were not nearly his equal, some of them even quite untalented imitators.[34]

Similar defenses can be found in many histories of German Jewry. But what did it mean to be a translator, or, even more important, an educator or layperson, awaiting that new translation? I quote further from the correspondence between educator and reformer Samuel Meier Ehrenberg (1773–1853), principal of the Samson Free School in Wolfenbüttel, and his former student Leopold Zunz:

> In your letter I read the words, "I give lessons, and hope [to] *translate. . . .*" *What* is it that you are translating? Should you be occupied with translating the Tanach (Hebrew Scripture), you would be satisfying a desideratum that has yet to be satisfied, and earn the gratitude of a large audience. Oh, if only I could live to see a critical school edition of the Old Testament in the German language! But not the botched works (*Machwerke*) such as those of Schalom Kohen Heinemann, and others.[35] I'm told the preacher Dr. Salomon and Mannheimer are working together on such a work: But I doubt that the former would be up to the task, the latter one I don't know at all.[36]

Ehrenberg's communication tells us a number of things about the new Bible industry. We hear a plea by one of the foremost educational reformers of the time for a "critically prepared" Bible for classroom use, because the new translations on the market are inadequate. He notes the difficult labor involved in such an undertaking and the ease with which someone without the proper training could botch the job. And he observes that a widespread demand exists for such a work, that Salomon and Mannheimer are competing for the same market, though he is suspicious of the competence of these radical reformers. Such observations give a good idea of forces that influenced the upsurge in Bible translation.

Another set of considerations appear in a letter by publisher Moritz Veit at a very early stage of the Zunz Bible project:

> A Bible for Israelites—an Old Testament. First: In which translation? The Christian has a canonical German Bible—Luther's: should we follow Mendelssohn or Heinemann? To prepare a new translation that would be *at the same time popular and scholarly* would be a monumental project—even Sachs is not considering this. It would be much more difficult to get the right tone than in [his] Psalms translation. What national value such a translation could possibly have, I know not: if we took the New Testament out of the Hanewald Bible—that could be Bible for Israelites. I am likewise not in favor of steel engravings: it doesn't really accomplish much and even Asher [publisher in Berlin] has stopped doing them, since there is nothing edifying for soul or body. These perfect little figures in a Bible! And what kind of pictures do you want? Copies of Jewish-national masters, or of Christian painters, who composed out of an anachronistic fondness for Old Testament things, but seldom without adding Christian elements?[37]

These concerns lead to the larger question: given the immense amount of knowledge and labor such a project demanded, was Mendelssohn's translation really no longer viable? Was it not also popular and scholarly? And how was a Jewish publisher to meet the new demands for illustrations of the sort beginning to appear in all printed books?

Surprising as it sounds, a central objection was that the *Be'ur* had become too German. Of course, the original page layout was entirely in Hebrew, including the German translation. But three of the Hebrew elements had been omitted from the 1815 edition of the Mendelssohn Bible—the edition widely in circulation when Johlson began translating. Even in Mendelssohn's lifetime, the translation had been reprinted in German script, and the demand for this version only grew. Subsequent editions, such as an 1852 one published in Saint Petersburg with commentary by L. J. Mandelstamm, followed suit (fig. 2.1). In these later editions, some of which even failed to acknowledge Mendelssohn as the original translator, Hebrew had utterly disappeared.

As faithful as it was to the *pshat*, the straightforward sense of the Torah, Mendelssohn's literary and explanatory German style provided no access to the form of biblical Hebrew. Mendelssohn had many reasons to suppress the foreignness of Scripture; all eighteenth-century translators strove to scuttle the Hebraisms and produce a modern-sounding German Bible idiom. The dominant belief was that a "true, faithful" translation should not be slavish (*sklavisch-treu*). No less than Martin Luther in his day did Mendelssohn, writing for a Yiddish-speaking readership, use translation to create a new German idiom—the language that an educated, cultured German Jew should speak. If his translation was, in fact, going to model German style, it had to display the richness and versatility of the new language.

The new translations were literal, *worttreu*. The next generation actively sought to invent a more Hebrew-sounding German Jewish biblical idiom; as trained philologists and scholars of Jewish literature and history, they were well suited to design a more authentically Hebraic German Bible. They were comfortable enough to tolerate, and even celebrate, the ambiguity and foreignness of ancient Hebrew. With greater distance from their Ashkenazi/Yiddish-speaking origins, this generation was less concerned about being associated with Judendeutsch (though Christian reviewers did hold that against the Zunz translation). In its time, the Mendelssohn Bible looked, but could not sound, like a Jewish Bible. Once the visual trappings of the traditional Jewish Bible were removed—Hebrew Torah and Hebrew commentary—the *Be'ur* was indeed too German, at least to the eyes and ears of the next generation.

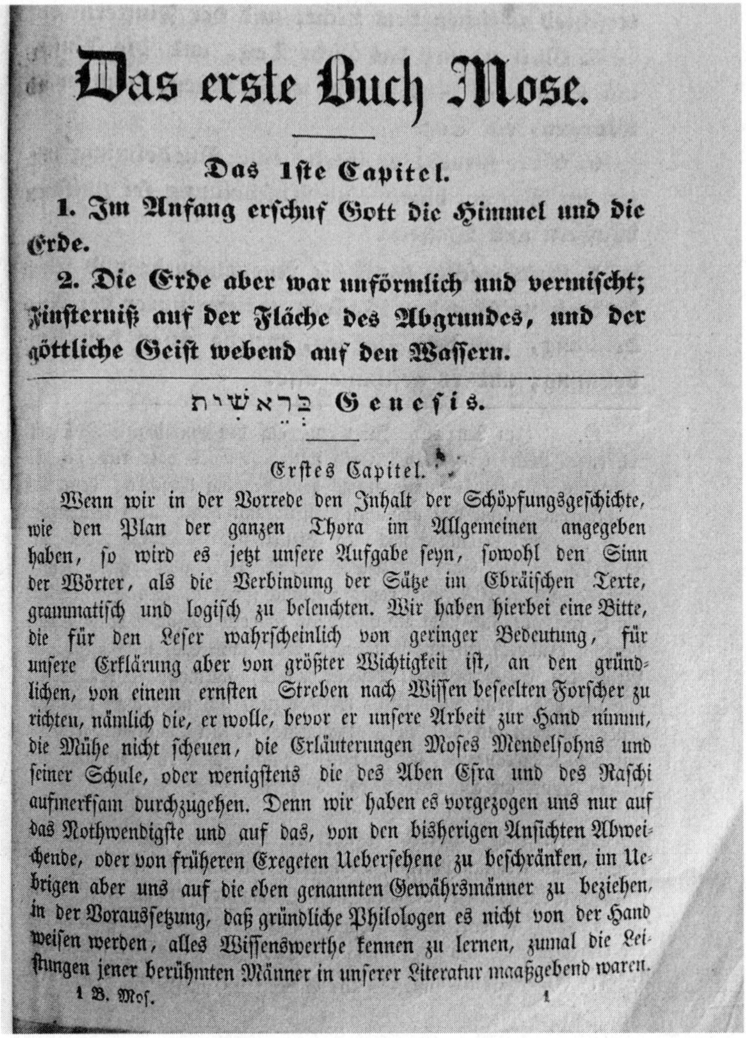

Das erste Buch Mose.

Das 1ste Capitel.

1. Im Anfang erschuf Gott die Himmel und die Erde.

2. Die Erde aber war unförmlich und vermischt; Finsterniß auf der Fläche des Abgrundes, und der göttliche Geist webend auf den Wassern.

בְּרֵאשִׁית Genesis.

Erstes Capitel.

Wenn wir in der Vorrede den Inhalt der Schöpfungsgeschichte, wie den Plan der ganzen Thora im Allgemeinen angegeben haben, so wird es jetzt unsere Aufgabe seyn, sowohl den Sinn der Wörter, als die Verbindung der Sätze im Ebräischen Texte, grammatisch und logisch zu beleuchten. Wir haben hierbei eine Bitte, die für den Leser wahrscheinlich von geringer Bedeutung, für unsere Erklärung aber von größter Wichtigkeit ist, an den gründlichen, von einem ernsten Streben nach Wissen beseelten Forscher zu richten, nämlich die, er wolle, bevor er unsere Arbeit zur Hand nimmt, die Mühe nicht scheuen, die Erläuterungen Moses Mendelsohns und seiner Schule, oder wenigstens die des Aben Esra und des Raschi aufmerksam durchzugehen. Denn wir haben es vorgezogen uns nur auf das Nothwendigste und auf das, von den bisherigen Ansichten Abweichende, oder von früheren Exegeten Uebersehene zu beschränken, im Uebrigen aber uns auf die eben genannten Gewährsmänner zu beziehen, in der Voraussetzung, daß gründliche Philologen es nicht von der Hand weisen werden, alles Wissenswerthe kennen zu lernen, zumal die Leistungen jener berühmten Männer in unserer Literatur maaßgebend waren.

1 B. Mos. 1

Fig. 2.1. Mendelssohn Bible, Gen 1:1 (Saint Petersburg, 1852).

Of course, it was not that simple. Michael Sachs commented that his more observant friends accused him of "annihilating Mendelssohn" through his retranslation. Ultimately, second-wave translators had to make a case for a new translation without seeming to lessen their admiration for Mendelssohn's accomplishment. Each found a way to praise him and his legacy and still pinpoint some shortcoming that mandated a retranslation. Thus, in his 1829 essay commemorating Mendelssohn's one-hundredth birthday,

Gotthold Salomon offered a mixed account of Mendelssohn's legacy. He emphasized that the merit of the *Be'ur* lay in its longevity, popularity, and success as a vehicle of enlightenment. He praises the work for holding fast to the Masoretic tradition and avoiding philology and biblical criticism—for not being revolutionary—and for introducing the nation to language, with the Bible as a kind of "preschool" for (real) education. Interestingly, he regards the Psalms as even more successful by aesthetic measures and also in terms of their German vocabulary. However, the *Be'ur* has "linguistic, hermeneutical, and archeological errors." He concludes his tribute by asserting that Mendelssohn did not aspire to "shine among the philologists" but, rather, to spread "light and research" among the Jews, and "his goal was fully achieved (*vollkommen erreicht*)."

> Mendelssohn, seeing the fruits of his work flourishing, went further to translate and write commentary on the Psalms, with a greater expansion of his German vocabulary, with even higher aesthetic sense, and with even more brilliant success; the Psalms was crowned with general acclaim.
>
> He intended to continue translating the remaining books of the Holy Writ, but taken by death too soon, he left only the Song of Songs in a beautiful translation that was much admired.—We do not want to examine the critical value of these works and stress their defects; *we only take into account their impact on the Jews.*[38]

Ten years later, Salomon Herxheimer did a similar dance when he described what his own "faithful translation" entailed: "As much as we value the translations of Mendelssohn, de Wette, and the most recent Israelite Bible translators, they didn't satisfy me."[39] Herxheimer spelled out his own priorities, each of which has a subtext that I note in parentheses: Herxheimer selected the most accurate German expression (= he is loyal to Mendelssohn's mission); he retained the integrity of the German by banning all willful neologisms and word combinations (= he corrects and improves upon Mendelssohn's German—see Ex 12:11); he sought as much as possible to preserve the nuances of the Hebrew original (= he is in line with the New Hebraism of the second-wave translators), but did not distort German (= as do the more scholarly translations of Zunz, Sachs, maybe Johlson), this in deference to children, because exposure to bad German during the early years stamps children's memories, and has an indelible influence on their spoken and written German and on their entire thinking (= he is in line with modern pedagogy).[40]

These translators' apologias lacked the confidence and authority exuded by Blitz, Witzenhausen, and Mendelssohn, for reasons that go beyond "anxiety of influence." Competition was the new reality. The authors wanted sales and popularity, and they manipulated language, design, and format to target specific populations. However, they shared an inescapable obstacle: any translation that promised to be *worttreu* was bound to sound awkward in German. Moreover, a philologically honest version would have to retain the ambiguity of the Hebrew—and might even let on that the meaning of a verse or word was up for grabs, even among scholars; this too would hurt their popularity. Thus, each of the translators found ways to compensate for (or supplement) his waning authority. It might be said that the stand-alone translation format pioneered by Salomon and Zunz exuded a new type of confidence, by suggesting that a Jewish translation did not have to be a study Bible: it could just be, without aspiring to teach anyone anything or to justify its choices.

THE NEW HEBRAISM: THE BIBLES OF JOSEPH JOHLSON AND LEOPOLD ZUNZ

Joseph Johlson and Leopold Zunz consistently approached translation with the express goal of re-Hebraizing the German Jewish Bible. They reintroduced the sound and syntax of Hebrew into the translation itself to make it impossible for the reader to forget that the original was an ancient Hebraic document. These two are the unacknowledged initiators of the linguistic and aesthetic approaches associated with the Bible translation of Martin Buber and Franz Rosenzweig in the 1920s. But the chapter begins back in the early 1830s, when Johlson, living in Frankfurt, added a humble postscript to a long and flattering letter to his dear friend in Berlin: "Might my German translation of the Pentateuch already be known to you?"[41]

Joseph Johlson: Translator-Pedagogue

Less well-known than Zunz, Joseph Johlson, or Asher ben Joseph Fulda, was the son of the Fulda rabbi (1777–1851). Johlson taught at the Philanthropin in Frankfurt, and authored the first German-language textbooks for Jewish children. His curriculum was called *Joseph's Sheaves* (*Alumei Yosef*), subtitled *Lessons in Mosaic Religion for Israelite Youth of Both Sexes* (*Unterricht in der mosaischen Religion für die israelitische Jugend beiderlei Geschlechts*). The first volume, a catechism titled *The Teachings of the*

Mosaic Religion (1814), was not only the primary textbook at the Philanthropin, but it also became the most widely used Jewish textbook in the first half of the century.[42] Questions ranged from the philosophical ("How does reason lead us to the existence of one God?"), to the factual ("Which are the Ten Commandments that we received on Mount Sinai?"), to the interpretive ("How does the Talmud convey that loving one's neighbor is the foundation of all the laws?").[43] Johlson also published *Songs of Jeshurun: Israelite Hymnbook for Devotion and Religious Instruction* (1816); *Toldot Avot: Biblical History in the Original Language of Scripture, Chronologically Arranged* (1820); and *Yesodei Halashon: The Foundations of the Language: Grammar and Dictionary of the Hebrew Language* (1833). He later published *Erek Millim*, a biblical Hebrew dictionary (1840; second edition, 1870), and a controversial pamphlet, "On Circumcision in Historical and Dogmatic Perspective" (1843) under the pseudonym Bar Amithai.[44]

Johlson's approach to the Hebrew Bible, and his understanding of how pedagogical needs had evolved since the first wave of translation, become clear in his preface to the *Toldot Avot: Biblical History*.

> Since the topics in the Israelite schools have multiplied to the degree that far less time can be used for instruction in Hebrew language, the need for goal-oriented textbooks and readers has become more apparent. In the past, when there was a dearth of pedagogic materials and it was sufficient to study the Pentateuch and to regard it erroneously as a textbook, so much had to be skipped over, due either to linguistic forms or the content. Nor did students gain exposure to other biblical histories and textbooks. That the type of instruction we practiced was unmethodical and counterproductive . . . is all too well known.[45]

Mendelssohn also knew that the Torah on its own was no textbook; this led him to include the commentary. Johlson's curriculum reconfigured the Bible to serve as a textbook for two typically neglected subjects, Hebrew language and Jewish history. His *Toldot Avot* weaves selected verses together to form a chronological narrative, providing an overview of biblical history. It also, by way of footnotes on every page, provides useful lists of the roots of numerous Hebrew vocabulary words. The preface goes on to boast that the book contains other user-friendly features: a table of contents, headers, an expanded vocabulary section, clear punctuation, diacritical marks, and special stress marks to aid pronunciation of individual words. *Johlson's Toldot Avot* exemplifies what one might call "applied Enlightenment."

Leopold Zunz, Scholar-Translator

Yom Tov Lipmann Zunz was born in Detmold into a traditional Jewish family. After his father died in 1802, his mother sent him to the Samson Free School in Wolfenbüttel, where children lived in very primitive conditions. They were poorly clothed and housed. German books were strictly forbidden and only four hours each week were devoted to secular studies. In 1807, Samuel Meier Ehrenberg took over the yeshiva and transformed it according to the model of schools founded by Mendelssohn's followers. "The school was renovated, the children properly clothed, and the curriculum broadened. Talmud was reduced to a few hours per week to make room for German literature, French, history, and geography."[46] Ehrenberg introduced liturgical reforms, such as a confirmation ritual for children past the age of bar mitzvah. On 22 August 1807, a thirteen-year-old Leopold Zunz was confirmed, in a ceremony that involved "a public oral catechism culminating in the thirteen articles of Maimonides, a blessing by Ehrenberg, and an original Hebrew prayer by the confirmand."[47] Zunz became the first Jewish student to attend the Wolfenbüttel gymnasium. He attended the University of Berlin from 1815–19, studying with the classical philologists Friedrich August Wolf and his disciple August Boeckh, as well as Old Testament scholar Wilhelm de Wette. He obtained his PhD from the University of Halle in 1821. In Michael Meyer's words, Zunz "gradually came to see it as his life's task to create a Jewish philology utilizing the principles and methods of modern scholarship."[48] His groundbreaking pamphlet "On Rabbinic Literature" (Etwas über die rabbinische Litteratur, 1818) audaciously analyzed rabbinic writings as literary texts, demonstrating also that rabbinic literature—demeaned by Jews, especially during the Haskalah—contained ideas about medicine, astronomy, and other topics of universal relevance. Zunz's critical, philological study of Jewish homiletical literature, *The Sermons of the Jews* (1832), launched the type of scholarship associated with the Wissenschaft movement. Zunz published the first Jewish literary history (*Zur Geschichte und Literatur*, 1845) and a biography of Rashi (Rabbi Solomon ben Isaac, 1040–1105), the first medieval commentator on the Bible and Talmud. Two studies of names (*Die Namen der Juden* and *Hispanische Ortsnamen*) emphasized the cultural and linguistic interplay between Jews and their environments throughout history. Zunz's scholarship exemplifies the uses of history in the Jewish nineteenth century.

How is it that just a few decades after the Haskalah sought to "dethrone the Talmud" and reject the authority of the rabbis, a young Jewish scholar saw fit to compose "modern" scholarly studies on rabbis and rabbinic literature? This point gets to the heart of what Wissenschaft des Judentums sought to accomplish. Judaism, which they called "Judentum," would no longer be defined primarily as a religion, but rather as a vital force in human history—culturally distinct, yet universally relevant. All aspects of Jewish history merited critical investigation in order to distill these essential contributions. Only through objective analysis could one discern which aspects of the past were usable and which might be discarded. The ultimate goals of the Wissenschaft des Judentums were not all that different from those of the Haskalah: to bridge the gap between Jewish religion and modern secular European culture through education; to convince the world that Judaism was integral to world history and that the study of Judaism was an academic discipline worthy of scholarly attention.[49]

The Johlson and Zunz Bibles

Within the complete title, *The Five Books of Moses According to the Masoretic Text Literally Translated, with Notes*, the words "with Notes" signal Johlson's original contribution. Footnotes took the place of commentary. Two paratextual elements, the table of contents and preface, exemplify the precarious and bold self-understanding of second-wave translators (fig 2.2). "Contents" divides the Pentateuch according to *parashot* (weekly synagogue portions), but also by chapter, giving capsule descriptions of each one. The descriptions are studded with Hebrew keywords (*mabul* = flood, *challah* = bread-dough, *olah* = burnt offering) and important years listed according to the Jewish calendar (2006, Noah dies; 2668 or 2448, the Israelites leave Egypt).[50] These features are hallmarks of modern scholarship. They suggest readers who are in transition: they lack intimate knowledge of the Scripture, yet are able to decipher Hebrew script and are familiar with key terms; they look to Scripture as a reference guide, yet are in need of a navigator—to use Herder's image—to help them do so.

Johlson's preface is brief and comprehensible. (Mendelssohn's preface was a lengthy treatise composed in Hebrew, directed at scholars and written in a rabbinic idiom; Zunz's preface, composed a few years later, says next to nothing about the methods and motives of the translators.) Johlson wrote to situate the new translation as a necessary successor to that of "the unforgettable Mendelssohn." The preface pays homage to Mendelssohn's *Be'ur* as a great work for its time—then goes on to explain that it needs to be supplanted. It also criticizes the proliferation of "false" successor-translations,

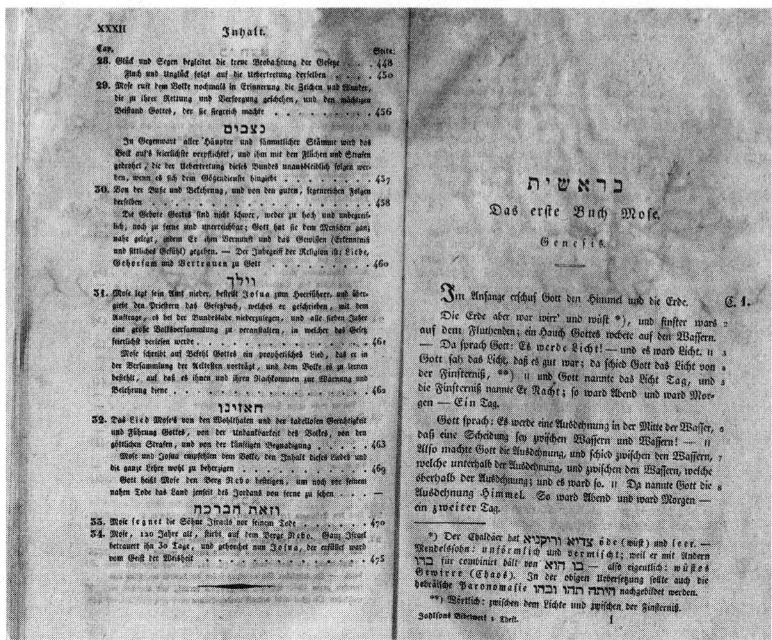

בראשית

Das erste Buch Mose.

Genesis.

Im Anfange erschuf Gott den Himmel und die Erde. C. 1.
Die Erde aber war wirr' und wüst *), und finster wars 2
auf dem Fluthenden; ein Hauch Gottes webete auf den Wassern.
— Da sprach Gott: Es werde Licht! — und es ward Licht. ‖ 3
Gott sah das Licht, daß es gut war; da schied Gott das Licht von 4
der Finsterniß, **) ‖ und Gott nannte das Licht Tag, und 5
die Finsterniß nannte Er Nacht; so ward Abend und ward Morgen — Ein Tag.

Gott sprach: Es werde eine Ausdehnung in der Mitte der Wasser, 6
daß eine Scheidung sey zwischen Wassern und Wassern! — ‖
Also machte Gott die Ausdehnung, und schied zwischen den Wassern, 7
welche unterhalb der Ausdehnung, und zwischen den Wassern, welche
oberhalb der Ausdehnung; und es ward so. ‖ Da nannte Gott die 8
Ausdehnung Himmel. So ward Abend und ward Morgen —
ein zweiter Tag.

*) Der Chaldäer hat צדיא וריקניא öde (wüst) und leer. — Mendelssohn: unförmlich und vermischt; weil er mit Andern בהו für combinirt hält von בו הוא — also eigentlich: wüstes Gewirre (Chaos). In der obigen Uebersetzung sollte auch die hebräische Paronomasie היתה תהו ובהו nachgebildet werden.

**) Wörtlich: zwischen dem Lichte und zwischen der Finsterniß.

Johlsons Bibelwerk 1 Theil. 1

Fig. 2.2. Johlson Bible, Gen 1:1 (1831). Photograph: Rae and Joseph Gann Library, Hebrew College.

"careless and inaccurate" editions of the Mendelssohn Bible printed in German characters, without the Hebrew and sometimes without any attribution to Mendelssohn.

Johlson's goals are to provide a "literal" translation of the Masoretic text, to follow the word order of the original Hebrew, to imitate instances of "wordplay" wherever possible, to clarify difficult passages in notes, and to use notes also to mention alternate translations. The preface begins, "The approving reception found by my German translation of the Twelve Minor Prophets [1827] encouraged me to publish the present *Bibelwerk*, undertaken in the same spirit . . . to translate the complete Masoretic Text, faithfully and **literally**, in [accordance with] its simplicity and terse conciseness."[51] Apologizing for the scholarly apparatus (i.e., footnotes), Johlson writes, "I could not avoid doing this [including alternate versions], due to love of truth and respect for the Holy Scripture."[52] These comments convey the modest, pious tone of the preface as a whole. The translator feels a need to justify his decisions twice over, in both secular and religious terms, but in so doing, he also admits forthrightly that his authority as translator is far from absolute. Of central concern for Johlson is to explain how and why it diverges from its predecessor. "It will astonish no one," Johlson continues, that the translation bears little affinity with Mendelssohn's "free" translation: Mendelssohn's goal was the education (*Bildung*) of his coreligionists by foregrounding the beauty, power, and fullness of the German language, and by displaying the perfection and richness of his own language.

Then comes the hitch—"*Nur so läßt sich erklären*"—"this is the only way to explain" why Mendelssohn's approach to the form of the Hebrew is so problematic. Johlson enumerates: Mendelssohn omits many words from the original Hebrew and elsewhere adds others that are not present in the original; he ignores word order and syntactic inversions in the Hebrew; he "anxiously" avoids repetition. Alert, however, to the cultural forces that shaped previous Bible translations from beyond the parameters of the Jewish world, Johlson notes that Mendelssohn couldn't have done otherwise: in an age where the standard in Bible translation was represented by Johann David Michaelis, it would have been impossible for Mendelssohn to elicit in readers an appreciation for a Bible that sought to be "identical to the original." Johlson claims that Mendelssohn himself regarded his translation as "temporary, dictated by the needs of his time" (*transitorisch und von den Bedürfnissen seiner Zeit geboten*). Johlson even cites a famous dictum of Goethe from 1819 to justify the Mendelssohnian position on translation: "the translator identifies so strongly with the original that he more or less gives up the uniqueness of his own nation."[53]

Johlson illustrates his fundamental departure from Mendelssohn's method by quoting the first nine words of Moses's "Song of the Sea" in Exodus 15:1, in Mendelssohn's translation.

> Exodus 15:1: אָשִׁירָה לַיהוָה כִּי-גָאֹה גָּאָה סוּס וְרֹכְבוֹ רָמָה בַיָּם
>
> JPS: I will sing to the LORD, for He has triumphed gloriously; Horse and driver He has hurled into the sea.
>
> Mendelssohn: Ich singe dem Ewigen. Der hoch erhaben sich zeigt. Roß und Reiter stürzt er ins Meer.
>
> Johlson: Singen will ich dem Herrn, denn hoch ist Er erhöht— / Roß und Reiter stürzet Er ins Meer.

To those not acquainted with Mendelssohn's translation, this may seem like a dubious way to depose it. At issue, after all, is the rendering of one half-verse, only five Hebrew words, because Johlson copied the second half exactly (*Roß und Reiter. . . .*). The phrase has neither theological nor doctrinal significance; or does it? First and foremost, this was an exemplary line of biblical poetry, difficult to translate, and, as such, the place to assert a more current approach to the literary aspect of Scripture. Johlson's critique suggests that he was familiar with Gesenius's *Hebrew Lexicon to the Old Testament Scriptures* published in 1810–12. Johlson spells out five challenges to Mendelssohn's rendering of the first five words of Exodus 15:1:

1. Mendelssohn's "*ich singe*" is wrong because the Hebrew verb "*ashira*" is in the volitional first person. Johlson adds the modal verb, changing "I sing" to "I want to sing" (or "Let me sing").
2. "*Erhaben*," sublime, is not an accurate translation of *ga'ah*, which means "lifted up."
3. Mendelssohn erred in translating the third word, *ki*, as a relative pronoun when it is a conjunction. Johlson changes "*der*" to "*denn*" ("because").
4. Mendelssohn's "*hoch erhaben*" falls short because the doubling in the Hebrew of *ga'oh ga'ah* requires an equivalent doubling in the German. Johlson translates "*hoch . . . erhöht*." (Johlson's version is even more accurate, in fact, than those of Buber and Rosenzweig ("*hoch . . . hoch*") and Robert Alter ("surged, O surged"), because Johlson's "*hoch erhöht*" conveys that the two verbs *ga'oh ga'ah* are not identical: the first is infinitive absolute, the second is a finite verb.)
5. Mendelssohn's last words, "*sich zeigt*" (shows itself), are nowhere to be found in the original.

The contrast between Mendelssohn's and Johlson's renderings of Exodus 15:1 indeed exemplifies the difference between their translations. Recall that both Mendelssohn and Johlson desired to emphasize the literary character of the Hebrew Bible. Both formatted lyric passages in stanzas with line breaks and both used some type of meter to emulate the Hebrew. Lamech's cryptic lament to his wives (Gen 4:23–24) had prompted one of Mendelssohn's first excurses on poetry.[54]

But was not poetry also Mendelssohn's goal? Here a single word in Exodus 15:1 represents the generational divide between Mendelssohn and Johlson: *erhaben* (sublime). Mendelssohn interpolated this adjective into Torah by way of the Song of the Sea, fostering the implicit association between biblical (and Jewish) poetry and sublimity. It was a gambit that had the potential to resonate far beyond Jewish circles. In his review of Bishop Lowth's study of Hebrew poetry, Mendelssohn praised Lowth for presenting "the rules of art by which the divine poets among the ancient Hebrews awaken the most sublime feelings inside of us." Moreover, as Jonathan Sheehan demonstrates, in Christian circles it was poetry as the bearer of sublimity that redeemed the Old Testament for modern life—and, that made it translatable, to boot.

> What characterized the sublime was its power to move the passions in a way beauty never did. Imagination is stirred, even violated, by the sublime, a violation that produces passions ranging from awe to sheer terror.
>
> Exactly this power of sublimity—what one might call the extra-textual aspect of sublimity, its direct appeal to emotions—allowed the Bible to vault the distance between ancient and modern.[55]

What is more, sublimity does not get lost in translation. Classicist Reverend Anthony Blackwall wrote in 1725: "The true sublime *will bear translation into all languages*, and will be great and surprising in all languages."[56] The idea was put into practice by writers such as Friedrich Klopstock, author of the epic poem *The Messiah* (*Der Messias*, 1749), and his disciple Johann Cramer, who published *Poetic Translations of the Psalms* (*Poetische Übersetzung der Psalmen*) in 1755. Sheehan concludes, "For Cramer, like Blackwall, only Hebrew poetry burned bright enough to pierce the veil of time. And because of this glow, the Bible was assured of its easy expression in all tongues. We do not have to become David to be moved by his poetry."[57] It was easier to be moved by the Psalms than by the odes of Pindar; thus was born the notion that sacred poetry could bridge ancient texts and modern souls, and vernacular translation was the medium by which such magic would occur. But what kind of translation would actually accomplish this blending of Hebrew and German, or of Hebrew and English? Paraphrase was not adequate to the task. In Christian circles in the eighteenth century it was the concept of sympathy, associated with the biblical book of Job, that replaced sublime pathos, leading to a "Job revival." In sum: Johlson knew what he was doing when he eliminated the word *erhaben* from the Song of the Sea, and made a federal case about it in his preface. In the German Jewish nineteenth century, translators like Joseph Johlson, Michael Sachs, and others renounced the quest for sublimity, and turned their attention to the poetic or lyrical qualities of language itself.

Most noteworthy in the case of Joseph Johlson is the way in which his poetic sensibility operated in tandem with his educator's impulse. (This is a noteworthy accomplishment in the history of Jewish Bible translation, since a recent tendency has been to oppose the poetic and the explanatory translation.)[58] In describing the world prior to creation (Gen 1:2, *tohu va'vohu*), where Mendelssohn made his first bold break with the German tradition, Johlson asserts his own literary-poetic style, replacing Mendelssohn's "war unförmlich und vermischt" with the alliterative "war wirr' und wüst" and adding a footnote to explain why.

Gen 1:1–2: וְהָאָרֶץ הָיְתָה תֹהוּ וָבֹהוּ
JPS: the earth being unformed and void
Mendelssohn: Die Erde aber **war unförmlich und vermischt**.
Johlson: Die Erde aber **war wirr' und wüst,*)**

Johlson's footnote: *The Chaldean [Targum Onkelos] has *tzadia v'rakania*, "öde (wüst) und leer."—Mendelssohn: unförmlich und vermischt [unformed and mixed]; because he, like others, sees *vohu* as a combination of *vo-hu* [in it]— Thus: wüstes Gewirre (Chaos). In the above translation, the Hebraic paranomasia *hayta tohu va'vohu* is meant to be re-created.

Johlson's very first footnote is also his longest. Startling in its honesty, it encapsulates the factors shaping the translator's praxis. Johlson first cites the Aramaic targum (just as Mendelssohn had) on the assumption that that version still matters for the reader. He then pays homage to Mendelssohn and explains how the latter arrived at the odd word *vermischt* ("mixed")—that is, by way of a rabbinic midrash that interprets the Hebrew word *vohu* as a composite of two words. Only then does Johlson provide a rationale for his innovation: paranomasia, a phrase that echoes the sound of the Hebrew rather than its sense. Like his predecessor, Johlson links the decisions translators make to larger issues in the history of Jewish exegesis and to the aesthetics of the Hebrew. Something of the *Be'ur* remains in this terse footnote, though in a much more abbreviated form and in German.

Johlson's rendering of Genesis 4:13 exemplifies the use of translation to carry on multiple arguments simultaneously. At stake is the exact meaning of Cain's protest upon hearing his punishment for committing fratricide.

Gen 4:13: וַיֹּאמֶר קַיִן אֶל-יְהוָה גָּדוֹל עֲוֹנִי מִנְּשֹׂא
JPS: Cain said to the Lord, "**My punishment** is too great to bear."
Luther: Kain aber sprach zu dem Herrn: **Meine Sünde** ist größer, denn daß sie mir vergeben werden möge.
Mendelssohn: Kajin sprach zu dem Ewigen, **meine Strafe** ist zu groß, um sie zu ertragen.
Johlson: Kajin sprach zu dem Ewigen: Zu gross is **meine Verschuldung**, um sie zu ertragen.*)

Johlson's footnote:* גָּדוֹל עֲוֺנִי מִנְּשֹׂא means both my sin is too great to forgive and also my punishment is too great to bear. In the above translation, one hopes to express both.

The difficulty here is that the noun *avon* could mean "sin" (Luther) or "punishment"—a thing or its correction. Mendelssohn uses *Strafe*, but adds a long explanation of how the Hebrew word "sin" means "sin that brings on punishment." Johlson manages to capture the ambiguity with *Verschuldung*, "debt" or "indebtedness," using a footnote to tell the reader that the verse is ambiguous, but without an arcane explanation. Johlson educates his readers about biblical Hebrew in a way that was heretofore unavailable to speakers of German.

In his preface, Johlson chastises Mendelssohn for fearfully avoiding repetition. In the Hebrew Bible, repetition is inescapable as one of the most frequently used methods for expressing certainty or emphasis. This priority, entirely in keeping with his commitment to the literary, prompts Johlson's lively approach to the "red, red stuff" that Jacob gives the hungry Esau in exchange for a birthright (Gen 25:30):

וַיֹּאמֶר עֵשָׂו אֶל יַעֲקֹב הַלְעִיטֵנִי נָא מִן הָאָדֹם הָאָדֹם הַזֶּה כִּי עָיֵף אָנֹכִי עַל כֵּן קָרָא שְׁמוֹ אֱדוֹם:

JPS: And Esau said to Jacob, "**Give me some of that red stuff to gulp down**, for I am famished"—which is why he was named **Edom**.

Mendelssohn: Da sprach Esaw zu Jaakow, **laß mich doch von disem rohten Gerichte kosten**, denn ich bin abgematet. Darum nent man ihn **Edom**.

Johlson: . . . sprach Esau zu Jakob: **Lass mich doch kosten** von dem rothen—von diesem rothen da!** denn ich bin ermattet. Darum nennt man seinen Namen Edom **[der Rothe]**.

Johlson footnote: ** Or to swallow (*verschlucken*). Or acc. to others: pour into me (*Schütte mir doch ein*).

Johlson borrows Mendelssohn's *kosten* (to taste)—other German versions simply used *essen* (eat); he changes the word order from German to Hebrew; and hedges his bet, yet again, by citing alternate meanings ("to swallow" or "pour into") in the footnote. The ambiguity here stems from the fact that the Hebrew verb translated as "gulping down" is a hapax legomenon—a word that appears only once in the Bible.

In a final example that also pertains to naming, Johlson takes extreme measures to transport the multiple nuances of Genesis 35:18 into German. In this passage, the matriarch Rachel is dying as she gives birth to her second son, and in her last breath she names her boy Ben Oni. What does this name mean, and why does Jacob rename the child Benjamin? Since there is almost no consensus, translators scramble to compensate.

Gen 35:18: וַיְהִי בְּצֵאת נַפְשָׁהּ כִּי מֵתָה וַתִּקְרָא שְׁמוֹ בֶּן אוֹנִי וְאָבִיו קָרָא לוֹ בִנְיָמִין

JPS: But as she breathed her last—for she was dying—**she named him Ben-oni***; but his father called him **Benjamin.****

*Understood as "son of my suffering (or, strength)." **I.e., "son of the right hand," or "son of the south."

Mendelssohn: Es war eben als ihr die Seele ausging, den sie starb, **darum nennte sie ihn Ben Oni: Sohn meiner Schmerzen**. Sein Vater aber nennte ihn **Binjamin, Sohn des Alters**.

Johlson: Und es war als ihr die Seele ausging, denn sie starb: **da nannte sie seinen Namen Ben-Oni [Sohn meines Schmerzens]**. Sein Vater aber nannte ihn **Benjamin [Sohn der Rechten].**)**

Johlson footnote: **She was to me like my right hand. —Others have: son of strength (*Kraft*) (because *Ben-Oni* can also mean this). Others have: Son of the days (of old age).

Zunz: Und es geschah, als ihr die Seele ausging, denn sie starb, da nannte sie seinen Namen: Ben-Oni (Sohn meines Schmerzes), und sein Vater nannte ihn: Binjamin.

Oni: *on* sometimes connotes suffering, but other times, particularly when conjoined to "son of," it connotes strength. The translator also must decide how to explain Jacob's name Benjamin. JPS uses two separate footnotes to explain the options. Mendelssohn's rendering, which interprets the vav as *darum* (that is why) makes only one interpretation available. Perhaps to solidify this interpretation over others, Mendelssohn takes the unusual move (for him) of inserting his view of the meaning of the two names into the text itself. Johlson's brackets and footnote provide the reader with the linguistic information needed to observe an interplay of patriarchal and matriarchal voices and intentions. In the square brackets, Johlson provides the literal meaning of the two names. In the footnote, he supplies a countertraditional interpretation, according to which the "right hand" can refer to Rachel, and "son of my right hand" by extension can be seen to echo the alternate meaning of "Ben-Oni," namely "son of my strength." The countertraditional reading holds that the different names arise out of Jacob and Rachel's common experience and shared strength.[59]

Four verses from Genesis begin to convey Johlson's technique, which involved crafting something wholly new by incorporating, in moderation, strategies of the Mendelssohnian Enlightenment, the educational reformers, and the Wissenschaft movement. Johlson made no effort to conceal his rejection of Mendelssohn's approach, but he does so with respect. Moreover, though his priorities are fidelity to the form and rhythm of the original Hebrew, he does not go as far as Zunz in this regard. Johlson anticipated Buber and Rosenzweig in his attention to the oral character of Scripture and the nuances of its language. Yet he did not share the intentions of twentieth-century translators to estrange the reader from past translations, or to situate the Bible in an existential present. Johlson evokes the word artistry of the Hebrew for the same reason that he includes brackets, informative footnotes, page headings, and a table of contents: these are ways of opening up the riches of the source text and granting access to its many layers of meaning. To reveal the Bible as a great work of literature is not an end in itself, after all, but a testament to its potential to speak to a wide range of people. While the textbooks would instruct his students in grammar and Jewish history, no textbook could adequately convey the art of the biblical narrative. The literary genius of the Bible would be the best argument for a return to Scripture.[60]

Zunz's *Twenty-Four Books*

Whereas the Haskalah translators boasted that they had created something new and modern, the translation edited by Leopold Zunz actually aspired to sound old. Where Mendelssohn embellished biblical language, shunned repetition, and cushioned everything in layers of explanation, this work did the exact opposite. The most important goal of Zunz was to replicate the formal characteristics of ancient Hebrew in German, but without footnotes, parentheses, or commentary (fig. 2.3). The audience remained much the same: teachers (*melamdim*) with poor knowledge of German; educators in new Jewish schools who had to translate difficult passages for their students; women and girls at home who (still) didn't have the opportunity to learn Hebrew and relied on Yiddish Bibles. This time, consistent fidelity to Hebrew was the key to Torah: this would make Torah accessible to those uneducated readers, and even, one hoped, to scholars who might consult it "in secret, borrowing from its treasures."[61]

What I (and most historians) call the Zunz Bible was a collaborative effort with three extraordinary young scholars who did almost all the translations. The impetus for this Bible came from Michael Sachs, an important translator in his own right. Sachs was one of the most admired preachers in Germany, well known for his lectures on Proverbs and on the literary and cultural

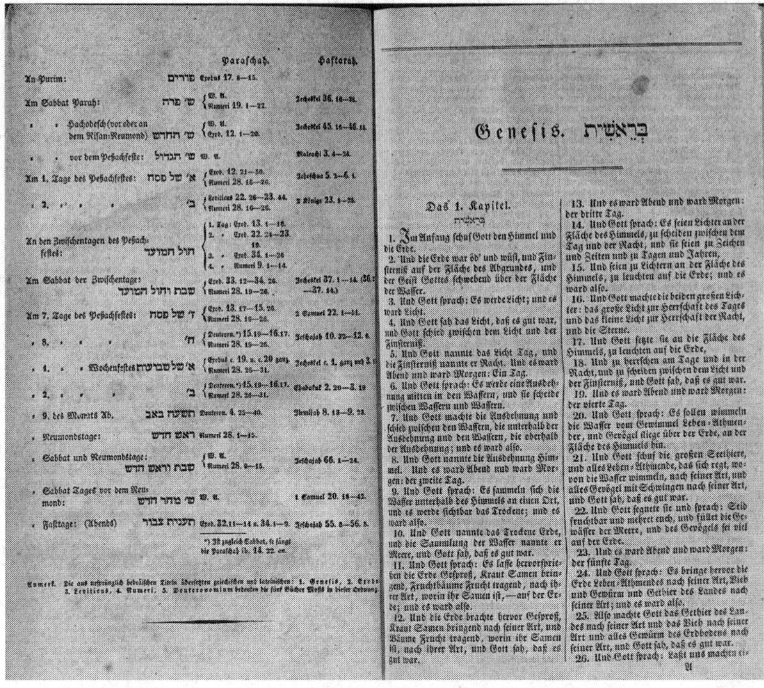

		Paraschah.	Haftarah.
An Purim:	פורים	Exodus 17. 8–16.	
Am Sabbat Parah:	ש' פרה	W. A. / Numeri 19. 1–22.	Jecheskel 36. 16–38.
" " Hachodesch (vor oder an dem Nisan-Neumond)	ש' החדש	W. A. / Exod. 12. 1–20.	Jecheskel 45. 16–46. 18.
" " vor dem Pesachfeste:	ש' הגדול	W. A.	Maleachi 3. 4–24.
Am 1. Tage des Pesachfestes:	א' של פסח	Exod. 12. 21–51. / Numeri 28. 16–25.	Jehoschua 5. 2–6. 1.
" 2. " " "	ב'	Leviticus 22. 26–23. 44. / Numeri 28. 16–25.	2 Könige 23. 1–25.
An den Zwischentagen des Pesachfestes:	חול המועד	1. Tag: Exod. 13. 1–16. / 2. " Exod. 22. 24–23. 19. / 3. " Exod. 34. 1–26 / 4. " Numeri 9. 1–14.	
Am Sabbat der Zwischentage:	שבת וחול המועד	Exod. 33. 12–34. 26. / Numeri 28. 19–25.	Jecheskel 37. 1–14. (36. 37–37. 14.)
Am 7. Tage des Pesachfestes:	ז' של פסח	Exod. 13. 17–15. 26. / Numeri 28. 19–25.	2 Samuel 22. 1–51.
" 8. " " "	ח'	Deuteron.*) 15. 19–16. 17. / Numeri 28. 19–25.	Jeschajah 10. 32–12. 6.
" 1. " " Wochenfestes	א' של שבועות	Exodus c. 19. u. c. 20 ganz. / Numeri 28. 26–31.	Jecheskel c. 1. ganz und 3. 12.
" 2. " " "	ב'	Deuteron.*) 15. 19–16. 17. / Numeri 28. 26–31.	Chabakuk 2. 20–3. 19
" 9. des Monats Ab.	תשעה באב	Deuteron. 4. 25–40.	Jirmijah 8. 13–9. 23.
" Neumondstage:	ראש חדש	Numeri 28. 1–15.	
" Sabbat und Neumondstage:	שבת וראש חדש	W. A. / Numeri 28. 9–15.	Jeschajah 66. 1–24.
" Sabbat Tages vor dem Neumond:	ש' מחר חדש	W. A.	1 Samuel 20. 18–42.
" Fasttage: (Abends)	תענית צבור	Exod. 32. 11–14 u. 34. 1–9.	Jeschajah 55. 6–56. 8.

*) Ist zugleich Sabbat, so fängt die Paraschah ib. 14. 22. an.

Anmerk. Die aus ursprünglich hebräischen Titeln übersetzten griechischen und lateinischen: 1. Genesis, 2. Exodus, 3. Leviticus, 4. Numeri, 5. Deuteronomium bedeuten die fünf Bücher Mosis in dieser Ordnung.

Genesis. בְּרֵאשִׁית

Das 1. Kapitel.

בְּרֵאשִׁית

1. Im Anfang schuf Gott den Himmel und die Erde.

2. Und die Erde war öd' und wüst, und Finsterniß auf der Fläche des Abgrundes, und der Geist Gottes schwebend über der Fläche der Wasser.

3. Und Gott sprach: Es werde Licht; und es ward Licht.

4. Und Gott sah das Licht, daß es gut war, und Gott schied zwischen dem Licht und der Finsterniß.

5. Und Gott nannte das Licht Tag, und die Finsterniß nannte er Nacht. Und es ward Abend und ward Morgen: Ein Tag.

6. Und Gott sprach: Es werde eine Ausdehnung mitten in den Wassern, und sie scheide zwischen Wassern und Wassern.

7. Und Gott machte die Ausdehnung und schied zwischen den Wassern, die unterhalb der Ausdehnung und den Wassern, die oberhalb der Ausdehnung; und es ward also.

8. Und Gott nannte die Ausdehnung Himmel. Und es ward Abend und ward Morgen: der zweite Tag.

9. Und Gott sprach: Es sammeln sich die Wasser unterhalb des Himmels an einen Ort, und es werde sichtbar das Trockene; und es ward also.

10. Und Gott nannte das Trockene Erde, und die Sammlung der Wasser nannte er Meere, und Gott sah, daß es gut war.

11. Und Gott sprach: Es lasse hervorsprießen die Erde Gesproß, Kraut Samen bringend, Fruchtbäume Frucht tragend, nach ihrer Art, worin ihr Samen ist, — auf der Erde; und es ward also.

12. Und die Erde brachte hervor Gesproß, Kraut Samen bringend nach seiner Art, und Bäume Frucht tragend, worin ihr Samen ist, nach ihrer Art, und Gott sah, daß es gut war.

13. Und es ward Abend und ward Morgen: der dritte Tag.

14. Und Gott sprach: Es seien Lichter an der Fläche des Himmels, zu scheiden zwischen dem Tag und der Nacht, und sie seien zu Zeichen und Zeiten und zu Tagen und Jahren,

15. Und seien zu Lichtern an der Fläche des Himmels, zu leuchten auf die Erde; und es ward also.

16. Und Gott machte die beiden großen Lichter: das große Licht zur Herrschaft des Tages und das kleine Licht zur Herrschaft der Nacht, und die Sterne.

17. Und Gott setzte sie an die Fläche des Himmels, zu leuchten auf die Erde,

18. Und zu herrschen am Tage und in der Nacht, und zu scheiden zwischen dem Licht und der Finsterniß, und Gott sah, daß es gut war.

19. Und es ward Abend und ward Morgen: der vierte Tag.

20. Und Gott sprach: Es sollen wimmeln die Wasser vom Gewimmel Leben-Athmender, und Gevögel fliege über der Erde, an der Fläche des Himmels hin.

21. Und Gott schuf die großen Seethiere, und alles Leben-Athmende, das sich regt, wovon die Wasser wimmeln, nach seiner Art, und alles Gevögel mit Schwingen nach seiner Art, und Gott sah, daß es gut war.

22. Und Gott segnete sie und sprach: Seid fruchtbar und mehret euch, und füllet die Gewässer der Meere, und des Gevögels sei viel auf der Erde.

23. Und es ward Abend und ward Morgen: der fünfte Tag.

24. Und Gott sprach: Es bringe hervor die Erde Leben-Athmendes nach seiner Art, Vieh und Gewürm und Gethier des Landes nach seiner Art; und es ward also.

25. Also machte Gott das Gethier des Landes nach seiner Art und das Vieh nach seiner Art und alles Gewürm des Erdbodens nach seiner Art, und Gott sah, daß es gut war.

26. Und Gott sprach: Laßt uns machen ei-

A

Fig. 2.3. Zunz Bible, Gen 1:1 (1838). Photograph: Rae and Joseph Gann Library, Hebrew College.

history of German Jews. He served as rabbi in Prague and, after 1844, in Berlin, pursued scholarship and translation on the side. He expressed opposition to reform, and frustration with the new tendency to see Judaism as basically an Israelite religion—not *Judentum* but *Mosestum*, a creation of Moses—on the premise that everything that followed was only an "afterbirth," as if Jews were not capable of further development.[62] Sachs had studied in Berlin (1827–35; PhD, 1836), and he heard Zunz lecture on the Psalms in 1834–35. He published his translation of Psalms in 1835 (*Die Psalmen: Uebersetzt und erläutert*), in the same year that Heinrich Ewald's Psalms appeared (published in *Die Dichter des Alten Bundes*). He published a revised edition of Gesenius's Hebrew grammar, and in 1836, he applied (unsuccessfully) to the Oriental Translation Committee in London to translate two Hebrew books. He was the first to publish an edition of Spanish Jewish poetry, initiating the mania among German Jews for translating and anthologizing Sephardic poetry. The two-volume *Religiöse Poesie der Juden in Spanien* (Berlin, 1845) included "Religiöse Dichtungen" (Religious poems) with translations from

Ibn Gabirol, Ibn Abitur, Ibn Ghayyat, Behai b. Joseph, Jehuda Halevi, R. Ḥalfon, Ibn Ezra, and Moses b. Naḥman; the second volume contained the essay "Historical Development of Religious Poetry of Spanish Jews in the Middle Ages." He included the original Hebrew poems at the end of the work. In 1855, Sachs published a nine-volume German-Hebrew *Mahzor* (festival prayer book), which was reissued five times throughout German-speaking lands. Sachs used "*der Ewige*" for "Lord" in the *Mahzor*, further popularizing Mendelssohn's appellation for God in Jewish communities in Germany and in the Austro-Hungarian Empire.

Sachs's Psalms, reviewed by Zunz, led to the Zunz Bible. Sachs dedicated the book to Friedrich Rückert, "the west-east poet, the powerfully eloquent master of translation and explication, with deepest admiration and veneration." His preface extolls Rückert's "energetic and undimmed" grasp of the "world of the Orient," as well as his ability to imitate that world "in a lively, fresh reproduction."[63] His intention is to challenge paraphrastic translation and remain faithful to Hebrew meter and word choice. Sachs's language describes the new code of translation into the nineteenth century: "This book will attempt, first, a scholarly, philologically rigorous interpretation of the Psalms, undertaken from a linguistic perspective that is appropriate from a scholarly standpoint, and second, make a contribution to a rational, grammatical, and lexical approach to the language."[64] Sachs's jubilant letter to Zunz conveys his hope that a positive review by the older scholar would be a great asset; it begins: "You are reviewing me! Best friend! I am cheering with joy to be introduced by you into the world of Jewish learning!"[65] Zunz wrote a very positive review, expressing the hope that Sachs's translation would revive interest in the Bible. In another letter, Sachs pays Zunz the ultimate tribute, noting that everything he wrote was already present in Zunz's work.

In 1835, correspondence shows Sachs began discussing a complete Bible translation with two publishers, Moritz Veit and H. Prausnitz. Veit came from an important and wealthy Jewish family. He was a scholar, a writer, and, as head of the Jewish community, a *Landtagsabgeordneter*, member of the state parliament. Veit sought to make sure the design of the Bible was appealing and the price moderate.[66] Letters suggest that Prausnitz initiated the project, enlisting Sachs and Heymann Arnheim (1796–1869), another teacher (and eventual rabbi) from Glogau. Arnheim was an autodidact who had risen from poverty through tutoring to become a talented translator and linguist, knowledgeable about biblical and modern Hebrew. Arnheim had published his own Job translation (*Das Buch Ijob, übersetzt und vollständig commentirt*) in 1836. At the beginning of 1836, Veit offered Zunz the position of editor and learned his conditions for the project; in April 1836, they reached an agreement.[67] Zunz then reached out to Julius Fürst (1805–73), a philologist from Leipzig and author of an Aramaic grammar book who was working on a concordance. Fürst agreed to take on the Aramaic sections of the Bible in Daniel and Ezra. Arnheim translated nineteen books (including the Pentateuch); Sachs did fifteen.[68] Jeremiah was a joint effort. Sachs revised his Psalms translation by toning down some of his more radical expressions to fall in line with Zunz's linguistic criteria.[69] Zunz translated Chronicles I and II, and, as editor, guaranteed the unity of the translation.

Veit's correspondence gives further insight into the factors shaping a Bible translation in the 1830s; above all, the need to balance scholarly and popular desiderata. Veit keeps coming back to the phrase "principles of translation," but without naming those principles. He tries to persuade Sachs to sacrifice scholarly precision for the sake of fluency and appeal. He worries that their work will be branded "incomprehensible, un-German, and suitable only for scholars, or at the most, educated people [*Gebildeten*]."[70] He even suspects that Salomon was spreading such rumors—ostensibly to promote his own popular translation. Above all, Veit insists that the readers *deserve* a readable, German-sounding Bible. In sum: the dual mandate—be scholarly and be popular—was the new impossibility. Translators pushed for greater historicity, at the expense of clarity; the publishers pushed back in the interest of readers (and sales). Sachs describes one remarkable case of self-restraint: instead of beginning Genesis 1:1 with *Im Anfang* (In the beginning), Heymann Arnheim wanted to begin with the word *Früher* (Earlier). Zunz agreed with Arnheim's translation but refused to incorporate it, lest the very first word of the Bible deter readers or make them mistrustful of its innovations.[71] Above all, the translators agreed that any translation for German Jews would have to follow the Masoretic text, even more so since they (unlike Mendelssohn) were determined *not* to reprint the Hebrew or the Scribal Corrections on the page. Elsewhere in his scholarship, Zunz disapproved of the uncritical attachment to the Masoretic text; however, for obvious reasons, he agreed to such a policy for the Bible translation.

Zunz's *Twenty-four Books* has long been regarded as a classic German Jewish translation. The reference to twenty-four books in the title was a Jewish, but value-neutral designation. Zunz was a mathematician, and he used numbers as sources of authority and authenticity. For the first time, a translation included neither a translator's apology nor a rationale for new methods. A brief preface addressed the reader more like a consumer, testifying to the credibility of the authors, the integrity of the process, and the "correctness" of the finished product. After listing the four translators, their cities of residence, and the books translated by each one, Zunz continues:

> The works of these gentlemen translators, who, by strict adherence to the *masorah* and accents, took on themselves the task of reproducing the established, correct sense (*den ermittelnden richtigen Sinn*) faithfully, clearly, and appropriately, are mutually advised and hereby essentially completed. Dr. Zunz, who held responsibility for the editing, looked through all the handwritten translations, made changes where necessary for meaning or expression, and strove to produce evenness and unity of tone through the work as a whole. The text was carefully revised once again in page proofs.
>
> That this work, undertaken for the sake of the Holy Writ, be worthy of its object, is our wish; that it not pass ineffectively by school and home, is our hope.

Note the lack of reference to previous translations, new methods, or any other framing narrative. All that one needs to know about the process is that it was conscientiously undertaken and dutifully carried out. Only in the final lines does the "indifferent" writer shed his confident stance to voice the hope that this work not be met with indifference.

In the Bible of Wissenschaft, facts and numbers take the place of the metadiscourses of prefaces and commentary. Front matter includes "A List of Parashas and Haftarahs for Holidays, Fast Days, and Special Sabbaths," almost always present in synagogue Bibles.[72] Back matter included a unique feature: "Chronology (*Zeittafel*) of the Complete Holy Scripture."[73] This timetable dated biblical history twice, according to the "the years counting from Creation" and "the years from the beginning of the Common Era." Judging from the materials framing this Bible, the implied reader is in tune with three different calendars: Jewish sacred time, Jewish historical time, and the secular calendar. From its title onward, the Zunz Bible draws upon numbers and dates to forge an impartial and authoritative framing context.

To convey the overdetermined use of numbers in the Zunz Bible, I contrast Zunz's detailed chronology of the events of 1656 BCE with the comparable section in Johlson's table of contents:

Johlson:

Chapter 7. The flood (*mabul*) breaks out. Noah goes into the ark (1656)

Chapter 8. End of the flood. Departure from the ark (1657) Expression of Noah's gratitude.—His sacrifice is favorably accepted. God's promises.

Zunz:

1656/2332. On the 10th of the 2nd month, announcement of the great flood.

Noach and his three sons: Jefet, Shem, Cham with their wives go into the ark.
On the 17th of the 2nd month, beginning of the flood.
On the 17th of the 7th month, i.e., after 150 days, the ark rests on Mount Ararat.
On the 1st day of the 10th month, the mountaintops become visible.
1657/2331. On the 1st day of the 1st month, the dry earth is being restored through the 27th day of the 2nd month.
Noach's agriculture and viniculture.
Population of the earth by Noach's progeny.

In Johlson's table of contents, the primary events are concisely noted: Noah enters the ark, Noah departs from the ark. Years are an afterthought, since the organizing principle is the sequence of events as narrated in the Bible itself. Zunz's chronology puts years first, and turns the flood into a full-fledged historical occurrence, the phases of which are carefully dated down to the month and day. As is typical of historical writing in the age of Wissenschaft, the individual story ("His sacrifice was favorably accepted") is subsumed within large-scale developments ("agriculture and viniculture"). Ismar Schorsch pinpoints why "the category of time" held such significance for practitioners of the new Jewish science:

> At the core of modern Jewish scholarship there is a new way of thinking about Judaism. Emancipation exposed Jews inexorably to the historical perspective: to understanding the present in terms of the past and the past in terms of itself. A religious tradition indifferent to the category of time in comprehending itself, that indeed made a virtue of leveling chronologically all its literary strata—*ein mukdam u-meuhar ba-Torah* [There is no early or late in the Torah]—was suddenly confronted with a mode of cognition that rested on contextual interpretation. Dating became the key to eliciting the meaning of a text and no contemporaneous piece of evidence—Jewish or non-Jewish—could be arbitrarily dismissed in the interpretive exercise.[74]

By this rationale, Zunz's "Chronology" endowed both the translators and the translation itself with new authority, which was especially useful in the case of a foreign-sounding German rendering that omitted all notes from the pages. As Schorsch notes, chronology eliminates the perception of arbitrariness on the scholar's (and translator's) part. On the premise that all the evidence has been considered and organized, no justifications are needed.

How did the translators of the Zunz Bible replicate Hebrew syntax and form? Their most dramatic intervention was to preserve the Hebrew word order, even in the case of syntactic inversion, at the expense of correct German. Of the three German versions of Genesis 34:1, Mendelssohn and Johlson place the verb "went out" where it properly belongs in German: in the second position. Zunz places the verb in the first position following the Hebrew: "And out went Dinah. . . ."

Gen 34:1: וַתֵּצֵא דִינָה בַּת-לֵאָה אֲשֶׁר יָלְדָה לְיַעֲקֹב לִרְאוֹת בִּבְנוֹת הָאָרֶץ

JPS: Now Dinah, the daughter whom Leah had borne to Jacob, **went out** to visit the daughters of the land.

Zunz: Und **ausging** Dinah, die Tochter Leahs, die sie geboren hatte dem Jaakob, um sich umzusehen unter den Töchtern des Landes.

Johlson: Als Dinah **ausgieng**,[75] die Tochter der Leah, welche Sie dem Jakob geboren, sich umzusehen unter den Töchtern des Landes

Mendelssohn: Dinah Leahs Tochter, die sie dem Jaakow gebohren, **ging aus**. Sich umzusehen unter den Töchtern des Landes.

Second, the translators transliterated all proper names, rather than incorporate Luther's distorted Greek and Latin versions. The decision to render biblical names as Hebrew *Fremdwörter* meant that Noah became *Noach*; Isaac became *Jizchak*; Moses, *Mosche*; and Rebecca, *Rivkah*. Consider Genesis 3:20:

וַיִּקְרָא הָאָדָם שֵׁם אִשְׁתּוֹ חַוָּה כִּי הִוא הָיְתָה אֵם כָּל חָי:

JPS: The man named his wife **Eve**, because she was the mother of all the living.

Zunz: Und es nannte Adam den Namen seines Weibes: **Chawah**, denn sie war die Mutter alles Lebenden.

Johlson: Adam nannte den Namen seines Weibes **Eva [die Belebende]**; denn sie ward eine Mutter alles Lebenden.

Compare the yields of Zunz and Johlson. The former gives the Hebraic form Chawah. The latter gives two names—the German Eva, and its translation *die Belebende* (the giver of life). Zunz's reader gains knowledge of the actual name; Johlson's reader will not learn the Hebraic form but will be able to understand the verse in its entirety, "because she was the mother of all living." The difference encapsulates the disparity between these two visions of what a Hebraic translation could accomplish: Zunz targets the linguistic form of the Hebrew, whereas Johlson targets the aesthetic sense of the Hebrew. Buber and Rosenzweig borrowed *both* of these techniques, consistently giving both the Hebraized form and its translation.

> BR: Der Mensch rief den Namen seines Weibes: **Chawwa, Leben**! Denn Sie wurde Mutter alles **Lebendigen**.

But Buber and Rosenzweig were the exception; according to David Rosin, these innovative techniques did not catch on. German Jews in the nineteenth century retained the familiar names in scholarship and in pedagogical texts. "School and Life proved to be more powerful than the better knowledge." A review by the Christian scholar and translator Karl Freiherr von Bunsen (1791–1860) may also explain their reluctance: Bunsen called this approach to biblical names *Judendeutsch*—a criticism he leveled at the work as a whole.[76]

A third innovation in the Zunz Bible is the reintroduction of the conjunction *und* (and) as a consistent marker of the letter vav that is appended to most Biblical Hebrew verbs. In using this marker, Zunz restored the convention introduced by Martin Luther and the Amsterdam Yiddish Bibles, which the eighteenth-century German translators had so vehemently rejected. Genesis 25:34:

> וְיַעֲקֹב נָתַן לְעֵשָׂו לֶחֶם וּנְזִיד עֲדָשִׁים וַיֹּאכַל וַיֵּשְׁתְּ וַיָּקָם וַיֵּלַךְ וַיִּבֶז עֵשָׂו אֶת הַבְּכֹרָה׃
>
> Zunz: **Und** Jaakob gab dem Esav Brod und ein Gericht Linsen, **und** er aß **und** trank **und** erhob sich **und** ging weg. Also verachtete Esav die Erstgeburt.
>
> KJV: **Then** Jacob gave Esau bread and pottage of lentiles; **and** he did eat **and** drink, **and** rose up, **and** went his way: **thus** Esau despised *his* birthright.
>
> Alter: **Then** Jacob gave Esau bread and lentil stew, **and** he ate **and** he drank **and** he rose **and** he went off, **and** Esau spurned the birthright.

In contrast:

> Mendelssohn: Jaakow aber, gab dem Esaw, Brod, und ein Gericht Linsen, diser aß, trank, stund auf, und ging davon. So verachtete Esaw die Erstgeburt.

> Michaelis: Esau aß, trank, stand auf, ging davon, und verachtete sein Erstgeburt.
>
> JPS: Jacob then gave Esau bread and lentil stew; he ate and drank, and he rose and went away. Thus did Esau spurn his birthright.

In recent times, Robert Alter has been a vocal proponent of the biblical "and," not in the name of grammatical accuracy, but as an acoustic necessity dictated by biblical cadence. The letter vav is indeed part of the narrative structure, but, in the opinion of most biblical scholars, it is best left untranslated. It has two specific functions: in some cases it has a conjunctive or "consecutive" function; in others, it plays a conversive role, signifying "but." Reintroducing the slavish use of the conjunction *und* restored the paratactic rhythm and served to defamiliarize biblical syntax for the modern German reader.

Zunz's most important break with Mendelssohn may have been his exchanging the pose of translator-exegete for that of translator-historian. *The Twenty-four Books of the Holy Scripture* is a primary source rather than a study Bible. It does not supplement the Hebrew Bible as much as replace it. Zunz's hebraism was not an end in itself but a means to the ultimate goal of restoring, perhaps even resanctifying, the ancient dignity and historical authenticity of Hebrew Scripture by means of piety and scholarship.

RECEPTION OF THE JOHLSON AND ZUNZ BIBLES

Early Reception

Perhaps the most important and illuminating review of Johlson's Pentateuch was that of Abraham Geiger (1810–74), one of the most eminent intellectuals to emerge from the Frankfurt Philanthropin. Geiger, who had been Johlson's pupil, went on to become a scholar, rabbi, theologian, and leader of the Reform movement in Germany. Geiger reviewed Johlson's *Bibelwerk* in 1837, in the wake of the publication of *Former Prophets*, a second volume of the Johlson Bible. Geiger cites Johlson's notes as the distinctive feature of his translation, and he reprints them in a footnote to his review. He also praises Johlson's "pluralistic" renderings and the precision with which he approached difficult passages. Geiger continues:

> The precision and careful implementation of the details, which are known to be the most valuable quality in all the author's works, are here, too, everywhere in evidence: the poetic passages are, in all their literalness,

> metrically rendered, and the chronologies and explanations of the locations and borders are given in extreme brevity in the table of contents. May the efforts of the author meet with general praise and recognition so that he can quickly bring the next parts [of his project] to completion.[77]

Since this review, Johlson's *Bibelwerk* has received little scholarly attention, most likely because it has been overshadowed by important translations of complete Bibles by Zunz, Herxheimer, and Philippson. Unlike his textbooks, which went through many printings in German and even in English, Johlson's Pentateuch was never reprinted. Its status as a minor work may reflect the contentious nature of Jewish community life in Frankfurt, where Johlson was based, as well as competition from the contemporaneous translations. Salomon's translation took hold in Hamburg, Zunz's in Berlin, and other, inferior Bibles were also in circulation. After the 1840s, monumental translations by Salomon Herxheimer (Bernburg), Ludwig Philippson (Magdeburg), and Samson Raphael Hirsch (Frankfurt) had entered the fray.

Philipp Ehrenberg wrote the following letter upon receiving the first volume of the Zunz Bible:

> The first volume of your Bible is in our hands, and it is very pretty on the outside. What I have thus far read of the translation I admire, mainly because of its correctness and literalness (*Richtigkeit und Wörtlichkeit*)—that which the Mendelssohn translation tends to paraphrase, from which one has to extricate oneself. But it seems to me that this striving for a close correlation of words at times goes too far to the opposite extreme and sometimes even makes a comical impression. I don't like "Und es ward der Mensch zu einem *Leben-Athmenden*";[78] even less do I like "*Gevögel*" instead of *Geflügel*;[79] "Die Sache *war leid* in den Augen,"[80] "Durch Deinen *Mund* werde mein Volk verpflegt"[81] (here the German is clearly incomprehensible; *peh* [mouth] has to be translated otherwise than with *Mund*). I think that this kind of a translation, intended for a popular audience [*Volk*], would definitely not have to distance itself from common German usage, even if it retains its simple oriental color. The union of these two demands is enormously difficult, and perhaps only achievable by continuing your efforts. Forgive me for this comment; I would really like you to translate one of the books yourself as a model for the young editors. Isn't Dr. Sachs the editor of the first volume?[82]

Ehrenberg's belief that the "union of these two demands," scholarly and popular, was virtually impossible, and that perhaps common usage need not be violated in the process of retaining the exotic color, eventually won the day. In a postscript to the letter, Ehrenberg père also weighs in:

> I have only enough time to tell you that I agree completely with the above, and in particular with the evaluation of the Bible translation. I turn for example to Exodus 15:7. Why is the perfect and not the present tense used? This would follow better from verse 6, und would be more appropriate to the *atid* [future tense] than the perfect (according to the spirit of the Hebr. language.)

Both Ehrenbergs are attuned to the competing priorities affecting the Bible translator. The language had to sound authentic ("oriental color") without being laughable and without digressing too far from common parlance. Another tension emerges in Samuel Eherenberg's postscript, where he accuses Zunz of violating the "spirit of the Hebrew language" by being obsessively attentive to verb tense. The risk of producing a translation that tries so hard to replicate the source language is the distortion of the target language, and Zunz was apparently vulnerable to this critique.

A further set of standards emerges in an anonymous 1840 review, most likely authored by Michael Hess (1812–75), in the Jewish periodical *Der Orient*. The reviewer notes that he is interrupting his serial review of the Salomon translation of 1839 in order to give a full account to the "Bible-reading public" of the accomplishments of both Bibles, "since neither is published with notes." He begins by praising "Dr. Zunz's *Bibelwerk*" for its "great elegance" and precise attachment (*Anschmiegen*) to the original.[83] He also comments that the Zunz Bible will have the authority to shape the creation of a "correct" (i.e., Hebrew) Bible, something "which we do not yet have." To support this claim, he singles out 1 Chronicles 24:8. He notes that both Zunz and Salomon deviate from the Masoretic text, and also from the Septuagint, the Vulgate, the Luther Bible, "the English," from "all Bibles" and also Gesenius's *Lexicon*—by writing the word "**Sch**eorim," with a *shin*, rather than "**S**eorim," with a *sin*. The reviewer wonders whether this is an error or an emendation. All translations throughout the nineteenth century were scrutinized for their adherence to the Masoretic text, but this reviewer reflects the liberal Jewish view that the establishment of a correct Hebrew scripture is an ongoing, positive process. Orthodox rabbis, on the other hand, banned any translation that veered from the letter of the Masoretic Bible. Both Zunz and Johlson make a point of referring to the Masoretic text on the title pages of their Bibles.

Der Orient's reviewer goes on to cite numerous verses and comment on accuracy and consistency. Hebrew-German transliteration—perhaps because this was one of this Bible's innovations—is a special concern. Within the very first paragraphs, he praises Zunz for doing away with the Greek letters "ph" and "th" in names such as *Naftali*, *Josef*, and *Efron*, but then asks, "but why '*Pharaoh*'?," concluding that in the case where the letter *peh* (p or f) comes at the beginning of the word, Zunz's Bible alternates: "*Frat*," but also "Pelischtim."[84]

> The proper names are rendered exactly as they are expressed in the Hebrew text, with few exceptions, which one would like to wish away. Thus, throughout, as in Genesis 22 and 23, "Rebekah" is written, but consistency requires either "Ribkah," as Salomon and Herxheimer write, or "Rivkah," as Philippson writes. But such abnormalities are few and far between. Here may be all of them: Gen. 46, 9, the same person is called Falu who in Ex. 6, 14 is Phalu and Num. 26, 5 is Fallu. Gen. 10, 16, Jebusi, Ex. 13,5 Jewisi.—Ex. 28, 18 Sapir and 24, 10 Sapphir.—Gen. 29, 34 Levi, but 34, 25 Lewi. Gen. 46, 10 Charmi, but Num. 26, 6 Karmi. Gen. 46, 10 Jachin, but Num. 26, 12 Jakin.—Gen. 46, 21 Becher, but Num. 26, 35 Beker.[85]

Transliteration is no simple matter!

The reviewer appears to have scanned the entire translation, verse by verse, for other errors, irregularities, and inconsistencies, and relishes listing them in the review. The first error is in Genesis 1:2, where Arnheim writes "water" as a plural; but in Genesis 7:7, "water is masculine singular." He also takes him to task for Genesis 1:8, "the second day," which should be "a second day"—only the sixth day is given the definite article—noting also that Salomon, Herxheimer, and Philippson got this one right. He continually compares Zunz to Herxheimer; Mecklenberg (*Scriptura ac Tradition*); David Marin (an English translation); Mendelssohn (of course); Dubno; Philippson; Fürst (*Concordance*); Heidenheim; Bochart; Sachs; the Vulgate; the Septuagint—and even an unnamed French version. Some translations, such as Genesis 6:16 or 9:20, he finds outright meaningless.

Later Reception of the Zunz Bible

The Zunz Bible went through six editions by 1855 and twelve by 1889.[86] Of the many German Jewish translations published between 1783 and 1937, only the Zunz Bible became an authoritative translation for German Jewry across the generations. David Rosin distinguished Zunz's enterprise, above all, as the first Hebrew Bible printed in German letters for Jews (Israelites), without the *Urtext*, that incorporated new research into exegesis, lexicography, and grammar, and that provided students, teachers, and friends of biblical literature an aid for the study of the Hebrew text.[87] More than any other, Zunz's translation demanded that its readers simply make peace with the Bible's awkward tone, the linguistic asymmetry, and those opaque passages. This may be why only Zunz's, of all the translations in the second wave, achieved true longevity. In Weintraub's Hebrew monograph *The German Translations of the Pentateuch*, Zunz's is the only second-wave translation to be included. Rabbi and scholar W. Gunther Plaut (1912–2012), who was raised on the Zunz Bible, speculates that its lack of smoothness, of being at home in the language, was precisely why this work in particular became his community's vade mecum:

> Zunz's translation reminded the reader that the original was Hebrew and that, while it was cast in the German tongue it never hid its origin. It proclaimed thereby that the Bible, even in its German garment, was essentially a Hebraic document. . . . I think it is not unreasonable to speculate that the work reflected, however subconsciously, the feeling of most German Jews that they were not fully German, not yet anyway, a judgment which they knew was vigorously reciprocated by the Gentiles. I see the wide acceptance accorded to Zunz to reflect the fact that German Jews on the whole treated the attempted German/Jewish symbiosis with caution.[88]

In essence, one could not open the Zunz Bible without being reminded that, as Theodor W. Adorno wrote, "The *Fremdwörter* are the Jews of language."[89]

The philosopher Hermann Levin Goldschmidt (1914–98) offers a contrasting assessment of Zunz's legacy.

> Zunz's achievement . . . was unable to spur a deepening of interest in the Bible of any consequence, and failed to become a subsequent reference point for Judaism's religious sector. This phenomenon, of course, is hardly unique to the Jews. Movements hostile to any form of religion had already taken hold, and created divisions within Judaism that became ingrained, preventing his work from gaining any impact.[90]

Given these two "eyewitness" assessments, one might say that the Zunz Bible succeeded as a cultural work, but it failed as a religious work. The attribution of this failure to the polarization of the Jewish community later in the nineteenth century is likely applicable also to the case of Johlson.

The Zunz Bible is the only German-language Bible currently available at a Jewish bookstore in Brookline, Massachusetts. This 1997 edition, which restores the Hebrew text alongside the German, was printed in Israel—a joint effort of Israeli and German publishers.

American Legacies of the Johlson and Zunz Bibles

An important legacy of both the Johlson and Zunz Bibles was their influence on the first American Jewish Bible translation (1853–54). The translator, Isaac Leeser (1806–68), was a modern Orthodox German Jew who immigrated to America in 1822. Leeser "was the most important Jewish religious leader in the United States during the Ante-bellum Period." In 1830, Leeser published an English translation of Johlson's catechism *Instruction in the Mosaic Religion* in Philadelphia (another English edition appeared in 1867). However, his major work was a Bible translation for American Jews, the authoritative English translation until the first Jewish Publication Society translation appeared in 1917.[91] As its title indicates, Leeser modeled *The Twenty-four Books of the Holy Scriptures* upon Zunz's *Die vier und zwanzig Bücher der Heiligen Schrift*. The translator, says the postscript to Leeser's Pentateuch, "feels it his duty to acknowledge that he has received the greatest aid from the Pentateuch of Arnheim, and the Bible of Zunz, even to a greater degree than from the works of Mendelssohn, Hochstatter, Johlson, Heineman, and several anonymous contributors to our biblical literature." In instances where Leeser did not follow Zunz, Arnheim, Sachs, and Fürst, he frequently cited their renditions in his notes.[92]

GOTTHOLD SALOMON'S *VOLKS- AND SCHULBIBEL* (1837)

In 1840, Julius Fürst's newspaper *Der Orient* published the first of a multipart series, "Notes on German Bible Translations That Appeared in Recent Years," comparing the new translations by Salomon and Zunz. The reviewer, a Hungarian scholar named Lazar Skreinka, was immensely conscientious; he treats each translation separately and both of them together, at one point juxtaposing a long passage from Leviticus in both versions and in his own translation. He opens by noting what surprised him about these two new translations: their stand-alone format.

> The almost simultaneous appearance of two Bible translations that are as literal as possible (*möglichst wörtliche Bibelübersetzungen*) without the accompanying [scriptural] text and commentary, yet explicitly des-

> ignated for the public and for school, is, with respect to that designation, a new phenomenon in Judaism. *Volksbibeln* (popular Bibles) for the secular masses were always ventured in one manner of presentation, in order to be as appealing as possible in light of the norms and tastes of the time—an explanatory [style]—to prevent any kind of mistake or misinterpretation. . . . Because even in former times, the interpreters of the chanted Scripture in the public worship service had to connect translation with the business of exegesis through paraphrase. But in that way, the fleeting word, animated by tone, was less subject to the dangers of abuse than the fixed, dead letter is. Even Martin Luther, with his major efforts to return to the pure word of the teaching, could not avoid giving explanatory notes to his translation.[93]

Without using the word "Yiddish," this reviewer assumes that Zunz and Salomon translated for uneducated men, women, and children—as did the *meturgeman* in the ancient synagogue, the Old Yiddish paraphrases, and Luther. It thus surprises him that these pedagogical Bibles have no notes, no commentary, nothing "to prevent misinterpretation." How could such works be useful to the "secular masses"? Perhaps this explains why the reviewer takes it upon himself to subject even the smallest units of these translations to minute analysis and critique. To scrutinize the language of a freely rendered or exegetical bible was pointless. But in a translation that claimed to be literal (*worttreu, möglichst treu*) and aspired to be used in schools each word had to be accurate. Six issues later, this reviewer took aim at Zunz's Bible in "Die Bibelübersetzung unter Redaktion des Dr. Zunz."

Like many biurists, Gotthold Salomon (1784–1862) began life in very impoverished conditions in Sandersleben, a small town in eastern Germany, and received neither gymnasium education nor university training. Nonetheless, he became learned in both rabbinical and philosophical literature. He taught for sixteen years at one of the early Jewish schools, the Free School in Dessau, during which time he also started preaching and translating, completing the Minor Prophets together with four other followers of Mendelssohn.[94] After delivering a guest sermon at the Beer Synagogue in Berlin, Salomon was called to lead the new Israelite Temple in Hamburg, where he remained for thirty-eight years. In an 1853 tribute marking twenty-five years of service, with a beautiful new synagogue under construction,[95] Salomon was celebrated for his oratory, teaching, charitable work, and his efforts on behalf of his coreligionists. Salomon was called the "father of modern Jewish homiletics," because, though he learned to preach by studying Christian sermons, he developed a genuinely Jewish mode of preaching, and was invited to preach in London, Vienna, and Prague. Twelve of his sermons were published in English translation in London in 1837. Salomon was also the first to compose religious songs in German; ninety-five of these songs were included in the collection *Religiöse Lieder und Gesänge für Israeliten* (1818–21).[96] But Salomon's main legacy is as a brilliant orator, and—when debating Jewish politics—an exceptional polemicist "who made use of lively language, humor, satire, and great eloquence."[97]

Gotthold Salomon's *Volks- und Schulbibel für Israeliten* preceded Zunz's Bible by one year, thus winning the race to become the first Jewish translation of the entire Hebrew Bible in German characters. Salomon worked on it for ten years and referred to translation as his most challenging undertaking.[98] To the best of my knowledge, Salomon's translation has never been studied systematically; its fame derives primarily from its status as the translation with which Zunz was competing, even before publication. Both books were stereotyped for inexpensive printing. By Salomon's account, rabbis and teachers responded very positively to his solicitations for subscribers. Assisting him in this effort was Rabbi Mannheimer, who had authored two books of the translation, and the Hamburg philanthropist Salomon Heine (Heinrich Heine's uncle), who subsidized its publication.[99] A third, multivolume edition (1868) added features for synagogue use (Haftarot; scrolls; and a prayer book). In the long run, by measure of popularity, Zunz won out. One reason was political: Salomon "was identified with the revolutionary Hamburg temple and therefore his work was suspect in many circles. No such odium adhered to Zunz."[100] In their time, both translations were reviewed together and, apparently, subject to the same criteria. Over Zunz, with its multiple translators, biographer Phöbus Philippson praised Salomon's idiom as coming from "*one* mold," capturing the spirit of both Hebrew and German, and even at times "schwungreich und erhaben" (buoyant and sublime).[101]

As reviewers noted, Salomon's goal and methods were distinctly different from those of Zunz. Salomon aspired, above all, to produce an affordable and accessible Bible that would appeal to the common Jew. Harking back to Luther, but also aspiring to the longevity of Mendelssohn, he strove for simplicity, clarity, and comprehensibility. He did not dare to alter German word order to reflect Hebrew syntax, but other features do reflect his generation's new attention to Hebrew. He preferred a strong mistranslation of the text to something stilted. Salomon's tribute to Mendelssohn in his commemorative monograph of 1829 also captured his own ambition as a translator:

> We are not inclined to investigate the critical value of these works [Mendelssohn's translations of Pentateuch, Psalms, Song of Songs] or to

> emphasize their deficits; what concerns us is their impact on the Jews. That is incalculable; it lives on to this day, and will serve to disseminate light and research for a long time to come. That was his intention, not to shine among the philologists; and his purpose has been completely achieved.[102]

In translating the first verses of Genesis, Salomon strove for natural expression and casual diction, pushing back against Mendelssohn's innovations in order to restore a Luther-like tone (*wüst und leer*; *der Geist Gottes*). Genesis 1:1–3:

> Im Anfang erschuf Gott den Himmel und die Erde. **Doch** die Erde war **wüst und öde**, und es war finster auf der Fläche des Abgrundes; **der Geist Gottes** aber schwebte über dem Wasser: Gott sprach: Es werde Licht! Da ward Licht.

Genesis 2:4:

> Dies die **Geschichte** des Himmels und der Erde, als sie erschaffen worden. Als **Gott, der Herr**, Erde und Himmel gemacht—keinerlei Feldgewächs war noch auf der Erde; keinerlei Kraut des Feldes war aufgekeimt, denn noch hatte **Gott, der Herr**, nicht regnen lassen auf der Erde, und kein Mensch war da, zu bearbeiten den Erdboden—Da stieg ein Dunst auf von der Erde, und tränkte die ganze Fläche des Erdbodens.

Salomon was the only second-wave translator who rejected *der Ewige*, out of his commitment to unpretentious language and probably also anxiety of influence. He was also the only one to reintroduce Luther's *der Herr* for the generic name of God in cases when it was followed by the proper Name, which he renders *Gott*. Salomon also simplified Mendelssohn's vocabulary. Where Mendelssohn writes *Entstehunggeschichte* (history of the origins) for *toldot* in Genesis 2:4, Salomon writes *Geschichte* (history or story). In Exodus 2:2, where Mendelssohn writes that Moses was *wohlgebildet* (well-formed, Heb. *tov*), Salomon uses *schön* (beautiful). But Salomon retained Mendelssohn's German neologism for Passover, though he placed the word in quotation marks, suggesting that although the term had become well known, it was not to his liking. Zunz of course used the Hebrew *Peßach*.

Exodus 12:11:

> JPS: it is a passover offering to the LORD.

Mendelssohn: es ist das Überschreitungsopfer dem Ewigen zu Ehren.
Salomon: Es ist das "Ueberschreitungsopfer" Gott geweihet.
Zunz: Peßach ist es dem Ewigen.

Like Mendelssohn (and unlike his contemporaries), Salomon would never alter German word order to replicate Hebrew syntax. Recall Zunz and Johlson's creative approaches to Genesis 34:1:

Zunz: Und **ausging** Dinah, die Tochter Leah's
Johlson: Als Dinah **ausgieng**, die Tochter Leah

By contrast, Salomon follows Mendelssohn almost verbatim.

Salomon: Und Dina, die Tochter Lea's, die sie dem Jakob geboren, **ging aus**.
Mendelssohn: Dinah Leahs Tochter, die sie dem Jaakow gebohren, **ging aus**.

Salomon did not use hebraized names, as a rule, but occasionally he used calques from Hebrew, such as *Mond* (moon) instead of "month." Does Exodus 12:2 announce a new month, or new moon?

JPS: This **month** shall mark for you the beginning of the months; it shall be the first of the months of the year for you.
Zunz: Dieser **Monat** sei euch das Haupt der **Monate**: der erste sei er euch unter den **Monaten** des Jahres.
Salomon: Dieser **Mond** sei euch der Anfang der **Monde**; der erste sei er euch unter den **Monden** des Jahres.

Salomon's innovations appear to have been unprincipled. He often preferred to follow Mendelssohn or Luther or do something idiosyncratic, and this stylistic naturalism brought enormous popular success, as did his popular hymns. A distinct statement was made by retaining Mendelssohn's *erhaben* (sublime) in Exodus 15:1, but he rewrote the verse so that it would rhyme like a folk song. Herxheimer, who preserved *der Ewige*, also managed to eke out a rhymed couplet. Mendelssohn likely turned over in his grave (Exodus 15:1):

JPS: I will sing to the LORD, for he has triumphed gloriously;
Horse and driver he has hurled into the sea.

Salomon: Ich will singen Gott, denn **erhaben, erhaben** ist er,
das Roß sammt seinem Reiter stürzte er ins Meer.
Herxheimer: Ich sing dem Ewigen, daß er hehr, war hehr,
Roß und seinen Reiter, warf ins meer!

Reception of Salomon's Bible

Salomon's *People's Bible* may have been popular, but the two reviewers who evaluated it for Jost's scholarly journal *Israelitische Annalen* attacked him brutally.[103] These were not the Orthodox rabbis who tried to shut down the Hamburg Temple and ban its prayer book; these were liberal rabbis: M. Hess from Trier and Leopold Schott, the district rabbi of Randegg in Lower Austria. In three issues of Philippson's *Allgemeine Zeitung des Judentums*, Salomon penned two long articles to defend his translation. It must have been unusual for the journal to provide room for an *Antikritik* (reply to a review in a different publication), because editor Ludwig Philippson, student and ally of Salomon, explains that he regarded it as his duty to provide the "respected author" an immediate opportunity to defend himself. I cite some examples from this exchange to illustrate the type of philological and stylistic scrutiny to which all of these translations were subjected. Whether writing in scholarly or popular journals, reviewers often went verse by verse to point out errors or disagreements.

Hess and Schott accuse Salomon's translation of being *undeutsch und sinnlos* (un-German and senseless); opposed to the genius of the German language; incomplete; against the Masorah; and full of linguistic and typographical errors. Schott groups Salomon's errors into seven "rubrics": strange and uneven translations, among them the use of *Gott* for the *nomen proprium* in lieu of Luther's *Herr*, because *Elohim* means *Herr*; inconsistencies; distortions of meaning; imprecision; violations of the Masorah; disregard for the original text (*Urschrift*); and again, *undeutsch und sinnlos*.

Salomon's refutation is rife with sarcasm, but he does bring substantive evidence to support his choices and illuminate his motives. On some level, the negative attention was flattering: he draws consolation from the memory that rabbis endorsed (or permitted) the burning of the Mendelssohn *Be'ur*. To the charge of inconsistency, he wrote that this was never his intent, noting the lack of consistency in Luther and De Wette, and in the Bible itself. To the claim that he disregarded the *Urschrift*, he scoffed: "as if there was an *Urschrift*!" And he is particularly indignant about Herr Schott's self-righteous critical tone, claiming that he never pretended that his translation was infallible, or that it aspired to make the original superfluous. Four brief excerpts from Salomon's *Antikritik* (the first three responding to Hess's criticisms, the fourth, to those of Schott) give an idea of what Salomon meant by not wanting to "shine among the philologists":

> Genesis 29:2, *grossen Stein*. In this translation, I followed the Chaldean [Targum] *avna rabata*.[104]
>
> Genesis 41:45. ["Zaphenath-paneah" in JPS] both words—which are not Hebrew, despite all philological blather that one reads in broadsides—are of Egyptian origin, hence my translation, which differs from all other translations (see Ibn Ezra's commentary to this passage).[105]
>
> Exodus 21:16. ["He who kidnaps a man—whether he has sold him or is still holding him—shall be put to death" in JPS.] My translation supposedly diverges from the Tradition. I respect the Tradition; but first, not everything that calls itself Tradition has traditional authority; second, Tradition is not permitted to do violence to the text; third, I distinguish whether the object of Tradition belongs to past times or to Israelite life in the present. In any case, the teaching of the Tradition that is under discussion does not come from Exodus 21:16 but from Deuteronomy 24:7 (as we see in Maimonides' Hilchot Genevah par. 9 § 2). But the translation of the latter verse agrees wholly with the Tradition.[106]
>
> I translated Genesis 6:3, the extremely difficult passage "*lo yadun ruchi*" ["my breath shall not abide in man forever" in JPS] as "*Nicht ewiglich soll mein Geist* ***herabgewürdigt*** *werden im Menschen . . .* " Since this passage, as noted, is one of the most difficult, I permitted myself to derive the verb *yadun* from the Arabic and translate accordingly. I admit that philologists might not validate this translation; but does that make it **un-German**? Is it **senseless**?! Is the spirit of God in the human being *not* degraded (*herabgewürdigt*) through sin?[107]

Salomon's method, or lack thereof, is best captured by this one retort: "I admit that philologists might not validate this translation; but does that make it *undeutsch*? Is it *sinnlos*?" That accusation rankled the most; he ends the first article with it and takes it up again in the sequel.

Salomon's boldest legacy may be his refusal to abide the Jewish mistranslation of Exodus 21:24 (JPS): "eye for eye, tooth for tooth, hand for hand, foot for foot," traditionally interpreted to mean monetary compensation.

> Salomon: Auge um Auge, Zahn um Zahn, Hand um Hand, Fuß um Fuß
>
> Blitz: Gelt far oyg in plats dos oyg; gelt far tson in plats den tson. Gelt far hand in plats di hand. Gelt far fus in plats dem fus [fig. 2.4].

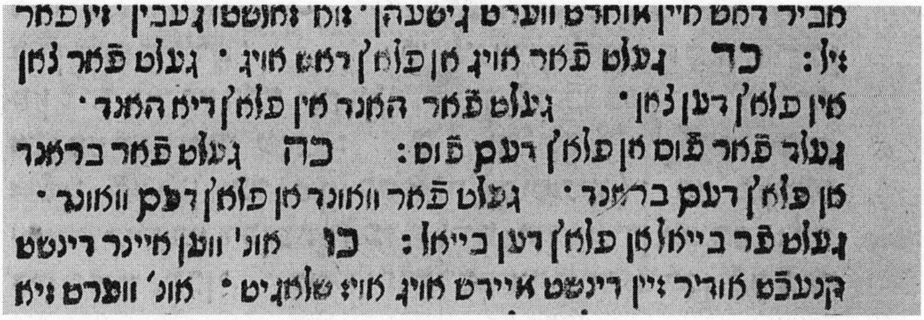

Fig. 2.4. Blitz Bible, Ex 21:24, "Gelt far oyg in plats dos oyg . . ." (1678).

Mendelssohn retains the striking Hebrew formulations but frames the verse on either end with explanatory words "By rights," "thus the perpetrator must give money for it." "**(Rechts wegen sollte)** Auge für Auge (seyn), Zahn für Zahn. Hand für Hand, Fuss für Fuss. Brandmal für Brandmal, Wunde für Wunde, Beule für Beule **(daher muss der Täter Geld dafür geben)**." Even Buber and Rosenzweig had to compromise and add *ersatz* (substitute): "Augersatz für Auge, Zahnersatz für Zahn, Handersatz für Hand, Fußersatz für Fuß."

SALOMON HERXHEIMER'S BIBLE (1840–1848): A *BE'UR* FOR JEWS AND CHRISTIANS

If Salomon's affinities with Mendelssohn, lack of method, and popularity place him to the left of the New Hebraists, the comprehensive approach of Salomon Herxheimer puts him to the right of this cluster. Though trained in Oriental studies, Herxheimer was not translating the Hebrew Bible merely to serve scholarly or national interests. He expanded the reach of the second wave in several ways: he sought to appeal to Christians, and to achieve the moral betterment (*Erbauung*) of all readers. He adopted the two-column format pioneered by Salomon and Zunz, but reinstated Hebrew Scripture on the right side and added numbered footnotes on the bottom of the page, somewhat like those of Johlson, but more numerous (fig. 2.6). Herxheimer's ambition is captured by the lengthy title of the first volume (1840): *Five Books of Moses in Correct Hebrew Text with Literal Translation, Continuous Explanation, and Edifying, Homiletically Useful Allusions, Adapted for Jews and Christians*. The title contains keywords of the second and third waves. The translation was "correct and literal," but this would be more than a scholarly work, as it promised not only explanation (a nod to Mendelssohn) but also something edifying and practical. A reviewer of

בראשית

Das erste Buch Mose.

בראשית

Die Schöpfung. — Der Garten in Eden. — Der bestrafte Ungehorsam. — Kain und Hebel. — Die Geschlechtsfolge. — Die Ausartung des Menschen.

Cap. 1—2; 3.

1. Im Anfang erschuf Gott den
Himmel und die Erde. 2. Doch
die Erde war wüst und öde, und
es war finster auf der Fläche des
Abgrundes; der Geist Gottes aber
schwebte über dem Wasser: 3. Gott
sprach: Es werde Licht! da ward
Licht. 4. Als Gott das Licht sah,
daß es gut sei, da schied Gott
zwischen dem Lichte und zwischen
der Finsterniß. 5. Und Gott nannte
das Licht Tag, und die Finsterniß
nannte er Nacht. Und es ward
Abend, und es ward Morgen Ein
Tag.

6. Da sprach Gott: Es werde
eine Ausdehnung inmitten des Wassers, und scheide zwischen Wasser
und Wasser. 7. Und es machte
Gott die Ausdehnung, und schied
zwischen dem Wasser, das unterhalb der Ausdehnung war, und zwischen dem Wasser, das oberhalb der
Ausdehnung war, und es blieb also.
8. Und Gott nannte die Ausdehnung Himmel. Und es ward Abend,
und es ward Morgen ein zweiter
Tag.

9. Da sprach Gott: Es ziehe sich
zusammen das Gewässer unterhalb
des Himmels an Einen Ort, auf
daß sichtbar werde das Trockene.
Und es ward also. 10. Und Gott
nannte das Trockene Erde, und den
Zusammenfluß des Wassers nannte
er Meere. Und Gott sah, daß es
gut sei. 11. Da sprach Gott: Es
sprieße die Erde Sprossen, Samen-
tragendes Kraut, Fruchtbäume,
Fruchttragend nach seiner Art, worin der Samen ist, auf der Erde.
Und es ward also: 12. Die Erde
brachte hervor Sprossen, Samen-
tragendes Kraut, nach seiner Art,
und Fruchttragenden Baum, worin
der Same ist, nach seiner Art. Und
Gott sah, daß es gut sei. 13. Und
es ward Abend, und es ward Morgen ein dritter Tag.

14. Da sprach Gott: Es werden
Lichter in der Ausdehnung des Himmels, um zu unterscheiden zwischen
dem Tag und zwischen der Nacht.
Auch sollen sie sein zu Zeichen für
Zeiten, so wie für Tage und Jahre;
15. sie sollen aber auch sein zu Lichtern in der Ausdehnung des Himmels, um zu leuchten auf die Erde.
Und es ward also. 16. Und Gott
machte die zwei großen Lichter: das
große Licht für das Reich des Tages, und das kleine Licht für das
Reich der Nacht, und die Sterne.
17. Und Gott gab sie in die Ausdehnung des Himmels, um zu
leuchten auf die Erde, 18. und zu
herrschen am Tage und in der
Nacht, und zu unterscheiden zwi-

1

Fig. 2.5. Salomon Bible, Gen 1 (1837). Photograph: Judaica Collection, Harvard University Library.

Herxheimer's translation clarified why the time had come to restore—not *the Be'ur*, but a *be'ur*, onto the pages of the German Jewish Bible:

> In Jewish religion, exegesis is not the exclusive property of the theologian, or even the scholar, as in Christianity, but the common property of all pious Jews; the merchant, the manual laborer, tended to sit down on the Sabbath and read the Pentateuch with Rashi or another old commentary, and they were comfortable in that because that understanding was one of the first elements of their instruction. Since Mendelssohn's time, the *Be'ur*—more appropriate for *die Neuzeit* (modernity)—replaced Rashi, until, finally, in our day, when Europeanization of Judaism matured so abruptly that even this became almost repressed and was no longer comprehensible.

First there was the targum, then Rashi, then the *Be'ur*. What would be next? Perhaps the "edifying, homiletically useful allusions" of Rabbi Herxheimer, whose portrait had been painted on a porcelain cup, in good Biedermeier fashion?[108] As the review above suggests, commentary, to be accessible, had to take a new form. First and foremost, it had to be written in German. Second, it had to be marketable to different constituencies. Herxheimer included two sets of notes on the page: scholarly and homiletical. He boldly claimed that his was a translation for Jews and Christians, for women as well as men. Both of these assertions reflect a very modern state of affairs. With the growth of a middle-class reading public, as Jonathan Hess writes, male and female readers continued to read different types of Jewish and secular books. A scene that exemplifies the new reading mania is found in Moritz Daniel Oppenheim's portrait "Sabbath-Ruhe auf der Gasse" (Sabbath rest, 1866), which depicts a father and son dozing off clutching their religious books, a mother engrossed in the *Tsene-Rene*, and in the far back, a young girl reading her novel in privacy.[109]

Salomon Herxheimer (1801–84) was a moderate reformer best known for his oratory skills, numerous publications, and pedagogical accomplishments.[110] He was born in Dotzheim, near Wiesbaden, studied at a yeshiva in Mainz, and eventually studied Oriental languages, history, philosophy, and pedagogy at the University of Marburg and in Göttingen. In 1827, he became a religion teacher, and in 1830, district rabbi (*Kreisrabbiner*) in Eschwege. In March 1831, he became a teacher, preacher, and regional rabbi (*Landesrabbiner*) in Anhalt-Bernburg.[111] He was called to the position by Duke Alexius Friedrich Christian, an advocate of Jewish emancipation who, in 1810, had published an edict on the betterment of the moral and civil condition of the Jewish subjects of Anhalt-Bernburg. Because the duke appointed him, he paid two-thirds of his salary and the congregation paid one-third. Protection by the government enabled Herxheimer to implement his reforms. He introduced confirmation of boys and girls into the synagogue; six boys and five girls participated in the first confirmation ceremony during Sukkot 5593 (1832). Together with Gotthold Salomon and Ludwig Philippson, he participated in rabbinic conferences of the 1840s in Braunschweig, Frankfurt, and Breslau, and in the synods in Leipzig. Many years after the duke had died, the Konsistorium zu Bernburg recognized Herxheimer for leading the Jewish community school, instituting confirmation, and excellent German sermons.[112] Like his contemporaries, Herxheimer authored many widely used and influential textbooks. The Prussian minister of education commended one of his catechisms "for its Kantian and Lessingian spirit" in 1886; this was a book that had already gone through twenty-nine editions, and had been translated into English in the United States.[113] Another of his missions was encouraging Jews to leave commerce and devote themselves to agricultural pursuits, crafts, art, and science.

Herxheimer's *Bibelwerk*, the product of ten years' labor, was published in four volumes in 1840 and in a single volume in the following year. Despite damage to his eyes, he worked until 1850 to complete all twenty-four biblical books. The translation was praised as rational, clear, accessible, and nonpartisan. Like Zunz and Johlson, Herxheimer restored the *and*s (connective vav) to the text, on the grounds that the Bible speaks in a "childlike, simple" language.[114] Genesis 1:1–2:

> Im Anfang **schuf** Gott den Himmel und die Erde. **Und** die Erde war **eine Oede und Leere**, **und** Finsterniß über der Fläche der Wassermasse, **und** der Hauch Gottes schwebend über der Fläche des Wassers. **Und** Gott sprach.

He breaks with his contemporaries in stating that *tohu va'vohu*, which he renders "a desolation and an emptiness," are nouns that emphasize not chaos but emptiness (*Leere*), and which evoke Luther's "*wüst und leer*." Perhaps in deference to Christian readers, he notes that the word *schuf* (created) alludes to 2 Maccabees 7:28, and that the primary meaning is creatio ex nihilo. In a note to Genesis 1:1, he broke new ground by quoting Rashi's vocalization of *bara* as *b'roa* (i.e. "of the creating," rather than "created"), which had been rejected by Mendelssohn, who in turn relied on Herder and Ewald for support. What stands out in all of this is the fine balance of rabbinic and scholarly concerns on each and every page.

Herxheimer's preface begins by expressing the confusion with which this chapter began:

> Amidst the chaos and agitations in religious life of our age, and particularly in the Jewish domain, there can be no more important step toward an all-satisfying truth and clarity than to investigate, in an unbiased way, the contents of the Holy Scripture, which forms the basis of our destiny in all matters of belief and religion, and bring it to secure and clear consciousness.

There is (still) no book more important for the Israelites, nay, for all confessions, than the Holy Writ. Herxheimer designates his readership as preachers, teachers, men and women who understand Hebrew and who seek *Erbauung* (edification) in the home and synagogue, and people who want to know whether this or that practice is found in the Torah.

Herxheimer follows this declaration by listing four highlights of his work. First, "the *Urtext* of the Holy Writ is included in the most correct possible form." Like Mendelssohn, he begins with a long defense of the punctuation, orthography, and accents of the Masorah. "It was a matter of conscience to present the Masoretic text as completely and correctly as possible." For whom is this necessary? Pious ones, the biblical researchers, the scribes, the cantors, and those who chant from the Torah, and teachers whose students translate the text. Second: he boasts of "a faithful (*getreu*) translation." The critical line: "As much as we value the translations of Mendelssohn, de Wette, and the most recent Israelite Bible translators, they didn't satisfy me."[115] He lists the reasons why not: a good translation must select the most accurate German expression; retain the integrity of German by avoiding willful neologisms and word combinations; and reflect the nuances of the Hebrew original without giving children a distorted German text. His translation is intended "to mirror the idea, the uniqueness, and the fine nuances of the Hebrew original as faithfully as possible"—all hallmarks of the second wave. Toward the end of the preface, he situates himself beautifully by explaining why the extant Jewish and Christian works are inadequate. Jewish translations are too old-fashioned (Mendelssohn? Zunz?), not scholarly (*wissenschaftlich*; Salomon?), and not progressive, and their exegesis and translation are superficial (Salomon?) Christian translations are too scholarly, too extreme, "one-sided," and far removed from most readers due to their Hebraic or Latin "garb." His own Bible will serve a combination of needs: provide the most "up-to-date scholarship, while making the Holy Book understandable in a brief and easily accessible exegetical commentary, expanded on through translation that reflects the spirit and ideas of the original as faithfully as possible, and also adding practical, fruitful allusions."[116] The emphasis on translation with commentary implicitly recommends this Bible as a *Be'ur* for the next generation. Herxheimer concludes by referring to his work as the "first German Pentateuch commentary in Israel": a project that brought him many hours of devotion and bliss, intended to bring "justice, truth, and peace" to Israel. He ends with a traditional blessing, "*Baruch hatov v'hametiv, Gepriesen sei Gott, der Gütige und Wohlthätige!*" (Blessed is God, who is good and makes good).

Taking Zunz's chronological tables to the next level, Herxheimer's twenty-page introduction resembles an encyclopedia article on the Hebrew Bible. Of particular interest is the reference guide to Jewish and Christian translations and exegetical sources. A section on "translations of the Pentateuch" includes subsections on Aramaic translations (which corrects the confusion Mendelssohn wrote about between Targum Yerushalmi and Targum Jonathan ben Uzziel), as well as Syriac, Arabic, Persian, and Latin ones. A section on "commentaries and aids to the Pentateuch" lists both Jewish and Christian sources alphabetically—among them, Ludwig Philippson (only Genesis and Exodus had come out), Michaelis, and Mendelssohn.[117] Under "other resources," Herxheimer names all the important works of biblical scholarship produced by German Orientalists since Mendelssohn's time.[118] He follows this with "Chronological Table of the Pentateuch," which again gives two time frames: "years of the world" and "years of the common era [CE]."

Herxheimer advertises his commentary as "complete, concise, and contemporary" with the emphasis on "concise." But—in a familiar paradox—concision was achieved through consultation of abundant sources: translations of the Alexandriner (Philo) and the Chaldeans (targumim); Luther; the exegeses in the Talmud, midrash, Rashi, Rashbam, Ibn Ezra, Kimchi, Ramban, and Abarbanel, as well as those of Herder, Michaelis, Vater, Rosenmüller, de Wette, Gesenius, Ewald, and Bohlen, and those in Josephus and *More Nevuchim* (Maimonides), also those of Mendelssohn and Heidenheim. He specifies that no commentary, Jewish or non-Jewish, Eastern or classical, should be excluded, with the exception of kabbalistic and antiquated, and newer sources.

But I propose that the distinguishing feature of this Bible is what Herxheimer called a bonus (*Zugabe*): "practical and homiletically suitable allusions (*Die praktischen und homiletisch benutzbaren Andeutungen*)" to address the dearth of solid Jewish *Erbauungsschriften*. Homiletical notes would appeal to preachers, teachers, and the female gender. *Bildung* and

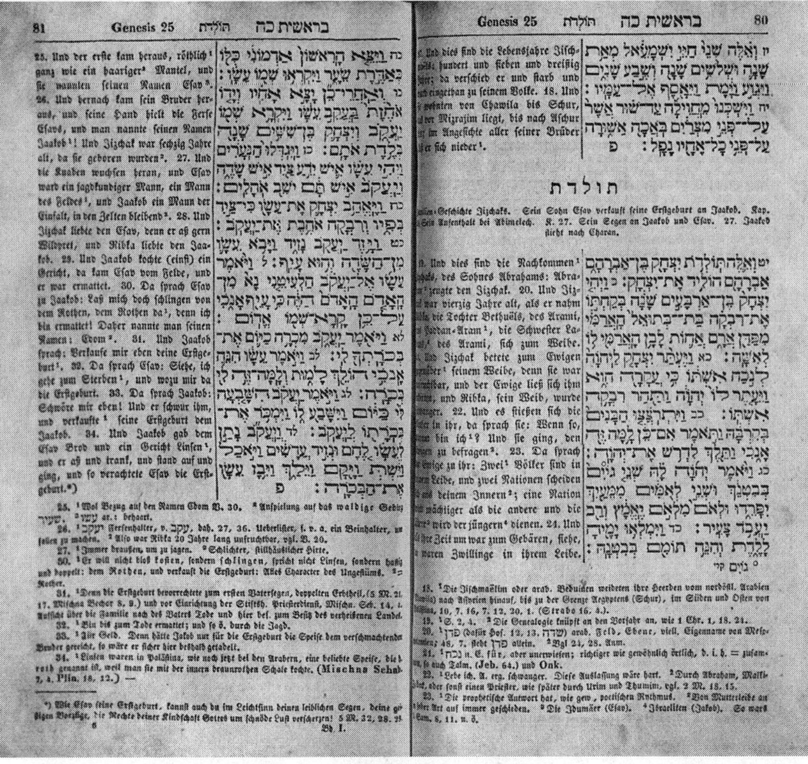

81 Genesis 25 תולדת בראשית כה

25. Und der erste kam heraus, röthlich[1] ganz wie ein haariger[2] Mantel, und sie nannten seinen Namen Esav[3]. 26. Und hernach kam sein Bruder heraus, und seine Hand hielt die Ferse Esavs, und man nannte seinen Namen Jaakob[1]! Und Jizchak war sechzig Jahre alt, da sie geboren wurden[2]. 27. Und die Knaben wuchsen heran, und Esav ward ein jagdkundiger Mann, ein Mann des Feldes[1], und Jaakob ein Mann der Einfalt, in den Zelten bleibend[2]. 28. Und Jizchak liebte den Esav, denn er aß gern Wildpret, und Ribka liebte den Jaakob. 29. Und Jaakob kochte (einst) ein Gericht, da kam Esav vom Felde, und er war ermattet. 30. Da sprach Esav zu Jaakob: Laß mich doch schlingen von dem Rothen, dem Rothen da[1], denn ich bin ermattet! Daher nannte man seinen Namen: Edom[2]. 31. Und Jaakob sprach: Verkaufe mir eben deine Erstgeburt[1]. 32. Da sprach Esav: Siehe, ich gehe zum Sterben[1], und wozu mir da die Erstgeburt. 33. Da sprach Jaakob: Schwöre mir eben! Und er schwur ihm, und verkaufte[1] seine Erstgeburt dem Jaakob. 34. Und Jaakob gab dem Esav Brod und ein Gericht Linsen[1], und er aß und trank, und stand auf und ging, und so verachtete Esav die Erstgeburt.*)

Genesis 25 תולדת בראשית כה 80

תולדת

Fig. 2.6. Herxheimer Bible, Gen 25 (1841–48). Photograph: Judaica Collection, Harvard University Library.

Wissenschaft (like Talmud study in Ashkenaz) were male pursuits; by contrast, *Erbauung* was what one found in the pages of the women's Bible (the *Tsene-Rene*) or in a good sermon: wisdom applicable to everyday life. Herxheimer, like Philippson and Hirsch, wrote in a rabbinic idiom. This little postscript signals Herxheimer's status as a transitional figure who bridges the agendas of the second and third waves.

What did an edifying Bible commentary look like? For one thing, it had to be concise (unlike the comments in third-wave translations.) Secondly, it had to relate to everyday cares. Herxheimer's two comments about Esau's request for that red red stuff is a case in point (fig. 2.6). Second-wave translators used this passage to open up the naturalism of the exchange and the etymology of the name "Edom." Herxheimer uses the linguistic nuance of "red red" to draw a lesson about character and bad behavior. His commentary on Genesis 25:30 reads:

> He does not say, let me eat but rather, gulp down (*schlingen*); out of fierce hunger and greed he cannot call the lentils by their name, but speaks hastily and in doubled form about "that red stuff," and gives away the birthright. Everything characterizes his impetuous character.

Herxheimer's homiletical note:

> Like Esav with his birthright, you too, in a moment of recklessness, can forfeit your corporal blessing, your spiritual assets, the rights of your divine filiation, for the sake of vile pleasure.

Edification is found neither in language, nor in sense. Herxheimer's homiletical notes speak in the second-person singular to address people of all faiths and ages. Genesis 1:1:

> Creation and Scripture begin with God; so shall all beginnings be with God! And when you begin your youth [by celebrating confirmation], your marriage, every undertaking, begin every day with God, then you will never begin anything bad, anything with a bad intention.

Genesis 2:25:

> The introduction of the Sabbath is already a testament to the divine origins of the Holy Writ. Holy Day! Through thousands of years, you have saved millions of people from physical exhaustion and spiritual death. Please also be for me a day of strengthening healing for my body.

Genesis 22 (Binding of Isaac):

> God demands sacrifice from each and every one of us: from one a beloved son, from another a dear daughter, a dear mother, a beloved friend, a good wife—and to each person, religion and conscience call out: sacrifice the last sinfulness that remains in your heart, tear out of your (heart) the mistakes of your youth, education, and desires! And to some. . . . give your blood for the fatherland. . . . May each of us be able to cry out, "Lord, I am here . . ." and believe that his faith renders him protected before God and Man.

This voice belongs to one who reportedly gave his first sermon at age seven, and who later studied the homiletic techniques of Christian preachers—Schleiermacher and others.[119]

Fifteen years later, when Herxheimer undertook to "revise and much expand" his original *Bibelwerk*, he was no longer writing in confused times, but in a period of renewed interest in the Hebrew Bible. He had been encouraged by the positive reception of the earlier edition—both by Christian ministers and Jewish principals and rabbis, who valued its succinct, useful, nonpartisan explanations.[120] This third edition was published in Leipzig in one volume, with a slightly different title page, the same introduction, and a shorter preface and commentary. The revisions seem to be consistent with how Ludwig Philippson revised his translation in the 1870s; perhaps Herxheimer was competing once again with Philippson. The use of the familiar *du* and an authorial narrator replaced the "Rashi style" neutral voice in the commentary, thereby extending the homiletical impact even further.

Reception[121]

Herxheimer's critics valued his application of the principles of Wissenschaft des Judentums to the sources of Judaism and his efforts to popularize biblical scholarship through notes. An early reviewer praised his precision and competence, but complained about the print being "unattractive and impractical," because despite the low price, people would prefer to pay more for a book that is *schön ausgestattet*—a possible allusion to Philippson's Bible.[122] Alone among the second-wave translations, Herxheimer's was purchased for Protestant ministers by the consistories of Bernburg and Sondershausen who also recommended that the local princes subscribe; "truly good signs for our time . . . for the authorities, clergy, and the rabbis!"[123] Reviews appeared even in non-local Christian papers, in the *Hengstenberg'sche Kirchenzeitung*, *Bremer Kirchenbote*, and *Frankfurter katholische Kirchenzeitung*, whose authors praised the work itself but thought it rather "un-Christian" that the consistory had asked them to purchase it.[124]

Herxheimer's was the only second-wave German Jewish Bible that opened from right to left, as Hebrew books do.

However, Herxheimer's *Bibelwerk* did not find the readership it hoped for among German Jews. Apparently, the publisher had neglected to advertise, so Herxheimer decided to lower the price and to advertise it himself in *Der Orient*.[125] Perhaps it could not compete with the aesthetically breathtaking Philippson Bible. The disappointing reception is summed up in a tribute in the Leipzig community newspaper in 1935, on the fiftieth anniversary of Herxheimer's death, that follows up its extensive praise with "Nonetheless, it could not break a new path, and save for the Pentateuch, it did not find a way to a [broad] public" and a plea for someone to produce new edition.[126]

LEGACIES OF THE SECOND WAVE

I have sought to understand four German Jewish Bible translations of the 1830s–1840s in conjunction with intellectual and religious trends in Germany at large. This generation had to transform Mendelssohn's "ephemeral solution" (Meyer) into an educational, social, and modern religious program. It did so by creating schools, curricula, and textbooks, and by producing Bible translations with an unmistakably Hebraic character that sought, albeit in different ways, to become popular. In nineteenth-century Germany, nationalism replaced universalism for German Christians as for German Jews. As Meyer writes (echoing Fichte), "The child must receive a specifically *national* education, not a universal one."[127] In the nineteenth century, moreover, the ideal of Pure Science replaced the ideal of Liberal Arts, and this "was accompanied by the transformation of the cosmopolitan ideal of humanity into the particularist ideal of the nation."[128]

The enduring accomplishment of this decade was what I have called the New Hebraism. While both Johlson and Zunz were driven to highlight the national origins of the Hebrew Bible, the differences between them correspond to the distinct priorities of the Jewish educator and the philologist of *Judentum*. Johlson followed Mendelssohn in viewing Bible translation as a pedagogical opportunity, but for him instruction was about form as well as content. Johlson used footnotes—the hallmark of modern scholarship—in lieu of commentary to open up the richness and the ambiguities of the language. Zunz, by contrast, had no interest in translation as a form of literary criticism or commentary; he had no need for footnotes. Nor did he aspire to supply preachers with ideas for their weekly homily. Zunz emphasized philological and numerical correctness and producing a scholarly Jewish Bible in German that would present itself as an authorless source text. Thus, though both Johlson and the translators of the Zunz Bible aspired to render the German more transparent to Hebrew, Hebrew served a different strategic function in each case. Johlson introduced Hebrew to make possible an intimate encounter between the reader and the original fertile, multimeaning text. Mendelssohn's free rendering had also sought to make the text as accessible as possible, but by taking the opposite approach—by using parentheses and paraphrase to disambiguate the Bible and its language. In the Zunz Bible, translation foregrounded the inaccessibility and foreignness of the Hebrew idiom, widening the distance between modern speech and biblical syntax and thereby endowing the Jewish *Urtext* with an aura of historicity.

Salomon's and Herxheimer's translations frame the second wave. On one end, Salomon's *Bibelwerk*, like his career as a whole, represented the ambition of radical Reform. The format of his Bible (identical to that of Zunz)—bifurcated all-German layout, with brief subject headers at the top of each *parsha*—was a complete innovation. Salomon started out as a biurist; perhaps he fundamentally believed he could produce a work as inspired as Mendelssohn's translation, though his critics saw little more than a hodgepodge of the new and the old. A few years later, Herxheimer retraditionalized the format of the German Jewish Bible. He understood the criticism with which this chapter began, namely, that a modern Jewish translation, in order to be popular, must include commentary. "Translation with commentary" became the motto of the German Jewish third wave, and it remains the method of choice in the American-Jewish twenty-first century.

CHAPTER THREE

The Third Wave: The Bible as *Gesamtkunstwerk*

WORKS DISCUSSED

Ludwig Philippson. *Die israelitische Bibel: Enthaltend—Den heiligen Urtext, die deutsche Übertragung, die allgemeine, ausführliche Erläuterung mit mehr als 500 englischen Holzschnitten* (The Israelite Bible). 3 vols. Leipzig: Baumgärtner, 1839–54; 2nd ed., 1858; 3rd ed., *Prachtbibel der Israeliten*, with Doré illustrations. Stuttgart: Halbergersche Verlagsbuchhandlung, 1874.

Samson Raphael Hirsch. *Der Pentateuch. Übersetzt und erläutert von Samson Raphael Hirsch* (The Pentateuch). 5 vols. Frankfurt am Main: J. Kauffmann Verlag, 1867–78; 3rd ed., 1899.

INTRODUCTION: REDESIGNING THE GERMAN JEWISH BIBLE

The first (August 1839) installment of Ludwig Philippson's *Israelite Bible*—published in fascicles over a fifteen-year period—opened with a two-page advertisement. Beyond offering subscribers the usual assurances that the translation is accurate and literal, Philippson and his publisher called special attention to form (*Gestalt*), design, and other aids (*Hilfsmittel*), which would "spread, for every man, the greatest possible light on [its] contents." Philippson boasted of the Bible's "inner and outer *Ausstattung*," and his publisher's short blurb also used that word: "This work, interesting in every respect and most lavishly designed (*das auf's Reichste ausgestattete Werk*), is easily available in fascicles of five sheets in large lexicon format, printed on the finest vellum" for six Groschen. *Ausstattung* also referred to the illustrations: theirs was "the very first to include the finest English wood engravings (over 500 of them)," a sample of which, "Lebanon with Cedars, after Cassas," was printed in the ad itself (fig. 3.1). Baumgärtner concludes, "We and the author take responsibility for the expeditious progress of the work."[1]

Dieses in jeder Beziehung interessante und von uns auf's Reichste ausgestattete Werk, erscheint zur Erleichterung des Ankaufs

in Lieferungen von 5 Bogen gr. Lexicon-Format

auf feinstem Velinpapier gedruckt

zum Preis von 6 Groschen für jede Lieferung

welche in möglichster Schnelligkeit in die Hände der verehrl. Subscribenten gebracht werden sollen.

Der Libanon mit den Cedern, nach Casas.

Zur Beurtheilung der künstlerischen Ausführung der Vignetten, haben wir eine solche hier beidrucken lassen.

Sowohl der Herr Autor als wir stehen für den prompten Fortgang des Werkes.

Leipzig, im August 1839.

Baumgärtner's Buchhandlung.

Druck von Bernh. Tauchnitz jun.

Fig. 3.1. Philippson Bible, "Prospectus: Lebanon with Cedars" (1839). Photograph: Harvard Divinity School, Andover-Harvard Theological Library (SCR 319 Philippson).

Above and beyond the linguistic and stylistic improvements of the first two waves, the translators of the third wave added *Ausstattung*: special design features that they believed to be necessary for a German Jewish Bible in the mid-nineteenth century. In each case, the outer elements pointed to the Torah's internal design. Philippson's publisher used folio format and vellum paper—smooth, white, parchment-like paper that made for clear contrast and durability and was often used for luxury books.[2] It also contained an extensive, wide-ranging commentary that incorporated a large number of diverse illustrations in its narrative. Philippson was quick to note that the images were not just for fun—*nicht für das Spiel der Phantasie*, not for women and children—but "for the comprehension and the teaching itself." We have seen this move before. Mendelssohn had also realized that a modern Jewish translation required *Hilfsmittel*—above all, an explanatory commentary—to achieve his goals. He too highlighted the aesthetic aspects of the Bible, while insisting that biblical poetry was for the heart, not the ear. And Mendelssohn (or his publisher) also printed poetry from Exodus, Numbers, and Jehuda Halevi in the prospectus ("Leaves for Healing," *Alim l'Terufah*) to attract subscribers. Taking their cue (albeit in very different ways) from Mendelssohn, the two translators of the third wave made exaggerated use of the peripheral space, adding commentary, illustrations, and more. These extraneous features were designed to illuminate not only the text of Scripture but also the translators' worldview and a view of the world.

The role of the translator is nicely captured by the image of "Lebanon and the Cedars, in the style of Cas[s]as" on Philippson's advertisement: a wood engraving of a painting by Louis-François Cassas, the French landscape painter who traveled throughout the Mediterranean and Middle East with French ambassadors and painted many historic and ancient sights for the first time.[3] The snow-capped Mount Lebanon in the background gives the scene a majestic alpine backdrop. Those cedar trees occupying the central swath were familiar to Jewish consumers, at least by name, from a Sabbath Psalm: "The Lord's voice breaks cedars, the Lord shatters the cedars of Lebanon." Beneath the trees are the travellers, marching erect in Oriental garb, emerging out of the dark Romantic past into a bright clearing—figures for the Jewish readers of the German Bible, entering a bright new landscape, with the translator as their tour guide and teacher. Philippson wrote about them in his closing commentary to Genesis:

> Thus, the first book of Moses has opened for us the gates of holiness . . . like the schoolteacher for the still-tender child, it has led us through the halls of nature, and through the winding ways of history, where we are supposed to become infused with the whole teaching. But just like nature, which teaches us without wanting to teach, which proclaims its truths without naming them as such, it laid the essence in the hand of our spirit, throughout, with clarity and simple dignity, without adding to it the form as a pressing burden. *In this way, everything appears to us in it, not as ideal and isolated thought of the subject, but rather as the objective truth as it forms itself and goes on to form [others], a true growth sprouting from godly ground.*[4] (emphasis added)

Philippson's approach combines the Romantic idea of nature as teacher with Friedrich Schiller's philosophy of aesthetic education. His final sentence subtly justifies a new approach: the "ideal and isolated thought of the subject" takes aim at the rationalism of the Haskalah and the second wave. Torah in this new form shows "the objective truth as it forms itself and goes on to form [others]." Such was the road taken by the translator who uses outer design as a bridge to inner design.

Samson Raphael Hirsch's innovations did not take the form of fine paper and illustrations. Hirsch added a narrative commentary on the pages of his translation, but instead of pictures, he incorporated an intricate system of *Lautverwandtschaften* (phonetic, aural affinities) that allowed him to cluster Hebrew words with similar sounding roots and showcase the language of the Bible as an internally logical, closed network of cognates. Hirsch's aural affinities were embedded in translation and commentary, and yet they constituted a discourse in their own right—a tension he did his best to sublimate. Hirsch (like Philippson) believed it was no longer enough to know *what* the Bible was saying (*pshat*); a translation had to highlight the deep symbolic sense of Scripture, which had both an ideal and an imagistic (object-like) character. Hirsch had articulated this rationale almost forty years earlier:

> [The Hebrew Torah] describes but little, but through the rich significance of its verbal roots it paints in the word a picture of the thing. . . . It presupposes the listening soul so watchful and attentive that the deeper sense and profounder meaning, which lie not upon, but below the surface, may be applied by the independent action of the mind itself. It is, as it were, a semi-symbolic writing.[5]

As translator and commentator, Hirsch took his reader on a journey into the inner workings of the Holy Book—a symbolic universe encoded in words and letters—to open up the Torah as a gallery of those pictures painted by words. As many have noted, at the root of Hirsch's speculative etymology was a Romantic notion that the *Volksgeist* lies in the heart of language. Hirsch was an established figure in Orthodoxy, whose staunch alliance with the rabbis of the Talmud and classic hermeneutic methods was beyond reproach. But neither Torah, nor the Talmud, nor Maimonides, all of whom Hirsch quotes, could make an adequate case for a Jewish way of life in nineteenth-century Germany. The *Lautverwandtschaften* served also as bulwark against the intrusion of Wissenschaft, Semitics, history, and modern scholarship into the pages of the Jewish Bible—and above all, against the types of knowledge of art history, nature, Hellenism, and Orientalism that Philippson had introduced. Hirsch's excurses on phonetic affinities were not accessories, but art in the service of the Torah, or in Hirsch's motto, "Torah with *derech eretz*," with a worldly path. They amplified the inner grandeur as well as the unity of the biblical text: in this respect, they enabled the translator to construct the Torah as an ancient Jewish *Gesamtkunstwerk*, a total work of art.

The concept of a total work of art was invented in Germany in 1827 and used most famously by Richard Wagner in 1849, in connection with musical theater.[6] I do not mean to suggest that the translated Bible metamorphosed into a festival play at Bayreuth; but rather that it took on characteristics of a mythic performance, synthesizing various elements into a unified whole, in order to do justice to the genius of a nation—as viewed through the eyes of an individual genius. New supplementary features were needed to accomplish something that the neither the plain text of Scripture nor the scholar-translators of the second wave could accomplish: the portrayal of the Bible as a vessel for a religious and national worldview with world-historical significance—a "coherent cultural system" in Clifford Geertz's sense. The added elements tipped over into ethnography. Jacob Neusner (following Geertz) captures the message of the third-wave Bibles: "A Judaism is not a book, and no social group took shape because people read a book and agreed that God had revealed what the book said they should do."[7] In Germany in the nineteenth-century, the heyday of Orientalism and history, Judaism began to be studied as a religious system comprising three interrelated elements: a cogent worldview, a way of life, and a social group.[8] The Bibles in the third wave aspired to showcase the entirety of that Jewish religious system. Translation, undertaken in this expansive mode, sought to bring the system as a whole—the idea, the way of life, and the *Volk*—into clear view.

CONTEXTS OF THE THIRD WAVE

Antoine Berman ascribes the immense appetite for translation among eighteenth- and nineteenth-century German intellectuals to a void within the collective self, which Herder, Goethe, Schlegel, Hölderlin, and others sought to fill by rendering foreign and ancient literatures—Greek, Latin, Asian, Shakespeare—into a foreignized German. In this way, translation played an essential role in national *Bildung*.[9] A similar hunger plagued the German Jewish intellectual parvenu. The use of the Bible to expand Jewish culture that began with the Amsterdam Yiddish Bibles reaches its apex midway into the third wave, and Berman's notion of translation as self-expansion comes into play.

The third-wave translators restored commentary to the pages of the German Jewish Bible. The sheer quantity of commentary signals its importance: an ocean of words and ideas occupies the bulk of each page, while the text proper, in German and Hebrew, hovers above (figs. 3.2 and 3.3).

Compare the bottom-heavy layout of these pages with the balanced foursquare layouts of Mendelssohn's *Be'ur*, modeled on the layout of the Rabbinic Bible (*Mikraot Gedolot*), which encircled Scripture with a conversation among commentators of various centuries. Recall also that second-wave translations had redefined the role of the religious commentator, replacing it with front and back matter, occasional footnotes (Johlson) or "homiletical insights" (Herxheimer), tables of contents and chronologies, all of the which situated Torah squarely within a scholarly framework. But Philippson and Hirsch wrote commentary in a new key. They wrote as rabbis first, scholars second. The overabundance of commentary suggests that theirs were the most important voices on the pages. It signifies their calculated use of translation to expand the Hebrew Bible in terms of contents, relevance, and significance.

The insertion of an encyclopedic commentary had clear parallels in Christian Bibles. More broadly, translations of the third wave took shape within an intellectual milieu in which history, myth, art, symbolism, and new media were shaping biblical scholars' understanding of Hebrew Scripture and the ancient world. Developments in printing and publishing and the changing reading habits of Christians and Jews also played a role.

The long nineteenth century has been called the "century of words."[10] Improvements in print technology and techniques for illustrating books, and the expansion of mass markets, literacy, and forms of print media—newspapers, journals, encyclopedias—"aspired to represent and chronicle in minute and rich detail the totality of the world."[11] In her introduction to *Publishing Culture and the "Reading Nation,"* Lynne Tatlock describes the shift away from religious books in the German publishing boom of the nineteenth century. "These new readers sought, in addition to edification, entertainment and information in books."[12] Philippson and Hirsch were both producers, and avid consumers, of these new media. For example, Philippson is best known as the editor (for fifty-six years) of what was arguably the most popular source of information, entertainment, *and* edification for German Jews—the newspaper *Allgemeine Zeitung des Judentums* (AZdJ). But his paper, founded in 1827, shared its name with a trendsetting fashion

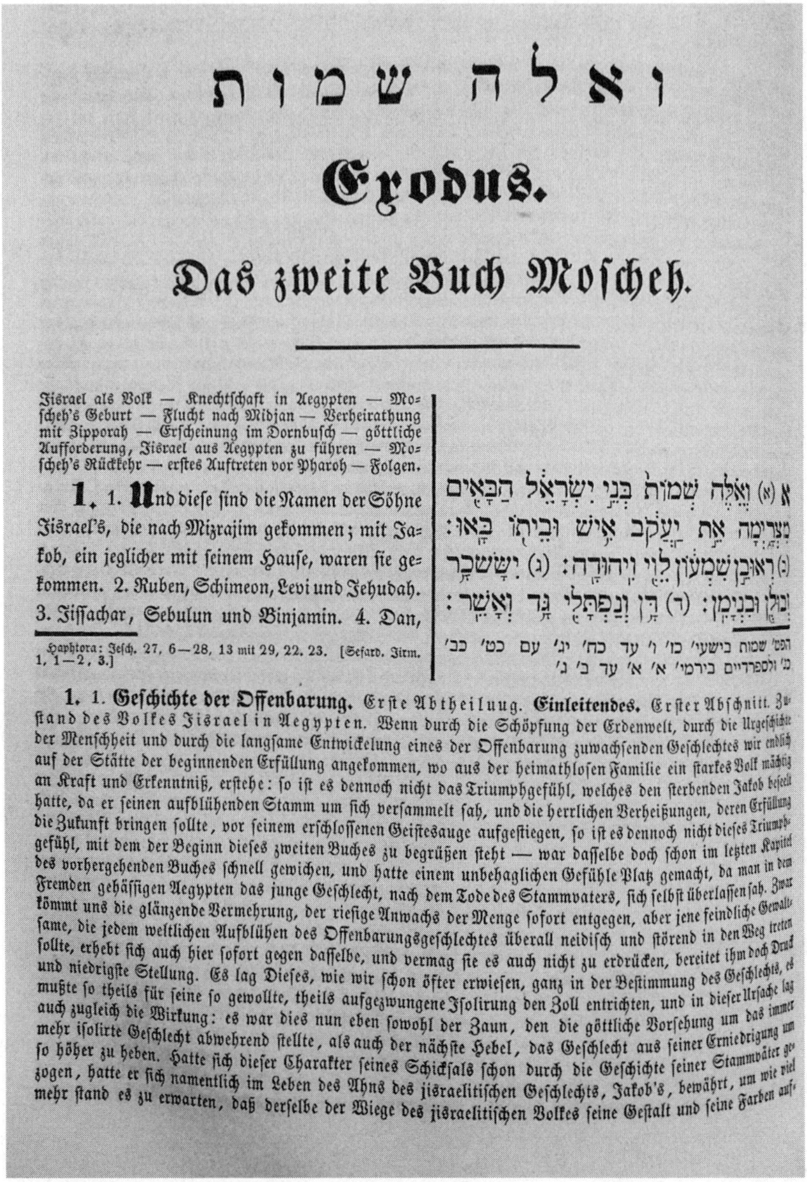

ואלה שמות

Exodus.

Das zweite Buch Moscheh.

Jisrael als Volk — Knechtschaft in Aegypten — Moscheh's Geburt — Flucht nach Midjan — Verheirathung mit Zipporah — Erscheinung im Dornbusch — göttliche Aufforderung, Jisrael aus Aegypten zu führen — Moscheh's Rückkehr — erstes Auftreten vor Pharoh — Folgen.

1. 1. Und diese sind die Namen der Söhne
Jisrael's, die nach Mizrajim gekommen; mit Jakob, ein jeglicher mit seinem Hause, waren sie gekommen. 2. Ruben, Schimeon, Levi und Jehudah.
3. Jissachar, Sebulun und Binjamin. 4. Dan,

Haphtora: Jesch. 27, 6—28, 13 mit 29, 22. 23. [Sefard. Jirm. 1, 1—2, 3.]

א (א) ואלה שמות בני ישראל הבאים
מצרימה את יעקב איש וביתו באו:
(ב) ראובן שמעון לוי ויהודה: (ג) יששכר
זבולן ובנימן: (ד) דן ונפתלי גד ואשר:

הפט' שמות בישעי' כז' ו' עד כח' יג' עם כט' כב' כג' ולספרדיים בירמי' א' א' עד ב' ג'

1. 1. **Geschichte der Offenbarung.** Erste Abtheilung. **Einleitendes.** Erster Abschnitt. Zustand des Volkes Jisrael in Aegypten. Wenn durch die Schöpfung der Erdenwelt, durch die Urgeschichte der Menschheit und durch die langsame Entwickelung eines der Offenbarung zuwachsenden Geschlechtes wir endlich auf der Stätte der beginnenden Erfüllung angekommen, wo aus der heimathlosen Familie ein starkes Volk mächtig an Kraft und Erkenntniß, erstehe: so ist es dennoch nicht das Triumphgefühl, welches den sterbenden Jakob beseelt hatte, da er seinen aufblühenden Stamm um sich versammelt sah, und die herrlichen Verheißungen, deren Erfüllung die Zukunft bringen sollte, vor seinem erschlossenen Geistesauge aufgestiegen, so ist es dennoch nicht dieses Triumphgefühl, mit dem der Beginn dieses zweiten Buches zu begrüßen steht — war dasselbe doch schon im letzten Kapitel des vorhergehenden Buches schnell gewichen, und hatte einem unbehaglichen Gefühle Platz gemacht, da man in dem Fremden gehässigen Aegypten das junge Geschlecht, nach dem Tode des Stammvaters, sich selbst überlassen sah. Zwar kömmt uns die glänzende Vermehrung, der riesige Anwachs der Menge sofort entgegen, aber jene feindliche Gewaltsame, die jedem weltlichen Aufblühen des Offenbarungsgeschlechtes überall neidisch und störend in den Weg treten sollte, erhebt sich auch hier sofort gegen dasselbe, und vermag sie es auch nicht zu erdrücken, bereitet ihm doch Druck und niedrigste Stellung. Es lag Dieses, wie wir schon öfter erwiesen, ganz in der Bestimmung des Geschlechts, es mußte so theils für seine so gewollte, theils aufgezwungene Isolirung den Zoll entrichten, und in dieser Ursache lag auch zugleich die Wirkung: es war dies nun eben sowohl der Zaun, den die göttliche Vorsehung um das immer mehr isolirte Geschlecht abwehrend stellte, als auch der nächste Hebel, das Geschlecht aus seiner Erniedrigung um so höher zu heben. Hatte sich dieser Charakter seines Schicksals schon durch die Geschichte seiner Stammväter gezogen, hatte er sich namentlich im Leben des Ahns des jisraelitischen Geschlechts, Jakob's, bewährt, um wie viel mehr stand es zu erwarten, daß derselbe der Wiege des jisraelitischen Volkes seine Gestalt und seine Farben auf-

Fig. 3.2. Philippson Bible, Ex. 1:1 (1858). Photograph: Harvard Divinity School, Andover-Harvard Theological Library (SCR 319 Philippson).

שמות א

Kap. 1. V. 1. Und dies sind die Namen der Söhne Jisraels, die nach Mizrajim kamen; mit Jaakob kam jeder und sein Haus.

2. Reuben, Schimeon, Lewi und Jehuda,

1. וְאֵלֶּה שְׁמוֹת בְּנֵי יִשְׂרָאֵל הַבָּאִים מִצְרָיְמָה אֵת יַעֲקֹב אִישׁ וּבֵיתוֹ בָּאוּ׃

2. רְאוּבֵן שִׁמְעוֹן לֵוִי וִיהוּדָה׃

שמות

Kap. 1. V. 1. Mit dem zweiten Buche beginnt die Geschichte des jüdischen Volkes. Aus der Einzel- und Familiengeschichte wird in die Volksgeschichte hinübergeleitet durch erinnernde Nennung der einzelnen Männer, die uns bereits als die „Grundstöcke" der jüdischen Volksgesamtheit bekannt sind. וְאלה es sind dies ganz dieselben, in ihren gesonderten Eigentümlichkeiten, aus welchen nunmehr das jüdische Volk erwuchs. Einen gemeinsamen Grundzug brachten sie mit, der die Grundbasis der jüdischen Nationalität bildet: את יעקב איש וביתו! Wenn später, als die durch pharaonische Mißhandlung zerstückte Volksleiche, wie sie einst dem Ahn prophetisch gezeigt war, dem Aasgeier der Geschichte zu willkommenem Fraß am Boden zu liegen schien und durch Gottes Weckerruf „in ihrem Blute" zu unsterblichem Leben erstehen sollte, Gott den Aufbau seines Volkes nicht mit den Giebelspitzen, sondern mit der Granitbasis des „Hauses" — שה לבית אבות שה לבית — mit dem Familienband der Kinder aufwärts, mit dem Familienband der Eltern abwärts begann: so wird uns hier gezeigt, daß diese Grundbasis des ewigen Gottesvolkes nur gewaltsam geraubt und zerstört war zur Zeit des erlösenden Aufbaues, mitgebracht war sie von vornherein, als die Söhne Israels hinabzogen in den egyptischen Mutterschoß, in welchem sie unter Leid und Weh zum Volke geboren werden sollten. את יעקב איש וביתו: obgleich sie schon alle ein selbständiges Haus ausmachten, hingen sie doch noch alle fest und innig an Jakob! — את יעקב ist eine viel innigere Verbindung als עם יעקב. (את, Wurzel אתת. Es ist eigentümlich, daß im Hebräischen Wörter, die eine Verbindung ausdrücken, größtenteils auch eine Trennung bezeichnen. So פהל und בדל, so את und אֵת Plural אתים; es läßt sich keine innige Verbindung ohne Sonderung von andern denken.) את יעקב איש וביתו: alle zusammen an dem alten Stamm, und doch jeder wieder für sich ein eigener, selbständiger Zweig, ein eigener, selbständiger Mittelpunkt für einen eigenen Kreis; alle Kinder Jakobs, und doch wieder selbst Väter für eigene Kinder; dieser Familiengeist und dieses Familienherz, das jeden Sohn sein Haus nur als Zweig des eigenen Elternhauses bauen, und jeden Vater in Kind und Enkel fortleben läßt, das Eltern mit Kindern und Kinder mit Eltern auf ewig und innig vereint, das ists, worin Israels ewige Blüte wurzelt, darin liegt das Geheimnis des jüdischen Stammes.

V. 2. Charakteristisch ist die Gruppierung: die ersten vier sind die ersten, von vornherein der Lea zugedachten Söhne; nach Juda heißt es: ותעמד מלדת. Jissachar und Sebulun waren gleichsam als Lohn besonderer Bestrebung gewährt. Benjamin ist ihnen als Sohn Rahels angeschlossen und in der folgenden Gruppe sind die Söhne der שפחות zusammengenommen. Befragen wir die Aussprüche Jakobs über die Bedeutsamkeit seiner Söhne für die nationale Zukunft, so sind auch dort (ויחי Kap. 49) Reuben, Schimeon, Lewi, Jehuda, Jissachar, Sebulun, Benjamin (— mit Uebergehung Josefs, der bereits in Mizrajim war —) die bedeutsamsten, wie wir dies dort zur Stelle gefunden zu haben glaubten.

Fig. 3.3. Hirsch Bible, Ex. 1:1 (1903).

magazine, the *Allgemeine Moden-Zeitung* (1806–1903), also edited by a scholar, Johann Adam Bergk. Bergk, like Friedrich Arnold Brockhaus, founder of the famous *Conversations-Lexicon*, "belonged to Leipzig's reform liberal elite, who set the tone for the most popular newspapers of their time."[13] The goal of these periodicals was the diffusion of useful knowledge, as announced in the title of *Das Heller-Magazin: eine Zeitschrift zur Verbreitung gemeinnütziger Kenntnisse, von einer Gesellschaft Gelehrter* (Heller magazine: a journal for the dissemination of socially useful knowledge, by a society of scholars), edited by Dr. F. A. Wiese. *Das Heller-Magazin* was modeled upon the French *Magasin Pittoresque* (1833–1938), edited by French publisher and saloniere Martin Bossange (1766–1865), which was in turn modeled on the English *Penny Magazine*, an illustrated British magazine for the working class published every Saturday starting in 1832 for the Society for the Diffusion of Useful Knowledge (fig. 3.4).

Diffusing useful knowledge was also the domain of the encyclopedia. *Das Grosse Brockhaus* was a distinctively modern type of book in that it addressed a popular audience; presented history, science, and technology; gave a "presentation of the contemporary world vis à vis German interests"; and incorporated "illustrations to produce a totalized view of the world."[14] Kirsten Belgum points out that encyclopedias were not antique volumes, but "repositories of historical knowledge and the shaping of meaning" that went through many editions.[15] Belgum's conclusion about nineteenth-century encyclopedism, based on a comparison of two multivolume editions of the *Conversations-Lexicon* from the 1820s and the 1880s, has a bearing upon the mandates of both Philippson and Hirsch:

> The recipe for success in the nineteenth century was for an encyclopedia to be *both* universal and national, that is, to keep up with the latest information about the world while also explicitly addressing the national audience and furthering a coherent story of national progress.[16]

When considering the evolution of the German Bible into a kind of national or religious encyclopedia, two eighteenth-century precursors become relevant. The Berleburger Bible (1726–42), the culminating work of the Pietist Bible translations, "spanned eight folio volumes, topped over 8,000 pages, and took some sixteen years to complete."[17]

> The Berleburger Bible . . . stepped boldly onto the path of scholarship. Its goal was to produce the perfect translation solely by means of accumu-

THE PENNY MAGAZINE

OF THE

Society for the Diffusion of Useful Knowledge.

147.] PUBLISHED EVERY SATURDAY. [July 19, 1834.

THE BISON.

[North American Bison.]

This remarkable species of ox is peculiar to North America. Until of late years, it was very generally considered that the domestic ox, the wild bull (*urus*) of Europe and Asia, and the American bison were only varieties of the same species, or, in other words, that the domestic ox was the urus altered by civilization, and that the bison was the urus altered by climate. This was the opinion of Buffon, Pallas, and other distinguished naturalists. The identity of the urus and the bison being assumed, it became a question of somewhat difficult solution how these animals migrated from the old to the new world. Many ingenious theories were framed to meet the circumstances, but the necessity for these speculations has been superseded by the discovery made by Cuvier, that the bison of America is really a species distinct from the urus; and he has indicated the very important differences by which the distinction is established.

We may consider the bison as characterized by fifteen pair of ribs; (the wild bull has only fourteen,) and by the immense disproportion between its fore and hind quarters. The latter distinction is partly occasioned by the great hump or projection over its shoulders. This hump is oblong, diminishing in height as it extends backward, and giving a considerable obliquity to the outline of the back. The hair over the head, neck, and fore part of the body is long and shaggy, forming a knee in a tuft. The hair on the summit of the head rises in a dense mass nearly to the tip of the horns, and directly on the front is curled and strongly matted. The ponderous head, rendered terrific by its thick shaggy hair and streaming beard, is supported upon a massive neck and shoulders, the apparent strength of which is more imposing from the augmentation produced by the hump and the long fall of hair by which the anterior parts of the body are covered. This woolly hair is remarkable not less for its fineness than its length. The difference between the winter and the summer coat of the bison consists rather in the length than in the other qualities of the hair. In summer, from the shoulders backward, the surface is covered with very short fine hair, smooth and soft as velvet. Except the long hair on the fore parts, which is to a certain extent of a rust colour or yellowish tinge, the colour is a uniform dun. Varieties of colour are so rare among the species, that the hunters and Indians always regard any apparent difference with great surprise. The fleece or hair of a full-grown bison, when separated from the skin, is usually found to weigh about eight pounds, according to Charlevoix. The horns are shorter than in any other species, nearly straight, sharp-pointed, exceedingly strong, and planted widely asunder at the base, as in the common bull. The tail is almost a foot long, and terminates in a tuft which is black in the males and red

Fig. 3.4. Society for the Diffusion of Useful Knowledge, *The Penny Magazine* (1838).

lation, by arranging all the information any reader might need to make sense of the Bible, and subsuming it within an ostensibly unifying spiritualist commentary. More than anything, this new monumental Bible resembled that signpost of ostensible modernity, Pierre Bayle's *Dictionnaire historique et critique*, rendered in spiritualized prose.[18]

As Sheehan describes it, not only was the "perfect translation" to be achieved by means of "accumulation" of information, but equally important (as we shall see later), the information was embedded in an "ostensibly unifying spiritualist commentary." The blend of scholarship and unifying narrative exactly captures the common strategy of Philippson and Hirsch. In the Christian world, Michaelis had also expanded the role of the translated Bible beyond exegesis.

> A corollary to Michaelis's commitment to use cognate "Semitic" languages to understand ancient Hebrew was his conviction that the geography, botany, and zoology of contemporary "Arabia felix," along with the languages and customs of his Arab inhabitants, might help to explain some of the supposedly miraculous events or the *hapax legomena* of the scriptures. In 1756, he approached the Danish foreign minister, J. H. von Bernstoff, with a plan to send a scholarly expedition to this part of the world.[19]

As noted in chapter 2, Suzanne Marchand identifies an important difference between the ethnographic interests of Michaelis and Herder, and those of the nineteenth-century Orientalists. The key terms are *Altertumswissenschaft* and *Orientalistik* as practiced by Christian Hebraists such as Heinrich Ewald, Wilhelm de Wette, and Johann Gottfried Eichhorn, whom Philippson frequently cites.[20] The shift to "historical" rather than religious or theological truth had a lasting impact on the perception of the Jew in German scholarly circles. However, whereas Christian Orientalism fixed the Jew as an ancient type (and the Other of the Greek), and Judaism as Mosaism, Jewish Orientalism would emphasize the evolving, temporal character of the religion.

In a different trend especially relevant to Hirsch, liberal Protestants such as the young Hegelian David Friedrich Strauss and the rationalist historian Bruno Bauer interpreted the Bible as a source of symbolic truths. The history of ancient Israel acquired world-historical and also symbolic importance that justified its study.[21]

In order to appreciate why encyclopedism, history, Orientalism, and symbolism figured so centrally in Philippson's and Hirsch's commentaries, one must also understand the most important *negative* impetus for their translations: the mandate to displace methods and discourses of Wissenschaft des Judentums as the primary model of the modern Jewish intellectual enterprise. From Philippson's and Hirsch's standpoint, the second wave had unleashed a new Babel. Philippson described "modern Bible criticism" as a "hypothesis hunt," a "bottomless confusion."[22] "In einem mannichfaltigen Knäuel standen sich bereits die Hypothesen gegenüber; die eine widersprach der anderen."[23] The educated reading public, students and teachers alike, needed a new kind of Bible and commentary: something "not merely accessible, but also attractive, that elevates and warms the spirit, yet remains far from the entire scholarly apparatus."[24] The scholarly approach left us cold; the new one would be warm. This is not to say that Philippson renounced scholarship and research; he simply realized very early on that scholarship in the Wissenschaft mode would not inspire religious reform, and that it itself had become part of the problem.[25] The rational-scholarly model became inadequate for additional reasons. Zunz and other first-generation Jewish scholars (after the biurists) had tended to research the medieval period and cultural, rather than political, history. Despite their philological orientation, they were not interested in biblical history—perhaps because the Bible had been the focus of their precursors the Maskilim, or perhaps because they wanted to avoid the fraught territory of Christian Old Testament scholarship.[26] Finally, because they were excluded from German universities, their work was discriminated against, segregated, ignored. The consequences were devastating on many fronts, as Marchand summarizes: "Thus, during the critical decades in the evolution of orientalism and of German liberalism, those who were best suited to make the case for Judaism's cultural impact and scholarly traditions beyond the Old Testament were relegated to a sphere most Christian academics considered unscientific and of exclusively parochial significance."[27] Ironically, the scholarship of the second-wave translators was derided as too neutral to cure religious alienation in the Jewish community, and, at the same time, too parochial to be taken seriously by liberal Christian scholars, despite their renewed interest in ancient Israel.

Philippson and Hirsch redoubled their forebears' efforts to refute biblical criticism, not only by avoiding any emendations, but also by creating a visible platform, a fortress, on the page of Scripture, from which to defend the unity and integrity of the Torah. Philippson found an important ally in a Protestant scholar who opposed the documentary hypothesis, Wilhelm Ernst Hengstenberg (1802–69), professor of Old Testament theology in Berlin and author of *Die Authentie des Pentateuchs* (1836–39), who edited an influential journal, the *Evangelische Kirchenzeitung*, which Philippson quoted approvingly in his commentary. Hermann notes similiarities in the biographies of Philippson and Hengstenberg, who "aggressively criticized enlightenment liberal rationalism and idealistic cultural Protestantism."[28]

The second wave had treated Scripture as an ancient text that was too remote from the present, in the eyes of Philippson and Hirsch, to inspire religious renewal. But it was not enough to correct the errors of *die Neueren* (those recent ones). Scripture had to be rendered anew as a unified, organic totality with world-historical, even cosmic significance. How might one achieve this immediacy without sacrificing the nation? German Idealism provided a solution with the concept of *Geistesgeschichte*. This sense of a Jewish *Geistesgeschichte* or teleology finds concrete representation in both Philippson's and Hirsch's commentaries, as we shall see. The solution was not to give up history, but to fit the events of the past (and in Hirsch's case, the words of Scripture) into a teleological continuum leading into the present. Hirsch located a Jewish national telos within nature and the cosmos. For Philippson, it was a Jewish national telos within, and as part of, world history.

The need for a German Jewish *Geistesgeschichte* inspired new forms of literary and cultural production. Jonathan Skolnik's *Jewish Pasts, German Fictions* argues that historical fiction by Heine, Auerbach, Philippson, and others played an essential role in fostering minority identity and in closing the East-West (and Ashkenazi-Sephardi) divide.[29] Jewish reading habits were evolving, and, as both Skolnik and Jonathan Hess demonstrate, popular writers—and religious writers with aspirations to reach a popular audience—designed new genres and plots to meet the expectations of the nineteenth-century readership, framing the religious mission in artistic terms.[30]

The new Jewish appreciation for aesthetics goes partway in explaining why, a full two decades before Gustave Doré's images enhanced Bibles in all denominations and European languages in the 1860s, Philippson's publisher Baumgärtner incorporated over 500 woodcut illustrations in a German Jewish Bible. As for Hirsch: *derech eretz*, "the way of the land," only coexisted with Jewish ways, but it infused his thinking. Hirsch adopted the classical German view of culture as ennobling and edifying. Roland Tasch notes that Shakespeare, Lessing, Goethe, and Schiller were as much a part of Hirsch's repertoire as the rabbis of the Talmud; Hirsch had to "speak in many languages" in order to be taken seriously by people like Philippson. "Alongside the ardency of the religious Jew, he spoke with the inwardness of the Christian, the aesthetic sense of the Greek, the juridical sense of the Roman, the idealism of Kant, the Romanticism of Schleiermacher and the linearity of Hegel."[31] In his famous essay in honor of Schiller's centennial, Hirsch praises Schiller as an idealistic poet who, "had he known Judaism other than through the veil of his birth . . . would have been a Jew." Above all, Schiller offered a remedy for a social plague facing Germans, Jews, and Christians—materialism. Schiller did not bring "material enrichment. Rather, he knew how to inspire ideals in his nation. He taught them to love and treasure the ideals of the human heart as the most genuine, eternal, inalienable, and uplifiting possessions man can have. Thus, the exalted radiance of the Schiller Festival sheds a modest ray on the Jewish school."[32]

PHILIPPSON AND HIRSCH: BIOGRAPHIES

Most accounts treat Philippson and Hirsch as representatives of opposing Jewish *Weltanschauungen*: Reform and neo-Orthodoxy; historicism and traditionalism.[33] Philippson was a centrist; Hirsch, a separatist. Philippson was a realist; Hirsch, an idealist. Philippson defined himself as a "historical Jew,"[34] whereas Hirsch zealously guarded what he viewed as the ahistorical core of Judaism. It is not wrong to say that they stood on opposite sides with regard to the politics of translation, as Shavit and Eran note: "the polemic over the nature of the translations was an inseparable part of the deep disagreements between the neo-orthodox and the Reform movement about the essence of Judaism." Philippson's translation was "the major cause of the polemic."[35] And yet, a common ground supported this divide: a joint religious mission. The biographies of Hirsch and Philippson spanned the nineteenth century. Both lived many lives. Both enjoyed illustrious careers as modern rabbis, whose pulpits extended far beyond the sanctuary. They spoke out on social and political issues; advocated on behalf of Jewish emancipation in German-speaking lands and throughout Europe, in Russia, and in the Middle East; and promoted Jewish belles-lettres as well as German secular culture. As preachers, writers, journalists, and translators, they had numerous outlets at their disposal and invented new ones as needed.

Ludwig Philippson was a translator by patrimony. At age fifteen, he made his literary debut with a Bible translation—a *metrical* German translation of the prophetic books of Obadiah, Hosea, Joel and Nahum. The project must have been inspired by his late father Moses Philippson, the biurist, educator, publisher, and cotranslator of the Twelve Minor Prophets, who died in 1814 when Ludwig was only three.[36] (Hirsch also lost his father at a very young age.) Ludwig Philippson was the first Jewish student to attend the gymnasium in Halle. He studied at the University of Berlin with G. F. Hegel, Henrich Steffens, Eduard Gans, Friedrich von Savigny, and August Boeckh. He earned his PhD in Jena at the age of twenty-two (1833), with a dissertation on Aristotle's and Plato's philosophies of natural science. In 1830, he published German translations of two Greek-Jewish works from Alexandria, Ezekielus's *Exagogue, or Exodus from Egypt*, a drama in hexameters, and Philo's epic *On Jerusalem*, with passages about Abraham and Isaac, Joseph, and the city of David.[37]

The turning point in Philippson's career came about because Jews were unable to obtain university positions in Germany. Baptism was not an option. He was on the verge of moving to France when a rabbinic position opened up in Magdeburg where his mother and brother lived; there he discovered his true calling. Philippson's granddaughter wrote that in becoming a pulpit rabbi, Philippson made an "absolute break" with his philological studies and "never looked back," never contacted classicists later in his life, and thereby spared himself becoming bitter and pessimistic (like Zunz) or accepting baptism (as Eduard Gans had done).[38] When the Orthodox rabbi in Magdeburg resigned, Philippson's position expanded, and he remained there for twenty-eight years.

Philippson was a liberal rabbi and proponent of moderate reform. He is credited with convening rabbinical conferences and synods, gathering together rabbis across the spectrum, and holding the center together. He disagreed with Abraham Geiger, with Zechariah Frankel, and Moses Hess, with Zunz on the left, and also with extreme traditionalists on the right.

Ludwig worked with his brother Phöbus, a doctor, who translated the Early Prophets and collaborated with him on the second and third volumes of the *Bibelwerk* (Prophets and Writings). The Philippson Bible was reviewed in Christian periodicals, and it garnered international attention: after sending the Bible to Czar Alexander II in 1841, he received a ring in return; and in 1848, the Jews of Stockholm asked him to send a copy of the Bible to the Swedish King Oskar to ask for civil rights.

Philippson's desire to educate and disseminate knowledge led him to turn early to journalism. He first published a monthly journal for teachers, *Israelite Magazine for Preaching and School* (*Israelitische Predigt- und Schulmagazin*, 1834–36) with sermons and essays about improving Jewish education, which allowed him to develop a journalistic style that was clear and flexible yet principled.[39] Shortly thereafter, he took on a more popular journalistic venture, becoming editor (and the primary author) of the longest-running German Jewish newspaper, the *Allgemeine Zeitung des Judentums* (AZdJ), published three times per week in tabloid format beginning 2 May 1837. The word *allgemein* represents Philippson's nonpartisan approach to Judaism and Jewish identity in a period when, as Hans Otto Horch writes,

political writings of Heine and other young Hegelians were subject to censorship. This was not the first German Jewish broadside, but it was groundbreaking in combining religious and secular topics, a program of religious reform and advocacy for Enlightenment and emancipation. The paper covered local politics, world news, theology, scholarship, and belles-lettres. When it became fashionable, he added a family insert. The paper's contribution to literary criticism alone has been widely studied. Philippson wrote every editorial and many of the articles. "Every copy of his paper is full of himself. He advertises his works, he tells the story of his own life, he tells of every success he had."[40] To be fair, there was a shortage of writers willing to write for a Jewish paper. "The paper's true objective, however, was to complete the emancipation of the Jews by adding religious emancipation to their political emancipation."[41] In print until 1921, this paper continues to be regarded as beginning of the modern Jewish press; as it was also read by Eastern European Jews, its influence is truly incalculable.

Philippson founded many cultural institutions, such as Jewish book-of-the-month club (1855–74), which he called the "institute for the promotion of Jewish literature." When his eyesight weakened, Philippson moved to Bonn, where he engaged in many other cultural activities. He authored a prayer book, a play about Beethoven's life, an essay on the "religious idea" in Judaism, Islam, and Christianity, and so much more. He printed a full summary of his work in AZdJ volume 60 (1877).

Samson Raphael Hirsch came from a traditional Jewish family in Hamburg; he was older than Philippson by three years, yet turned to translation only late in life. His early mentor was the Hakham Isaac Bernays (1792–1849), one of the first rabbis with a university degree, who became chief rabbi of Hamburg. Bernays's *Der Bibel'sche Orient* (1820), influenced by Schelling, Herder, and Hamman, argued for a reformation of religion on the basis of the Bible as the "national scripture of a Volk," with an almost Hammanian view of language as encoding the original national spirit.[42] Bernays preached in German, and he reformed the old-style Jewish school (which eventually became a public school). He also challenged the radical efforts of the Hamburg reformers. Hirsch later adopted many of Bernays's practices. Hirsch studied for five years with the famous talmudist Rabbi Jacob Ettlinger, obtaining his rabbinical degree in 1828, then began to study classical languages, philosophy, and history at the University of Bonn, where his famous friendship with Abraham Geiger developed. For reasons that are unclear, he left the university after one and half years when offered the position of district rabbi of Oldenberg, which he occupied for eleven years (1830–41).

In this period, instead of writing a dissertation, Hirsch experimented with two other genres of writing that were perhaps better suited to his ambitions. He first wrote *Horeb*, a long treatise on Judaism and Jewish law. But his Christian publisher balked at the size of the book and urged him to begin more modestly. For his literary debut, *Nineteen Letters on Judaism* (1836), Hirsch used a pseudonym (Ben-Usiel) and the epistolary form—a genre made famous in classical German letters by Goethe's novel *The Sorrows of Young Werther* (1774) and Schiller's philosophical *Letters on Aesthetic Education* (1794). Hirsch had been urged to publish in Hebrew or Yiddish, but he opted for German—the language of his target readership. The *Nineteen Letters* was a bestseller, and became one of the most influential religious works of German Jewry. *Horeb*, subtitled "Essays on Yisrael's Duties in the Diaspora, Written for Yisrael's Thinking Young Men and Women," came out the following year, under Hirsch's own name.[43] In these works and elsewhere, Hirsch expounded the ideas and values underlying the commandments. His overarching thesis was that Jewish law (Halakhah), which liberal Jews denigrated as "Rabbinism" or "Shulkanarukism" (after the name of a famous medieval law code, the *Shulhan Arukh*) was not only the sine qua non of Judaism, but also immanently livable in the modern world. His genre was neither theology nor speculative religious philosophy (like Mendelssohn or Maimonides), but rather "a philosophy of Jewish historical experience."[44]

Hirsch opposed the Reformers but also angered observant Jews. Gil Graff suggests that in his second and third rabbi positions, in East Friesland and as district rabbi of Moravia, his constituents found him too liberal and criticized his clean-shaven appearance, and that it was his failure there "after four frustrating years" that led him to give up a prominent post in exchange for leading a small group in Frankfurt where he could, in effect, preach to the converted.[45] As head of the Israelite Religious Society in Frankfurt, he built a community from the ground up: another form of *Gesamtkunstwerk*. His first task was to create a Jewish day school for both sexes that embodied his educational philosophy, "Torah together with a worldly path" (*derech eretz*): a weltanschauung that remains the motto for Modern Orthodoxy to this day. No less famous and highly controversial, Hirsch's society formally seceded from the united *Gemeinde* when secession became a legal option in Prussia in 1876, against the fierce opposition of Rabbi Bamberger.

As with Philippson, journalism proved to be an important steppingstone to translation. In 1854 Hirsch founded the journal *Jeshurun*, the complete title of which echoes the title of Philippson's publications with the word *Förderung* (promotion, advancement).[46] Hirsch edited *Jeshurun* (1854–70) and wrote most of the articles himself, among them "Grundlinien einer jüdischen Symbolik" (detailing his "science of symbolism"), which appeared serially over a three-year period (1857–60) and was later incorporated into his Pentateuch. It was not only these articles that found their way into the Bible commentary, but also lectures given over many years, which "attentive listeners were kind enough to transcribe"[47] and led to its long-winded form: "Repetitions are intentionally not avoided, in order to devote to each textual passage what is necessary for its explication."[48] In 1870, *Jeshurun* merged with another neo-Orthodox journal, *der Israelit*, edited by its founder Dr. Marcus Lehmann.[49]

Philippson's entire *Israelite Bible* came out over fifteen years; Hirsch's *Pentateuch* absorbed his energies for eleven years. The common mission of both Bibles can be summed up in Philippson's words: "The Bible has fallen out of the hands of modern Jews. They must possess it once again."[50] When he penned these words in 1859, he was justifying the creation of a Jewish Bible society that would make inexpensive Jewish Bibles available to those without means—to keep the cheap, widely available Christian missionary Bibles out of Jewish hands. But the motive applies to both men's work as rabbi-translators. What had fallen out of Jewish hands was not the Bible, but the Torah: the core religious teaching within. Philippson and Hirsch's approach to translation extended from the determination to restore the Torah to the German Jewish Bible, in the name of religious regeneration. But they also knew that Torah could not make the case on its own terms, especially in the nineteenth century. To invoke the chain of transmission from God to Moses to the Masoretes down to the present day was no longer sufficient; clear language, grammar, and poetry were no longer compelling rationales for retranslation. Instead, they called for unity. Translation would restore the religious authority of the Bible for the masses by rendering the Torah as an internally unified book. This, above all, would be the argument of these two distinctly nineteenth-century *be'urim*.

PHILIPPSON AND HIRSCH: MISSION STATEMENTS

Thirty years separated the translations of Ludwig Philippson and Samson Raphael Hirsch, yet they articulated their agendas in uncannily similar terms around 1836, when they were twenty-five and twenty-eight years old. The second wave was about to crest, but neither of these two were on board.

The clearest statement of how Philippson viewed his place and his mission is found in the preface to the first volume of his *Schulmagazin* from 1836—the same year in which, according to Meyer Kayserling, Philippson went to the publisher with his plan for the Bible translation. Ever the historicist, Philippson sets up his agenda by narrating a summary of German Jewish history—all fifty years of it!—to ground his perception of the present as a period of religious crisis. The history begins, of course, with Mendelssohn urging Jews to elevate study of Scripture over the Talmud, and with the efforts of the Maskilim to improve Jewish education. Philippson's account pays special tribute to the "bridge generation" of Maskilim, among them his teacher Gotthold Salomon and his late father Moses. But these Maskilim provided a short-lived approach to the challenge of integration, and moreover, the first wave of social and religious reform in the wake of the Napoleonic wars came "too early." A schism resulted: those who were educated in the modern schools found the rabbinic forms too oppressive, but by giving up rabbinic Judaism, they had no way to connect to God. At the same time, traditionalists became alienated from the new Jewish society and were unable to benefit from these advances. "This *Indifferentismus*, the result of a 'Hyperbildung,' such as that which took place in the previous century generally in the world, and which proceeded from the French 'Hyperculture,' destroys the good and the beautiful results of education with more severe damage than they would have incurred had they stayed behind on the old plateau."[51] As a result, Orthodoxy became more entrenched, and the community became polarized—and polarity is just about the worst thing that can happen, in Philippson's mind. Philippson blames the Reform movement, and modernity more broadly, exuding a very German bias against French culture and drawing a parallel with how the Protestant Reformation left Catholics behind. One point captures Philippson's educational agenda above all: if Reform is unable to create spiritual renewal for *all* Jewry, it fails.

> Oneness and Unity, supporting itself on one side through the veneration of the old, the extant, in which Judaism moved through the millennia, in which it lived and through which we have inherited it; and on the other hand, an admiration of ennoblement, continued education, and relevance. History and Reason: both, in concert, are the basis of the human race; both, when isolated, fall apart; both, when unified, preserve the truth, preserve justice, preserve religion!

This passage encapsulates the dialectical mission of the third wave: to correct the excesses of early modernization and the Haskalah by advocating for a reintegration of the traditions that had sustained Judaism for centuries. Notice that the remedy Philippson proposes—a yoking together of history and reason—is not for Jews only; it is the double foundation of the entire human race, the essential path to truth, justice, and religion as such. This critique of his own time as the aftermath of the *failure* of the Haskalah and the "indifferentism" bred by over-hasty religious reform gave Philippson his identity as a very particular kind of mediator. Kayserling's biography describes his legacy in these terms: "Just as Mendelssohn introduced Jews into the mainstream cultural life, so did Philippson rouse the Jewish masses from their religious sleep, wage a struggle against spiritual inertia and religious indifference."[52] Rejecting the second wave meant reappropriating the first, especially when it came to translation. In the afterword to volume three of the *Israelite Bible*, Philippson wrote:

> Epoch-making was the pure-German translation of the Pentateuch by Moses [Mendelssohn], which was published in 1780. If on the one hand, this was the language instructor for countless Jews, on the other hand, its greater merit is to have forged a path for *simple, rational exegesis* among the Jews, to which the commentary appended to the translation essentially contributed. In recent times, we highlight translations by Salomon, Zunz, and Herxheimer.[53]

To my reading, what Philippson admired in Mendelssohn was precisely that which had no place in the Bibles of Zunz, Johlson, or Salomon: "rational commentary." He aspired to produce nothing short of a nineteenth-century *Be'ur*.

> Already in 1835 . . . I decided to write and edit the first comprehensive (*umfassend*) commentary of the whole Bible by a Jewish author, and I made the arrangements. The guiding thoughts of the undertaking were: to compile the main results of exegetical research on every scriptural verse, both from old translations and Jewish commentaries, and from the most prominent Christian exegetes; to add explanatory notes, from the great [corpus of] travel literature about the relevant lands, as well as from works of natural science; then, to provide an understanding of the text from my own perspective and from a scholarly standpoint. Supporting these explanations would be numerous illustrations—not artistic or imaginary images (*Phantasie- und Kunstgebilde*), but those which served antiquarian, topographical, and natural-historical purposes.[54]

The impetus behind the illustrations—at least in Philippson's mind—was not aesthetic education for its own sake, but rather a path into Torah. In other words, the goal of this type of translation could be achieved only by commentary.

Samson Raphael Hirsch likewise positioned himself to correct the errors of the recent past—from the Middle Ages onwards—by resurrecting the distant past. In *The Nineteen Letters on Judaism,* Hirsch makes a powerful case for reviving the Oral Torah, defined as the lost or hidden spirit of the Law, which "went into exile" sometime after the canonization of the Babylonian Talmud, without which there could be no complete, cogent understanding of the whole of Judaism.

> The Law went into exile, the letter and its external practical fulfillment were saved; but the spirit, preserved only in the symbolical concealment of the letter, disappeared. The spirit can be discerned only by deduction from the letter and from the symbol that veils it, and *with the help of the higher insight* that certain individuals had preserved.[55] (emphasis added)

Maimonides may have rescued the philosophical spirit, but for the most part, the field of *ta'amei ha-mitzvoth* (the science of the commandments) was lost, or disintegrated into "dialectic subtleties and hairsplittings."[56] Jehuda Halevi's *Kuzari* and Nachmanides made noble attempts to comprehend Judaism from within. But many other negative developments—here unnamed—predominated in the German Jewish world.[57] Mendelssohn, in Hirsch's account, "showed the world that it was possible to be a strictly religious Jew and yet to shine forth as a German Plato."[58] He was useful in defending Judaism against Christianity, but "he did not build up Judaism as a science from within itself."[59] The subsequent misunderstanding of Judaism as "soul-killing priestcraft" was inevitable, as only the most pedantic, base interpretations of Jewish laws became popular: the Sabbath is simply to give us a day off of work; sacrifices are simply to give something back to God, etc.

In an especially striking echo of Philippson, Hirsch diagnosed a dialectical struggle for the soul of Judaism as he experienced it:

> And what is our present state? Today, two opposing parties confront each other. The one party has inherited uncomprehended Judaism as a mechanical habit, *mitzvoth anashim melumodoh* without its spirit. They bear it in their hands as a sacred relic, as a revered mummy, and fear to awaken its spirit. Some of the others are indeed filled with noble enthusiasm for the welfare of the Jews, but they look upon Judaism as a lifeless framework, as something which should be interred in the grave of a past long since dead and buried. They seek its spirit and find it not, and are in danger, with all their efforts to help the Jew, of severing the last life-nerve of Judaism out of sheer ignorance. *And today, when, de-*

> *spite a thousand shades and variations of difference, these two opposing elements are alike in the one great respect, that they are both in the wrong—what shall be done?*[60] (emphasis added)

Like Philippson, Hirsch positions himself at a distance from two opposing camps. Philippson saw the good in both; Hirsch found both wrong. Hirsch also mocks the notion that a way forward can be forged by the logic of dialectic—what Philippson sought to convey with his battle cry of unity, blending, unification. Hirsch asks:

> Does it suffice for the salvation of Judaism to establish our schools upon such a twofold basis, and to reform our mode of worship? The spirit, the inner harmonious principle of life, is lacking, and that you cannot supply by polishing the outer frame.[61]

With the suggestion that the reformers are merely polishing the hardware of religion, Hirsch advocates starting over: "forgetting" both "inherited views and prejudices concerning Judaism" and going back to the "true sources of Judaism, to the Bible, the Talmud and Midrash; to read, study, and comprehend them in order to live by them." This is the heart of the matter:

> to know Judaism out of itself; to learn from its own utterances its wisdom of life. The beginning should be made with the Bible. Its language should first be understood, and then, out of the spirit of the language, the spirit of the speakers therein should be inferred. The Bible should not be studied as an interesting object of philological or antiquarian research, or as a basis for theories of taste, or for amusement. It should be studied as the foundation of a new science. Nature should be contemplated with the spirit of David; history should be perceived with the ear of an Isaiah, and then, with the eye thus aroused, with the ear thus opened, the doctrine of God, world, man, Israel and Torah should be drawn from the Bible, and should become an idea, or system of ideas, fully comprehended. It is in this spirit that the Talmud should be studied. We should search in the Halachah only for further elucidation and amplification of those ideas we already know from the Bible, and in the Aggadah [midrash] only for the figuratively disguised manifestation of the same spirit.[62]

The Bible is not just giant container of all things Jewish, but the primer for a new kind of world education, a curriculum incorporating Jewish texts, nature, and history. The Bible comes first as a foundation of the new science, which provides a lens that can be then turned to nature (through the imagery of David's Psalms) and history (Isaiah's accounts of the destruction of the Temple, exile, messianic time); only then do rabbinic law and lore elucidate what is known from the Bible.

For Hirsch and for Philippson, translation became that hermeneutic, whereby a new, all-encompassing foundation was forged—not just for Jewish life, or even Torah, but for knowledge of the world as such.

PHILIPPSON: UNIFYING THE HEBREW BIBLE

In the introduction to the *Israelite Bible*, under "inner unity," Philippson writes:

> So we see in the Five Books of Moses one unifying idea (*eine einige Idee*) predominate, the pursuit of one specific intention from beginning to end, a precise continuous teaching running through it, and all these through a regular process that is conditioned in itself and brought to explication in the entire contents. These form a totality, a whole, in which beginning and end and the entire development mutually determine each other, in which no part can be missing without rendering the entire whole incomplete, and in which each part corresponds to the whole and as a necessary limb is interdependent on the organism of the whole.[63]

Unity was the highest priority: it was a religious and also an aesthetic concern. How else to explain the overabundance of front matter: three titles;[64] three tables of contents; an eighteen-part introduction; and a steel engraving of Moses for the frontispiece or "author portrait"? Why three tables of contents? The first divides the Pentateuch according to the Hebrew *sidrot*, or weekly portions in the synagogue calendar. The second, *Inhalt* (contents), divides the Pentateuch by themes, subthemes, and sub-subthemes: History of Creation, page 1; Before the Flood, page 10; The Flood, page 28; After the Flood, page 42. On through Moses' death, page 992. Remarkably, this index uses the terminology of a legal document, with Roman numerals, Latin and Hebrew letters, and categories of story (*Geschichte*), part (*Abtheilung*), paragraph (*Abschnitt*), article (*Artikel*). Under "History of Revelation: second section: revelation on Sinai," we find three paragraphs: "The Theogony," "The Ten-Words as Foundation," "Explanatory Laws." Under the last of these are eight articles: "The Rights of Slavery," "Injuring the Body," "Injury to Property," "Injury to Virginity," "Prohibition against Magic," "The Rights of the Stranger, Widow, Orphan and the Poor," "About Debts," "About Justice in the Court." Items are not listed in order of appearance, but according to a

Philippsonian rationale; this reorganization speaks to Philippson's anxiety about sequence and order.

A third index, *Holzschnitte* (Woodcuts), numbered 1–197, had been advertised in the prospectus and on the title page. "English" woodcut illustrations referred to the technique of wood engraving invented by Thomas Bewick (1753–1828), still used to this day, whereby plates were made out of boxwood cut against the grain, rather than metal. Whether or not a special index for illustrations was commonplace at the time, it was needed here, because the images tell a story of their own.

Philippson's thirty-page "Introduction to the Five Books of Moses" includes sections devoted to names, division, and contents, as well as philosophical topics: idea, ideological agenda, teaching, process/structure, inner unity;[65] the Bible is once again sliced up every which way. Philippson must have been hyperconscious of how his reader would approach the translation, and he must have been equally certain that the Bible does not speak for itself, and that it needs his assistance to communicate its message effectively. For Philippson was not interested in word symbolism, or in creating a more Hebrew-sounding German version; Philippson even apologizes for incorporating the Hebraized names of biblical characters, lest these create dissonance for his audience. A monumental Jewish *Bibelwerk* would redefine the Bible of the Jews as a work interconnected with ancient civilizations and societies, inseparable from the geographical and natural landscapes of the modern world, and laden with information, knowledge, and meaning. Philippson's methodology as a translator and commentator was to highlight the overarching ideas and continuous themes, always with the big picture in mind. No individual word, verse, or episode, however troubling, should distract one from the grand vision. Prioritizing the particular at the expense of the whole is a hallmark of the "critical spirit" that was anathema to Philippson. As the tables of contents illustrate, the key to this totalizing vision was smoothing out any difficulties.

Improving the Bible's paratactic syntax, we have seen, had been the challenge of each and every translator since the Haskalah. Prior translators added conjunctions "however," "namely," or "that means," and also explanatory parentheses. Philippson took on a different challenge. To promote the unity of the Bible as whole, he would have to master transitions *between* episodes, and explain the hierarchical or causal relationships among disparate events. Philippson absolutely relished making these clarifications and left nothing to chance. One of the earliest transitional verses is Genesis 2:4, thought to be a composite of the end of the first Creation story and the beginning of the second. How did he gloss this transition?

> *From the general to the particular.* The Holy Scripture follows precisely this path. It begins with the creation of the entire world, then deals with the specifics of the creation of human beings, gives their first story, leads then to the development of humans into a human race, the education of peoples and races, then again singles out the origins of Abraham, in order to follow the development of the Abrahamic race into the people of Israel—here as there, in order to recount the history of revelation. *When this goal of Scripture is summarized in such a sharp and precise way, then all of its parts appear closely connected as one whole, and the minor difficulties easily dissolve if one avoids seeking the representation of something new that is in its smallest details systematic and consistent.* (emphasis added)

Read: don't be like the modern scientist who seeks consistency even on the minutest of levels. If one keeps in mind the larger purpose, all lesser difficulties dissolve—Philippson's hermeneutic in a nutshell.

The question of why the Israelites had to endure slavery in Egypt requires an explanation of a different order. Philippson draws an analogy from natural science, where a "conglomerate of atoms" dissolves fixed elements in a "great chemical procedure": the people's circumstances had to become so unbearable that all the ties that bound them would dissolve. Just as famine drove them down to Egypt, so would slavery drive them out and prepare them to receive revelation.[66] In response to an even thornier theological conundrum, to wit, why does God harden Pharaoh's heart? and why were twelve plagues needed in Egypt instead of just one?—Philippson answers impatiently, in essence saying, "because that was God's plan, that's why."

> to the question of why God did not bring about the exodus from Egypt immediately, with one miraculous expression, it should be countered that his acts need to be related to the mental condition of Pharaoh, from whom the stubborn refusal emerged, but without being concerned that speculating grandchildren would turn it into a metaphysical question.[67]

Philippson's comment betrays an anti-intellectualist agenda. Pharaoh's stubbornness serves the larger plan: the need to present a series of increasingly great miracles, to prepare the Israelites for revelation, and also to impress the Egyptians with God's power. Accept the simple answer and resist drawing "metaphysical" conclusions, or "speculating" too closely about God's ways.[68]

The Philippson Bible is filled with facts. But when it comes to ideas, the commentary is ideological, rather than scholarly. He opens up the debates and hard questions, but ultimately, there is no room for ambiguity. The question remains whether he gives real answers to the questions he raises, or whether he arbitrarily draws a line (*Schlussstrich*) out of sheer impatience or need for closure.

PHILIPPSON: PICTURING THE NATIONAL STORY

Philippson used "over five hundred" images (close to two hundred in volume 1 alone) as hermeneutic tools for explaining Scripture, much as he used translations of Mendelssohn, Zunz, Johlson, De Wette, the Septuagint, the targumim, Philo, Josephus, Symmachus, and Albo, and the exegeses of Talmud, Midrash, and medieval commentators. Of critical importance: unlike the pictures in Gustave Doré Bibles, the large majority are *not* illustrations of this or that scene, episode, or figure; rather, they depict the realia of the Hebrew Bible: its locales, trees, animals, clothing, jewelry, and customs (fig. 3.5). Thus, the first images in volume 1 include a fig leaf, the sheep that Abel sacrificed, and the dove and olive branch from Noah's

Fig. 3.5. Philippson Bible, "The Ox, the Camel, and the Donkey" (1858). Photograph: Harvard Divinity School, Andover-Harvard Theological Library (SCR 319 Philippson).

story. By comparison, Old Yiddish Bibles (following Protestant Bibles) include illustrations of the snake tempting Eve, Cain slaying Abel, and the diluvian landscape. A large majority were reproductions of artworks and museum relics, travel literature, archaeological and ethnographic works. Though little is known about the origins of Philippson's "antiquarian, topographical, and natural-historical" illustrations, evidence suggests that they may not have been produced for this Bible alone. Mary Bergstein speculates that there may have been an image depository from which publishers drew. Baumgärtner's Buchhandlung was a publisher in Leipzig, the center of liberal publishing, who also published Philippson's broadside and other periodicals dedicated to the dissemination of knowledge among the masses such as *Das Heller-Magazin*, which included illustrations similar to those in this Bible. Most of the scholarship on these illustrations is by Freud scholars and art historians who study Freud's visual culture.[69]

Within this "great archive of image-text interface,"[70] how does Philippson deploy the images as translator-exegete? Zoological, botanical, and geographical images, such as Mount Ararat, the Dead Sea, and Edom, serve to naturalize biblical stories, shifting the focus from the supernatural to natural and historical domains. A classic example is Genesis 11, the story of the Tower of Babel. Philippson's illustration captioned "Birs Nimroud (Babel)" follows the phrase, "and that is why it is called Babel" (fig. 3.6). His comment describes the history of Babylon, then moves on to identify the ruin that, in his view, was without a doubt the one referenced in the text:

> Babylon was conquered by Cyrus and Darius, later sank more and more into ruin. Among these widely spread out ruins there are three points which must be considered in connection with the tower mentioned here in scripture, one so-called Nimrod-tower, which is in fact a ruin of Akad; Mujelibe; and Birs Nimroud. All factors point to the last [choice]. This ruin is an oblong (elongated) form, 762 English yards around, on the western shore of the Euphrates. On the east side it is enclosed by a deep water pit, and it is only 50–60 feet high; on the west is a cube of 198 feet, upon which is a pile of bricks at 371 feet high and 28 feet wide. It is broken through with small, square openings. The stones are decorated with cuneiform, and the cement is so strong that one cannot even break one off.[71]

It is not that Philippson ignores the story and its theological and moral messages, but that the story is rounded off with facts and information: the geographical location and dimensions of a physical tower, followed by a discussion of the etymology for "Babel."

dreißig Jahre gelebt, zeugte er den Peleg.
17. Dann lebte Eber, nachdem er Peleg gezeugt, vierhundert und dreißig Jahre, und

וארבע מאות שנה
ס (טז) ויחי־עבר ארבע ושלשים
שנה ויולד את־פלג: (יז) ויחי־עבר
אחרי הולידו את־פלג שלשים שנה

Birs Nimroud. Für den Letztern sprechen alle Gründe. Diese Ruine ist von länglicher Form, 762 engl. Yards im Umfang, auf dem westl. Ufer des Euphrat. Auf der Ostseite ist sie von einem tiefen Wassergraben eingeschlossen, und nur

Birs Nimroud (Babel)

50 bis 60 F. hoch, auf der westlichen ist sie ein Würfel von 198 F., auf dem ein Stoß Ziegeln von 371 Höhe und 28 F. Breite. Sie ist durchbrochen von schmalen, viereckigen Oeffnungen. Die Backsteine sind mit Keilschrift versehen, ihr Zement ist so stark, daß man keinen ganz abbrechen kann. — Der Name בבל für בלבל, wie Onk. stellt, wie man im Syr. und Chald. mehrere Beispiele von solchen Auslassungen des ל bei Reduplikationen hat. Die dagegen erhobenen Zweifel und die Ableitungen von בב בל verwirft Fürst in der Konkordanz p. 138 und führt das Beispiel מֵמֵל für מַלְמֵל an, so daß die Ableitung der Schrift völlig gerechtfertigt ist. Die Gegner zeigen auch wenig Takt, da offenbar hier die Ueberlieferung an den Namen sich knüpfte. — 10. Hiermit ist die Universalgeschichte geschlossen; es bedarf nur eines Ueberganges noch zur Spezialgeschichte der Offenbarung und ihrer Träger; so war denn das Zurückkommen auf die Urquelle noch einmal nothwendig, um in genauer Folge zu Abraham zu gelangen. Obgleich nun dies erst von dem 10, 25 verlassenen Peleg nothwendig war, so sollten hier doch zugleich die chronologischen Angaben hinzugefügt werden. Wir haben nun hier von der Sündfluth bis Abraham wieder 10 Geschlechter, wie von Adam bis Noach, und stellen hier sogleich die Tabelle auf.

Schem	geb. 1558*) J. d. W.	gest. 2158 J. d. W.	alt 600 J.	(98 J. vor der Fluth, die 1656 d. W.)
Arpachschad	— 1658 — — — —	2096 — — — —	438 —	
Schelach	— 1693 — — — —	2126 — — — —	433 —	
Eber	— 1723 — — — —	2187 — — — —	464 —	
Peleg	— 1757 — — — —	1996 — — — —	239 —	

Fig. 3.6. Philippson Bible, "Birs Nimroud (Babel)" (1858). Photograph: Harvard Divinity School, Andover-Harvard Theological Library (SCR 319 Philippson).

At the same time, extensive Orientalist imagery—the large majority of which depicts Egypt, then Israel, followed by Rome, Persia, Greece, and Syria—exemplifies the Romantic thrust of nineteenth-century historicism.[72] Oriental figures, such as "Bedouins Camping in the Desert by Carne and Laborde," from travel literature or ancient art, take the place of biblical

174 1 Mos. 33, 1—4.

Spannader, die auf der Hüftpfanne sitzt, bis auf diesen Tag, weil er stieß auf die Hüftpfanne Jakobs, auf die Spannader.

33. 1. Und Jakob erhob seine Augen, und schaute, und siehe, Esav kam und mit ihm vierhundert Mann; da vertheilte er die Kinder um Leah und um Rachel und um die beiden Mägde. 2. Und er stellte die Mägde und ihre Kinder vorn an, und Leah und ihre Kinder dahinter, und Rachel und Joseph zuletzt. 3. Er aber ging ihnen voraus, und beugte sich zur Erde sieben Mal, bis er seinem Bruder nahe kam. 4. Da lief ihm Esav entge-

Orientalische Art zu grüßen.

175 1 Mos. 33, 5—10.

gen, und umarmte ihn, und fiel ihm um den Hals, und küßte ihn, und sie weinten. 5. Und er erhob seine Augen, und sah die Weiber und die Kinder, und sprach: Wer sind diese bei dir? Da sprach er: Die Kinder, womit Gott deinen Knecht begnadigte. 6. Da traten heran die Mägde selbst und ihre Kinder, und bückten sich. 7. Und auch Leah trat heran und ihre Kinder, und sie bückten sich, und danach trat Joseph heran und Rachel, und bückten sich. 8. Dennsprach er: Was wolltest du mit jenem ganzen Lager, auf das ich gestoßen? Er sprach: Gunst finden in den Augen meines Herrn. 9. Und Esav sprach: Ich habe genug; mein Bruder, dein sei, was dir gehört. 10. Aber Jakob sprach: Nicht doch,

Ein Perser, sich vor dem Könige beugend; nach Moriers zweiter Reise in Persien.

Fig. 3.7. Philippson Bible, "Oriental Greetings" (1858). Photograph: Harvard Divinity School, Andover-Harvard Theological Library (SCR 319 Philippson).

characters. In Genesis 33:3, when Jacob returns home to Canaan after his long sojourn, he "bowed low to the ground seven times until he was near his brother." Philippson must have believed these gestures require explanation, since he includes three different images of bowing (fig. 3.7).[73]

His commentary reads:

> The seven-time deep bowing, which probably occurred in intervals, is the sign of submission that is typical between younger and older brothers in the Orient. If this was already natural in the relationship between Jacob and Esau, now Jacob, since he was at last secure about his Abrahamic declaration of faith, was more easily able to observe these outer signs of the younger brother. At an audience before the Sheik of Persia, those who enter have to bow nine times in six pauses (Johnson). When David walked toward his cousin Jonathan, he bowed three times 1 Sam 20:41. In the Orient, the common manner of bowing as a sign of respect is threefold, either the complete falling on the floor, like the Arabs in our picture, like the Mohameddan at prayer, or with crossed arms, the right hand over the heart like the position of the slave before the master, or

> the bowing of the upper body with hands on the knees, like the Persian in our illustration.—We have a similar scene in which brothers' rancor disappears at the sight of a brother's face, and the one who reconciles takes them into his arms and to his breast, in the story of Jacob's sons in 45:3 and 50:18.

This passage captures the essence of Philippson's commentary. The ethnographic comments about Oriental bowing customs are framed by comments about biblical bowing of Jacob, Joseph's brothers, and David. They provide the realia of the biblical story. Even so, the bowing figures in the pictures are not Israelites, but Persians and Arabs, enabling Philippson, as Mary Bergstein observes, to "universalize ancient history in order to 'make a world that unified the Jew, the Christian, and the Mohammedan.' "[74]

Among these illustrations are some of the earliest modern images of Jewish ceremonial and ecclesiastical practice from *Ceremonies des Juifs* by Bernard Picart (1630–1733), a Christian designer and engraver in Amsterdam. Leviticus 9:14 is illustrated by a Passover seder; the commandment for wearing fringes on the corner of one's garment is followed by an extraordinary image, "A Jew with prayer shawl and fringes, after Picart."[75] Jews are in the distinct minority, however. Philippson carefully describes the contents of the image, but also, in the manner of ekphrasis, the image as image.

In the case of a Rosselini painting of an ancient cave drawing of slaves making bricks, he goes into detail about Rosselini's use of color and other details that would not be visible to the reader (fig. 3.8). Notice also his use of the first person plural:

> Let us take this occasion to give a highly interesting scene of the preparation of Egyptian bricks that Rosselini copied from a painting on the walls of a mausoleum near Thebes. Rosselini himself is convinced that it is a representation of the oppressed Israelites. In support of this, first, is that four of the Egyptians are different than the other persons; while the Egyptians are consistently painted in brick red color, in contrast, the others are in bright yellow paint . . . The representation is very clear and portrays the entire preparation of the bricks. A few men prepare the mortar, others carry the mortar in baskets to those who press it into the form of bricks; once the bricks are formed, they are laid out to dry in rows, and when they are dried, they are piled up in an orderly way. In the original, the formed and dried bricks are clearly differentiated, as the former are pale gray, the latter are pale red.[76]

Fig. 3.8. Philippson Bible, "Egyptian Slaves" (1858). Photograph: Harvard Divinity School, Andover-Harvard Theological Library (SCR 319 Philippson).

Philippson's note implies that both the ancient image, and the painting thereof, would be of interest to his reader.

The Philippson Bible was a *Gesamtkunstwerk*, where past and present, Europe and the Orient, religious and secular, nation and nature, culture and history, word and image were analogized, reconciled, brought into correspondence.

COMMENTARY OF PHILIPPSON AND HIRSCH

The translation and commentary of Samson Raphael Hirsch opposed both Jewish scholarship and Protestant Bible criticism. He emphasized that the Torah is a unique document, not part of "classical" or ancient literature, and thus not comprehensible by way of the tools of modern scholarship.[77] Philippson's contribution was to translate the Jewish religious idea into universal terms and pictures; Hirsch responded by resegregating the Jewish Bible from the outside world by treating the Hebrew language as something that only Jews could understand.

In both cases, commentary consists of many different elements: esoteric details and specialized information are juxtaposed with didactic and even polemical comments. Citations are important, but in each case for different reasons. Hirsch quotes only from Talmud and Midrash with attribution; when disputing an idea, he does not name its author. Philippson quotes more liberally and extensively than any commentator before or since, and punctiliously names each source. Hirsch's rhetoric is homiletical and at times tendentious. Philippson relishes the process: he *assembles* ancient, medieval, and modern voices, Christian and Jewish exegetes; *organizes* them (a, b, and c hold this view; d, e, and f hold that view), just as he did when setting up the rabbinical conferences in the 1840s; and only then identifies the "correct" interpretation. Of both it can be said that the ultimate goal is to privilege one interpretation over all others.

My leading-image is that of a purple-flowered plant, commonly called oregano or zaatar, that plays an important role in the story of the Exodus from Egypt (Ex 12:22) (fig. 3.9). In Exodus 12: 1–14, the beginning of the Jewish national story, God commands the Israelites to slaughter a lamb at twilight of the fourteenth day of the month, paint its blood on the lintel and doorposts of the house, and that night, eat the roasted lamb together with unleavened bread and bitter herbs; in short, the Israelites are commanded to celebrate Passover before there has been any passing-over, before the bread didn't have time to rise, before the Exodus even transpired. A few verses later, in Exodus 12:21–22, Moses repeats the information to the elders, but adds a few extra details, such as that they should use "branches of hyssop" for the dipping and smearing of the lamb's blood on the doorposts and upper threshold of their homes. Moses Mendelssohn merely pauses to note the similarity between the Hebrew *ezov* and the German word *Hysop*. But this innocuous instance of almost repetition led both Philippson and Hirsch to see an opening for a lesson.

Exodus 12:21–22 (JPS):

> Moses then commanded all the elders of Israel and said to them, "Go, pick out lambs for your families, and slaughter the passover offering. Take a **bunch of hyssop**, dip it in the blood that is in the basin, and apply some of the blood that is in the basin to the lintel and to the two doorposts. None of you shall go outside from the door of his house until morning."

Philippson's commentary on "A Bundle of Hyssop":

> Even as the Greek ὑσσωπος sounds like the Hebrew *ezov*, which commonly leads one to explain it as *Hyssopus officinalis*—a plant that grows on ruins and walls (I Kings 5:13), with lanceolate leaves, 1 to 1½ feet high stem, blue flower—however, the tradition (Talmud Pesachim 11.7 [fol. 118a]) distinguishes the hyssop of this law explicitly from Roman and Greek hyssop. Maimonides and Saadia translate with the Arabic *zaatar*, which is صعتر Origanum (*Dosten*), an aromatic plant with a one-foot-high straight stem and many downy leaves that commonly grows in Palestine, Syria, Egypt, and Arabia. A completely different interpretation was attempted with *Phytolacca decandra*, which is frequently found near Aleppo and in Abyssinia, and has a long and attenuated stalk and an unusual number of salty parts (compare Psalm 51:9). According to the tradition (Parah 11.9), a "bundle" contains three stems, according to Maimonides (commentary on Pirkei Avot 3); it is the amount that can be grasped by a hand.[78]

Philippson's commentary reads like a nineteenth-century German encyclopedia entry, as its prime concern is the precise identification and classification of the plant. But is there any other agenda? One can perceive that he gives too much information here—far more than is needed to understand the verse. The illustration further gives cause for wonder. Incidentally, the detail of the ribbon is meant to convey that the plant is not in a natural setting. Most of the natural and ethnographical, historical illustrations in the Philippson Bible incorporate a trace of human presence, in line with the place of nature in German realism. Is this torrent of information coupled with the picture intended to cover up or prettify what is otherwise a rather disturbing episode? Perhaps it was meant to sublimate the national drama, to distract the reader from the sacrificial blood and the plague of the killing of the first-born children. Other than the parting of the sea, there is no moment in the drama of the Exodus that demarcates so clearly the

ich herausgeführt eure Heere aus dem Lande Mizrajim, so beobachtet diesen Tag, für eure Geschlechter eine ewige Satzung. 18. Im ersten Monat, am vierzehnten Tage des Monats, am Abend, sollt ihr ungesäuertes Brod essen, bis zum ein und zwanzigsten Tage des Monats am Abend. 19. Sieben Tage soll Sauerteig nicht gefunden werden in euren Häusern, denn Jeglicher, der Gesäuertes ißt, dessen Person soll ausgerottet werden aus der Gemeinde Jisrael's, sei's Fremdling, sei's Eingeborner des Landes. 20. Nichts Gesäuertes sollt ihr essen, in all' euren Wohnungen sollt ihr ungesäuertes Brod essen. 21. Und Moscheh berief alle Aeltesten Jisrael's, und sprach zu ihnen: Rüstet euch, und schaffet euch Schafe für eure Familien, und schlachtet das

הזה
מצרים ושמרתם את־היום הזה
לדרתיכם חקת עולם: (יח) בראשן
בארבעה עשר יום לחדש בערב תאכלו
מצת עד יום האחד ועשרים לחדש
בערב: (יט) שבעת ימים שאר לא
ימצא בבתיכם כי | כל־אכל מחמצת
ונכרתה הנפש ההוא מעדת ישראל
בגר ובאזרח הארץ: (כ) כל־מחמצת
לא תאכלו בכל מושבתיכם תאכלו
מצות: פ [חמישי]
(כא) ויקרא משה לכל־זקני ישראל
ויאמר אלהם משכו וקחו לכם

Schluß gezogen, daß schon am 14ten das Gesäuerte hinweggeschafft sein müßte. Vgl. 1 M. 2. — 16. Ueber die Bedeutung des מקרא קדש und die Unterlassung der Arbeit werden wir ausführlich beim Sabbat- und Festritus sprechen. — 17. ושמרתם את המצות wird von den trad. Komm. zu wörtlich erklärt, man soll darauf achten, daß die Mazzoth nicht säueren, da hier das Fest, das Essen, die Verordnung der Mazzoth verstanden werden. Samar. und Septuag. lasen המצוה. — 18. בחדש הראשן für בראשן (Rabe). — In sorgfältigster Erklärung für V. 15. — 19. Die Ausdrücke häufen sich der genauesten Bestimmtheit wegen. שאר „Sauerteig" für חמץ V. 15. לא ימצא für תשביתו. Das Verhältniß zwischen אורח und גר beim Peßach wird hier erst flüchtig berührt, und findet unten weitere Auseinandersetzung. — 20. בכל מושבתיכם genauer für בתיכם. Nach der tradit. Erkl. bedeutet der Ausdruck בכל מושבתיכם auch außerhalb des heiligen Landes (חוץ לארץ) Kidduschin 37. 1. — 21. Da eine allgemeine Volksversammlung nicht in Aeg. statt finden konnte, so bediente sich Moscheh der Aeltesten (s. Anm. zu 3, 16.) — משכו Raschi, wer Schafe besitzt, hole sich ein Lamm, וקחו wer keine besitzt, kaufe sich eines. T. Jon. und Midr. משכו „ziehet die Hand von den ägypt. Götzen ab." — 22. So gleichklingend auch das griechische ὕσσωπος mit dem hebr. אזוב ist, so daß man es gewöhnlich mit hyss. officinalis erklärt, einer auf Schutt und Mauern wachsenden Pflanze (1 Kön. 5, 13.), mit lanzetförmigen Blättern, 1 bis 1½ Fuß hohem Stengel, blauer Blume: die Trad. (Pesach. 11. 7.) [fol. 118. 1.] unterscheidet dennoch den Ysop des Gesetzes ausdrücklich vom röm. und grich. Ysop, Rambam und Saad. geben es mit dem arab. צעתר, welches صعتر Origanum (Dosten), eine aromatische Pflanze mit 1 Fuß hohem, geradem Stengel und vielen wolligen Blättern, bezeichnet, die in Palästina, Syrien, Aeg. und Arab. sehr häufig wächst. Eine ganz andere Deutung versuchte

Fig. 3.9. Philippson Bible, "Hyssop" (1858). Photograph: Harvard Divinity School, Andover-Harvard Theological Library (SCR 319 Philippson).

painful uprooting of the Israelites from the diaspora context. It is easy to understand that this is *not* a message that nineteenth-century German Jews would care to broadcast to the world.

When Hirsch looks at that hyssop, what is it that catches his attention? I cite from his commentary:

> Here, right at the very first *Mitzva*, we have a concrete example of *Torah she b'al peh* (the spoken, traditional Torah). Here we have recorded in the "written Torah" that Moses gave additional details of the procedure to be carried out, which are not mentioned above in the "written" record of God's commands [i.e. the type of plant to be used for the dipping and smearing of the lamb's blood]. In the same way, at all the later laws, Moses had to receive and transmit more detailed explanations which were not given in the written record of God's words, which only contain a general reference to the law, and leave these detailed explanations to verbal transmission.[79]

Though he does discuss the characteristics of the hyssop plant, what Hirsch fixates on first and foremost is that the hyssop is *not mentioned* in the initial command to the masses. Hirsch picks this up again in his commentary on the verse "And the Children of Israel went and did as *God* had commanded Moses and Aaron, so did they do." (Ex 12:38):

> Moses and Aaron remitted it faithfully and truly, Israel accepted and carried it out faithfully and truly, and so Israel's act completely corresponded to God's command. This shows incidentally, how, from the very beginning, the Law came to be kept solely on the base of verbal tradition. Out of the six hundred thousand men who had to bring the Pessach only the elders had the order direct from Moses, the others only got it through a whole series of intermediate transmitters, and nevertheless the Torah tells us that the order was carried out completely in accordance with the command that God had in the first place given to Moses and Aaron.[80]

Like the Yiddish translators and to some extent Mendelssohn, Hirsch does not miss an opportunity to invoke the Oral Law, which is the essential key to Jewish practice. However, a subtext to Hirsch's defense of the Oral Law is his own poetics of translation: his commitment to locating the significance of Torah *beyond* the text proper, building up his own authority as a translator-commentator-artist, claiming all the while that this meaning is wholly internal to it.

Compare their approaches to Genesis 22:13, a difficult verse with a long tradition of emendation. The confusing word is the adverb *achar*, "after," as in: "he saw, and behold a ram after," which most translations render as "behind," "*hinter*," "after that," or "thereafter."

> KJV: And Abraham lifted up his eyes, and looked, and behold ***behind him*** a ram caught in the thicket by his horns: and Abraham went

and took the ram, and offered him up for a burnt offering in the stead of his son.

Mendelssohn: und sahe einen Widder (vorbeylaufen), **hernach** ward er in den Hecken mit seinen Hörnern verwickelt.

Zunz: und schaute, und siehe da ein Widder, der **hernach** hängen blieb im Dickicht an den Hörnern;

Philippson: und sah, und siehe ein Widder, **nachher** verwickelt in Dickicht mit seinen Hörnern; und Abraham ging hin und nahm den Widder, und brachte ihn zum Opfer statt seines Sohnes.

Hirsch: . . . und sah, da war ein Widder; **darauf**, wurde er durch das Gehege an seinen Hörnern festgehalten. Da ging Abraham und nahm den Widder und brachte ihn zum Opfer an seines Sohnes Stelle.

BR: da, ein Widder hatte sich **dahinter** im Gestrüpp mit den Hörnern verfangen.

Philippson's comment shows us how he struggled. "The word *achar* is difficult." It is difficult. "Not only the ancient versions but many Heb. manuscripts read *'hd* for *'hr*, in other words, they change *achar* (behind, thereafter) to *echad* (one)." Philippson faced the temptation to depart from the *textus receptus*.

Mendelssohn, Zunz, and Philippson use the German *hernach*, *nachher*, "after that," "afterwards," suggesting that the ram was initially moving (see Mendelssohn's addition of "walking by") but became trapped after Abraham spotted him. Hirsch uses *darauf*, "after which," to the same effect. The significance of this translation emerges from the commentators (above all Abarbanel) who note that the "trapping" was a second, later miracle brought about by the angel.

Following twenty lines of commentary that begin "The word *achar* is difficult," Philippson concludes, "*achar* is best understood as a time expression that was somewhat lightly thrown in." In other words, accept it, and don't obsess. The interpretive tradition matters, and as Peter Machinist observes, Philippson had to work hard to *not* reject *achar*. He first quotes the Septuagint which emends the text to *achad* (*ein einzelner*, a single one). Then: "According to the well-known critical principle, this easier reading testifies to interpolation." In other words, he rejects the emendation by relying on the principle of lectio difficilior vs. lectio facilior (the more difficult reading is preferable to the easier reading). He goes on to give the interpretations of Onkelos, Abarbanel, and Ibn Ezra, and to agree with the "more difficult" Jewish exegetical reading of "after which" (*achar kach*).[81]

Hirsch shifts the focus from *achar* to the end of the verse, "instead of

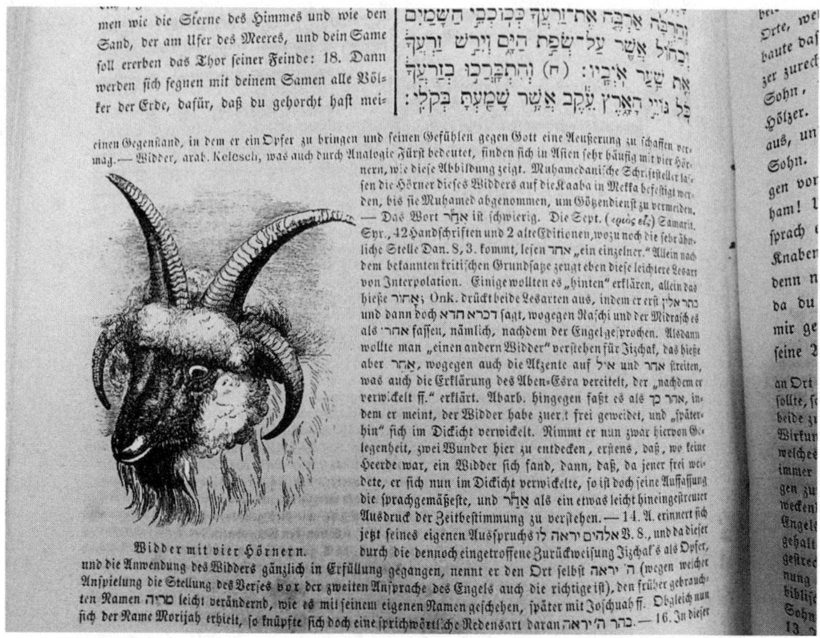

men wie die Sterne des Himmes und wie den Sand, der am Ufer des Meeres, und dein Same soll ererben das Thor seiner Feinde: 18. Dann werden sich segnen mit deinem Samen alle Völker der Erde, dafür, daß du gehorcht hast mei-

וְהַרְבָּה אַרְבֶּה אֶת־זַרְעֲךָ כְּכוֹכְבֵי הַשָּׁמַיִם
וְכַחוֹל אֲשֶׁר עַל־שְׂפַת הַיָּם וְיִרַשׁ זַרְעֲךָ
אֵת שַׁעַר אֹיְבָיו׃ (ח) וְהִתְבָּרְכוּ בְזַרְעֲךָ
כֹּל גּוֹיֵי הָאָרֶץ עֵקֶב אֲשֶׁר שָׁמַעְתָּ בְּקֹלִי׃

einen Gegenstand, in dem er ein Opfer zu bringen und seinen Gefühlen gegen Gott eine Aeußerung zu schaffen vermag. — Widder, arab. Kelesch, was auch durch Analogie Fürst bedeutet, finden sich in Asien sehr häufig mit vier Hörnern, wie diese Abbildung zeigt. Muhamedanische Schriftsteller lassen die Hörner dieses Widders auf die Kaaba in Mekka befestigt werden, bis sie Muhamed abgenommen, um Götzendienst zu vermeiden. — Das Wort אַחַר ist schwierig. Die Sept. (κριὸς εἷς) Samarit. Syr., 42 Handschriften und 2 alte Editionen, wozu noch die sehr ähnliche Stelle Dan. 8, 3. kommt, lesen אחד „ein einzelner." Allein nach dem bekannten kritischen Grundsatze zeugt eben diese leichtere Lesart von Interpolation. Einige wollten es „hinten" erklären, allein das hieße אָחוֹר; Onk. drückt beide Lesarten aus, indem er erst בתר אלין und dann doch דכרא חדא sagt, wogegen Raschi und der Midrasch es als אחרי fassen, nämlich, nachdem der Engel gesprochen. Alsdann wollte man „einen andern Widder" verstehen für Jizchak, das hieße aber אַחֵר, wogegen auch die Akzente auf איל und אחר streiten, was auch die Erklärung des Aben-Esra vereitelt, der „nachdem er verwickelt ff." erklärt. Abarb. hingegen faßt es als אחר כך, indem er meint, der Widder habe zuerst frei geweidet, und „späterhin" sich im Dickicht verwickelt. Nimmt er nun zwar hiervon Gelegenheit, zwei Wunder hier zu entdecken, erstens, daß, wo keine Heerde war, ein Widder sich fand, dann, daß, da jener frei weidete, er sich nun im Dickicht verwickelte, so ist doch seine Auffassung die sprachgemäßeste, und אַחַר als ein etwas leicht hineingestreuter Ausdruck der Zeitbestimmung zu verstehen. — 14. A. erinnert sich jetzt seines eigenen Ausspruchs אלהים יראה לו V. 8., und da dieser durch die dennoch eingetroffene Zurückweisung Jizchak's als Opfer, und die Anwendung des Widders gänzlich in Erfüllung gegangen, nennt er den Ort selbst ה' יראה (wegen welcher Anspielung die Stellung des Verses vor der zweiten Ansprache des Engels auch die richtige ist), den früher gebrauchten Namen מריה leicht verändernd, wie es mit seinem eigenen Namen geschehen, später mit Joschuah ff. Obgleich nun sich der Name Morijah erhielt, so knüpfte sich doch eine sprichwörtliche Redensart daran בהר ה' יראה. — 16. In dieser

Fig. 3.10. Philippson Bible, "Ram" (1858). Photograph: Harvard Divinity School, Andover-Harvard Theological Library (SCR 319 Philippson).

his son," in order to extol the symbolic meaning of religious sacrifice. "That was why Abraham looked for an animal, for words were insufficient, and see, there stands a ram, *and* achar, *afterwards, after Abraham had first seen it*, it became caught by its horns in a bush." Then Abraham took it and brought it as "an offering *in place of his son*." Up until this point, Philippson and Hirsch agree. But Hirsch goes on to make a polemical point (without naming his antagonist).

> These words which we have stressed are a striking refutation of that narrow- minded or malicious misconception which disputes the symbolic meaning of our offerings, so as to be able to launch into a proud disparagement of the 'bloody ritual of offerings.' If offerings had no symbolic meanings, if the offering of this ram did not express a much higher and much more meaningful giving oneself up to God, what a blasphemy, yea, what an absurdity would it be to say *tachat bno*; instead of the dearest, most precious thing, for which one would sooner have suffered death oneself ten times over, to substitute an animal that just happens to be

running wild in the forest, so that it has not even the value of one's own possessions! Somebody has generously given me a million pounds, and I pick up a pin and say, well at least take this for it![82]

The tendency of these two commentators to take the same text and run in opposite directions is seen, for example, when the Bible reports that the Israelite tribes encamped, "each man with his division and each under his standard" (*ish al diglo*; Num 1:52) (fig. 3.11). Philippson wonders "what the standards and signs of the camps, the branches, were made of," and takes us on a mini-tour of the ancient Near East in an effort to find out. "The invention of standards is attributed to the Egyptians by ancient authors, and Diodorus reports that the Egyptian standards were composed of an animal image at the end of a pole. Among the Egyptian sculptures and paintings there appear other standards that depict a spread-out, semicircular flag." Adorned with a striking array of Egyptian, Greek, Roman, Persian, and "modern Oriental" standards, the pages themselves become a museum, or a parade of the nations of the world.

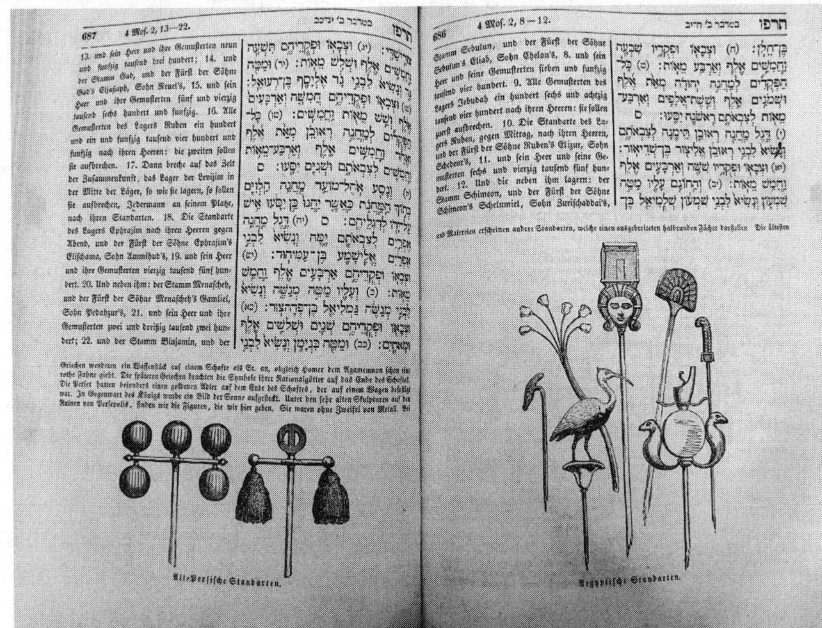

687 4 Mos. 2, 13—22.

13. und sein Heer und ihre Gemusterten neun und funfzig tausend drei hundert; 14. und der Stamm Gad, und der Fürst der Söhne Gad's Eljasaph, Sohn Reuel's, 15. und sein Heer und ihre Gemusterten fünf und vierzig tausend sechs hundert und funfzig. 16. Alle Gemusterten des Lagers Ruben ein hundert und ein und funfzig tausend vier hundert und funfzig nach ihren Heeren: die zweiten sollen sie aufbrechen. 17. Dann breche auf das Zelt der Zusammenkunft, das Lager der Levijim in der Mitte der Läger, so wie sie lagern, so sollen sie aufbrechen, Jedermann an seinem Platze, nach ihren Standarten. 18. Die Standarte des Lagers Ephrajim nach ihren Heeren gegen Abend, und der Fürst der Söhne Ephrajim's Elischama, Sohn Ammihud's, 19. und sein Heer und ihre Gemusterten vierzig tausend fünf hundert. 20. Und neben ihm: der Stamm Menascheh, und der Fürst der Söhne Menascheh's Gamliel, Sohn Pedahzur's, 21. und sein Heer und ihre Gemusterten zwei und dreißig tausend zwei hundert; 22. und der Stamm Binjamin, und der

Griechen wendeten ein Waffenstück auf einem Schafte als St. an, obgleich Homer dem Agamemnon schon eine rothe Fahne giebt. Die späteren Griechen brachten die Symbole ihrer Nationalgötter auf das Ende des Schaftes. Die Perser hatten besonders einen goldenen Adler auf dem Ende des Schaftes, der auf einem Wagen befestigt war. In Gegenwart des Königs wurde ein Bild der Sonne aufgesteckt. Unter den sehr alten Skulpturen auf den Ruinen von Persepolis, finden wir die Figuren, die wir hier geben. Sie waren ohne Zweifel von Metall. Bei

686 4 Mos. 2, 8—12.

Stamm Sebulun, und der Fürst der Söhne Sebulun's Eliab, Sohn Chelon's, 8. und sein Heer und seine Gemusterten sieben und funfzig tausend vier hundert. 9. Alle Gemusterten des Lagers Jehudah ein hundert sechs und achtzig tausend vier hundert nach ihren Heeren: sie sollen zuerst aufbrechen. 10. Die Standarte des Lagers Ruben, gegen Mittag, nach ihren Heeren, und der Fürst der Söhne Ruben's Elizur, Sohn Schedeur's, 11. und sein Heer und seine Gemusterten sechs und vierzig tausend fünf hundert. 12. Und die neben ihm lagern: der Stamm Schimeon, und der Fürst der Söhne Schimeon's Schelumiel, Sohn Zurischaddai's,

und Malereien erscheinen andere Standarten, welche einen ausgebreiteten halbrunden Fächer darstellen. Die ältesten

Fig. 3.11. Philippson Bible, "Standards" (1858). Photograph: Harvard Divinity School, Andover-Harvard Theological Library (SCR 319 Philippson).

As surely as Philippson's commentary inevitably moves outwards, Hirsch's follows a centripetal logic. After noting by way of the Midrash Rabbah that the color of each tribe's flag matched that of its stone on the breastplate of the High Priest, Hirsch hones in on what the Hebrew word *degel* sounds like. "*Degel* is likely related to *dekel* the Chaldean word for the palm tree, which grows straight up and with its spreading top is visible far away and so could easily express a military standard. Thus pillars of smoke rising high are also called 'smoke-palms' (Joel 3:3 and Song of Songs 3:6) *timrot ashan*."[83] The standards dissolve into smoke before our very eyes.

HIRSCH'S PHONETIC SYSTEM: EXPLAINING THE BIBLE FROM WITHIN

Hirsch introduces his method in the commentary to the first verse of Genesis. Recall that Mendelssohn commented on the direct object particle *et* in that verse to instruct about the accusative case; Hirsch uses the same *et* to explicate the interrelatedness of subject and object: the coming into being of the object in relationship to the acting subject; the Jewish downgrading of the thing-in-itself in favor of a veiled or secret nature that emerges only when a subject—like the ram in the thicket—becomes an object of some action.

> *Et* from the root *ot*, as is evident from *oti otecha* etc. *Ot* related to *od*, a handle, a lever, the means by which an action is accomplished, hence *ood*, a fire-rake, a piece of wood with which to stir the fire. *Odot* the causes, hence *al odot* [with regard to]. Hence, perhaps *id*, the bringer-about of the rain, the moisture that rises up from the earth. *Ot* the means for making something known (*Erkenntnis*), a sign, that is not the thing itself but leads to it. But this is then at once the particle of the accusative *et* which presents the object in all those phases (*vergegenwärtigt*) that represent its characteristics, its effect and relationship, by which its nature is to be recognized, which accordingly its sign, the means by which it gets known (*Erkenntnis*).[84]

What follows is a tacit reference to—and refutation of—the first lines of Mendelssohn's *Be'ur*:

> It is a deeply distinctive character of the thought that lies behind the Jewish language that *et* is used only for the accusative, the object, but never for the nominative, the subject. It is how the object appears with regard to something else, . . . how the object appears in the gaze of another. But the

> real nature of things is completely veiled, incomprehensible to anybody or anything else. We only know (*kennen*) things by their *otot* and their effect and doings by which they show their characteristics and which form the sole means by which they can be known. So that our sages, in their deep understanding of the language, find a significant difference if the object is expressed simply by its name or if by means of *et*. In the former case the effect extends to the object alone, in the latter, to all those factors by which its essential effect shows itself. Thus *kabed avicha* [honor thy father] would make only the father the object of the honouring, but *kabed et avicha* [honor **et** thy father] extends this honouring to all those who stand in such a relation to the father that the personality of the father is represented in them e.g, *eshet avicha* [the stepmother], and *equally et imecha* [**et** your mother] includes the stepfather. So that really *et* is a *ribui* [plural] that allows the object to be taken in wider sense. So, here too the *et* extends the conception *shamayim* [heavens] to include all the heavenly bodies, and the *aretz* [earth] to include all that is on the earth, which are just the effects which heaven and earth characteristically imprint on us.[85]

By the conclusion of this note, *et* is no longer a direct object particle, but the signifier par excellence: the quality of an object that mediates its being known, and also, the expansive character by which any singular one "expands" to include the many. The untranslatable word *et* becomes arguably the most significant word in Genesis 1:1—and the key to Hirsch's method of unfolding the meaning of scripture out of scripture itself.

In explaining the meaning of *et* by reference to similar-sounding Hebrew words meaning a lever, handle, fire-rake, and the earth's moisture, Hirsch demonstrates the hermeneutic of *Lautverwandtschaft* ("phonetic relationship" in Levy). The word appears in the very first sentence of the Pentateuch commentary about the first word of the Torah, *Bereshit*, noting that it has a root *rosh* (beginning, head) that is a cognate with *ra'ash* (movement in space) and *rachash* (inner movement). Hirsch then deduces that *rosh* is the "organ" that controls inner and outer movement and that moreover, *bereshit* connotes temporal but never spatial beginning. He moves on to talk about creatio ex nihilo. His commentary on the second word, *bara*, begins the same way, with a list of five related cognate roots, "which all have the meaning of striving to get out, or getting out of a state of being constrained or bound, [and] give *bara* the underlying conception of bringing something out into the open"[86] (fig. 3.12).

Hirsch's commentary often claims that a word does not mean what it appears to mean. Though the Bible states that Adam was formed from the

בראשית א 4

und beide, Welt und Mensch, werden das höchste Ziel des Guten erreichen, für welches sie beide erschaffen; denn der Gott, der ihnen dieses Ziel gesteckt, hat sie beide für dieses Ziel mit seinem allmächtigen, durch nichts gehinderten, freien Willen geschaffen. Er hätte sie anders geschaffen, wenn dies dem von Ihm frei gesetzten Ziele förderlicher gewesen wäre. Eine Wahrheit, die wir uns immer wieder auf's neue im קדיש in's Bewußtsein rufen, in welchem wir die Überzeugung aussprechen, daß Sein großer Name sicherlich die von Ihm gewünschte „Anerkennung und Heiligung in einer Welt gewinnen werde, די ברא כרעותיה, die Er ja ganz nach seinem Willen für dieses Ziel geschaffen." In diesem Sinne gewinnen auch die Sätze der Weisen: בזכות ישראל בזכות משה בזכות חלה מעשר ובכורים נברא עולם die alle ראשית genannt werden, oder der Satz: ה"ב"ה היה מביט בתורה ובורא העולם ihre tiefe Begründung. Wenn Israel und Moscheh als ganz neue Anfänge einer ganz neuen Phase der Geschichtsentwickelung erscheinen und daher ראשית genannt werden, oder diesen Namen als erste Verwirklichung des mit der Menschenschöpfung vorgesetzten Ideals, gleichsam als Erstlinge der Gottesernte verdienen; wenn חלה מעשר ובכורים nichts als die Ausdrücke sind für die huldigende Zurückgabe der Welt an Gott, deren Spender; wenn vor allem das Gesetz der erste Baustein für den mit der Schöpfung und aus derselben zu erreichenden Gotteszweck ist und darum ראשית genannt wird: so waren alle diese, wenn gleich spät sich entwickelnden Ziele schon mit dem Beginn der Welt gesichert, eben weil diese בראשית geschaffen ist, ganz aus Gottes Händen hervorgegangen, somit von vorn herein für diese höchsten Ziele gebildet worden. Gott, heißt es, schaute in die תורה und schuf danach die Welt. Wir erkennen somit in diesem בראשית den Eckstein unseres Gott- und Welt- und Menschen-Bewußtseins und begreifen, wie, als dieses Bewußtsein geschwunden war und wieder neu aufgerichtet werden sollte, das freie, unumschränkte Schalten Gottes mit der Welt, ihren Stoffen, Kräften und Gesetzen, durch Wunder zu konstatieren war, die eben als נסים, hochaufgesteckte Merk- und Leitzeichen, uns zur Wiedergewinnung des Bewußtseins von der durch nichts gehinderten freien Allmacht Gottes führen sollten, ein Bewußtsein, das, wie angedeutet, die Vorbedingung alles sittlichen Menschenbewußtseins, somit die Vorbedingung unseres ganzen Verhaltens zur תורה bildet.

ברא. Die verwandten Wurzeln: פרע, פרא, פרח, ברה, ברח, die sämtlich ein Hinausstreben und Hinaustreten aus einer Innerlichkeit oder einer Gebundenheit bedeuten, ergeben für ברא ebenfalls den Begriff des Hinaussetzens in die Äußerlichkeit; heißt ja auch Chaldäisch ברא ohne weiteres das Draußenseiende, draußen. ברא ist somit das Äußerlichmachen eines bis dahin nur im Innern, im Geiste Vorhandengewesenen. Es ist jenes Schaffen, dem nichts anderes als der Gedanke und der Wille vorangegangen. Es ist das eigentliche יש מאין und wird daher nur von dem Schaffen Gottes gebraucht. Ehe die Welt ward, war sie nur als Gedanke in dem Geiste des Schöpfers — menschlich zu sprechen — vorhanden. Der Schöpfungsakt machte diesen Gedanken äußerlich, gab diesem Gedanken ein äußeres, konkretes Dasein. Die ganze Welt im ganzen und einzelnen ist somit nichts als verwirklichte Gottesgedanken. Eine Anschauung, der wir auch in der Betrachtung der Wurzel ה'יה, dem jüdischen Begriffe des Seins (siehe V. 2) wieder begegnen. — (Von dieser Bedeutung des Äußerlich-, Konkret-, Tastbarwerdens ward dann auch ברא zur Bezeichnung des Feist-, Korpulent-, Gesundseins und davon ברה, בריה, ברית zur Bezeichnung des ersten Mahles, des Anbisses, Frühstückes, das den Menschen wieder äußerlich gekräftigt hinstellt, ihn gleichsam wieder fest, konkret macht. Auch das וּבראתו, ובראת לך שם (Josua 17, 15, 18) dürfte sagen: schaffe dir dort Raum, daß du dich ausdehnen kannst. Oder es hängt mit dem chald. Begriff ברא, das Draußenseiende, das Freie, die Weite zusammen und heißt dann: mache dir den Wald zum freien Raum. וברא אותהן בחרבותם (Ezech. 23, 47) heißt wohl nicht durchbohren, sondern aufschlitzen,

Fig. 3.12. Hirsch Bible, commentary on *bara* (1903).

dust in the earth (*adama*), Hirsch proposes an alternative translation of Adam: representative (*Stellvertreter*). He insists that the name Adam does *not* relate to "the earth"—this would be demeaning to human nature—but rather, earth derives its name and identity from the human being.

How does the festival offering called Passover get its name? Didn't God "pass over" the houses of the Israelites in Egypt? Mendelssohn and others translate the verb *passach* as "stepping over." But Hirsch adds a strange adverb, "haltingly" (*zögernd*) slowing God down considerably. Exodus 12:27:

> JPS: you shall say, "it is the **passover sacrifice** to the LORD, because He **passed over** the Houses of the Israelites in Egypt."
>
> Hirsch/Levy: Ye shall say: It is **a meal of a haltingly-passing over salvation**, dedicated to *God*, Who **haltingly passed over** the houses of the children of Israel in Egypt.
>
> Hirsch: So sollt ihr sagen: **Ein Mahl zögernd hinüber schreitender Rettung** ist es, Gott geweiht, der über die Häuser der Söhne Israels in Mizrajim **zögernd hingeschritten.**

Hirsch explains his odd translation of *Pesach* in his commentary on the earlier verse (12:11), deriving the meaning "to limp" through recourse to his theories of phonetic affinities and interchanging letters.

> *Pesach* is related to *pasa,* to step, and even, as it seems from Isaiah 27:4, to step out vigorously, Chaldean *psa, psiya,* simply to step, a pace. If then, *pasach* is "to limp" and piseach is "lame," we seem to have here . . . another example of the [letter] *chet* indicating a restriction, a hindrance, of the idea which is expressed by the [letter] *ayin noach* and *noa, chala* and *alah* in the root. In any case, as *pasach* **quite definitely** means to limp, and *piseach* **equally definitely** means lame, *pasach,* is a restricted, slow, halting stepping along. *Pasach al* would accordingly mean "to step haltingly over something" . . . It was only slowly and haltingly that the danger passed away from over their heads (*pasach*). So press on, delay not to make yourselves deserving for it to do so (*b'hipazon* [in haste]).[87]

To summarize: within Hirsch's system of interchanging letters, *pasach* (ending with *chet*) must denote the opposite of *pasa* (ending with *ayin*), meaning "to step"—hence: to step haltingly. The homily that evolves out of God's limping is that the redemption of the Jews involves a slow transformation, whereby the Israelites made themselves worthy of being redeemed.[88]

Has the author successfully explained the Bible from within the Bible? That was Hirsch's goal, as described in the brief preface to his Pentateuch:

> To derive the explanation of the text from the words themselves; to arrive at this explanation [in German: *schöpfen* = to create] from the

> nuances of the particular expression used in each case; to derive the fundamental meaning of the words from the rich fund of linguistic explanations which we possess in our traditional writings; out of these traditional disquisitions of the biblical text, and the halachic and agadic explanations of them, to explore and establish the facts out of which the Jewish outlook on the world and on life has formed itself, and which, for all time, form the norms of Jewish life.[89]

Here and in subsequent passages, Hirsch's traditionalist rhetoric proves to lay the groundwork for a creative approach to Scripture and translation. He writes of the "uniform spirit which pervades the whole of the Torah" a spirit that is not of the "antiquated past" but of the "vivid present," which is the "hope of the future of all human efforts." Through translation, Scripture should become "a saving of light and understanding for all those that would earnestly gather its fruit" (für alle, *die mit Ernst aus ihr schöpfen*). The use of the verb *schöpfen*, to create, here and above (and mistranslated by Levy), captures Hirsch's position. Although a traditionalist by most standards, Hirsch was an immensely creative translator; as I have shown, he had no qualms about inflecting the German language to convey his idiosyncratic interpretations. On the level of word choice, the Hirsch Bible can be more startling than the Bible of Buber and Rosenzweig.

Hirsch was not the first to develop a theory of "interchanging consonants," or "homo-organic consonants."[90] Underlying it all was profoundly logocentric or theological view of Hebrew as a universal *Ursprache*, "sui generis, a unique and holy system bearing the imprint of the Divine."[91] A. H. Lesser suggests that Hirsch's view of language originates in German philosophy, but also draws from "Wordsworth's attitude to Nature as a moral teacher—and Hirsch had written a thesis on Wordsworth."[92] It is not an exaggeration to call his system a "pseudo-philology." But does it add up to a "total work of art"?[93]

More than any other translator did Hirsch claim to model translation on a preexistent Oral Torah, transmitted to Moses, to the rabbis, to the elite of every generation. In earlier generations, that defense served to anchor translational practice to rabbinic interpretation. But I argue that Hirsch used it to liberate himself as practitioner of translation. Hirsch rejected the conceptual premise of the first and second generations of translators: dynamic equivalence of Hebrew and German. The unit of translation once again became the word, rather than the verse or sentence. Even more radical, he conveyed that the written Bible *absolutely could not make sense* by comparing it to a secretary's shorthand notes.

> The *Torah shebichtav* [Written Torah] is to be to the *Torah sheb'al peh* [Oral Torah] in the relation of short notes on a full and extensive lecture on any scientific subject. For the student who has heard the whole lecture, short notes are quite sufficient to bring back afresh to his mind at any time the whole subject of the Lecture. . . . For those who had not heard the lecture from the Master, such notes would be completely useless. If they were to try to reconstruct the scientific contents of the lecture literally from such notes they would of necessity make many errors.[94]

Moses is not the author of the text, only a divine secretary, and "this book was to be given into the hands of those who were already informed in the Law." Luckily, biblical hermeneutics were contemporaneous with or given even earlier than the Written Torah. These *midot* (measures of meaning) are likewise of divine origin, as are Written and Oral Law. Still, it doesn't happen automatically; the oral must be "remembered" or "reproduced" from the written text, and Hirsch positions himself as the heir to this mnemonic mandate. In effect, to interpret was to perform an act of translation internal to the language of the Torah, in a sense, by uncovering the inner code within. Translation is not subsumed within interpretation, but to translate is to provide the key for interpretation.

In other words, the written text needs to be decoded, translated, and the grammar or alphabet is the Oral Torah. But even so, why did Hirsch need the system of the phonetic affinities, as a secondary grammar for drawing out the forgotten sense of the Bible? This aspect bespeaks an aesthetic sensibility.

HIRSCH VERSUS THE ORTHODOX BIBLE SOCIETY

The road taken by Hirsch was not the only option available to an Orthodox Rabbi who sought an alternative to Philippson's enormously successful *Bibelwerk*. Hirsch's modern Orthodox contemporaries took a different route in the name of "tradition."

Anonymous reviewers and well-known rabbis in Germany and Switzerland attacked Philippson. Rabbi Seligmann Bamberger brought a petition against him opposing his Bible and the Bible Society.[95] Philippson wrote many bitter replies to his critics, calling them "inner enemies" of Judaism for trying to "ban research about the Bible . . . chain us for all time to the dead letter, and the Bible itself to the Talmud, which interprets the Bible one hundred times over."[96] Philippson identified with the attacks on Mendelssohn's Bible: "How mild is our time! Mendelssohn's Pentateuch translation was officially burned in Fürth, in its time; people today just bring a piece of paper." The attacks came in response to Philippson's call to "Bible-loyal Israelites" to support the production of inexpensive Bibles, which led to the publication of 100,000 copies of his translation in stereotype format with revised translation and commentary (and without illustrations).[97] The Orthodox protested vociferously, to the point that they founded their own bible society, the Orthodoxe Israelitische Bibel-Anstalt, for the "distribution of inexpensive Bibles with Hebrew text and a God-fearing German translation."[98] The most eminent rabbis, including Ettlinger, Bamberger, Hildesheimer, and Lehmann headed the society. Lehmann diagnosed the "urgent need" in his newspaper *Der Israelit*, with a nuanced perspective on the state of the Bible industry as it looked to a modern Orthodox Jew in 1861.

Lehmann asserts—no surprise—that the Tanach is barely known in many Jewish circles, because there is (still!) no adequate Bible translation for "godfearing Israelites." Cost was a prime obstacle. He laments that inexpensive Christian missionary Bibles are everywhere in Jewish schools. He even blames the continued use of "inexpensive Hebrew and Judeo-German Bibles"—works that "overstep their limits," i.e., are not pure translations—confirming the ongoing popularity of these medieval Yiddish works such as the *Tsene-Rene*.

> *There exists thus far no Bible translation that a godfearing Israelite can place in the hands the uneducated, women, and children, without any scruples.* Of course, the translation cannot absorb into itself the entire treasure of tradition; of course, the translation *cannot overstep its limits and claim to render midrashic or halakhic moments that are leaning on the word of Scripture.* What we want to produce is a translation that never runs afoul of tradition, and that, whenever possible, *without doing violence to the language,* takes into account the traditional view, and there, where that is not possible, makes the case [for that view], supplementing, through a brief commentary (*kurzgefassten Kommentar*). *The fact that our enterprise is completely different than [that of] the famous Philippson, even if the latter is being purified of the greatest offenses, is obvious.* By beginning this enterprise, we are not driven by the idea of creating a Vulgate, i.e., an authorized translation of the Bible, from whose translation one may not deviate. *We are a long way away from placing constraints on free research,* insofar as that takes place within the boundaries of religious law. *We only want to remedy an urgent need of our time by producing a translation which renders the authentic, i.e.,*

traditional spirit of the biblical word, we want to have printed a correct biblical text, and want to make certain that the unfalsified word of God becomes easily accessible even to those without means.[99]

In 1861, the only translation named as a competing work was Philippson's Bible, already in its second edition. What is striking here is the call for an affordable translation for their time; not a new *Be'ur*, but something current, up-to-date, in line with modern research.

Hirsch refused to participate. Mordechai Breuer asserts that Hirsch regarded the new translation as too connected to Zunzian scholarship; moreover, Hirsch was already preparing his own Pentateuch translation with commentary, which likely also influenced his reaction.[100] The following comparison of two passages in these translations by Hirsch, Philippson, and the Orthodox Bible Society (OBS) makes the differences patently clear. Hirsch diverged from the other two in syntax (use of "and"), word choice, and Divine Naming. First, compare their versions of the creation of man in Genesis 2:7.

KJV: And the **Lord God** formed man *of* the **dust of the ground**, and breathed into his **nostrils** the breath of life; and man became a **living soul**.

IB: Und **der Ewige Gott** bildete den Menschen, **Staub vom Erdboden**, und blies in seine **Nase** Odem des Lebens; da ward der Mensch zu **belebtem Wesen**.

OBS: Und da bildete **der Ewige, Gott**, den Menschen, **Staub von dem Erdboden**, und er blies in seine **Nase** Odem des Lebens, und es ward der Mensch zu **beseeltem Lebenden**.[101]

But

Hirsch: Da bildete **G o t t** den Menschen, **Staub von dem Menschen-Boden**, und hauchte in sein **Antlitz** Odem des Lebens, und so ward der Mensch zu einer **lebendigen Persönlichkeit**.

Hirsch/Levy: Then *God* formed Man, dust of the [human-]ground and breathed into his countenance the breath of life, and so Man became a living personality.

Hirsch departs from the others in four respects.

(1) Instead of two names for God, he writes *G o t t*. The others retain Mendelssohn's *der Ewige* for "Lord."

(2) He replaces "nostrils" with "countenance" (*Antlitz*), most likely to avoid the anthropomorphism, though he justifies it by relating the Hebrew *af* (nose) to *aiv* (bud, shoot).[102]

(3) He invents a word *Menschen-boden* (human-ground) as a play on the common word for earth, *Erdboden*, thereby challenging the folk etymology linking *adama* (soil, earth) and *adam* (human). Translators faithful to the pun render the verse "human from the humus" (Alter). Hirsch flips the etymology to convey that rather than inanimate matter shaping the character of humans, humans shape the earth.

(4) By extension of (3), "living personality" challenges the idea that human being is in equal parts physis and spiritus; rather, "it was only the Breath of God which made it into a living individual. That is where the freedom, the immortality, the whole greatness of Man comes from."[103]

One further example shows why Hirsch would not buy into the project of the Orthodox Bible Society; it demonstrates that what they produced was a scholarly second-wave translation. The first words of Genesis 37:32 describe what Joseph's brothers did with his coat after throwing him in the pit: "They had the ornamented tunic taken to their father . . ." (JPS). This is a potentially problematic verse, because the Hebrew for "sent, had taken" (*vayishalchu*) has been read by some as "they tore it with a knife." Philippson, the OBS, and Hirsch each felt compelled to comment on this word in their notes. But these are very different notes.

IB: Dann schickten sie den farbigen Rock, und brachten ihn vor ihren Vater, indem sie sprachen:

IB (note): Radak gives the word "they sent" the meaning that they tore the coat with a sword (related to the similar root *shelach*), which is contrary to usage.[104]

OBS: Und sie schickten den bunten Rock und (die Boten) brachten (ihn) zu ihrem Vater.

OBS (note): According to some: and they cut through it, following an analogy of Job 36:12, in order to bemoan their claim that he had been destroyed by a wild beast.

Hirsch: . . . schickten den verbrämten Rock, ließen ihn zu ihrem Vater kommen und sagen . . .

Hirsch/Levy (note): They did not send the cloak direct from them, but had it sent from elsewhere, and then came to their father.

Philippson deserves credit for mentioning the counterinterpretation, citing the exegete Radak, even if he rejects it. The OBS's note takes the most scholarly approach, including the alternate rendering with reference to Job, and leaving the decision up to the reader. Hirsch could not admit any doubt about what a word meant in a given context; certainty about definition was his priority. This he had in common with Philippson.

The OBS Pentateuch appeared in 1873 and went through seven editions through 1913.

PHILIPPSON AND HIRSCH: MENORAH

A final example captures the opposing agendas that Hirsch and Philippson brought to the enterprise of biblical translation and commentary, but also a distinct formal similarity in their approaches, which, when juxtaposed, illuminate each other.

Both Philippson and Hirsch found immense significance in the tabernacle and sacrificial cult at the end of Exodus (chapter 25 and thereafter). Philippson incorporated a series of extraordinary pictures, one even occupying a full-page that illustrates the encampment of the Israelites in the desert surrounding the tent of meeting ("Das Heiligtum mit dem Lager Yisrael's in der Wüste," I: 450), and others of the altar with the cherubim, the table with the twelve loaves, the candelabra. Philippson begins by noting that he finds it very strange that so many commentators have interpreted these institutions symbolically, beginning with Philo, the Church fathers, Abarbanel, interpreting the tabernacle as a microcosm of the created universe, and the earth as a parallel, material universe to the heavens. He even quotes Plato's Timaeus. Leading away from this train of thought was Maimonides, and also the "moderns," Hess, Gesenius, Bolkter, and Winer, who fail to appreciate the imagistic character of the Temple rite. Philippson—in direct opposition to Hirsch—insists that the Holy Word does not connect nature and religion; rather, it insists on the clear delineation between reality and God, nature and religion.

When he arrives at the menorah (candelabra), he refers to the Arch of Titus, and begins to describe the measurements in detail. The ultimate point of the holy candelabra (*Leuchter*) is the "idea (*Gedanke*) that the light of knowledge (*Erkenntnis*) is an eternal light that is always awake and working, and will always drive and create blossoms and fruit on the tree of life, just as the Word of God, as bearer of *Erkenntnis*, always blossoms and ripens."

Oddly enough, a candelabra is the one and only one "illustration" in the Hirsch Bible—a candelabra of his own design. As if in direct conversation with Philippson, Hirsch uses only dots and Hebrew words to illustrate and at the same time eviscerate the illustration. The dots convey that this is not a material candelabra, but rather the Platonic form of the candelabra. Suffice it to say, Hirsch holds the view that the menorah in fact has only six, not seven arms—corresponding to the six types of wisdom that Isaiah receives from God, all of which he literally maps on to the candelabra.

This pair of menorahs (figs. 3.13 and 3.14) represents what Philippson and Hirsch have in common, as well as the great divide between these two third-wave translations.

The essence of the opposition is that between centripetal and centrifugal approaches to Torah. Philippson sought to magnify and popularize the Torah among Jews and among humanity. Hirsch was educated and immersed in arts and philosophy, yet he sought to insulate Torah and establish its ongoing relevance for Jewish observance. The Torah was no less grand, yet its innermost teaching had to be worked out through an esoteric science whose rules followed the written and spoken (rabbinic) codes of law, though to some extent, the rules were truly accessible only to him. At least, this is how Philippson and his heirs regarded Hirsch's legacy.

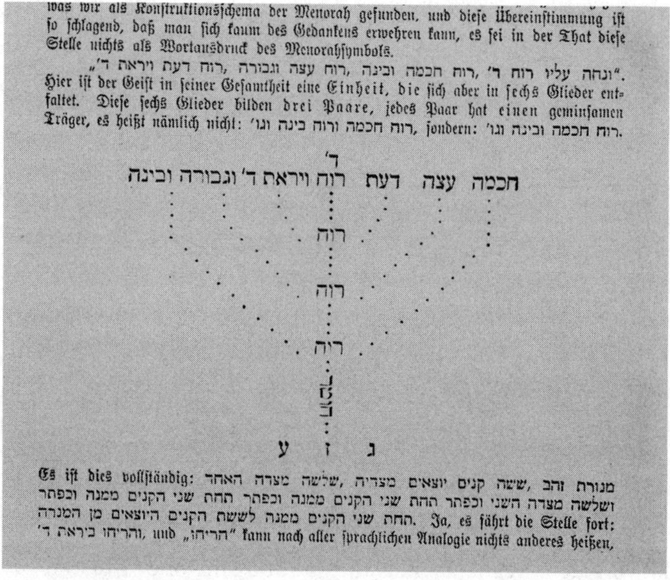
was wir als Konstruktionsschema der Menorah gefunden, und diese Übereinstimmung ist so schlagend, daß man sich kaum des Gedankens erwehren kann, es sei in der That diese Stelle nichts als Wortausdruck des Menorahsymbols.

"ונחה עליו רוח ד׳, רוח חכמה ובינה, רוח עצה וגבורה, רוח דעת ויראת ד׳". Hier ist der Geist in seiner Gesamtheit eine Einheit, die sich aber in sechs Glieder entfaltet. Diese sechs Glieder bilden drei Paare, jedes Paar hat einen gemeinsamen Träger, es heißt nämlich nicht: רוח חכמה ורוח בינה וגו׳, sondern: רוח חכמה ובינה וגו׳.

Es ist dies vollständig: מנורת זהב, ששה קנים יוצאים מצדיה, שלשה מצדה האחד ושלשה מצדה השני וכפתר תחת שני הקנים ממנה וכפתר תחת שני הקנים ממנה וכפתר תחת שני הקנים ממנה לששת הקנים היוצאים מן המנרה. Ja, es fährt die Stelle fort: והריחו ביראת ד׳, und „והריחו" kann nach aller sprachlichen Analogie nichts anderes heißen,

Fig. 3.13. Hirsch Bible, "Menorah" (1903).

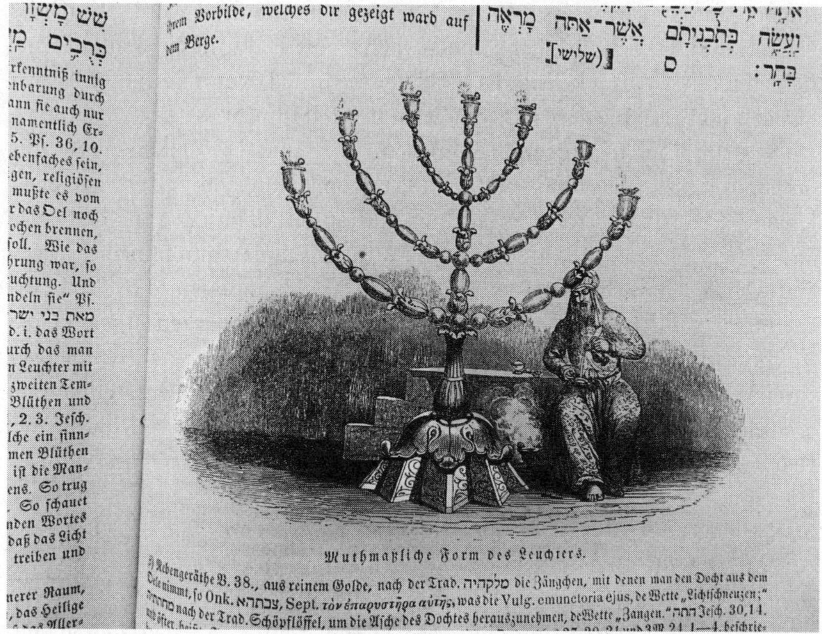

Fig. 3.14. Philippson Bible, "Menorah" (1858). Photograph: Harvard Divinity School, Andover-Harvard Theological Library (SCR 319 Philippson).

LEGACIES OF THE THIRD WAVE

In his obituary for his eighty-year-old colleague, the seventy-eight-year-old Dr. Ludwig Philippson commended Hirsch's efforts to "breathe new life into Orthodoxy" by arguing for the strict observance of *all* laws, customs, and rituals, and also by trying to resuscitate and "spiritualize" the commandments through symbol and allegory. It was a noble effort, though one that could not help but lead to "overstatements" (*Übertreibungen*) and "absurdities" (*Lächerlichkeiten*). According to Philippson's narrative, Hirsch waged the struggle on two fronts, first as a scholar, later as a rabbi. But Hirsch's writings (according to Philippson) had little impact beyond the community of his devotees, as would be the case with his later publications—his monthly periodical *Jeshurun* and his Bible translation and commentary. Ultimately, according to Philippson, advocating separatism and secession had a limited impact; Philippson is only aware of five communities that answered Hirsch's call. He concludes by noting that Hirsch was a formidable figure, memorable for his "zealous defense of his convictions," whose impact was, nevertheless, "limited."[105] Perhaps the final word, "limited," was unkind. Hirsch did many controversial things during his long life and fielded many an attack. Still, he would have turned over in his grave to hear himself memorialized as someone with limited impact.

Samson Raphael Hirsch is memorialized as one who staked everything on opposing *das Allgemein* and took every opportunity to oppose and challenge the efforts of reformers (such as Philippson) to broaden the relevance and appeal of Judaism. Alongside the critical scholarship, Hirsch's legacy and writings have been perpetuated in the Anglophone world by his heirs, the far-right Orthodox communities led by his descendants in London and in the United States—communities that became more right-wing over time.[106] It is surely a testament to his impact that Hirsch's Pentateuch with commentary is the only Bible described in this book that was published twice in *English* translation, first in a multivolume edition published in the UK, and then in the United States in Gertrude Hirschler's translation with an abridged commentary in the format of an American synagogue Bible.

Michael Meyer credits Ludwig Philippson with keeping the Reform movement unified, noting that he was "not a scholar-intellectual like Abraham Geiger or a radical like Samuel Holdheim," but rather "a talented publicist, man of the center, and inveterate optimist."[107] Tributes to Philippson often take an apologetic turn. In his centennial year 1913, Hermann Cohen called Philippson the great "media expert," but lamented his decision to turn his back on classical scholarship to become a popularizer of Judaism. The tenor of Philippson's reception can be summed in a 1989 tribute written on the one-hundredth anniversary of his death, subtitled "Ludwig Philippson—the 'Journalist' of Reform Judaism": "He took his stand as rabbi, preacher, journalist, writer, and popularizer; and as a fighter against prejudices and for equal rights, on the 'battlements of his time'—nothing more, but also, nothing less."[108] These interpretations do not do justice to the man's immense intellectual energy as evidenced in the *Israelitische Bibel.* He may not have followed the paths of Zunz, Gans, and Geiger, but he was more than a publicist. The *Bibelwerk* grew out of his knowledge, research, and imagination, applied single-mindedly to the cause of Jewish religious regeneration.

The Philippson Bible had its first afterlife as the "Doré Bible," as Philippson's translation was printed in the *Prachtbibel der Israeliten* along with illustrations by Gustave Doré (1832–83). The first Doré Bible was a French Bible published in 1866, with 230 illustrations.[109] Publisher Eduard Hallberger in Stuttgart saw the marketing potential and inserted Doré's illustrations into a Protestant, Catholic, and Jewish *Prachtausgabe*, or *Prachtbibel.* The

Old and New Testaments in Luther's translation appeared 1867–70 in two volumes, followed by the Catholic translation of Dr. Joseph Franz von Allioli with 230 Doré images in 1870, and, in 1874, the Jewish version with Philippson's translation and 154 illustrations.

But the Philippson Bible also became the Freud family Bible—a fact that has drawn new attention to the relationship between Sigmund Freud and his father, and also lent import to the Bible itself. When Jakob Freud began teaching his seven-year-old son Torah, his "textbook" was Ludwig Philippson's *Die israelitische Bibel.* In this volume, several of the figures are colored in, and there is every indication that Freud did the coloring. Freud mentions his own "deep fascination for the Philippson Bible" as a young reader in his *Autobiographical Study* (1925). He refers to it first in *The Interpretation of Dreams* (1900), when he recollects waking from an anxiety dream as young child and realizing that the scary people with birds' beaks carrying his mother had been "taken" (*entnommen*) from the illustrations in Philippson's Bible. In 1891, on the occasion of Freud's thirty-fifth birthday, his father presented him with a paperbound volume containing many fascicles from the first edition of the Philippson Bible (to which he had also subscribed), and a deeply personal handwritten Hebrew inscription. That Bible also contains a *Gedenkblatt*, a customary commemorative page upon which Jakob Freud had marked the death of his own father, the birth and circumcision of Sigmund, and lastly, the day upon which his son, "long may he live, got three teeth." Finally, for reasons unknown, Freud purchased his own three-volume Philippson Bible as an adult. Freud's editions of the Philippson Bible are precious palimpsests that, since the 1970s, have inspired research by biographers, psychoanalysts, cultural historians, and, most recently, historians of Freud's visual culture.[110] Meanwhile, the Philippson Bible has been revised and digitized in Germany, and it continues to be studied by historians and Bible scholars alike.

What are the common legacies of Philippson and Hirsch? It is not only that both rabbis used journalism and created new institutions to popularize their ideas and visions; they did those things in order to define and solidify their idiosyncratic middle positions. Both were conservative by temperament, averse both to older orthodoxy and to radical change. They took controversial stances that set them apart from their respective mainstream communities—Reform Judaism and neo-Orthodoxy. Philippson, like Hirsch, preached in German; he also introduced organ music into the sanctuary—a hallmark of Reform. He was mainly opposed to separatism. He liked totalities; he viewed Judaism as an organic corpus, each limb indispensable. Hirsch and Philippson thought big and acted expansively. They constructed vast all-encompassing conceptions of Judaism for their time, hoping to "promote" Jewish religious renewal (*Erbauung*), urging their followers to fix their vision on the forest rather than the trees. It was only the contents of their visions that differed. In Philippson's case, the forest was a grand vision of the Israelite nation evolving in history from an ancient *Volk* into a modern nation shaped by the nations of the world and serving as "light unto the nations." Hirsch's vision was no less grand. Each man used translation of Torah as a platform for making a persuasive rhetorical case for his vision.

The process of "translation as self-expansion" reached its apex with Philippson. The meaning of Torah expanded and expanded, until it could not take in even one more iota of knowledge, and suddenly the trend reverses dramatically—as if the Jews heeded Friedrich Nietzsche's critique in *The Uses and Disadvantages of History for Life*. Hirsch initiated the backlash, sealing the book, insisting that Torah was all that was needed to understand the Bible. Hirsch (neo-Orthodoxy), Buber and Rosenzweig (modernism), and Pappenheim (feminist Orthodoxy) had a far simpler understanding of Torah, one no less dependent on translation, but emphasizing the inward turn.

CHAPTER FOUR

The Fourth Wave: Reimagining the German Jewish Bible

WORKS DISCUSSED

Martin Buber and Franz Rosenzweig. *Die fünf Bücher der Weisung*[1] (The five books of instruction). Berlin: Schocken Verlag, 1925–27.

Bertha Pappenheim. *Zeenah u-Reenah: Frauenbibel: Bereschith. Übersetzung und Auslegung des Pentateuch von Jacob Ben Isaac aus Janow* (Women's Bible: Genesis). Frankfurt am Main: J. Kauffmann, 1930.

The Hebrew Bible itself is read as a translation—as a bad translation.
—Martin Buber

INTRODUCTION: REFRAMING THE HISTORY

The translators of the fourth wave gave up on the German Jewish Bible. They presented their efforts as a rupture with the tradition I have traced in this book; translation, as it had come to be known, was the problem they sought to remedy. Their translations would not be held to the criteria applied to translations during and after the Haskalah: clear, correct, and beautiful. Bible translation would not be a cultural activity, but nor would it be considered a religious one in the normal sense of the word, because, as Franz Rosenzweig wrote, "There is no 'religious sphere.'"[2] Where translators of prior epochs used translation to enhance or elevate the Torah, the translators of the fourth wave decried those efforts as shallow. Instead, they sought to elevate and enhance people's relationship to Scripture. Translation became a modern imperative, a *mitzvah*; they even dared to question the hierarchy of source and translation. When Rosenzweig wrote that it is the Bible's "destiny" (*Bestimmung*) to be translated and retranslated, he was not talking about Jewish history or even human history.[3] Buber and

Rosenzweig, and their older contemporary Bertha Pappenheim, were fierce religious renegades who broke with the mainstream with regard to translation, as on numerous other issues. Their aspirations were utopian and their methods paradoxical. They sought to untranslate the German Jewish Bible; to defamiliarize Torah in the extreme; to force modern people to see it with new eyes. They also produced groundbreaking translations before they turned to the Bible. Translation thus construed became a tool for redrawing the boundaries of the German Jewish *Kulturgut*, and for upending modern identity as such.

The translators' opposition to modern trends notwithstanding, the fourth wave was no less conditioned by history than were the other waves. Buber, Rosenzweig, and Pappenheim, like many other Jewish thinkers, artists, and activists of their generation, believed the obstacles to authentic Judaism in the early twentieth century to be as formidable as ever; perhaps they were right to think so. The internal pressures to define modern Jewish identity persisted, but the community also had to contend with the resurgence of anti-Semitism in the 1880s, the manifold crises of World War I, and Nazism. The solutions and strategies of the previous century and a half—Haskalah, Wissenschaft des Judentums, *Bildung*, historicism, religious reform, the rise of denominational Judaism—not only were no longer useful in the face of the "Jewish questions" of the twentieth century; these were themselves construed to be part of the problem. In response, German and Austrian Jewish intellectuals who had come of age in the late ninteenth century—Stefan Zweig's "golden age of security"—invented new political ideologies, avant-garde literary movements, experimental artistic forms, and radically new genres of social, religious, and philosophical thought. The context for the fourth wave is above all the fertile intersection of European and Jewish modernism: a world inhabited by Kafka and Agnon, Schnitzler and Peretz, Freud and Benjamin, Dvora Baron and Else Lasker-Schüler. In line with modernism's highly experimental character, the translations of the fourth wave differ in form and substance from those that came before, and also from one another. The striking difference between them corresponds to a divide in modernism itself. One on side, Buber and Rosenzweig—like Franz Kafka, Arnold Schönberg, Expressionist art, and Dada—devised something utterly new and alienating. On the other side, Pappenheim, akin to traditionalist modernists such as Hugo von Hofmannsthal, Hermann Broch, S. Y. Agnon, and Marcel Proust, reached deep down into the well of memory, history, and tradition. What these two modernist camps, as it were, have in common can be summed up with reference to the

Buberian notion of religiosity (*Religiosität*). Religion is preservative, and seeks to achieve many goals; religiosity is creative, with the singular goal of enhancing and imbuing rites and dogmas with new meanings, thereby serving the needs of a new generation. A comparison with Bertolt Brecht's conception of "epic theater" is not far-fetched. In contrast to dramatic theater, which fosters catharsis and complacency vis-à-vis the world beyond the theater, epic theater stimulates critical thinking and activism by tearing down the fourth wall and reaching out to viewers in their "contemporaneity," with the message that human beings change and the world too can be changed.[4]

In the last few decades, the story of the Buber-Rosenzweig Bible has been told many times.[5] Conceivably, they anticipated this kind of reception, since they left an extensive written record of their methods and goals. The translation's overall significance has become fixed over time, paradoxically endowing the project with a familiarity that is distinctly at odds with the translators' own view of Torah and their aspirations for the translation.[6] This reception history recalls that of Bertolt Brecht's *Threepenny Opera* in the 1920s, as bourgeois audiences applauded and cheered at performances of a theater play explicitly designed to mock them. What remains to be understood is exactly how Buber and Rosenzweig fit in to the history of German Jewish Bible translation—the lineage about which they said the least. Where they presented their approach as sui generis and unique, the affinities with the new Hebraism (chapter 2) suggest otherwise. Analyzing this project as part of the fourth wave brings out other surprising dimensions of a translation that was, after all, designed to surprise.

Pappenheim's translation poses the opposite challenge: to argue the significance of a work that has had no place in previous accounts of German Jewish Bible translation. In a photo from July 1934 with the caption "Lernwoche in Lehnitz" (week of learning in Lehnitz), Bertha Pappenheim sits on the sidelines as Martin Buber lectures (fig. 4.1). The scene represents the numerous educational programs offered by Buber, Ernst Simon, Pappenheim, and others under the Nazi regime. In 1934, Buber and Pappenheim had been intellectual acquaintances for eighteen years. They shared more than an educational mission; Pappenheim's translations were related to the Buber-Rosenzweig Bible in their ambitions and goals, and moreover, provide a new perspective on their efforts. Juxtaposed with Pappenheim's project, the Buber-Rosenzweig Bible seems less radical, less different in execution, than prior Bibles. Juxtaposed with the Buber-Rosenzweig Bible, Pappenheim's translations, which most write off as backward looking, acquire a progressive dimension. Finally, to

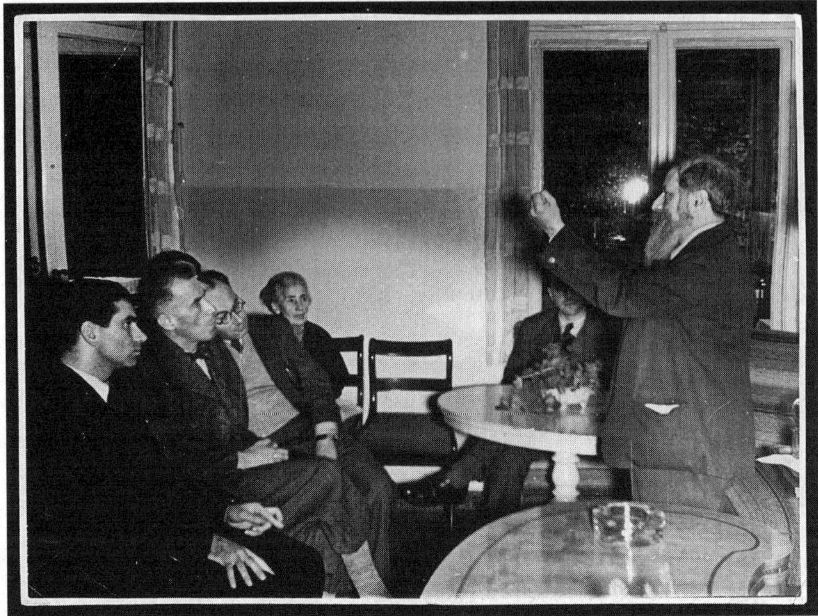

Fig. 4.1. Buber lecturing in Lehnitz ("Lernwoche in Lehnitz") (July 1934). Photography by Herbert Sonnenfeld. Martin Buber Archive (ARC Ms. Var. 350 series 350). Photograph: The National Library of Israel.

place Pappenheim's minor work as the second "bookend" lends the history of German Jewish Bible translation a whole a new frame.

A FRIENDSHIP IN LETTERS: BUBER AND PAPPENHEIM (1916–1936)

The fourth wave begins with Bertha Pappenheim's first letter to Martin Buber, 28 May 1916[7] (fig. 4.2).

> I don't know whether you know my name. I am a Jewish woman, an old woman with experience in social work, affiliated with Judaism and with Christian culture, who accepts and defends both the duties and the rights of that affiliation.

She was fifty-seven and he was thirty-eight. Both were Austrians by birth; both were then living in the environs of Frankfurt. Martin and Paula Buber had recently moved from Berlin to the small medieval town of Heppenheim,

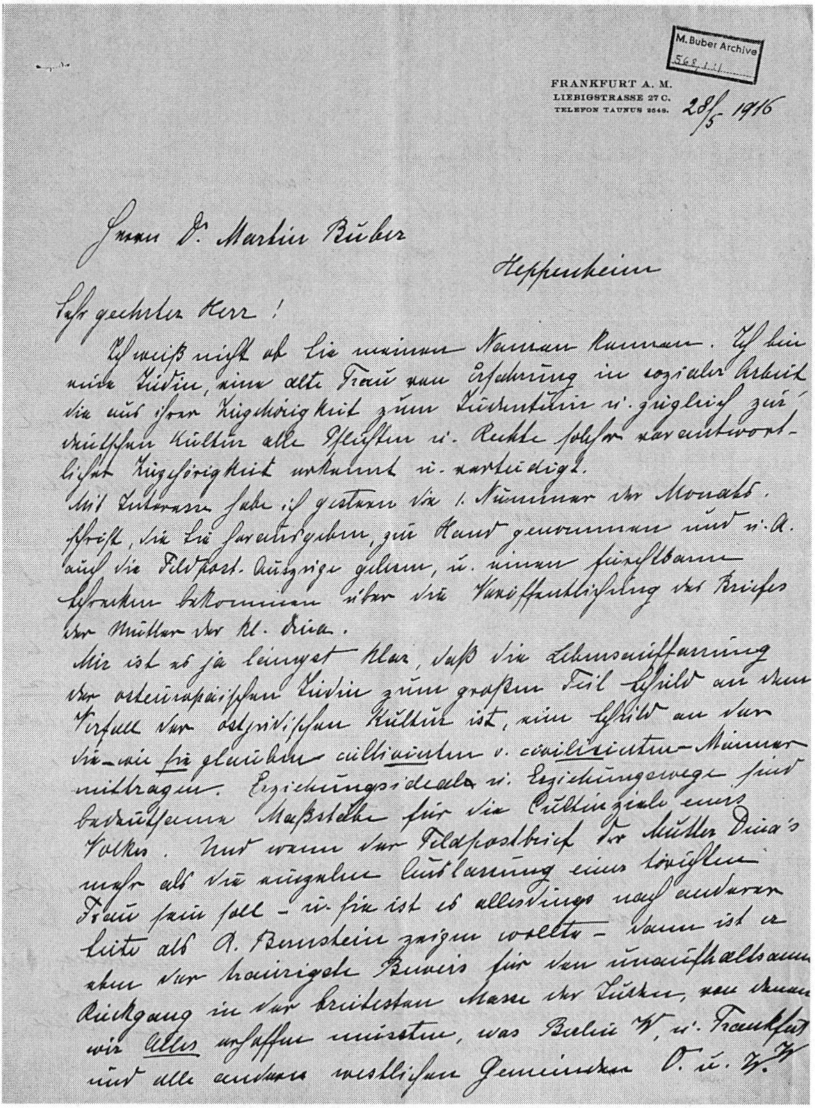

FRANKFURT A. M.
LIEBIGSTRASSE 27 C.
TELEFON TAUNUS 2549.

28/5 1916

Herrn Dr. Martin Buber

Heppenheim

Sehr geehrter Herr!

Ich weiß nicht ob Sie meinen Namen kennen. Ich bin eine Jüdin, eine alte Frau von Erfahrung in sozialer Arbeit die aus ihrer Zugehörigkeit zum Judentum u. zugleich zur deutschen Kultur alle Pflichten u. Rechte solcher verantwortlicher Zugehörigkeit erkennt u. verteidigt.

Mit Interesse habe ich gestern die 1. Nummer der Monatsschrift, die Sie herausgeben, zur Hand genommen und u. A. auch die Feldpost-Auszüge gelesen, u. einen furchtbaren Schrecken bekommen über die Veröffentlichung des Briefes der Mutter der kl. Dina.

Mir ist es ja längst klar, daß die Lebensauffassung der osteuropäischen Juden zum großen Teil Schuld an dem Verfall der ostjüdischen Kultur ist, eine Schuld an der sie – wie sie gleichen cultivierten u. civilisierten Männer mittragen. Erziehungsideale u. Erziehungswege sind bedeutsame Maßstäbe für die Kulturziele eines Volkes. Und wenn der Feldpostbrief der Mutter Dina's mehr als die einzelne Entladung einer törichten Frau sein soll – u. sie ist es allerdings nach anderer Seite als A. Bernstein zeigen wollte – dann ist er aber der traurigste Beweis für den unaufhaltsamen Rückgang in der breitesten Masse der Juden, von denen wir Alles erhoffen müssten, was Berlin W. u. Frankfurt und alle anderen westlichen Gemeinden O. u. W.

Fig. 4.2. Pappenheim's letter to Buber (28 May 1916). Martin Buber Archive (ARC Ms. Var. 350 series 350). Photograph: The National Library of Israel.

where they would live until 1938.[8] Pappenheim had resided since 1907 in Neu-Isenberg, outside of Frankfurt, where she would remain until her death in 1936.[9] With characteristic modesty, she introduced herself as "an old woman with experience in social work." With characteristic authority, she described her religious identity in un-Buberian terms as her *duties and rights*.

Pappenheim wrote in response to the inaugural issue of Buber's periodical *Der Jude: eine Monatschrift*.[10] It was not a fan letter. She wrote to complain about an article titled "Russian and Jewish *Feldpost*" (correspondence from the war zone). The article described a young Jewish girl named Dina as lazy, spoiled, and badly educated, even as her father was fighting on the Russian front. To Pappenheim, the story represented everything that was wrong with Jewish society, but above all, the "bad parenting and poor education" that she had witnessed firsthand during her travels in Eastern and Western Europe, in Berlin, London, and even Tel Aviv. "These Dinas are the downfall of our people," she wrote, exhorting him not to publicize such accounts to the non-Jewish world.[11] Buber's lead editorial challenged the Jewish community to prove their mettle in these terrible times. Pappenheim implored him to publish articles that would inspire such conduct. Though we don't have Buber's reply, we can infer from Pappenheim's second letter, dated two days later, that he had welcomed her critique and solicited further contributions to *Der Jude*. "You need not worry," she responded, "that I will exercise restraint (weakness) when the truth is what's needed—and truth is needed everywhere. I have only one tongue and only one pen." She concluded, "I would be happy if some kind of collaboration developed between us, at least as far as our conscience permits. I am an opponent of Zionism and, even more, of Zionists." Collaboration was nice, but principles were principles. These first letters shine light on Pappenheim's old-fashioned values, social activism, and critical temperament.

By 1916, Martin Buber was a prolific intellectual and well-known Jewish author. Who was this "old woman with experience in social work"? Bertha Pappenheim was born into a wealthy Orthodox Jewish family in Vienna in 1859. She entered history as the patient whom Josef Breuer and Sigmund Freud called Fräulein Anna O. in the first case history of their volume *Studies on Hysteria* (1895): a young woman suffering from hysterical symptoms in the wake of her father's illness and death, symptoms also "caused by a society that prevented educated women from using their talents and expertise in any meaningful way."[12] Her active role in her own "talking cure" led to her to be counted among the founders of psychotherapy. Pappenheim was hospitalized and given electroshock therapy. After moving with her mother Recha Goldschmidt to Frankfurt in 1888, she grew close to her mother's relatives, through whom she discovered the German woman's movement. A stint serving Galician refugees in a soup kitchen was the first chapter in what became an illustrious career as a social worker and pioneer. Her accomplishments as a founder and administrator of organizations—something she claims she never "intended" to become—are remarkable by any standard. She became a social and political activist who had founded a Woman's Welfare Association (Weibliche Fürsorge), as well as the Jewish Woman's Foundation (Jüdischer Frauenbund, or JFB), modelled on Catholic and Protestant women's foundations, to promote women's education and the reform of social work and charitable organizations. She founded a home for unwed mothers and their children (Heim des Jüdischen Frauenbundes), an un-modern Jewish residence for unmarried and pregnant women and their children, that she directed for thirty years, from 1907 until her death. If that weren't enough, Pappenheim also travelled extensively to the poorest Jewish communities all over the world, writing up reports about the dangers of poverty, laxity in Jewish education, and especially white slavery.[13]

Pappenheim's biographers have examined her contributions to psychoanalysis at very great length, and historians of German Jewish women and German feminism have likewise documented her extensive contributions as a social worker. New editions of many writings have recently appeared, as well as English translations; biographers, scholars, and artists (in both German and English) continue to be fascinated by her life story and extensive oeuvre.[14] But only recently has this pioneering figure begun to be appreciated as an intellectual, not only as an "author and activist," but as a Jewish thinker in her own right. Pappenheim was also a prolific writer in many genres: essays, fiction, drama, journalism, *Denkzettel* (short meditation), travel writing, and translation. She began publishing literature under the pseudonyms Paul Berthold and P. Berthold; even when she wrote under her own name, many writings were circulated only to friends and colleagues. Another type of writing she practiced might be called creative imitation, parable, or midrash. After 1922, she wrote increasingly in a religious vein, composing meditations and prayers; a new bilingual German-English edition of Pappenheim's prayers, edited by two women rabbis, was published in Germany in 2003.[15]

Pappenheim remained an observant Jew throughout her life. She called herself Orthodox "by birth and upbringing," and she never repudiated Orthodoxy, even as she challenged the Jewish community's exclusion and deprecation of women throughout history and in her own time, and advocated for equal rights and women's suffrage (instituted by the new German government of the Weimar Republic in 1918). She served together with Rabbi

Nehemiah Nobel on the commission set up by the board of the Frankfurt Jewish Community to draft a new community constitution, and she counted as one of her most important accomplishments that she convinced Rabbi Nobel—alone of all the Orthodox Rabbis—to support active voting rights for women within the *Gemeinde*.[16] She was also a life-long advocate on behalf of *agunot*, Jewish women unable to obtain a divorce. But it was social work—in the broadest sense—that she regarded as the Jewish mission par excellence and a direct extension of *Nächstenliebe*, the commandment to love the "near one" from Leviticus 19:18.[17] As early as 1897, in an article titled "The Question of Women's Rights and Careers for Women in Judaism," Pappenheim (as P. Berthold) urged upper-class women to work on behalf of others.[18] To be a liberated, educated women entailed "rights and duties." The obligations to help the needy and fight for social justice represented the core of Pappenheim's Torah.

With all her accomplishments, Pappenheim approached Buber as an uneducated Jewish woman, on behalf of others like herself. She read his work faithfully and aspired to learn from him. In her letter of 6 May 1918, she asked him to send her something on Judaism that she could study with her five young workers at the home—nothing "difficult or philosophical." She later thanked him for sending "intellectual nourishment, thankfully unrationed." But one detects something more in these letters: Buber's writings pushed her to develop her own Jewish worldview. Many letters begin with gratitude and end with disagreement. A striking example is another 1918 letter responding to Buber's seminal *Three Lectures on Judaism* (*Drei Reden über das Judentum*). Pappenheim upends her praise with this critique:

> Because if I don't understand so much of this, the girls also won't understand it, and I won't be able to answer their questions, because I have the same questions. . . . For something that is so self-evident, does one really require such a large scholarly apparatus, so many words and things that are unfamiliar to a woman like me, and to thousands of other Jewish women?[19]

Over the course of the correspondence, Pappenheim took issue with Buber for three main reasons: his ideas and writings were too abstruse for uneducated people; he was too lenient, too tolerant; and he was not enough of a feminist. These differences between them crystallized in a fascinating disagreement, carried on over many years, about how to interpret the commandment "Love your near one as yourself" (Lev. 19:18).[20] In another letter from 1918, Pappenheim proposes that this commandment, together with the Ten Commandments, constituted the "social thought" (*der soziale Gedanke*) that formed the essence of Judaism—not Zionism, not philosophical ideas—and that moreover, women have a more "severe" view of love than men:

> I read the commandment of loving thy neighbor to my children in a similar way you have explained it to me. But there is more to it: the hate of that which is not worthy of love. . . . it may seem strange that a man should proclaim leniency and a woman demand severity. And yet it is quite simple: a woman's love is far more all-embracing. She is to be the creator, or at least shaper, of life, transcending pain and woe. She has to bring forth the *re'a*, [neighbor], or at least shape him in inexhaustible love; she has to guide him, admonish him, purposefully develop divine seeds—hard, rigorous work. Destiny.[21]

And on the following day:

> Dear Professor Buber, in all modesty, I must confess that I don't understand the book you sent me. Probably I did not even understand your preface, and I was responding to something that you didn't even say—. . . . But I cannot understand why one should package concepts that should belong to everyone, even to many unintelligent ones, the highest and the nearest, to the point where they become as cold as ice and recede farther and farther from us and take our life from us. I believe in loving the best and the nearest, just as I hate their adversaries and opponents, every day, every hour! I would like to make this love and this hate accessible to all—to implant it. That is [what I call] "loving the near one," an educational goal with many pedagogies.[22]

The letter continues,

> Probably you will not suffer my inadequate [illegible word] and you'll snicker. But I refuse to allow that which is so simple, so true, so satisfying, to become so complicated.
>
> Perhaps I find so much to be simple and self-evident in the course of my life because I am so alone and always have been, with no one, no "near one" to complicate my existence.

In fact, Pappenheim's insistence on "severe" and "simple truths" finds clear parallels in the thought and praxis of both Buber and Rosenzweig. Pappenheim sought to educate and be educated, but the lessons had to be simple: follow the Ten Commandments and love those who are nearest—"an educational goal with many pedagogies." Love, if serious, also entails hate. Lastly, women, especially unmarried and childless woman, cannot help but see the world differently than men. Pappenheim associated femininity with rigor and discipline; justice, not mercy. She wanted her tombstone to read "Sie war streng" (she was strict); instead, her tombstone has a verse from Psalms 113:9, "He makes the barren woman to keep house, and to be a joyful mother of children."

It does not appear that Pappenheim ever did contribute to *Der Jude*, though she published widely in the German Jewish press, in pedagogical and feminist periodicals. But the surviving letters confirm that many forms of collaboration did develop, and that despite philosophical and ideological differences, mutual admiration and a strong kinship arose. Buber has been called Pappenheim's "closest male friend," but not much is known about the friendship. The letters testify to a serious intellectual dialogue, with regular exchanges of writings and books and occasional visits. In 1922, Pappenheim sent Buber a story titled "Another Story about the Baal Shem"; she had evidently read his anthology *Legends of the Baal Shem* and added one of her own.[23] In 1929, she asks him to recommend someone who could check over her translation from Yiddish.[24] In 1933, Buber had his publisher send her a copy of the Buber-Rosenzweig Bible, and in 1936, the Psalms (1936); Pappenheim replied, "My soul chuckled when I received the book."[25] The two crossed paths in Franz Rosenzweig's famous Center for Adult Jewish Education, the Freies Jüdische Lehrhaus. Rosenzweig invited Pappenheim and her assistant Hannah Karminski to lecture in 1921, and in 1923 she agreed to lead a working group on her research on *The Memoirs of Glückel of Hameln*. Buber was lecturing in those years as well. She became a regular auditor at the Lehrhaus, and led a second seminar on social work in 1933. From that fateful year forward, Buber and Pappenheim became not only "spiritual resisters" to Nazism, but educational and intellectual resisters, establishing a network of teachers and schools for Jewish children and adults across Germany. In a letter of 1935, Pappenheim thanked Buber for the "intellectual stroll" and expresses pleasure that he and his "better half" had finally visited the women's home she founded and directed.[26] Between 1933 and 1936 Pappenheim's letters to Buber reveal a deepening religiosity. Hannah Karminski reports that in her final days, she spoke fondly of "Professor Buber."[27] When she died, his obituary paid her the ultimate compliment, calling her "a female Moses." He also wrote, "I didn't just admire her as a representative of the true passion of the mind, a type that is growing ever rarer. I loved her and I will remember her with fondness for the rest of my life."[28]

These excerpts allow us to conjure other lively exchanges, in person and in letters, over a twenty-year friendship. We know they communicated about essential religious topics, personal and philosophical, and that his works inspired both criticism and imitation. At one point she observed that she was Buber's "near one," the one whom he had lovingly guided, admonished, and cultivated. Did Pappenheim's philosophy of "loving the near one" develop in response to Buber's philosophy of dialogue? Was her translation project undertaken in dialogue with Buber's own? In eulogizing her as a female Moses, Buber understood that Pappenheim's life and work were shaped by a vision of Torah. Like both Buber and Rosenzweig, she spurned the legacies of the Haskalah, of traditional and liberal Judaism; diagnosed the acute crises of her time; and responded to them as a thinker, educator "with many pedagogies," and translator.

EDUCATORS WITH MANY PEDAGOGIES: BUBER, PAPPENHEIM, ROSENZWEIG

> The Students of the Maggid of Mezritch did not visit him in order to hear him say Torah, but rather to watch the way in which he laced and unlaced his boots.
> —Martin Buber, *Tales of the Hasidim*[29]

> A new "learning" is about to be born—rather, it has been born.
> —Franz Rosenzweig, "Upon Opening the Jüdisches Lehrhaus"[30]

If one were to identify the most important commitment shared by Buber, Rosenzweig, and Pappenheim, it would be education in the sense of *Erziehung*. Unlike *Bildung*, a term associated with the age of Idealism and with cognitive learning, and *Erbauung*, moral or religious edification, *Erziehung* connotes good upbringing; the education of the social self, the forging of social identity, often with an emancipatory aspect.[31] Martha Friedenthal-Haase describes Buber's view of education as the key to "identity-formation, deep-seated regeneration, and transformation,"[32] and the same could be said of Pappenheim's ideas. These three educators, *Erzieher*, taught adults as well as children, founded schools and educational organizations, developed pedagogies and curricula, and reached out to the disenfranchised, striving to bridge the hiatus between intellectuals and laypeople. Pappenheim had no formal education, having grown up in a land where women were not admitted to universities until 1895. But all three shared an antipathy for Wissenschaft and devoted themselves to popular education through pamphlets, lectures, conference papers, essays, letters, fiction, anthologies, translations—and face-to-face teaching. Torah lay at the core of any concept of Jewish education; like the maggid in the Hasidic tale from Buber's anthology, they did not strive to say Torah, but to be Torah: to live their teachings and to educate through experience.

Buber and Pappenheim developed philosophies of education that favored experiential learning. His lectures on Judaism were a wake-up call to the young generation. The philosophy of Buber's *I and Thou*, written during the years of close friendship with Franz Rosenzweig and work in the Lehrhaus, became a basis for pedagogy, and his writings on education from before and after the war are voluminous. If anything, his teaching style in the Lehrhaus was criticized as too "student-centered." His many efforts in adult education in Germany and in Israel, as well as in other countries, have been well documented.[33] Pappenheim's philosophy was shaped in part by the German feminism of Helene Lange and Gertrud Bäumer, and specifically by other moderate (religious) feminists who made female education a central goal.[34] Many believed that the parent-child (mother-child) relationship—not a one-directional experience, but one of mutual nurturing, learning, and teaching—provided the best model of instinctual, nurturing education. The experience of being denied an education as a young girl in Vienna was certainly formative in Pappenheim's case. She railed against the "mental abstinence" traditional Jewish life enforced on women, but she was also convinced that the modern Jewish movements, Haskalah and emancipation, had left women behind, and that neither the Reformers nor the Zionists cared about education or family life. She blamed women and men equally for the decline of religious values and standards in the community. In her essay "Die jüdische Frau," she laments:

> Since the influence of the one and only Jewish educator and pedagogue, Moses, with his succinct commandments, has lost the force of law in the lives of Jews, the ethical atmosphere of Jews has dissolved. There is no *Erziehung*, there are no more *Erzieher*. Every bad habit, every misbehavior, every bad custom, every idiocy, every loss of inhibition, every tastelessness and inaction, every lack of character, is explained away through history or psychology; the explanation then becomes an excuse. Tradition is not erected as an obligation, but rather as a cowardly and comfortable backdrop or scenery. There are no demands made, not on men, not on women, not on men and women, not on children or youth, whom we miseducate (*verziehen*) rather than educate (*erziehen*).[35]

There is nothing warm and fuzzy about Pappenheim's concept of education: it goes hand in hand with "rights and duties," with *Verpflichtung*, obligation, and *Forderungen*, the demands on men, women, on youth and children. Pappenheim had no tolerance for the tendency of modern liberal religion to erode the hard edge of the commandments.

Buber and Pappenheim believed education to be the ultimate tool of Jewish renewal and survival, and they went to extraordinary lengths to make it so. Their extraordinary commitments to education are exemplified by Buber's work as coordinator of Jewish education across Germany from 1933 to 1938, and by Pappenheim's work as founder and director of a home for unwed mothers and their children. In both instances, they stretched the task of the educator to almost unimaginable bounds.

In 1933, Buber resigned his professorship at the University of Frankfurt before it was taken from him, and he took over the coordination of the Mittelstelle für jüdische Erwachsenbildung set up by Rabbi Leo Baeck's Reichsvertretung der deutschen Juden. The *Mittelstelle* opened centers for adult education throughout Germany, and set up what has been called a "traveling university," with prepackaged curricula in bible, history, sociology, philosophy, economics, and pedagogy and a staff of teachers, among them Ernst Simon, Alfred Kantorowicz, Abraham Heschel, and Karl Adler, who took these courses on the road to communities across the country. Buber describes the mandate of Jewish education in a time of crisis in article titled "The Children" of 1933:

> The children are experiencing what is happening, and are silent. But at night they awaken from their nightmares and stare into the darkness. The world has become so uncertain and untrustworthy. . . . What happened? No one seems completely competent to answer the child. Parents, educators—how can we help our children? Parents—you cannot dismiss the child with a mere verbal explanation. . . . However, you can conduct yourself in a way that may help your child. You can translate Jewish values into Jewish living. You can study our language-rich lore, Hebrew, and our heroic history . . . Nay, study is not enough, it must become part of our daily living . . . Teach your children Jewish values! Make your lives Jewish! Begin with yourselves—and your children will follow.[36]

Buber's work during this time is often framed as spiritual resistance to Nazism. This phrase, together with "inner immigration," has also been applied to Pappenheim's activities after 1933. I believe Buber and Pappenheim saw the crisis of the 1930s as an opportunity to redouble educational efforts already long underway.[37] In a short essay from 1933 titled "The Individual and the Community," Pappenheim admonishes the community to renew the bonds of family, religious life, Sabbath and holiday observances, to rededicate themselves to good books, music, art, nature, and above all, to the core value of "placing oneself in the service of the near one," concluding, "for this too, our time will find the proper forms."[38] The appeal to bridge Jewish learning and Jewish living was the guiding premise of the *Erziehungsgemeinschaft* (educational community) or *Erziehungsheim* Pappenheim founded in 1907 in Neu-Isenberg. The home was part orphanage, part reform school, part kibbutz; financed by her mother's family, the house itself had been donated and funded by the Rothschilds. Unwed mothers and their children lived in a community organized around Jewish values and also educational principles. There was an "unsentimental" emphasis on formal routines, daily chores, schooling, and religious observance. Every hour of the day was structured. The home had a spartan character, to discourage frivolity and promiscuity.

> In place of intimacy, love, and personal attention to the child, [she] valued creation of a just community, education, discipline, manners. [There was] strict regulation of hygiene, table manners . . . training young people to do chores . . . washing, ironing, knitting, cooking, darning. Music lessons, theater, lectures, reading out loud, storytelling on Shabbat, fine handcrafts.[39]

Shabbat and Jewish holidays were not just observed but celebrated joyfully, even in the final weeks of Pappenheim's life.[40] Pappenheim believed that rituals were the most powerful teaching tools. At meals, food blessings and Grace after Meals were recited and boys wore *kippot*. The children attended the local *Volksschule*, and a rabbi visited to provide religious instruction and Hebrew classes. One could say that Pappenheim was less the director of this mini–Jewish community than its rabbi. Over one thousand young residents lived in the home in the first thirty years: 252 pregnant women or mothers; 374 nursing babies; 441 small children; 199 schoolchildren; 399 young women.

Franz Rosenzweig only makes one reference to Bertha Pappenheim in his published correspondence, referring to her as a *Kratzbürste* (scratchbrush) while granting that the weight of her strong opinions and "prejudices against everything" did not impede her "aviatorial" powers.[41] Rosenzweig also valued traditional Jewish observance and a return to the sources. Though an explication of the philosophical basis of these values lies beyond the scope of this book, Rosenzweig's efforts to forge new forms of Jewish education over and against the available options—the university, Wissenschaft des Judentums—are essential parts of the picture. "'Learning'—the old form of maintaining the relationship between life and the book—has failed."[42] Rosenzweig found reason to praise the type of learning that took place in the *heder*, an institution much maligned by the Maskilim: "In its actual effect it corresponds much more to the ideal of an educational institution than any Western European school. The latter turns out fragmented human beings, disoriented and incapable of orientation; through the *heder* a nation constantly rejuvenates itself."[43] The singular goal of a Jewish education had to be living Judaism—a goal not yet met, in his view, by the likes of Mendelssohn, Zunz, Philippson, or Hirsch.[44] The Freies Jüdisches Lehrhaus in Frankfurt, which Rosenzweig helped found in 1920 and headed until his death in 1929, embodied his understanding of how his assimilated contemporaries, sophisticated in all areas yet ignorant of Jewish sources, might be reached through "a new sort of learning. A learning for which—in these days—he is the most apt who brings with him the maximum of what is alien."[45] Moreover: "There is no one today who is not alienated, or who does not contain within himself some small fraction of alienation."[46] How does that work? In his famous speech celebrating the opening of the Lehrhaus, Rosenzweig advocated "learning in reverse order. A learning that no longer starts from the Torah and leads into life, but the other way around: from life, from a world that knows nothing of the Law, or pretends to know nothing, back to the Torah."

Can it be said that these three educators shared a vision of Judaism and Jewish identity? There was distinct overlap among their respective agendas. For each one, *Erziehung* was an extension of a Jewish ethical and theological vision. It was a Jewish imperative but also a universal vision that transcended confessions. Each developed a philosophy of education in conjunction with current trends in German social thought and religious life, including religious feminism.[47] Second, they were, to use Rosenzweig's phrases, *Golusjuden* (exile Jews), *Deutschjuden*; they lived the German Jewish symbiosis. Third, they aspired to shake up the Jewish establishment by creating new (and always controversial) forms and institutions through which to disseminate Jewish knowledge, values, and culture. As Jewish leaders, they were in equal parts prophets and priests, Jeremiahs and Moseses. In a prayer she composed in 1933, Pappenheim echoed Jeremiah: "People have struck and hurt me many times—what does it matter? / Let me pick myself up so that I may take the only road—the way of kings . . . / Let me continue to speak and to say the truth."[48] Rosenzweig called the prophet the one who lives in the present—as the present must subsume, rather than serve, the past and the future. (In his Bible translation, Buber did not want to translate the

Hebrew *navi* with the German *Prophet* as too future-oriented, opting for an old-fashioned *Künder* [herald]). A tribute to Buber from 1953 echoes this idea: "He is not a prophet, but a student of the prophets. He did not invent his message, nor is he merely its medium or instrument. . . . One should rather refer to him as a translator—that would be the appropriate category. He translated his message for us into the idiom and the spiritual reality of our age."[49] It was their indefatigable Mosaic passion that drove Buber, Rosenzweig, and Pappenheim to become translators in more than just the figurative sense.

ROSENZWEIG AND JEHUDA HALEVI: FIRST STEPS TO TRANSLATION

Franz Rosenzweig took up translation after philosophy.[50] Even more so than for Mendelssohn was Jehuda Halevi's Hebrew poetry a major stepping stone to Bible translation. Recall that Mendelssohn reprinted his previously published German translation of Halevi's most famous poem, the sixty-eight-line rhymed "Ode to Zion" ("Tzion Ha'lo Tishali") in the prospectus for the *Be'ur*, both to advertise his competence as a Hebrew-German translator and to celebrate the very existence of postbiblical Jewish poetry.

Approximately midway between the 1780s and the 1920s, Halevi's complete poetic corpus was published and rapidly translated into German.[51] Halevi was a kind of Jewish Goethe; he was the most famous of the Sephardic poets who captivated Christian Hebraists, as well as Jewish scholars of Wissenschaft des Judentums who regarded medieval Spanish-Hebrew poems and *piyyutim* (liturgical poems) as far superior to native Ashkenazi hymns. By 1920 there were seventeen different German translations of the "Ode to Zion." Rosenzweig's intensive engagement with the poet had many facets, one of which was the use of translation to counteract this enormous cultural trend. He published translations of close to one hundred of Halevi's difficult Hebrew poems into German, dedicating the volume to Martin Buber.

Rosenzweig discovered Halevi while translating liturgical texts for Sabbath, such as the Grace after Meals, for houseguests who didn't know Hebrew.[52] Letters testify that he struggled to capture the tone, the *niggun* or melody, in German, and came to acknowledge that his German vocabulary, shaped by Luther and the hymns of Friedrich Hölderlin, was Christian.[53] Rosenzweig began consulting with Buber on translational matters. The exchanges of two thinkers both so deeply committed to *Verdeutschung*, to expressing the Hebraic genius in German, laid the groundwork for a collaborative translation of the Hebrew Bible.[54] But first, Rosenzweig published

The Hymns and Poems of Jehuda Halevi (1924) with sixty poems and an afterword, reissued in 1927 with ninety-two poems.[55] This second edition, *Zweiundneunzig Hymnen und Gedichte* (published by Lambert Schneider, who also initiated the Bible translation), is a large volume that includes the poems in German (but no Hebrew originals), detailed notes, and a mistitled "afterword," oddly sandwiched between the poems and the notes rather than after them.[56] Rosenzweig's notes were not for philological clarification or historical context; they provide rather a running philosophical meditation on the poems' themes.[57] Similarly, the afterword—arguably the most famous part of the book today—reads as though written to be anthologized alongside essays of Luther, Schleiermacher and Goethe. Much work remains to be done on the collection as a whole.[58] What did it mean to translate Halevi after Mendelssohn and so many others? Furthermore, how did these translations of poetry shape Rosenzweig's approach to translating the Bible?

To understand Rosenzweig's rupture with Mendelssohn, one need only compare their two versions of the first eight lines of the "Ode to Zion" (fig. 4.3). The fulcrum of Rosenzweig's version are two words found in the very first line: "Joch tragen" (to bear a yoke). *Joch* signals the subjection to form, rhyme, and meter; *tragen* initiates the poem's dominant rhyme scheme.

An Zion (Franz Rosenzweig)
Zion! Nicht fragst Du den Deinen nach, die Joch tragen,
    Rest deiner Herden, die doch nach Dir allein fragen?
West, Ost und Nordsturm und Süd,—o laß von ihnen den Gruß
    Dessen, der fern ist und nah, von ringsher Dir sagen.
Gruß des, den Sehnsucht umstrickt, des Träne wie Hermons Tau;
    O sänk' auch sie hinab zu Deinen Berghagen.
Wein ich dein Leid, Schakal werd ich; träum ich Dich fronbefreit,
    Bin ich die Harfe, zu Deinen Liedern zu schlagen.

The central point is that whereas Mendelssohn used translation to flaunt his own powers of language and imagination—expanding these eight lines into seventeen—Rosenzweig's fit the poem back into its original, rigorous mold of thirty-four distichs alternating thirteen and fourteen syllables, masculine and feminine cadences. The approach to form was justified as a condition of the address to "Zion!," and indeed the apostrophe holds the key to the rhyme scheme. Why is this so? Thirty-four of the sixty-eight lines of "An Zion" share the end-rhyme of line 1: in German, this suffix is *-agen*, and Rosenzweig faithfully rhymes line 1 and all of the even-numbered lines: *tragen, fragen, sagen, Berghagen, schlagen*. In Hebrew, the suffix is *-rayich*,

AN ZION

Zion! nicht fragst Du den Deinen nach, die Joch tragen,
Rest Deiner Herden, die doch nach Dir allein fragen?
West, Ost und Nordsturm und Süd, – o laß von ihnen den Gruß
Dessen, der fern ist und nah, von ringsher Dir sagen.
Gruß des, den Sehnsucht umstrickt, des Träne wie Hermons Tau;
O sänk' auch sie doch hinab zu Deinen Berghagen.
Wein ich dein Leid, Schakal werd ich; träum ich Dich fronbefreit,
Bin ich die Harfe, zu Deinen Liedern zu schlagen.
Nach Machanajim, nach Bethel, Pniel hindrängt mein Herz,
Und wo die Deinen noch sonst der Gottesschau pflagen.
Hier kam der Höchste zu Dir herab; und der Dich erschuf,
Brach Deine Tore gemäß den Himmelstor-Lagen.
Und Gottes Lichtglanz umstrahlte Dich, – wie konnten da noch
Sonne und Mond und der Sterne Lichter Dir tagen?
Wie könnt die Seel' ich da auszugießen, wo Gottes Geist
Auf Deine Großen sich goß – wie könnt ich wohl zagen.
Königspalast Du, du Gottesthron, wie dürfen des Knechts
Enkel, zu sitzen auf Deiner Herren Thron, wagen.
O trüge dort mich der Fuß, wo Deinen Sendboten Gott,
Deinen Propheten er Antwort gab auf ihr Fragen.
O hätt ich Flügel, wie wollt ich, mein zerrissenes Herz
In Deinen Rissen zu bergen, hin zu Dir jagen.
Aufs Antlitz sänk ich, auf Deinen Boden, und Dein Gestein
Herzt ich, und liebkoste Deinen Staub mit Wehklagen;

Fig. 4.3. Rosenzweig, "An Zion" ("Ode to Zion"). From *Jehuda Halevi: Zweiundneunzig Hymnen und Gedichte* (Berlin: Verlag Lambert Schneider, 1927).

where *r* belongs to the root of the Hebrew word and *-ayich* means "your," so: *asirayich, adarayich, avarayich, hararayich, shirayich*. Because each rhyme word contains "you" or "your" within it, the rhyme (and the second-person address), as Rosenzweig says, is not the "grout" but the "building material itself."[59] Rosenzweig also captures the alliteration and rhythm of the

Hebrew. The first couplet contains a chiasm: *fragen (nicht) nach* and *nach . . . fragen*—you don't inquire after us, but we inquire after you!—placing the sonorous *du den deinen* in the middle. The word ***fr**onbe**fr**eit* (free of drudgery) sounds like the Hebrew ***sh**ivat **sh**vutech*, which is itself a highly unexpected phrase that means "the return of your captivity" (not your captives) in a playful allusion to Psalm 126. (Mendelssohn has *Erlösung*, redemption). *Fronbefreit* mimics the paranomasia of the Hebrew, and the *f* and *r* sounds recur in the next line in *Harfe*.

Though some earlier translators incorporated a rhyme scheme—often making Halevi sound like Heine, or perhaps a church hymn—it was only in Rosenzweig's case that, as we shall see, the preservation of the rhyme scheme, meter, and the overall form of the elegy was elevated to a philosophical and even theological necessity, one not always appreciated by his readers. Gertrud Oppenheim called the poems "*mit Reimlexicon zusammengeschustert*," as if the translator was simply having fun with a rhyming dictionary.[60] A more serious criticism was voiced by poet and Hölderlin expert, Ludwig Strauß, who called the translations "*künstlich, gewunden*," artificial and unnatural. Strauß objected to the formalist approach to translation practiced by Rosenzweig, George, and many others, which he deemed an overly simple understanding of poetic language and form.[61] He was particularly offended by Rosenzweig's comments in the afterword that translators of Halevi who didn't replicate the meter were nothing but "lazy."[62]

But it appears to have been one of these lazy translators who provided the negative impetus for Rosenzweig to produce his own version of Halevi's poems. As he wrote to Buber (6 January 1923): "Moreover, I translated a slim volume by Halevi with an afterword and notes. . . . The rhyme and meter have been replicated precisely. This whole [project] owes its appearance to Emil Cohen (given to me by Michael), which offended me to such a degree that verses emerged."[63] Who was Emil Cohn, and why did his *Ein Diwan* of 1920 make Rosenzweig so angry?[64] Cohn rendered the "Ode to Zion" in a manner reminiscent of Goethe's *Sturm und Drang* poem "Prometheus," in unequal verses and stanzas, and placed the lyric self, *I* and *me*, rather than *you* and *your*, front and center. Cohn's translation had expanded the first eight Hebrew verses into twenty-two German ones. Cohn's was the most recent example of a long tradition of free renderings of Halevi, the method that Rosenzweig called *Nachdichtung*, which Mendelssohn had originated.[65] The main point, as I already suggested, is that the rivalry with Cohn epitomizes Rosenzweig's dispute with a tradition of translation going back to Mendelssohn.[66] What got him so angry, in other words, was the entirety of a translation tradition that in his view had led German Jews deeper into secular culture and to the margins of Judaism. Rosenzweig untranslated Halevi as a way of untranslating the Haskalah.

Rosenzweig's afterword is usually read for its pronouncements about the task of the translator as such, and for its fascinating excursus about the history of Bible translation in Germany in which Luther is celebrated as the exemplary German translator—the "religious genius" who became a "world-historical person" by translation. In the second half of the essay, Rosenzweig writes about a second religious genius, the poet-philosopher Jehuda Halevi. Those passages make absolutely clear that to fanatically translate one hundred poems of Halevi in rhymed couplets had nothing to do with formalism, and everything to do with forging a radically new poetics of Jewish translation, in which content and form were inseparable. (Translation does not transmit content.) Translation that strove for formal equivalence would have the power to estrange German Jewish readers from their assumptions about Hebrew, poetry, and Judaism altogether.

The main principle is announced in the first paragraph: "Basically, my intention was to translate literally" (*wörtlich*).[67] He mentions Mr. Cohn in passing, but his main counterexample is the school associated with classical philologist Wilamowitz-Moellendorff (1848–1931), known for making ancient texts comprehensible. Rosenzweig makes an incredible assertion, quoted many times since, that all Jewish poetry in exile, in its very nature, resists domestication.[68] Rosenzweig uses words such as *Unnatürlichkeit* (unnaturalness), *unnachbildbar* (inimitable), *Fremdheit* (alien nature), and *Ungewöhnlichkeitsgehalt* (unusual content) to describe Halevi's language, thereby constructing an *internal* rationale for his "unnatural" approach.

What was unnatural to German ears was Rosenzweig's use of meter, biblical language, word choice, and above all his approach to rhyme, which from his vantage point was the most misunderstood aspect of these poems, both by average readers and connoisseurs, such as the nameless reviewer from the newspaper *Wiener Morgenzeitung* whom he quotes. One reason rhyme is misunderstood is ignorance of Hebrew; another is ignorance about poetry, or failure to hear poetry. The afterword builds up to the crux of the matter: *just because a poet subjects himself to these rules—rhyme, meter,* Musivstil (mosaic style)*—must the translator re-create those conditions?* Rosenzweig answers that those unnatural features that make Halevi a stranger to a twentieth- or twenty-first-century reader have nothing to do with historical context; they form the core of Halevi's originality, which was about *using rhyme and repetition to express truth and love.* The "Ode to Zion" was a liturgical poem to be chanted and responded to in the synagogue! As liturgical texts, the raison d'être was "repetition and return," both within each poem, and year after year, across the cycle of the holidays. Such formal patterns—rhyme, rhythm, meter, refrain, and acrostic—were inspired by "truth" on one hand, and by the feeling inspired by that truth—love of God—on the other. Halevi's liturgical poems are love poems—but not of the Christian, Romantic, sort; not like Heine's *Dichterliebe*, where love comes to an end by the end of the cycle. "The lie has many possibilities, the truth only a few, in essence, only one. That [truth] never tires of repeating this in new ways—in that it attests to its true power. In the mouth of the lover, endearments never grow old."[69]

I believe that Halevi's verse, because so intricately interwoven with biblical allusions and citations, presented an even greater challenge to the Jewish translator than Scripture itself.[70] Yet, to become the German harp to Jehuda Halevi's exquisite Hebrew verse meant something quite different for Mendelssohn and Rosenzweig. Mendelssohn approached poetry as a Romantic, treating it as an elevated, aesthetic language with extraordinary power to move the soul and instruct the mind. Translating Halevi gave wings to Mendelssohn's own poetic imagination, which meant that when Mendelssohn translated a *qinah* (Hebrew elegy), it read like a German ode in free rhythms. It thus follows that his next project would be a nonsectarian translation of the Psalms, and that even in translating the Bible, he would pay extraordinary attention to poetic passages he claimed were superior to non-Jewish poetry "as heaven to earth." Rosenzweig, one might say, had the exact opposite aspiration: he used translation (and commentary) to distill the liturgical, theological essence of the poem. Rather than use free rhythms, he obeyed the strict meter and rigorous form of the original Hebrew. Essentially, he wanted to transform the nineteenth-century *Diwan* back into a book of *qinot*: literature back into liturgy, reinterpreted as love poetry. But there was nothing retrograde about this aspiration; it was a clear instance "traditionalist modernism," a hybrid of formalism and radical experimentation, much like the Bible translation project that diverted Rosenzweig's attention in 1925.

BUBER'S CREATIVE RETELLINGS

Rosenzweig staked everything on opposing the method of *Nachdichtung*, but Buber, who worked for many years as a writer and editor before becoming a professor, embraced the method of *Nacherzählen*, creative retelling. Using a technique that was not at all *wörtlich*, but perhaps no less powerful or theological, Buber rehabilitated mythic tales and mystical writings from the Hasidic masters and myriad other sources. His translations include *The Tales of Rabbi Nachman* (1906); *The Legends of the Ba'al-Shem* (1908); an anthology of mystical writings titled *Ecstatic Confessions* (1909); *Speeches and Parables of Chuang Tse* (1910); *Celtic Sagas* (1914); and a Finnish epic. Buber sought to place ancient wisdom in new vessels in the way that a storyteller channels memory, in Walter Benjamin's famous image, by leaving his handprints on the material, merging it with his own life experience.[71] Buber was reluctant to refer to his "retellings" of Rabbi Nachman of Breslov as translations, emphasizing rather that imagination played an important role in his approach—a common modernist trope. The preface begins: "I have not translated these tales [of Rabbi Nachman], but retold them with full freedom (*ihm nacherzählt, in aller Freiheit*), yet out of his spirit, as it is present to me."[72] Later, in the introduction to the anthology *For the Sake of Heaven*, he wrote, "I was forced to obey the law of these inner connections, to supply lacks according to the meaning of what preceded and what followed."[73] Using the imagination to fill in the gaps—and at the same time, disavowing control over the creative process—was consistent with the artistic approach to memory of many modernists. A comparison of a tale such as "The Rabbi's Son" in Buber's version and in those transcribed from oral sources within the Hasidic world demonstrates how he rounded off these raw, esoteric parables, so that they read like the literary tales (*Kunstmärchen*) produced by the German Romantics. Buber too insisted that his method was justified by the form. In combining an anecdote with a moral saying, the Hasidic tale "aims at the oneness of outer and inner experience, of life and teaching."[74] But achieving this multifacted give-and-take was also Buber's priority, and it anticipated what he aspired to make possible for the readers of the Bible through translation—an *Erlebnis*. The axiom that "the event must be narrated with extreme concentration, in order that the story or maxim may arise from it in pure *spontaneity*," corresponds exactly to his aspiration for the Bible. The upshot is that the translator assumed artistic license to refashion the text in such a way that this kind of old-new encounter would again become possible, though insisting all the while that the method is not artificial, but authentic; not imposed, but immanently justified.

LUTHER AND TORCZYNER: STEPPING-STONES OF THE BUBER-ROSENZWEIG BIBLE

In purely chronological terms, the most distant and most immediate stepping-stones of the Buber-Rosenzweig Bible were the translations of Martin Luther (1532) and Harry Torczyner (1935–37). As was the case in previous generations, the favoring of a precursor from the remote past became linked to the rejection of the near past and the present.

Less a stepping-stone than a provocation for Buber and Rosenzweig was the news that the Berlin Jewish Community under the leadership of Rabbi

Leo Baeck had mobilized to produce a new official Bible translation for synagogue use, with individual books assigned to scholars as well as liberal and conservative rabbis from Berlin, to be edited by the Hebrew philologist and Bible scholar Harry Torczyner (1886–1973). Rosenzweig responded in a letter to Buber that as a *Deutschjude*, he believed a new "official Bible translation was not only impossible but also forbidden, and only a Jewish revised (parts more, parts less revised) Luther Bible as possible and permitted."[75] Why impossible? Why forbidden? Rosenzweig opposed the production of another second-wave Bible: an up-to-date, scholarly German translation for Jews by Jews, whose efficacy would be limited to the "religious sphere," to school and synagogue. He noted that unlike Baeck's, theirs would be a "self-commenting translation," perhaps because there would be only two translators working "privately" as one.[76] Neither Buber nor Rosenzweig was invited to participate in what came to be known as the Torczyner Bible. This translation was published in Frankfurt in 1937, and Torczyner (known after his immigration to Palestine as Naftali Herz Tur-Sinai) revised it in the 1950s.[77] In his preface, he identifies the Zunz Bible, another collaborative project and a "valuable monument to Jewish scholarship (*Gelehrtenarbeit*)," as his model. The preface further paid tribute to the Buber-Rosenzweig Bible as its main competitor—"whatever one may think of it"—noting that it represented an "in sich geschlossenes starkes Wollen," a self-contained, strong will. The Torczyner Bible retained *der Ewige* for the name of God.

To identify the Luther Bible as the only "permissible" and "possible" precursor was an ideological statement with a kernel of truth. Christian publisher Lambert Schneider had just founded his own house, and he invited Buber in 1925 to produce a new translation of the Old Testament into German.[78] Initially, the task seemed "impossible." "Is the Bible translatable? Has it been in fact translated? What remains to be done? Little? Much? The crucial element? How can it be done? In editing a classic translation? In a daring new beginning? Does the age have room for a new beginning . . . etc."[79] Like all our modern translators, they embraced the impossibility and turned it into the very condition of their enterprise; as Rosenzweig wrote to Scholem, "Only he who is fervently convinced of the impossibility can translate."[80] They began by revising Luther's Genesis directly—ostensibly, this means that they were working from Luther's German version, rather than the Hebrew—until they realized that they could not overcome Luther's Christianity. In Buber's account, it took only a single day for them to realize that the efforts to revise Luther, verse by verse, produced not a new translation but "a heap of ruins" (*Trümmerhaufen*).[81] "Clearly, Luther's 'Old Testament' would remain in perpetuity a magnificent structure (*ein herrliches Gebild*); but for our time *it was no longer a Bible translation."* But Luther's language (*Bibeldeutsch*) was the ruin, so to speak, out of which they chiseled their own rendering, at least initially. They took Luther's "barbaric" Hebraism a step further when they decided to use Hebraic forms of names (though they chose to keep the orthography as familiar as possible). An important stylistic break occurred when Buber convinced Rosenzweig to renounce the *und* on the grounds that *Asyndese* (linking of syntactical units without conjunctions) was a fundamental characteristic of *Bibeldeutsch*, and moreover, the consecutive vav in Hebrew was a part of the verb and not to be replicated by an independent word.[82] (The *und*s had been removed by Mendelssohn and restored by Zunz.) After reading Buber's rendering of the first chapter of Genesis, Rosenzweig made the memorable comment, "it's astonishingly German. Makes Luther sound like Yiddish by comparison. Maybe too German??"[83] The quip anticipates criticisms of the Buber-Rosenzweig translation, and conveys the discrepancy between Luther's natural diction and their own archaic idiom, as well as their aspiration to be out of step with the present.

Was it disingenuous of Rosenzweig to claim that Luther, rather than any Jewish translator, represented the highest form of translation? The heart of the matter, as Rosenzweig wrote in "Scripture and Luther" (1926) and in the Halevi afterword (1924), is that a monumental Bible translation had to be inspired by a genuine religious vision rather than an intellectual or linguistic agenda. Luther's Christian perspective shaped his translation of certain verses and words that had doctrinal significance. A modernist Jewish approach would out-Luther Luther by treating each and every word as a potential gateway to Torah, and at the same time rebuff the source critics by highlighting the totality and unity of Scripture. But the identification with Luther also allowed Rosenzweig and Buber to deny other relevant legacies: to challenge the use of *der Ewige* that pervaded the prayerbook and to suppress their patent affinities with the Hebraizing tendencies of Johlson and Zunz in the 1830s and with Hirsch's roots-based translation of the 1860s and 1870s.[84]

PAPPENHEIM'S YIDDISH TANACH

Pappenheim's *Zeenah u-Reenah: Frauenbibel* was her third translation from Yiddish, and, in fact, her fourth rendering of a classic work by or for women into German. She first translated Mary Wollstonecraft's *Vindication of the Rights of Women* of 1797 and published it with the title *Eine Verteidigung der Rechte der Frau* under the name P. Berthold, at her own expense, in 1899. She learned of Wollstonecraft's book, never before translated into German, in the pages of *Die Frau*, the periodical of the German women's movement;

Wollstonecraft's influence is evident throughout Pappenheim's lectures and writings. In 1910, she translated the memoirs of Glückel of Hameln, the oldest memoir by a Jewish woman, and arguably the first Jewish autobiography, from Yiddish into German.[85] Pappenheim's decision to produce a new German translation of the memoirs was reportedly inspired by her discovery, during a visit with her brother in Vienna, that her mother Recha Goldschmidt was related to Glückel. In her preface, Pappenheim claims the same motive as Glückel: she wants her heirs to know "von was für Leute ihr her seid," from what kind of people they descend. Pappenheim went so far as to print six family trees in her translation; this edition was also privately funded and originally published for her family alone. But the project was part of a larger enterprise; she translated in order to "animate the image of a woman with many intellectual gifts who was true to her faith, her people, her family, and herself." In the way that Buber channeled the Hasidic masters and Rosenzweig championed Halevi over Heine, Pappenheim put forth Glückel as a better role model than the well-known salonières Rachel Varnhagen and Henriette Herz, who abandoned traditional Jewish life. In her preface, moreover, she praises the memoirist as an exemplar of womanhood as such: "Glückel of Hameln merits a place among those women who, modestly and unknowingly, embodied the best and worthiest of a woman's existence (*Frauendasein*)." Glückel and Wollstonecraft are thought to have been Pappenheim's two role models: a portrait of Wollstonecraft hung in her living room (and still hangs in the Pappenheim House in Neu-Isenberg), and a famous portrait of Pappenheim dressed up as Glückel was reproduced in some editions of the *Memoiren*.

Two more translations from Yiddish followed. In 1929 Pappenheim translated a classic of old Yiddish literature, the *Maasse-Buch*, a compendium of legends and folktales from the Talmud, regarded as a "Yiddish Gemara."[86] The book contained a brief historical foreword by Ismar Elbogen, a well-known Berlin rabbi and expert on Jewish liturgy whom Buber had recommended, which concluded by noting that the book was meant for the Jewish woman and mother, as an extension of Pappenheim's social advocacy.[87] In her introduction, Pappenheim also stresses the book's value for a female audience, partly due to the naïveté of its form. Using the same formulation as in her preface to Glückl's memoir, Pappenheim asserts that the book teaches us about the "important, and yet—modest (*bescheiden*) position of woman in Judaism"—a double characterization of Jewish womanhood, which recurs often in her writing. But there is more: the *Maasse-Buch* opens a window onto "the power of belief in a God-given Torah in the smallest everyday occurrences to the highest martyrdom," as well as to other "evidence of the life-affirming power of the Jewish teaching: pleasure, possession, joy, and above all, the great purity and chaste-ness in the outlook of those life expressions which form the basis and the foundation of Judaism." The book has sociological and linguistic value, but above all, she presents it as a pedagogical resource for "parents, educators, and teachers": "a bridge to a renewed understanding of the significance of traditional Jewish cultural and religious assets." Her method, it was emphasized, is *anspruchlos* (unassuming); "the book makes not even the slightest claim to *Wissenschaftlichkeit*."

One year later, in 1930, the same year in which the second edition of Buber's and Rosenzweig's Pentateuch translation appeared, the Jewish Women's Federation published volume one, Genesis, of Pappenheim's *Zeenah u-Reenah* with a foreword by Dr. Pessach Goldring. Editions of Exodus, Leviticus, and Numbers were in progress at the time of her death.

These three works together make up a women's Tanach—the acronym that designates the three sections of the Hebrew Bible: *Torah*, *Nevi'im* (Prophets), *Ketuvim* (Writings). Pappenheim's Tanach also comprises three volumes: one dedicated to history, a second to rabbinic texts, and a third to the Bible.

Pappenheim had no intention to *replace* the Hebrew Bible. She would not have gone as far as Elizabeth Cady Stanton, the American suffragist, who created a women's Bible in 1895 that omitted the first twenty-five verses of Genesis. Nor was her goal to promote a Yiddish language revival among German Jews. Her Tanach was a "bridge" to Jewish religious culture, inspired by her feminism, her Orthodoxy, and the deepening religiosity of her last years.

EXCURSUS: THE *TSENE-RENE*, THEN AND NOW

The *Tsene-Rene* was less a translated Bible than a translated Bible curriculum. This Old Yiddish compendium of select verses and commentaries took the form of the narrative or contextualized Bibles discussed in my introduction. Turniansky writes:

> The *Tsene-Rene*, like the previous [Yiddish language] word for word translations, included *khumash*, *megillot* and *haftarot* [Pentateuch, scrolls, and prophetic readings], although not in a translation or consecutive homiletic elaboration of the text. The *Tsene-Rene* discusses selected verses in a kind of *drashah* (sermon), interlaced with commentaries, *midrashim*, moral instructions, *halakhic* explanations and various other elements . . . The *Tsene-Rene* was not intended specifically to convey the biblical text, but to elaborate on certain topics in an expansive, enlightening com-

> mentary, instructing readers and broadening their knowledge of matters found in an array of other, post-biblical sources.[88]

Author Jacob ben Isaac Ashkenazi of Janow (Lublin), an itinerant preacher and scholar about whom little is known, titled the volume "go forth and look" (Song of Songs 3:11), based on a verse imploring the daughters of Zion to gaze upon King Solomon—perhaps because Janow incorporated many sayings from Solomon's Proverbs. As the second-person female plural verb form suggests, it was intended for a category of Jews referred to as "women and men who are like women," or women and uneducated men.[89] But this was not just another vernacular Bible; it became "a genre in itself," the core text of "Ashkenazic women's religion" into the modern period,[90] due to its lively and accessible style, which

> offered readers suspenseful and poignant stories from traditional sources in simple, comprehensible Yiddish prose. On Sabbath and holidays it was read and read aloud in Jewish families. The *Tsene Rene* was not read by women only, but was intended for all adults who didn't have access to sources in the original, Hebrew and Aramaic. Since reading aloud was a particular pleasure, practically all Ashkenazic Jewish children grew up with this book.[91]

The *Tsene-Rene* is widely known as the most often published Yiddish book of all time, with over three hundred editions from the early seventeenth through the twentieth centuries.[92]

How does the *Tsene-Rene* work?

Genesis 3:1—regardless of whether one reads about it in a Buber-Rosenzweig or Luther Bible, in the KJV or JPS, the fact tantalizes: "the serpent was the shrewdest of all the wild beasts that the LORD God had made" (JPS).[93] The *Tsene-Rene* cuts to the chase, "The snake was really bad and wanted Adam to die" (*Un der Schlang is gewesen sehr schlecht un hat gewollt, daß Adam sterben soll*), then moves on to a frequently asked question about Genesis 3:2–3: why does Eve misstate the divine prohibition of eating from the Tree of Knowledge to add a prohibition of touching the tree? "Hat Eva geantwortet: 'Gott hat nur verboten den Ez hadaas (Baum der Erkenntnis) nit zu essen. un ihn auch nicht anzurühren.'"[94] (Was she perhaps the Bible's first female mistranslator?) Why does she succumb to the snake? The *Tsene-Rene* eventually concludes, "Thus Eve didn't lie after all" (Darum hat die Frau keine Lüge gesagt). How does the Yiddish Bible manage to exculpate Eve? I shall quote the passage from Pappenheim's German version, then summarize. (Note Pappenheim's use of parentheses on ten occasions to translate Hebrew *Fremdwörter.*)

> Die Chachomim (Weisen) sagen: "Man darf nit reden, das was nit befohlen worden is, denn Gott hat nit verboten anzurühren, nur zu essen hat Gott verboten. Un Eva hat zugesetzt un hat ein Lügen gesagt. Darum is sie zu einer Aweroh (Sünde) gekommen. Dann der Schlang is gegangen un hat die Hand von Eva gestoßen zu dem Ez hadaas (Baum der Erkenntnis), un hat zu Eva gesagt: 'Sowie du nit gestorben bist vom Anrühren, so auch wirst du nit sterben vom Essen.' "
>
> Der Tauldaus Jizchak schreibt: man kann zwei Fragen auf den Injen (Sache) stellen: eine, warum hat Eva zu der Schlange Lügen gesagt? . . . Noch mehr koschoh (unverständlich) is: der Schlang hat die Hand von Eva gestoßen zu dem Baum un hat so gesagt: "Sowie du nit bist gestorben von dem Anrühren, so auch wirst du nit sterben von dem Essen." Un warum hat Eva dem Schlang geglaubt, un hat bald gegessen? . . . . Un noch eine Kaschje (Frage) kann man fragen: Gott hat zu dem Odom horischaun (ersten Menschen) gesagt: "Warum hast du gegessen von dem Baum?" Hat Adam geantwortet: "Das Weib hat ihn gegeben." Was für eine Tiruz (Erklärung) is das? Weil das Weib ihm gegeben hat, darum soll er poter werden (frei von Schuld), Gott hat es aber doch verboten?
>
> Der Rambam schriebt: Odom horischaun (Adam) hat zu Gott gesagt: "Du hast mir gegeben ein Weib zu einer Hilfe. Hab ich mir gedacht, was sie mich heißt, muß ich tun. Darum hab ich gegessen von ihr Hand."
>
> Kann man frägen darauf: "Is denn Adam ein solcher Schaute (Narr) gewesen . . . ?"
>
> Neiert der Pschat (Auslegung) is so: "Adam und Eva haben gemeint, Gott hat verboten zu essen von dem Ez hadaas (Baum der Erkenntnis), das is als von wegen weil der Ez hadaas is gestanden an einem sehr heiligen Ort, wo die Schechina (göttliche Herrlichkeit) pflegt dort zu ruhn. . . . Drum haben sie gedacht . . . wenn der Apfel von dem Baum soll herabfallen un soll sich heraus welgern (rollen) von dem heiligen Ort, dann mäg man ihn wol essen, wenn er sich welgert heraus von dem heiligen Ort.["]
>
> Un darum hat die Frau zum Schlang gesagt: "Von dem Baum inmitten Garten", klaumer (das heißt) weil er steht auf einem heiligen Ort inmitten. Sowie ein Melech (König), der inmitten von dem Land wohnt so auch ruht die Schechina (göttliche Herrlichkeit) inmitten von dem Garten. Darum dürfen wir von ihm nit essen, und drum hat die Frau

> zum Schlang gesagt: Gott hat verboten, den Baum anzurühren. Denn sie haben sich gedacht, das is Gotts Mein (Eigentum).
>
> Darum hat die Frau keine Lüge gesagt, auch nit ihr Deoh (Gedanken) nach.[95]

Janow begins with the assumption that Eve lied, and that her lie led to her sin (once she saw that nothing bad came of touching the tree)—the lesson being that lying leads to sinning. But other questions arise. Why did Eve believe the serpent? How could Adam be so callous as to blame Eve for giving him the fruit, and God for giving him Eve? *Is denn Adam ein solcher Schaute (Narr) gewesen?*—was he such a fool? Such questions awaken the reader's curiosity and indignation. The next step is to give the *pshat*, the simple answer that exculpates the first man and woman: Adam and Eve were both operating under the misconception that what was holy (and prohibited) was not the tree itself, or its fruit, but rather, the zone in the middle of the garden, where the Shechinah (divine presence) dwells, just as every king dwells "in the center of the kingdom." They assumed it was forbidden to approach (and touch) the tree in that zone, but once the fruit rolled away from the holy site, why not? By this logic, the narrative arrives at the conclusion that Eve's extra prohibition was logical, and Eve did not lie after all.

All this is to show that while the *Tsene-Rene* was designed for the uneducated, it is not a work for the unintelligent. "Readers of this literature could gain familiarity not only with the content of the traditional sources but also with the ways in which traditional Jewish exegesis uses sources and structures an argument."[96] It is easy to understand that a book that engages the reader in the hermeneutic process on such an elemental level would become so immensely popular. Not only do female characters that came to life; the same critical lens is trained on the Patriarchs—and on Scripture itself. Why does the Torah embarrass Leah by mentioning her flaw ("weak eyes")? Why does Jacob speak so coarsely to Laban about wanting to have intercourse with his future wife? Why did he love Rachel more than Leah? On Jacob's hurtful response to his wife Rachel's desperate plea for children:

> *Yaakov was angry at Rachel and said, "Shall I take God's place?"* (30:2). He asked if she thought that he was God who had withheld children from her. His father had prayed for Rivkah because he had no children from other wives, but he already had children from Leah!
>
> *Ramban* asks: How could Yaakov have answered her so? The righteous—such as Eliyahu and Elisha—even pray on behalf of total strangers. How much more should Yaakov have prayed for his own beloved wife!

> Further, it is difficult to understand Yaakov's anger, since Rachel had been justified in her request, for does God not accept the prayers of a *tzaddik* [righteous person]?
>
> The *Midrash* says that God told Yaakov, "You did not reply properly to Rachel, and so your other children will be forced to bow down to her child Yosef." But the simple explanation is that Rachel frightened Yaakov. She knew how much he loved her and so warned him that she would die of sorrow if she would have no children, hoping that he would fast and wear sackcloth and plead with God until He granted her children. Yaakov was angered, for he realized that she had tried to frighten him so that he would pray, in her certainty that through his prayers she would have a child. This is why he replied, *Shall I take God's place?*[97]

The women's Bible supplied far more than a corrective to the overly concise style of biblical narrative. Biblical figures become psychological characters and cryptic verses open up the drama of real life. The behavior of the Matriarchs and Patriarchs is continually interrogated and reevaluated. As recently noted, the *Tsene-Rene* makes the Bible read like Homer's *Odyssey* after Erich Auerbach's description in "Odysseus' Scar": it magnifies the inner life and leaves little to the imagination, but it also activates the imagination.[98] Psychological realism is juxtaposed with moral outrage, tough questions, and unmodern answers. Reading Scripture becomes experiential reading.

As we shall see from the reviews, Pappenheim's generation—the generation of the German Jewish cultural renaissance—appreciated the *Tsene-Rene* as an authentic source of religiosity. But Pappenheim was well aware of the fact that within traditional Jewish society, "the spheres of male Hebrew and female Yiddish literacy were not equal, but hierarchical," as Iris Parush reiterates. The system did not ensure that all women learned to read Yiddish and acquired the skills to gain access to texts.[99] The two spheres were "ranked" in terms of prestige, quality of instruction, status of the texts, and importance of the languages. Women did ultimately have an advantage moving into the modern world: learning to read in private was far more comfortable than in the ritualized space of the *heder*, which was often associated with shame and humiliation.[100]

And yet, the counter-modern stance of the fourth wave provided a platform from which the *Tsene-Rene* could be appreciated and taken seriously in German translation. One reason was its patent oral character; as Henri Meschonnic notes, twentieth-century translators celebrated orality, which became associated with issues of identity and alterity. An article by writer and scholar Bertha Badt-Strauß (1885–1970) under the Hebrew pseudonym

Bath-Hillel (daughter of Hillel), that preceded Pappenheim's translation, praises the *Tsene-Rene* and calls for a new translation on just these grounds.

> It is not a book I'm writing about here. It's about grandmother sitting by the window on a warm, summer Shabbos afternoon, wearing her Shabbos bonnet with a red ribbon, like the young rebbetzin she once was, though she's already eighty years old. Though her face is as wrinkled as parchment . . . her eye remains sharp, and she reads *sforim* [Jewish books] without glasses, as she does every Shabbat. Weekdays she works in the kitchen and house and has no time. Everyone, Jews and Christians, knows that Grandmother does more than eat bread. If a mother worries about her son abroad, a woman is close to childbirth, someone is ill . . . they are all sent to Grandma. She knows what to do: Psalms for the sick, blessings for the healthy, she looks in her books and "paskenet" (issues a ruling) as if she were a rabbi. . . . Generation after generation of Jewish women read this book, "leyned" on Saturday afternoon, even as they do today. Eagerly the lips move . . . the ribbons on the bonnet move to the rhythm. Whoever wants to can listen.

There were others before *Tsene-Rene*, but none as beloved. Why?

Bath-Hillel's answer, in a word, is orality. The aural nature of the Buber-Rosenzweig translation—divided into breathing units, rather than numbered verses—is well known. Orality—in stories, lessons, sermons, exegesis, and dialogue, the Jewish "national form"—was also the priority of the *Tsene-Rene*. "Here we have a moral lesson, such as the Rav would give on Shabbos Hagadol [the Great Sabbath before Passover]; there we see a collection of life experiences that a grandmother shares with her grandchildren. Then there is the 'Afikoman,' or bonus: a fairytale, a miraculous tale (*maasse*) or parable (*moshelchen.*) Because 'It's not only to children that one feeds stories.' "[101] The book is filled with questions—so essential to Jewish pedagogy (*Erziehungskunst*). Lastly, this book fills in the story between the lines of Scripture. Whereas the Bible depicts its heroes in the "great episodes of their lives—being chosen, being tested, transformation," the *Tsene-Rene* teaches us what happened before and after: "A new kind of Bible, a true Lay Bible." Bath-Hillel criticizes a recent German edition of Rabbi Kraus from Lakompak, Hungary, which undertook to "transform the 'corrupted' German of the Zenne Renne into a pure German." The *Tsene-Rene* cannot be translated into pure German just as *Weiberdeutsch* (*Vaybertaytsh* = German in Hebrew characters) cannot be translated into pure Hebrew. "The *Judeo-German* dress belongs to the Zenne Renne as the Sabbath Bonnet belongs to grandmother." The comment that this book exemplifies *Golus-schicksal*, the diasporic condition, recalls similar comments in all three of Pappenheim's prefaces, as well as Franz Rosenzweig's comment that all Jewish writing in the diaspora "disdains to ignore its state of being-in-exile." Bath-Hillel concludes with an appeal for a publisher to reissue the book.

It is also critical to appreciate that in their original historical context, Pappenheim's translations were evaluated as religious texts. The clearest evidence of this lies in reviews that appeared in her lifetime: these establish that her contemporaries took her seriously as a translator of Torah.[102] These reviewers also channel, in an uncanny way, the voices and priorities of German Jewish Bible translators throughout history, allowing us to imagine what they might have thought of her project.

The pedantic priorities of Mendelssohn, Zunz, and others come to the fore in a 1934 review by Bernard Heller published in a preeminent scholarly journal explicating the contents of the *Zeenah u-Reenah* and assessing the quality of the translation. Heller lists the commentators referred to in the original and the page numbers on which they appear, for reference purposes, and a note about the commentators who are *not* included, Saadia, Abulwalid, Ibn Ezra, Samuel b. Meir, Maimonides (not true). Heller corrects information in Pappenheim's preface, as well as her style and usage. There are long lists of errors in spelling and transliteration, as well as typographical and other types of mistakes; in short, Heller's was exactly the type of review accorded to translations by Zunz, Salomon, and others. Ultimately, Heller praises Pappenheim, but with reservations. He approves of her decision to retain the expressive flavor and lively tone of the original, as in the verses "Deine Schelter sollen gescholten sein, deine Segner sollen gesegnet sein" and "Gott soll dich leutseligen, mein Sohn." Interestingly, Heller assumes that Pappenheim's translation was intended for a female readership—a decision to which he objects: "The task of reconstructing a Jewish folk-book from the early seventeenth century for the Germanophone Jewish woman of the twentieth century raises linguistic, aesthetic, and ethical concerns," he begins.[103] "Much more of value could be offered to our women from Talmud and Midrash, and by no means should this book be given to our young daughters, even though the good Jakob ben Isaak of Janow himself used a number of euphemisms, as when he wrote that a woman should decorate herself 'like a bride,' p. 29, 30, when when the source Genesis Rabbah XXIII:2 says 'like a prostitute.'" Ultimately, he praises the book, not for its intellectual content, but as a source of edification, *Erbauung*, which he finds in the descriptions of old Jewish folk customs, in its moral sensiblity and judicious treatment of biblical characters and episodes (Noah and Lot get a good name), its hard questions ("Tamar shall be burned, why not Judah?"), and its promotion of good conduct (i.e., one is permitted to lie in the name of peace). Heller's review captures the reasons why this book was rejected by Maskilim in the first place and also why it survived nonetheless.

In the newspaper that Samson Raphael Hirsch had founded, *Der Israelit*, a reviewer of Pappenheim's second translation (*Allerlei Geschichten*) notes that the "naïve rhymes" with which the narrator sums up each story are especially important, and that the book will be a useful pedagogical tool (*Hilfsmittel*) for the "teacher and educator" who is attempting to show to those entrusted to him [*sic*] "what old-Jewish piety (*altjüdische Frommigkeit*) demands," and he concludes that the book is suitable for instruction as well as entertainment.[104]

What one might call the modern liberal reception—one that exemplifies the priorities of the fourth wave—was that of Margarete Susman, the scholar of philosophy who had tutored Pappenheim in Ancient Greek. Susman elaborates on many of the points in Pappenheim's own preface, emphasizing not only the historical value of the *Tsene-Rene*, but also its value as a source of Torah. As in the Torah, no detail is irrelevant: individual letters and numbers are as signficant as precepts and events. Susman captures the force and function of questioning displayed in the excerpt cited above: "The great Jewish spirit of questioning (*Fragegeist*) keeps everything in constant motion, and over and over, wrests from every truth discovered yet a new truth."[105] And it is Susman who here observes that the little fable about the assignment of *bet* as the first letter of the Bible (*bereshit*) and *alef* as the first letter of the Decalogue (*anokhi*) is not merely a rivalry of two letters but a philosophical debate about the status of creation with regard to Torah. She also grasps the paradoxical value of many such anecdotes: "out of the shell of the everyday, the powerful primal truth of Judaism breaks forth."[106] Above all, Susman is attuned to the book's double-sided nature: "how much and how little" it has to offer. For all its naïveté, she emphasizes, the book demands substantial "intellectual preparedness and mental capacity" on the part of its female readers. It required only "a little" in respect to learned knowledge. It demands much (and offers much) when one attends to the "internal cohesion of all these stories and interpretation," out of which emerges the "unusual mixture of naïveté and depth, folksiness and greatness" that characterizes the book. Unlike Heller, who echoes the typical appraisal of the *Tsene-Rene* as a book for woman, Susman notes that "present-day readers—women and men—must be grateful to Bertha Pappenheim" for making accessible this book, which contains "an authentic and inexhaustible significance for the Jewish soul, far beyond the folkloristic or historical interest."[107]

Bertha Pappenheim fundamentally shared the view that the *Tsene-Rene* was an exemplary, untranslatable book, if to translate meant what it did in the first wave of translation, namely, to render a Jewish text in the pure, correct language of the majority culture. Franz Kafka said something similar about Yiddish in his "Introductory Lecture on Jargon" of 1912. But there is more. As we shall see, Pappenheim already knew what Iris Parush's research bears out: the Yiddish women's Bible became a stepping-stone to enlightenment and culture. The faded Yiddish books found on grandmother's bookshelf had contributed to the shift in reading habits in the middle of the nineteenth century.[108] Women who read religious literature in these narrative genres also read Yiddish fairy tales (*Bove Buch*, *Centura Ventura*), then novels, "and onward to reading the maskilic periodicals." In later generations, women read secular books written in Yiddish and European classics in Yiddish translation.[109] Since women's reading had never been supervised, the transition from religious to secular reading occurred naturally.[110] Finally, as many memoirs of Maskilim and poets testify, the reading habits of mothers and grandmothers inspired many a son and grandson to turn to literature.[111] The *Tsene-Rene* was a first step to culture.

MISSION STATEMENTS: BIBLES FOR PEOPLE TODAY

> How do we mediate between such people and the biblical message? Where is the bridge here?
> —Martin Buber, "People Today and the Jewish Bible"

> In the hand of parents, educators and teachers, the *Allerlei Geschichten* can become a bridge to the renewed understanding of the significance of traditional Jewish cultural assets and treasured beliefs.
> —Bertha Pappenheim, *Allerlei Geschichten*

The premise of the fourth wave was that people's *relationship* to the Bible had become problematic. Modern life was largely to blame. Buber came up with the audacious formulation that "the passage of time had largely turned the Bible into a palimpsest. The original traits of the Bible, the original meanings and words, had been overlaid by a familiar abstraction . . . *The Hebrew Bible itself is read as a translation—as a bad translation, as a translation into a smoothed-over conceptual language, into what is apparently well known but in reality only familiar"* (emphasis added).[112] Pappenheim, who insisted that she was no Bible expert, objected on feminist grounds: "Dear Daughters: If I might permit myself a bit of Bible criticism, I would say that based on the unjust position that the Bible designates for women, it is patently clear that this is the transcription of a genial but masculine person, and not divine dictation, that is, the logical, necessary result of the divinely willed division of the sexes."[113] The Torah within the Bible had become hopelessly buried and misconstrued, due to overfamiliarity, sexism, and other errors of history. The fundamental common ambition of these translators was not to produce an improved translation, but rather to transform the *relationship* between text and reader through translation. The difference is subtle but consequential. Their predecessors had sought to update what came before, often by importing external knowledge or content, be that grammar and poetry, scholarly insights, illustrations, or religious philosophy into the pages of the Bible. But these thinkers formulate their aspirations in terms of discovery and intimacy. They thought about translation dynamically, pedagogically, and also psychologically. They cared how people "reach for, relate to, are with [the Bible], through it"; about how they might "take it up as if they had never seen it before," and place it at their "beck and call." If only translation could re-create the fertile encounter with Scripture that past generations took for granted; if only it could inspire an *Erlebnis*—the kind of startling life-altering experience privileged by modernists of their day.[114] With a combination of hubris and humility, they imagined that their efforts could channel the Ur-voice and make it heard to contemporary ears: "to take care that a human ear which the voice reaches from any passage of Scripture be able to receive that voice more easily and more clearly."[115] Three formulations from the years 1926 (Buber), 1929 (Rosenzweig), and 1936 (Pappenheim), demonstrate that the possibility of transforming *how and why* people read the Bible exerted a powerful grip on their imaginations.

In his 1926 lecture "People Today and the Jewish Bible," Buber criticizes the status quo in terms of spiritual decadence and intellectual torpor. "People today resist scripture because they cannot abide revelation." "By 'people today' I mean 'intellectuals.' . . . The intellect's freedom from real obligation is the signature of our time."

> "Religion" today is itself a thing of unattached *Geist*—one of its departments, a clearly privileged department of the superstructure of life, an especially impressive chamber among the upper rooms. It is not a life-encompassing whole . . .

> People do not in the manner of earlier generations stand before the biblical word in order to hear it or to take offense at it; they do not any longer confront their lives with the word. Rather they store the word in one of the numerous secular warehouses, and rest contented.[116]

Buber laments, in other words, that the Bible has become Emily Dickinson's antique volume. His words call to mind the crowd of laughing nonbelievers in Nietzsche's parable "The Mad Man" and Hugo von Hofmannsthal's critique of aestheticism in the verse drama *Death and the Fool*, which Buber knew well. How to shatter this complacency? Buber goes on to imagine an unheard-of encounter with the text:

> They too can . . . open themselves up to this book and let themselves be struck by its rays wherever they may strike; they can, without anticipation and without reservation, yield themselves and let themselves come to the test; they can receive the text, receive it with all their strength, and await what may happen to them, wait to see whether in connection with this or that passage in the book a new openness will develop in them. For this, of course, they must take up Scripture as if they had never seen it, had never encountered it in school or afterwards in the light of "religious" or "scientific" certainties; as if they had not learned all their lives all sorts of sham concepts and sham propositions claiming to be based on it. *They must place themselves anew before the renewed book, hold back nothing of themselves, let everything happen between themselves and it, whatever may happen. They do not know what speech, what image in the book will take hold of them and recast them, from what place the spirit will surge up and pass into them, so as to embody itself anew in their lives; but they are open . . . They read aloud what is there, they hear the word they speak, and it comes to them; nothing has yet been judged, the river of time flows on, and the contemporaneity of these people becomes itself a receiving vessel.*[117] (emphasis added)

Buber envisions an active, open-ended, and potentially life-altering engagement with the words of Scripture, made possible through the experience of reading and hearing the words. He discards the content-oriented and intellectual goals of his predecessors, in favor of an indeterminate and unpredictable outcome. His terms recall those of *Lebensphilosophie*, of Henri Bergson's duration and Ernst Mach's neoempiricism. The acknowledgment that the most powerful encounter with the Bible just might be a matter of chance has important affinities with the modernisms of Agnon, Proust, and Freud.

Can receiving the Torah really be so spontaneous and anarchic? In a famous section of *I and Thou*, Buber made the controversial assertion that divine revelation—not a one-time event, but an ongoing possibility—has no fixed content. "Man receives, and he receives not a specific 'content,' but a Presence, and Presence as power. . . . It is not prescribed, it is not specified on any tablet, to be raised above all men's heads. The meaning that has been received can be proved true by each man only in the singleness of his being and the singleness of his life."[118] Rosenzweig concurred with Buber's existential, *relational* understanding of revelation, and his rejection of the notion of Scripture as divine legislation. As Neil Gillman summarizes, "Both thinkers understand revelation as God's entering into relationship with Israel. . . . What was revealed, then, was not a text, not a body of doctrine, and certainly not a set of laws. The only content of revelation is God's self-disclosure, the fact of His presence, and thereby, His concern with Israel."[119] Yet Rosenzweig did not accept the antinomian consequences of this model; he rescued the binding, authoritative aspect of Torah through the concept of "being commanded." An individual can freely to choose to obey a commandment. "The relationship itself commands."[120] Rosenzweig thereby retained the major function of Torah within normative Judaism, namely as the authoritative guide to Jewish observance.

In a remarkable article on "Bible," written for the *Encyclopaedia Judaica* in the last year of his life, Rosenzweig identified the historical present as shaped indelibly by Mendelssohn and the Haskalah. In an insight that bears out the argument of this history as a whole, he avows that the importance and scope of Scripture increased in direct proportion to the diminishing roles of (Christian) dogma and (Jewish) law in modern life.

> It is quite possible that the secularization of religious communities, which began a hundred and fifty years ago, will march on, and that church and synagogue in the old traditional sense will persist only for a small nucleus . . . . If this should happen, the significance of the Holy Scriptures would not lessen but would even grow—as has been shown by both church and synagogue in the last century and a half. When dogma and Law cease to be the all-embracing frame of the community and serve only as props from within, the Scriptures must not merely fill the task of all Scriptures: to establish a connection between generations; they must also assume another which is likewise incumbent upon all Scriptures: they must guarantee the connection between the center and the periphery of the community. Thus, even if church and synagogue no longer arched the portal on the road of humanity, the Bible would still continue

> to be at beck and call, so that humanity could consult it about this very road, "turn its pages again and again," and find "everything in it."[121]

Rosenzweig envisions the Bible today as the new sanctuary. A century and a half since the age of enlightenment and emancipation, when religious communities no longer cohere through faith and obedience, Scripture provides everyone with everything. He reiterates the need for "reverse learning": the Bible is not only a "path to peace," a bridge between generations, but a two-way street from the margins to the center. To illustrate reverse learning, Rosenzweig closes with a rabbinic adage from Mishnah Avot, "Turn it and turn it, for all is contained within it," giving the mishnah a new, if ironic, meaning.

Bertha Pappenheim's most serious complaints about "people today and the Jewish Bible" are found in letters she wrote to Buber during her final illness. It is possible that she had his piece of that name in mind. Her tone reflects her own physical condition, as well as the political situation in Germany, 1936. Most significant (and most surprising), she implicates Buber and Rosenzweig's Bible translation, as well as the educational program of the *Mittelstelle*, in the overintellectualization of the Bible.

> Since yesterday I have been preoccupied with why the Bible means something entirely different to Christians than to us. In all circles and classes there have been, and there are, Christian people who read the Bible with original, naïve (or primitive) faith, and who found in it edification, strengthening, and comfort in difficult times—the path to God—to God, not to HIM (den Weg zu Gott—zu Gott, nicht zu IHM).
>
> I can't recall ever meeting a person I would have thought capable of having a relationship to the Bible such as the one depicted so movingly, so beautifully, by Rembrandt in the portrait of his mother reading the postil. Peaceful, quiet, devoted we are not with respect to the Bible, with it, through it. (I don't even know a single pious Jew.) In the best of cases the Bible is a kind of history book in which we are supposed to find appeasing analogies to our fate from past times, but not a path to—to what, to whom?
>
> In our times, one would have to love the Bible, to reach for it, but I believe that many (Jewish) people in true times of need would rather reach for their Goethe than for their Bible. (I am allowed to say this because I am neither a Goethe expert nor a Bible expert.) But what you do in the Center for Adult Learning: you intellectualize the Bible to an extreme. One needs to acquire it through hard work [*Man soll sich sie erarbeiten*]. How awful.

> That is how I would like to be able to read the Bible. But that is something that cannot be learned, just as one cannot learn to believe, to be pious.[122]

To "intellectualize" the Bible, treat it as a history book, as a source of "appeasing analogies to the present" as rabbis and exegetes did, rather than a path to God, is all too easy; what Pappenheim stresses is the "hard work" of *Frommigkeit*, pious devotion. She admires the faith she sees in "Christian people, who, in their original, naïve (primitive) belief," read the Bible and "found in it edification, strengthening, and comfort in difficult times—the way to God," noting with sarcasm, "I don't even know a single pious Jew." Pappenheim does not yearn for an immediate Buberian dialogue with the words of Scripture, nor does she fantasize (as Rosenzweig did) that the Bible should be everything for everyone at all times. Her vision is not anarchic. She wishes only that Scripture could fulfill its most simple purpose: offer comfort in times of need. She insists that this naïve encounter with the Bible can neither be taught, nor learned—not even by her.

Pappenheim's rhetoric marks a definitive rupture with the German Jewish translation tradition, and a spiraling, by way of Rembrandt's mother, to the Old Yiddish Bibles designed to meet the needs of pious, uneducated women and men. Her appeal for a Bible that would meet primal religious needs—long since replaced by culture ("they reach for their Goethe")—stands in stark contrast to the exuberant intellectuality found in the commentaries and introductions of Mendelssohn, Philippson, even Hirsch. It is hardly surprising that Pappenheim's ideal Bible reader is female—the unlearned, pious older woman, reading the postil—a collection of homilies.

Quite possibly, Pappenheim had in mind Rembrandt's famous painting "Old Woman Reading a Book," though she may have been referring to other paintings with similar titles, such as the one by Rembrandt's apprentice Gerrit Dou (1613–75). It is not certain that this woman is Rembrandt's actual mother, Neeltgen van Zuytbrouck; the image is a "tronie," a kind of picturesque genre painting that was common in the 1630s. Among the many portraits of old women reading, this one has unique features that have led to its interpretation as Hannah the Prophetess or "an allegory of Faith or Piety."[123] Pappenheim narrated this woman's life and faith in her essay "Die jüdische Frau." Whoever she is, it seems likely that the religious book she reads is a translated book.

Gender surfaces again in Pappenheim's comment that reading the Bible should provide "a path to God—to God, not to HIM," using all capital letters to mimic Buber's and Rosenzweig's use of pronouns, usually marked as masculine, in capital letters, *Ich*, *Er*, *Ihm* (I, He, Him) as equivalent to the Lord (Hebrew *Adonai*, Luther *der Herr*, Mendelssohn *der Ewige*). For example, Genesis 2:4:

> BR: Am Tag, da Er, Gott, Erde und Himmel machte.
> KJV: In the day that the Lord, God, made the earth and the heavens.

and Genesis 2:7:

> BR: Und Er, Gott, bildete den Menschen, Staub vom Acker
> KJV: And the Lord God formed man of the dust of the ground.

Pappenheim hints here that these pronouns gratuitously exaggerate God's masculinity. Although biblical Hebrew uses male verbs and pronouns when referring to God, their approach hypostatizes God's maleness, making gender impossible to ignore. To my knowledge, this is the only time Pappenheim commented on the Buber-Rosenzweig Bible (other than her joy upon receiving the Psalms translation). Her subtle comment relates to the view expressed on several occasions that Buber's philosophy—despite its dialogic character and reliance on universal, elemental concepts—furthered a patriarchal, overly abstruse view of religion, God, and the Bible that closed off access to Torah (and to God) to the uneducated and to women. By relating the question of gender to the problem of intellectualization, Pappenheim's coy accusation implicates Buber and Rosenzweig in the century-and-a-half-long tradition of German Jewish Bible translation instigated by the Haskalah. "You intellectualize it. *Wie furchtbar.*"

Each of these expressions of frustrations with the modern relationship to the Bible shaped the desire to radically reimagine the German Jewish Bible. What does that mean? First of all, they were not translating content. They sought to inspire a second naïveté; to convey that, contrary to the modern religious sensibility, the Torah is first and foremost a personal path to God. They knew that only an unmodern type of translation could have an impact. To a degree, Samson Raphael Hirsch also belongs in the fourth wave, as he also rebelled against the modern, "enlightened" tradition of Bible translation that extended from the seventeenth-century Amsterdam Bibles and Mendelssohn to Philippson. Those translations were no longer a usable past, as far as they were concerned. Like Hirsch, both twentieth-century translations announced their distance from the Enlightenment Bible by adopting a foreignizing approach to the German language that was meant to shock a bourgeois Jewish readership. Buber and Rosenzweig followed Samson Raphael Hirsch in three other respects: in their belief that modern biblical scholarship had a become an obstacle to Torah; in promoting an ahistorical, almost existential view of Scripture; and in their conscientious, even pedantic effort to locate Torah immanently in the Hebraic word, in a way that was not related to modern philology. At the same time, Buber and Rosenzweig departed from Hirsch in viewing translation as a universalizing project, rather than an activity fully consonant with the Oral Law and rabbinic Judaism. Pappenheim followed Hirsch in her traditionalism; both of them used translation to foster a neo-Orthodox Jewish-religious *Weltanschauung*, to transmit the Jewish exegetical tradition and rabbinic lore, in lieu of modern knowledge of the text. She, like Hirsch (and unlike Buber and Rosenzweig), cared about the religious praxis of her readership. Yet she departed from Hirsch by promoting a model of devotion (and a corpus of knowledge) that was coded female and—in the eyes of many—"unintellectual"—in stark contrast to Hirsch's abstruse philosophical and pseudo-linguistic apparatus. Pappenheim alone placed gender front and center, although her feminism coexists with, was part and parcel of, the quest, common also to her male counterparts, to devise forms that would meet the religious needs of "simple people," and also, the "simple" needs of all people. In Rosenzweig's words, "But beside the expert and the teacher, one thinks also of the many simple souls among Jews and Christians who have lost access in the one case to the original and in the other to Luther. It is these people—serious, painstaking, striving—whom one wishes as readers."[124] In Pappenheim's words, "But the Bible would have to be brought so near to the Jews—even the most simple among them—that they would learn to love and to hate (which are after all the same thing), nothing more."[125] For Pappenheim, "simple ones" (die Einfältigen) referred most immediately to the women to whom she devoted her life: unwed mothers, prostitutes, victims of white slavery; Jewish women denied education, equality in the *Gemeinde*, and basic welfare support; orphans, *agunot*, immigrants from the East. The model of faith she put forth—for men and women, educated and uneducated—was *Frommigkeit*, the unsophisticated piety exuded by Rembrandt's portrait, coupled with the core obligation of Torah, which was also the simplest universal value: loving one's neighbor. Buber and Rosenzweig also desired to create a translation that would reach all humans, religious and alienated, Christians and Jews, on an equal footing, and that would enable them to hear God's voice through the biblical text. They did not seek to enlighten people in the manner that their predecessors did, by teaching them *something*—German prose, Hebrew grammar, Torah, botany. Inasmuch as this common priority—to place the simplest things at the center—shaped their approaches to Bible translation in Frankfurt in 1920s and 1930s, Buber and Rosenzweig and Pappenheim make up the fourth wave in the history of modern German Jewish Bible translation.

METHODOLOGICAL CONSENSUS IN THE FOURTH WAVE

As different as they are, the Buber-Rosenzweig and Pappenheim Bibles share a methodological similarity: they radically defamiliarized the target language, and rejected the idiom of Jewish *Bibeldeutsch*. Correct and current German had been the hallmark of each new translation since the Haskalah, ever since Blitz announced that his translation was "clear, correct, and beautiful," and Mendelssohn claimed to "make the crooked straight." The fourth-wave translators shared the conviction that in their day and age, a new translation of the Bible would have an impact only if it were *not* written in good German. Instead, they invented a Hebraized German in one case and a Yiddishized German in the other.

Pappenheim stated that her German renderings remained as close as possible to the "old form" (vii), because to domesticate the original language would have "sterilized" it. She gave her readers what Scholem called the *niggun* (melody) of Yiddish. In the passage on Genesis 3 cited above, Pappenheim retains key words in Hebrew and Yiddish and gives the German in parentheses: *Ez hadaas* (Tree of Knowledge); *Injen* (topic); *Kaschja* (question); *Odom horischaun* (Adam, the first man); *Schaute* (fool), *Schechina* (feminine divine glory); *melech* (king); *Deoh* (opinion); *Koschoh* (difficult); *Tiruz* (solution). Parentheses had been a staple of this book since medieval times, and we have seen them in the first and second waves.[126] Pappenheim used them to translate key words and exegetical vocabulary (difficult question; solution), adding layers to an already layered text. Her style conveyed what Elizabeth Loentz calls a folksy "old-new language," neither pure German nor pure Yiddish, but resembling Yiddish dialect.[127] This approach was consistent with a greater trend. "Yiddish dialect writing in Latin letters" had been popular since the second half of the nineteenth century among Jews who no longer spoke or wrote in Yiddish. According to Steven M. Lowenstein, "Yiddish dialect was used either as a specifically humorous device, or as a means of evoking a lifestyle treated as already dead."[128] In her short fiction and plays, Pappenheim cast undesirable characters as Yiddish-speakers. She had no interest in promoting Yiddish language and literature, with which she was undoubtedly familiar. In her view, neither Yiddish nor Hebrew could qualify as the Jewish national languages, since these were not languages of culture.[129] Loentz summarizes:

> In order to negotiate these contradictions, Pappenheim compartmentalized: good Yiddish was securely rooted in the past and bad Yiddish refused to disappear from the present. This clear separation enabled her to idealize Yiddish-speaking female ancestors (even to render translations of their literature in something resembling *Mauscheln*) while dismissing modern Yiddish as an uneducated *Jargon* and working to transform its speakers into speakers of a *Kultursprache*.[130]

The important insight here is not only about language politics. Pappenheim retained the flavor of Yiddish in her Tanach to signal its distance from the German Jewish Bible, from language and culture; to announce it as a source of Torah as it had been learned and lived by Jewish women for centuries.

Buber and Rosenzweig also created an old-new German idiom for their translation, one replete with unexpected and archaic words excavated from various Germanic linguistic periods. Such words had various purposes: they were meant to Hebraize the German text, displace "smoothed-over conceptual language" of other translations, and evoke a primordial biblical reality. For "sacrifice," they replaced *Opfer* with *Darnahung, Darbringung* = bringing near; instead of *Monat* for month, they used *Mondneuung*, Moon-Renewing. Their German followed Hebrew on the level of word (especially with regard to names and words with common Hebrew roots) and syntax, but with a different goal than Zunz and Johlson. The extreme literalism was ontological, not philological. It extended out of their desire to reproduce the spoken character of Scripture: to turn a book back into a voice. The plural "voices" would be more accurate, given that in their model of open-ended revelation and reverse learning, each word could have a voice of its own. Their famous *Leitwort* method, as Mara Benjamin explicates it, served many goals: to highlight the dynamic unity of Scripture; bring out "subversive or ironic" undertones in a particular passage; "illuminate a subterranean stratum"; and "show the indivisibility of biblical content and form and the irreducibility of language itself in apprehending the Bible's meaning."[131] Buber believed that a hermeneutic inspired by the hearing of repeated keywords (more exactly, keyroots), "bridges of words,"[132] was retroactive rather than prescriptive or didactive. His description of the method recalls the scenario of Franz Kafka's parable "Before the Law"; he claims it does not bring one to some "true" meaning, but rather points one "towards something that is to be perceived in its actuality, but not paraphrased in language or thought."[133] Buber performed the method in a lecture titled "*Leitwort* style in Pentateuch Narrative," demonstrating that seven *Leitworte* bridge the two parts of the story of the Tower of Babel (Gen 11:1–9), and three *Leitworte* circulate in multiple configurations throughout the story of Korah's rebellion (Num 16:1–17:5). These passages recall the experiences of connecting the dots to view a figure, or staring at the stars until the Big Dipper becomes visible. That figure, Torah, is embedded in "revealed" written language, but not in the way that Hirsch or Philippson identified it; for them, a cumulative body of knowledge external to Scripture per se was needed to decode the signs. Buber's translator has more authority than a rabbinic exegete to identify the patterns, and ultimately, the reader of the translation has authority equal to or greater than that of the translator. In the fourth wave, creation, revelation, and interpretation were not one-time events, but continual experiences.

Buber and Rosenzweig and Pappenheim aspired to produce translations that Goethe referred to as the "final and highest" type: the "third kind of text for which the taste of the masses has to be developed," that is possible only once a translator "gives up" on his or her nation.

> In such periods, the goal of the translation is to achieve perfect identity with the original, so that the one does not exist instead of the other but in the other's place (*sodaß eins nicht anstatt des andern, sondern an der Stelle des andern gelten solle*).
>
> This kind met with the most resistance in its early stages, because the translator identifies so strongly with the original that he more or less gives up the uniqueness of his own nation, creating this third kind of text for which the taste of the masses has to be developed.[134]

METHODOLOGICAL DISSENSUS IN THE FOURTH WAVE

The two projects diverge most dramatically in their attitudes towards history. Pappenheim's translation was thickly historical. It spiraled back to the prehistory of German-speaking Jewry, taking as a prototype a form of the Old Yiddish Bible that Blitz and Witzenhausen had rejected—a translation that was still so popular in the eighteenth century that Mendelssohn did not want to call attention to it.[135] Pappenheim claimed to transmit into the present the aura of religiosity and female piety surrounding those texts. In stark contrast, Buber and Rosenzweig *purported to* create a radically original translation with no precedent, other than, ever so briefly, the Luther Bible. Mara Benjamin uses the terms "transhistorical" and "post-historicist" to describe Rosenzweig's philosophy of translation.[136] While all translators struggled with the anxiety of influence, Buber and Rosenzweig were the most daring in this regard. They did not present their translation as the next chapter in the rich tradition of German Jewish Bibles described in this volume; they called it a *Verdeutschung* rather than an *Übersetzung*, and gave new names to the biblical books.[137] Alan T. Levenson notes their "hostility" to translation; by this he means that they did not want to be viewed as translators rendering the text from one language into another to supplement the Hebrew text, or meet the needs of a particular linguistic, national, or religious community.[138] Detaching their project from history served an existentialist and universalistic agenda. As I hope to have shown, it was not an honest representation of their endeavor.

The visible symbol of this fundamental difference in the two approaches is the contrast in the page layouts. The page of the Buber-Rosenzweig translation displays the pure text formatted in cola: a stripped-down Torah, unmediated, surrounded by white space (fig. 4.4). Pappenheim went in the diametrically opposite direction to render a very cluttered page of Torah, where verses from Scripture are interwoven with commentaries, legends, questions and answers about matters that preoccupied the medieval imagination such as pride, charity, women's religious practices (fig. 4.5). Pappenheim's *Frauenbibel* did away with the careful separation of Written and Oral Torah, Scripture and commentary—the singlemost radical innovation of modern Jewish translations. Buber and Rosenzweig erased commentary altogether, for much the same reason: to snub their precursors. With regard to layout, the projects under discussion represent the two extreme positions among all of the translations in this study.

Why would Buber and Rosenzweig's stripped-down Torah be the perfect work for people today? The white space surrounding the text is the most prominent symbol of the translators' very unhistorical (areligious?) approach to translation. To unmoor Scripture from its anchoring contexts—commentary, chapter and verse numbers, the "chains of the written word," i.e., punctuation—was to create a Brechtian *Verfremdungseffekt* (alienation effect). The format was designed to estrange the readers from Scripture as a book, first visually, as the eye followed the division of the text into cola, and then aurally, as the ear followed unfamiliar renderings and *Leitworte* that highlight patterns or constellations of meaning. The white space surrounding the Torah signals that the guardians of the text—scholars and rabbis, masoretes and exegetes—had surrendered their authority; that territory was open to one and all. As Rosenzweig wrote in "Scripture and Luther" (1926): "For the voice of the Bible is not to be enclosed in any space . . . Rather this voice seeks again and again to resound from outside—from outside this church, this

Dies sind die Reden die Mosche redete zu all Jiſsrael
jenseit des Jordans,
in der Wüste, in der Steppe,
gegen Sſuf zu, zwischen Paran und Tofel, Laban,
Chazerot, Di-Sahab.
Elf Tagreisen sinds vom Choreb, auf dem Weg zum
Gebirge Sſeïr, bis Kadesch Barnea,
aber es war im vierzigsten Jahr:
in der elften Mondneuung, am ersten auf die Neuung
redete Mosche zu den Söhnen Jiſsraels
allwie ER ihn an sie entbot,
nachdem er geschlagen hatte
Sſichon König des Amoriters, der in Cheschbon saß,
und Og König des Baschan, der in Aschtarot saß, –
bei Edreï.
Jenseit des Jordans, im Lande Moab
unterwand sich Mosche diese Weisung zu erklären,
sprechend:

ER unser Gott
redete zu uns am Choreb, sprechend:
Genug eures Sitzens an diesem Berg!
Wendet und zieht ihr,
daß ihr ins Gebirg des Amoriters kommt und zu all
seinen Anwohnern
in der Steppe, im Gebirg, in der Niedrung, im Mittag
und an der Küste des Meers, –
das Land des Kanaaniters, und der Libanon, bis zum
großen Strom, dem Strom Euphrat:

1,1–7] 7

Fig. 4.4. Buber and Rosenzweig Bible, Deuteronomy 1:1. From *Das Buch Reden. Die fünf Bücher der Weisung*, vol. 5 (Berlin: Schocken Verlag, 1927).

people, this heaven. It does not keep its sound from echoing in this or that restricted space, but it wants itself to remain free."[139] Elimination of commentary promised not only an unmediated encounter with Scripture, but also a freeing of the voice of the Bible to reach any reader at any time. In Buber's words: "We the translators of Scripture have a more modest task: to take care

Bereschith

Im Anfang

Im ersten Beschäffenis von Himmel un Erd is gewesen die Erd wüst un leer un der Kissehakowaud (erhabene Thron) von Gott hat geschwebt in der Luften über dem Wasser. Un warum hebt die Thauroh an mit der Beth? (B)? Um zu weisen, daß der Beth is Broche (Segen). Darum hat Gott angehoben mit der B. Da is die Aleph (A oder O) vor Gott geflogen un hat gesagt: „Heb mit mir die Thauroh an, denn ich bin das erste Aus (Zeichen) von dem Alephbeth (Alphabet). Hat Gott ihr geantwortet: „Auf dem Berge Sinai werd ich die Zehngebote geben; da will ich anheben mit dem Aleph, אנכי ה' אלהיך (Ich bin der Ewige dein Gott). Un darum hebt die Thauroh an mit dem Wort Bereschith um uns zu lernen, daß die Welt is beschaffen von wegen der Thauroh un daß sie heißt Reschis Darkau (Anfang seines Weges).

Rabbi Jizchak sagt: „Warum hat die Thauroh angeschrieben wie Gott hat die Welt beschaffen? Die Thauroh is doch nur Mizwaus (Gebote). Darum hat sie nur anfangen sollen von Mizwaus. Neiert wenn die sieben Umaus (Völker) werden nachher zu Jisroel sagen, ihr seid Gaslonim (Räuber) denn ihr nehmt uns Erez Jisroel, dann werden ihnen die Jisroel antworten: „Gott hat die Welt beschaffen; er hat sie erst euch gegeben, un heut will er sie uns geben." Unsere Chachomim (Weisen) haben gesagt, von wegen drei Sachen hat Gott die Welt beschaffen: von wegen der Thauroh, die heißt Reschis Darkau (Anfang seines Weges); un wegen die Korbonaus (Opfer) die man hat im Tempel dargebracht, der heißt Reschis (Anfang), weil er is beschaffen worden vor der Welt; un wegen der Maaßraus (Zehnten), die die ersten des Getreides heißen.

Weil die Thauroh dort auf das Bethhamikdosch (Tempel) hingewiesen hat, drum weist sie uns auch wie das Bethhamikdosch zerstört werden wird. Drum sagt der Posuk (die Schrift) die Erd wird sein verwüstet, denn die Schechina (göttliche Herrlichkeit) wird sich vom Chorbon (Zerstörung) abtun. Un darum sagt der Posuk (Vers): „Der Geist Gottes schwebt über den Wassern", das weist darauf, sogar daß wenn wir schon im Golus (Verbannung) sein werden, wird uns doch die Thauroh nit abgetan sein. Un darum sagt er (der Vers) auch, Gott sprach: „Es werde Licht." Das weist darauf, daß nach dem Golus Gott

Ze' enah u- Re' enah 1

Fig. 4.5. Pappenheim, *Bereschith* (Genesis). From *Zeenah u-Reenah* (*Frauenbibel*) (Frankfurt am Main: J. Kauffman, 1930). Photograph: Courtesy of the Leo Baeck Institute.

that a human ear which the voice reaches from any passage of Scripture be able to receive that voice more easily and more clearly."[140] The white space, in other words, was to be filled in by the reader's imagination, much as the young Sigmund Freud used the pictures in the Philippson Bible as a coloring book—pictures that then found their way into his dreams.

THE LIMITS OF REIMAGINATION

THE PATINA IS GONE

Two related tensions mark Buber and Rosenzweig's project, especially when juxtaposed with Pappenheim's. First, although they insisted that they were doing something revolutionary, their enterprise was in many respects continuous with the history of German Jewish Bible translation. Second, some of their central claims, such as that they had freed the voice within Scripture (the Torah within the Bible), or that they had gone where no translator had gone before, bespeak a Romantic ideology that limited if not undermined their achievement. Rejecting history led them to rely on Romantic tropes of depth and surface. They claimed that their particular method enabled them to cut through the ossified reception and lay bare a pure, original spoken text. Another formulation posits that the "book" lies beneath "history."[141] Elsewhere, they penetrate the written text to its "spokenness" (*Gesprochenheit*).[142] They refer to magical revelations of an "original text" and even a "naked text." Was it not disingenuous to claim "Our work illuminates the palimpsest; it gets beneath the waxen surface upon which nations have inscribed the 'Bible' of their religious needs and expressive forms, and the original text appears"?[143] What exactly lies beneath what, and who gets to see—or hear? The tension recalls Odysseus's false dilemma with regard to the Sirens' song in book 11 of *The Odyssey*. Are the translators Odysseus, who hears the song, or Homer, who composed the song? And what about the rest of us lowly sailors with wax stuck in our ears?

The tension is most marked in the genealogy Buber traces in a 1938 essay that describes in personal terms the path that led both him and Rosenzweig to their method. It was in Eduard Straus's Bible class, he writes, that Rosenzweig was

> "for the first time in his life actually standing before the pure text in its nakedness, without its traditional garments." Until that point he had, as he said, been reluctant to read the Torah and the Prophets except in the context of the millennia—the Jewish millennia . . . the millennia generally. Only now in Frankfurt did he dare "to take his place before the text and the text alone." Everything that the Bible became to him, everything that took place within the Bible, had its origin in this "naked" encounter.[144]

In a comparable passage in the same essay, Buber provides what one might call the confession of a future Bible translator. He explains that in his earliest years he studied Torah in Hebrew. But one day he discovered the Hebrew

Bible in German, through the "beautiful" Zunz translation, after which point he "began to get angry at the Bible."

> It was for me like what happens in a fairy tale, when a wicked spirit drapes a veil over a maiden and transforms her into something dreadful; and I have similar experiences here in the streets of Jerusalem sometimes, when I catch sight of the face of an Arab woman all covered by some multicolored veil and it seems to me the face of a ghost . . . soon after—shortly after my Bar Mitzvah—I suddenly noticed that I was reading the Bible with literary pleasure, and that fact so shocked me that I did not pick up a Bible translation for many years. I tried to return to the original text; now, though, it seemed to me hard and alien, the words had lost their easy and familiar movement. . . . It took thirteen years for anything new to happen. I had come home from Herzl's funeral . . . casually, without hope, I opened the Scriptures . . . I began again to read in the Hebrew Bible, not continually, only a passage from time to time. It was not familiar, as it had been in my childhood; but neither was it alien, as it had become afterwards. Every word had to be won, but every word could be won. From that time the Bible has meant in my heart nothing else but the untranslated book. I read it aloud; and in reading aloud I got free of the whole Scripture [*Schrift*], which was now only *miqra'* and nothing more.
>
> One time—again after several years—as I was in the middle of speaking a chapter aloud it seemed to me that the chapter was being spoken for the first time, that it had not yet ever been written down, that it did not at all need to be written down. The book lay before me; but the book was melting in the voice.[145]

The scenario reads like a Freudian case study. Discovering the Bible in the Zunz translation was coming-of-age rite/seduction that produced an admixture of pleasure, rage, and guilt. German translation had magically transformed the familiar religious text, the foundational text, into a ghost, or a veiled Arab woman Buber encountered on the streets of Jerusalem, to which he had just moved: something exotic and other—but distinctly female. The joy of reading the Bible as a novel for pleasure (as women did), in his native German, also entailed the loss of the youthful, naïve connection. With maturity, the joys of this feminine reading gave way to a new hard-won relationship to the (masculine) Hebrew text. In the manner of a Freudian screen memory, Buber associates his rediscovery of the Hebrew Torah with a traumatic event, Theodor Herzl's funeral in 1904, when he was twenty-six years old. He mentions that he "casually" opened the Bible to a random place, and a story about Jeremiah and King Jehoiakin had a surprising effect on him—the "let everything happen" moment referred to in the earlier essay. A new adult relationship to the "neither familiar, neither alien" Hebrew text begins to be forged, but it is painstaking work. In this phase, meaning must be wrestled (or wrested) from isolated words and passages by reading aloud and listening, until such point when the entire written text "melts" into the voice—in another magical metamorphosis. In sum, Buber's deeply personal journey to the Bible comprised a cycle of engagement and alienation, masculine and feminine reading, with defamiliarization ultimately giving way to unimaginable intimacy, as the hard book melts into the (warm? soft?) voice. Buber is like the biblical Jacob, losing one wrestling match after another. But the desire to gaze upon the "naked" unclothed Scripture—which both translators claimed to have themselves viewed at different times—is not the same as viewing the face of God. The passage exemplifies the Romantic dimension of the Buber-Rosenzweig Bible identified by Brenner, Loentz, Seidman, and others, one that stands in tension with what we know (and what translators elsewhere admit) about their research and use of precursors.

This tension relates to Pappenheim's hint that the Buber-Rosenzweig Bible, when all was said and done, was an intellectual translation by men, for men. Pappenheim looked to the Bible for "a path . . . to whom? To God, not to HIM."[146] Their use of male pronouns ER, IHM (HE, HIM), in capital letters for Lord/*Adonai* was intended to counter, above all, the distant, Platonic "Eternal" Deity introduced by Mendelssohn. Rosenzweig had argued that it was the Bible itself that proved Mendelssohn wrong; that "the only justifiable translation [of God's name] is one that makes prominent not God's being eternal but his being present, his being present for and with you now and in time to come."[147] By this reasoning, a modern person who relates to the God of Scripture pronomially as HE, YOU, HIM could achieve greater intimacy than one who addressed God as LORD or Eternal One. By what rights did Rosenzweig presume to know which divine name would have what kind of effect? The fact that these everchanging PRONOUNS could not become icons highlighted the Bible's relational potential. That these pronouns also had the effect of hypermasculinizing that relationship did not seem to bother Buber and Rosenzweig. Her critique is about more than gendering God. Pappenheim's challenge ("a way to God, not to HIM") implies that from the vantage point of an uneducated Jewish woman, they were just as guilty of inscribing distance between God and humanity as Mendelssohn. From a historical vantage point, whether or not Buber and Rosenzweig intended it, within the tradition of German Jewish Bible translation, the masculine pronouns go hand in hand with the emphasis on a pure, unmediated translation—the modern format of the German Jewish Bible—which leaves the authority squarely in the hands of the new Moses, the modern translator. Because Moses spoke face to face with God; he was also God's first secretary. In August Weger's steel engraving at the front of the Philippson Bible, Moses's head has two rays emanating from it, to signal that his encounter with the divine is already behind him, and the transcribing, the teaching, can begin.

LOVING AND HATING THE *TSENE-RENE*

No less was Pappenheim's Tanach the endpoint of a complicated personal journey. Like the author of the *Tsene-Rene,* who was an itinerant preacher, Pappenheim was an intermediary between the religious elite and the populace. Both directed their efforts towards the needs of uneducated Jews, seeking to make Jewish sources accessible to those on the margins of society—women and *amei-ha'aretz.* Pappenheim often referred to herself as the uneducated one, as she never attended a university, nor did she have formal Jewish education. Despite her brilliant mind, she expressed her dislike for intellectual and philosophical processes. In her dialogue with Buber, she stated that the most important ideas and values could and must be expressed simply, so as to be accessible to all. Pappenheim hoped her translations would become a medium, or bridge, to a more authentic Jewish experience. But here too, there is a tension. Could these classics plausibly make the case for religion to modern young women (let alone men) in the age of *die neue Frau* (the new woman), Zionism, and so many explosive cultural, intellectual, and political developments?

Perhaps this explains why, in her preface to *Zeenah u-Reenah,* Pappenheim likens the picturesque world constructed therein to a painting by Albrecht Dürer. "In medieval form . . . one experiences the motley characters and events of the Bible in quotations, explanations, and stories in a language that is indispensable if one does not want to destroy the charm of the presentation."[148] For her, it was a medieval book, but *not* a timeless one: as a mark of historicity, she likens it to a work of art that is "charming," "quaint," "multifarious." As was the case with Yiddish, Pappenheim neither romanticized nor glorified the past, nor did she believe the *Tsene-Rene* depicted an ideal image of womanhood.[149] She was not oblivious to the double-sided portrait of Jewish woman it provided. The book (like the Bible) represented Jewish tradition, the good and the bad. For worse and for better, this is the "tradition" that shaped women's lives, that they carried "in their blood and in their brains," in their DNA, albeit in ignorance.[150] Pappenheim grasped the essence of *Frauendasein* in the *Tsene-Rene* as Jean Baumgarten describes it: the representation of women

> provides a good example of the dynamic tensions which characterize the text. Women occupied an important role as pillars of textual transmission, and of education, and as the vital heart of the Jewish home. They were celebrated, like the matriarchs, as producers and dispensers of many kinds of knowledge. The *Tsene-rene* thus witnesses to a clear advocacy of women within Jewish society. Long left on the margins of religious Jewish literature, the female figure here bursts forth as the central character, both in daily life and as a motivating element in the process of messianic redemption. Even so, women are still belittled, even condemned as the source of sin and transgression.[151]

The *Tsene-Rene* offers a snapshot of premodern traditional Jewish life in all its conflicts and irreconcilable beliefs; in Baumgarten's words, "The *Tsene-rene* seems a mirror of the contradictions of the Jewish people, a work that brings together the most conflictual components of Jewish culture." The anachronistic portrayal of womanhood in medieval texts did not discourage Pappenheim; she captures it well in her preface: "How little, and at the same time, how much did one see fit to present women from the treasures at hand." *Wie wenig nun, und doch wie viel*: The wistful comment relates to her view of Torah as a book that taught one both to love and to hate, because love without hate would have no meaning. In translation, as in life, a continual balancing act is needed.

The tension within Pappenheim's translation project is that she values the Yiddish classics both positively, as repositories of Jewish women's spiritual experience, and negatively, as they codify the wound, the exclusion, a depreciation of women that "cast its fateful shadow onto the present day." She did not seek to reintroduce these books to modern German Jewish readers for their intellectual content, nor did she aim to awaken interest in Yiddish. She aspired rather to channel the aura of belief and devotion, the religious sensibility that imbued the pages of the *Tsene-Rene* and, even more important, that infused the souls and minds of the readers of that book over the centuries, for a new generation.

LEGACIES OF THE FOURTH WAVE: A FEMALE MOSES, A JEWISH LUTHER

Rosenzweig and Pappenheim were engaged in translating in the final years and months of their lives; and in fact, Buber completed the *Verdeutschung* in Israel in 1961, one year before his death at age eighty-four. Though they are not the authors' best-known works, translations of the Torah represented the culmination of their life work.

Pappenheim was working on the *Zeenah u-Reenah* when she died. Her final outing in 1936 was in response to a summons by the Gestapo. She did not live to see the vanquishing of the Nazis or the founding of the State of Israel. Despite her anti-Zionism, she came to realize the importance of Palestine and sent many girls there for training and research. The output of her final years and her remarkably constant temperament suggest that she did envision a world beyond the crisis or, at the very least, that she never doubted that the values that guided her life's work—and those of all the translators studied in this book—would triumph. In answer to the question "How will we survive the unexpected blow of 1 April 1933?," she wrote:

> Through suicide of individuals? Through collective suicide? By extinguishing the memory of the past? By complaining and surrendering, by wandering and regrouping, by marking time, by philosophy or levity?
>
> May each man or woman do what he or she must do, whether from weakness or strength. But we Jews will want to bear in mind that wherever we are in the diaspora—and even Palestine is *Golus* [exile] and diaspora—we can see the peak of Mount Sinai.[152]

Pappenheim left her correspondence and papers with her closest friend, Hannah Karminski, who succeeded her as director of the home. In 1942 the remaining residents were deported to Auschwitz, where Karminski is believed to have died. Though she had taken measures to safeguard Pappenheim's documents, they were destroyed during the war.[153] Pappenheim did not compose essays or make pronouncements about the art of translation, and her prefaces refer only briefly to matters of style and method. Biographers and critics have largely neglected her translations, though interest in Pappenheim's life and work continues to be strong.[154] Today, in the building in the Taunusstraße in Neu-Isenberg that housed the Heim des jüdischen Frauenbundes, the first floor houses a day care center, and the upper floor, a memorial and seminar site with a library, memorabilia, lectures and tours, and a studio for piano lessons and concerts.[155] An online archive with complete information about the history of the home and the names of all residents takes the form of a memory-book, *Gedenkbuch für das Heim des Jüdischen Frauenbundes in Neu-Isenburg* (1907–42).

Martin Buber continued translating after Rosenzweig's death in 1929. There was a hiatus during the war, but he resumed his work in Israel around the time of his seventieth birthday in 1948. He returned to Germany in 1949 and on many occasions in the 1950s in order to continue research for the translations, and also, as some have suggested, to cultivate a readership for the Bible translation and other German publications, since he had continued to write in German. Buber was awarded two important German prizes in those years, the Peace Prize of the German Book Trade and the Goethe Prize. He completed the *Verdeutschung* in Jerusalem in 1961, where at a famous ceremony Gershom Scholem, who had been critical of the translation in the early years, praised it highly in its revised form, even as he cynically called it a Jewish *Gastgeschenk* (parting gift) for Germans—a work whose readership had since been annihilated. But Scholem's verdict was shortsighted. With the efforts of Nahum Glatzer, Lawrence Rosenwald, and Everett Fox, the Buber-Rosenzweig Bible has become an established work of world literature.[156]

Buber's reference to Pappenheim as a "female Moses" acknowledges that as a translator and as leader, Pappenheim engaged in cultural cross-dressing. Her earliest literary works were published under the pseudonym Paul Berthold or P. Berthold. But she was not above essentializing the differences between men and women; she believed that men in general were too lenient. Men "speak," women "act." "Women have a more intense connection to humanity and to life—to destiny. Thus God gave women 'two hands'—one mild, one strict." Pappenheim, who spoke with one tongue and wrote with one pen, translated with both hands, marrying both sides of her agenda. She drew upon the power of German and Yiddish, religious teaching and picturesque folk customs, stringency and leniency, rising to the position of "female lawgiver." Her Tanach comprises the final chapter in her life-long quest for a Jewish voice.

Buber and Rosenzweig also translated with two (or four) hands. They too married diverse aspirations and conflicting agendas: Jewish and Christian, intellectual and popular, Romantic and modernist, Mosaic and Lutheran, theocentric and androcentric.

As the first wave traced the transition from Yiddish to High German, so does the fourth circle back to the Yiddish culture of Ashkenaz. Thus, Pappenheim's translations, which redirected modern German Jews back to the Torah of their ancestors, are a fitting last chapter in the history of German Jewish Bible translation. My study began with the shift away from translations intended for women and the uneducated. With Pappenheim's efforts, a corpus of writing that Moses Mendelssohn (and his heirs) regarded as unfit for German Jewry returns through the back door. In the 1920s and 1930s, the two traditions—German and Yiddish, male and female—emerge side by side.

EPILOGUE

Ma shemo? The Name of God in the German Jewish Bible

In this book I have sought not only to describe a series of Bibles, but to enter into translators' minds and illuminate the process of translating. The creative process was of the essence, because the translation revolution had turned the Jewish translator into an agent, author, and artist.

I began with Moses Mendelssohn's fateful decision to call God "the Eternal One," *der Ewige*—the name that became the "signature" of the German Jewish Bible into the nineteenth and twentieth centuries. Hermann Levin Goldschmidt notes that the name of God is the "ultimate test" for translators of the Hebrew Bible; Franz Rosenzweig wrote that the very unity of the Bible hinges upon the correct perception of God and rendering of the divine name. How did Mendelssohn arrive at that name? How did so many later translators, despite their disagreements with Mendelssohn, manage to retain it? On what grounds was *der Ewige* rejected by two other philosopher-translators, Samson Raphael Hirsch and Franz Rosenzweig?[1] The case of *der Ewige*, pro and contra, encapsulates the history recounted in the foregoing chapters.

Imagine that you were charged to translate the Tetragrammaton, YHWH, into the vernacular. Would you defer to the longstanding tradition of LORD? "LORD" is a translation of the Hebrew *Adonai*, a biblical appellation in its own right that ended up being used as the pronunciation of, and in place of the Tetragrammaton, by virtue of its frequent proximity to it in Scripture.[2] LORD was adopted by the Septuagint (*Kyrios*), the Vulgate (*Dominus*), the Luther Bible (*der HERR*), and of course, the King James Bible, who chose it over Tyndale's "Jehova." LORD also endures in the Jewish Publication Society Bible (1985) and in Robert Alter's *Five Books of Moses* (2008). Alternately, would you leave God's name untranslated? Choose a particular attribute, such as "The Holy One" or "The Eternal One"? Perhaps, rather than follow historical precedent, you devise a new name—as did Mendelssohn in the 1780s; Buber and Rosenzweig in the 1920s; or Marcia Falk in 1996, who refers to God as "Source of Life." Perhaps you would go as far as the authors of a controversial new Protestant German translation, *Bibel in gerechter Sprache* (Bible in just language, a "fair-trade" Bible), which prints multiple versions of the Name of God, one after the other in page headers so that the eye continuously encounters new and different names—

> Yud-Yud Sie Er die Eine die Heilige Schechina Gott E-L Adonaj

and never loses sight of the fact that "God's Name is untranslatable . . . God surpasses the possibilities of language. What human beings say about and to God is an ever-renewed attempt to approach [God]."[3] The story of Mendelssohn's *der Ewige* is but one chapter in an ongoing, universal story.

Mendelssohn chose the primal Mosaic scene of naming in Exodus 3 as the occasion for introducing *his* name. It was a brilliant move, because in Exodus 3, the name is actually revealed by God, in response to Moses's query:

> But Moses said to the Deity, "Suppose I come to the sons of Israel and say to them, 'Your fathers' deity has sent me to you,' and they say to me, 'What is his name?' (*ma shemo*)—what should I say to them?" (Ex 3:13, Anchor Bible)

Mendelssohn also understood that to translate the divine Name was to identify a divine attribute,[4] that which Hirsch called an "inner truth."[5] In other words, Moses's question *ma shemo*? does not only mean *what is His name?* or *how shall we call Him?* but rather, *who is He to us*? Perhaps that explains why God does not simply reply, "I am . . ." or "call me . . ."; instead, Scripture records three delphic answers, one after the other (JPS, Ex 3:14–15, emphasis added):

1. And God said to Moses, "*Ehyeh asher Ehyeh* (*I will be what I will be*)."
2. He continued, "Thus shall you say to the Israelites, '*Ehyeh* (*I-will-be*) sent me to you.'"
3. And God said further to Moses, "Thus shall you speak to the Israelites: the Lord, the *God of your fathers, the God of Abraham, the God of Isaac, and the God of Jacob*, has sent me to you: This shall be My name forever / This My appellation for all eternity."

The first, in Hebrew a kind of three-word palindrome, *Ehyeh asher Ehyeh,*[6] Mendelssohn paraphrased: "I am the being that is eternal" ("ich bin das Wesen, welches ewig ist"). His rendering departs from the Hebrew in diction, style, and meaning; he eliminates the "cagey" (Propp) undertone and forfeits the symmetry, replacing those with a straightforward definition or self-description. Three words in Hebrew become eight in German. In effect, Mendelssohn invented the clear answer Moses might have wanted, but one woefully far removed from the answer he got. For the second answer, Mendelssohn went even farther afield, translating one Hebrew word "I-will-be" (*Ehyeh*) into nine German words divided into three clauses: "das Ewige Wesen / welches sich nennt / ich bin ewig": "the eternal being which names itself 'I am eternal.'"

With regard to the first answer: how did Mendelssohn justify rendering "I will be what I will be" as "I am the being that is eternal"? As he explains it, it was an innovation born of compromise. In the following excerpt from the commentary, Mendelssohn arrives at the "only possible" German equivalent by interweaving two distinct discourses—rabbinic and philosophical:

> It says in a midrash, "The Holy One, Blessed be He, said to Moses: 'say to them, "I am the one who was, and now I am the same and will be the same in the future"'" [Exodus Rabbah 3:6]. And our teachers, may their memory be a blessing, say further: "I will be with them in this need, who will be with them in their bondage in the kingdoms to come" [Berakhot 9b]. Their meaning is the following: "Because past and future time are all present to the creator, since in Him there is no change and dependence and of His days there is no passing—because of this all times are in Him called by a single name, which embraces past, present, and future alike. . . ." Now in German there is no word that better unites the meanings of omnitemporality, necessity of existence, and providence, then does this holy name: "the eternal, necessary, providential being" (*das ewige, notwendige, vorhersehende Wesen*). So we have translated "the Eternal" (*der Ewige*) or "the Eternal Being" (*das ewige Wesen*).[7]

Mendelssohn begins with a midrash drawn from Rashi's commentary and the Talmud (i.e., I will be with Israel in their time of need); proceeds to a classical, philosophical notion about God's essence (eternal, necessary, providential); and ultimately claims that the German name "Eternal One" embraces them all: omnitemporality, necessity, providence, *and* the rabbinic attribute of being with Israel in their time of need—actually, in many times of need. Incidentally, the allusion to future bondages "in the kingdoms to come" refers to the aggadic (anecdotal) part of the Talmudic passage not quoted, in which a Woody Allen–esque exchange occurs between God's first and second answers to Moses at the burning bush:

> God: "'I will be' with them in this predicament 'what I will be' with them in their subjugation by other kingdoms."
>
> [Moses] said before [God], "O Lord of the universe! Why should I mention to them another trouble? They have enough [problems] with this one."
>
> [God] said to him, "You have spoken well. So shall you say, etc."[8]

Out of agreement with Moses—and out of sympathy for the nation—God decides to edit or curtail the first answer, "I will be whom I will be," into "I-will-be." Mendelssohn takes a similar kind of shortcut, if you will: he begins with the midrashic explanation, then restates the tension in philosophical terms, then claims that he was compelled to choose one attribute, "eternal," that would harness the others—necessity of existence, providence (and being with Israel in times of need)—because "in German there is no word" other than that one which captures all the qualities.

Franz Rosenzweig found this argument shaky. He claims that of the three attributes, Mendelssohn chose the wrong one: it was not about God's *eternality* that Moses and the enslaved Israelites most needed to hear, but about God's *providence*. Perhaps the harnessing of these concepts was possible prior to Kant. Rosenzweig goes so far as to suggest that Mendelssohn concealed his true source, which was not the Talmud, but rather Protestant French theologian John Calvin, who introduced *L'Éternel* into French Bibles; the term was used in the Geneva Bible from 1588 on.[9] Rosenzweig speculates that Mendelssohn violated "the sure instinct of Jewish tradition" to prove himself a "true citizen of Berlin," as Mendelssohn's Berlin was also the city to which Huguenots, Calvin's followers, fled in the seventeenth and eighteenth centuries. Rosenzweig concludes:

> So Mendelssohn made the wrong choice, influenced as he was by Calvin's example and made susceptible to that influence by the rationalizing, classicizing spirit of his century. (In Mendelssohn's case the spirit of the age made alliance with the Aristotelian spirit of Maimonides, whom Mendelssohn had honored all his life, against the sure instinct of Jewish tradition.)[10]

Whether or not Mendelssohn got the idea from Calvin, he clearly rejected other Christian options, such as *der Herr* (Luther) and *Jehova* (Schmidt and Michaelis).[11] Mendelssohn did not make reference to Christian options in his commentary. But in the continuation of the passage cited above, he boasted of having consulted many Jewish translations and philosophical works: Onkelos's Babylonian Targum (2nd–5th centuries), Maimonides's *Guide of the Perplexed* (13th-century Spain), Nachmanides's commentary on the Hebrew Bible (13th-century Spain), Saadia Gaon's Judeo-Arabic translation (9th century), and lastly, the Palestinian targumist Pseudo-Jonathan (4th century). Like many a Bible translator who made a controversial choice, Mendelssohn allied himself with a trustworthy precursor from the remote past in order to legitimize his break with the recent past. In this genealogy, Targum Pseudo-Jonathan (known in Mendelssohn's day as Jonathan Ben Uzziel) comes almost as an afterthought; the very last sentences read:

> And the present German translator decided to render the name with respect to eternity because for him the other meanings branch out from this central one. Similarly, I have found in Jonathan Ben Uzziel a rendering similarly oriented to this meaning: "I-who-am-and-shall-be has sent me to you."[12]

Targum Pseudo-Jonathan provides further legitimacy for Mendelssohn's controversial decision to paraphrase, rather than translate, "I will be what I will be." Moreover, in the complete Aramaic verse (which Mendelssohn does not quote), Pseudo-Jonathan connected the verb *to be* in "I will be what I will be" back to God's creative utterance "Let there be light." He translated: "And the Lord said unto Moshe, '*He who spoke, and the world was; who spoke, and all things were.*' And He said, 'This you shall say to the sons of Israel, I-who-am-and-shall-be has sent me to you.'" By linking Exodus 3 to Genesis 1, Pseudo-Jonathan established that the Deity speaking through the burning bush is not a Platonic Idea, but a deity who intervenes in history to create, and to redeem.

No less important, Mendelssohn's account, in tracing his approach back to Targum Pseudo-Jonathan, enables us to identify another road *not* taken: the approach used by the better-known Aramaic translator, Onkelos (whom he mentions first on his list). Onkelos initiated what I call the *alternative Jewish approach* to Exodus 3:14: he left the three Hebrew words untranslated (boldface added):

> וַאֲמַר יְיָ לְמֹשֶׁה **אֶהְיֶה אֲשֶׁר אֶהְיֶה** וַאֲמַר כִּדְנָן תֵּימַר לִבְנֵי יִשְׂרָאֵל **אֶהְיֶה** שַׁלְחַנִי לְוָתְכוֹן.

The Yiddish Enlightenment Bible translations of 1678 and 1679 by Jekuthiel Blitz and Joseph Witzenhausen followed Onkelos's approach. Witzenhausen used bold, large-font letters: **אֶהְיֶה אֲשֶׁר אֶהְיֶה**. Blitz set off the Hebrew words with parentheses. These two Yiddish translators modeled their efforts on the Luther Bible, admired for its expressive style, and the Dutch States Bible, admired for its fidelity to Hebrew. But when it came to the divine name, they took exception to these Christian models—both of which render Exodus 3:14 in clear German and Dutch prose, adding typographical marks for emphasis:

> Luther: Ich werde sein, der ich sein werde.
> Dutch States Bible: ICK SAL ZIIN DIE ICK ZIIN SAL.

Blitz and Witzenhausen must have concluded that in Bible translations that were to be marketed to traditional Jews in Amsterdam and Poland, "*Ehyeh asher Ehyeh* / I will be what I will be" should be retained in Hebrew. One century later in Berlin, Moses Mendelssohn arrived at a different conclusion. Mendelssohn did not retain the Hebrew *Ehyeh asher Ehyeh*: he paraphrased, "Ich bin das Wesen, welches ewig ist," and defended his bold innovation through the rhetoric of compromise. To his one rationale, I would add that Mendelssohn's priority as a translator was to disambiguate Hebrew Scripture. To leave *Ehyeh asher Ehyeh* alone would have violated his first principle, namely, that everything in Scripture could (and should) be translated as clearly as possible. Mendelssohn's formulation "I am the being that is eternal" seems designed as a statement that this opaque, enigmatic utterance does after all have a clear and unambiguous meaning. Furthermore, as a philosopher, there was no way he would *not* take up the ultimate challenge. This translation screams out: the Bible *does* do philosophy! Finally, Mendelssohn (perhaps opportunistically) used Exodus 3:14 (and also Deuteronomy 6:4, "Hear O Israel . . .") to authenticate his own choice of *der Ewige* for the proper Name of God throughout the Pentateuch, by having God dictate the Name by which God would be known: *I am the being that is eternal, and this is how you shall call me.*

German Jewish translators in the 1830s and 1840s produced a spate of translations that were far more true to the rhythm, syntax, and vocabulary of biblical Hebrew than Mendelssohn's. Yet, it was apparently not an option to dislodge *der Ewige*; the name had taken hold in the German Jewish religious imagination. These scholars found creative ways to do justice to the opacity of the original Hebrew, *without* giving up the word *ewig* and the association of God with omnitemporality. Johlson, Zunz, and Herxheimer relied on letter spacing, square brackets, parentheses, footnotes, backslashes, and other typographical marks in order to transmit the original Hebrew Name; provide a functional German rendering; *and* retain Mendelssohn's appellation:

Johlson (1831):[13] Und Gott sprach zu Mose: **Ehejeh-Ascher-Ehejeh. [Ich werde seyn, der ich seyn werde*).]** Und sprach: So sollst du sagen zu den Söhnen Israels: **Ehejeh [das ewige, selbständige Wesen]** sendet mich zu euch. Und sprach ferner Gott zu Mose, so sollst du sagen zu den Söhnen Israel's: **Der Ewige** . . .

Johlson's footnote: *) Oder: *Ich bin, der ich bin.*—(Ich bin und **werde ewig seyn**, *weil* ich seyn will.—**Ich allein bin *selbstständig* und kann sagen: Ich werde seyn! Ich bin und bleibe unveränderlich**—).

Zunz: Da sprach Gott zu Moscheh: **Ich werde sein der Ich bin**. Und sprach: Also sprich zu den Kindern Jisrael: **Ehejeh** sendet mich zu euch. Und ferner sprach Gott zu Moscheh: Also sprich zu den Kindern Jisrael: **Der Ewige** . . .

Herxheimer: Da sprach Gott zu Mosche: **Ich bin, der ich bin.*** Und sprach: So sprich zu den Kindern Jisrael: **Ehejeh**** sendet mich zu euch. Und Gott sprach ferner zu Mosche: So sprich zu den Kindern Yisrael: **Der Ewige** . . .

Herxheimer's two footnotes: *Mit diesen inhaltschweren [*sic*] Worten sagt Gott, dass er ein unveränderlich **ewiges** Wesen sei; dass also auch seine Verheißungen durch Moses, wie an die Väter, erfüllen werde. ** E h e j e h, d.h. **das ewige Wesen**; das sich selbst (in der ersten Person) nennt Ehejeh.

The second wave had a high tolerance for polysemy; their approach of laying out all the options remains the method of choice in contemporary American Jewish Bibles, such as *Etz Chaim Torah and Commentary* (2001, JPS translation):

And God said to Moses, "Ehyeh-Asher-Ehyeh."* He continued, "Thus shall you say to the Israelites, 'Ehyeh sent me to you.'"**

*Meaning of Heb. uncertain; variously translated: "I Am That I Am": "I Am Who I Am," "I Will Be What I Will Be"; etc.

** Others "I Am" or "I Will Be."

And *The Schocken Bible* (1983; trans. Everett Fox):

God said to Moshe: EHYEH ASHER EHYEH/I will be-there howsoever I will be-there. And he said: Thus shall you say to the Children of Israel: EHYEH /I-WILL-BE-THERE sends me to you.

The translators of the third wave approached the Name of God from opposing directions. In his *Israelitische Bibel*, Ludwig Philippson retained *der Ewige*. His translation of Exodus 3:14 took a literal, second-wave approach: "Ich werde sein, welcher ich werde sein" reproduces the Hebrew word order, and thus violates German word order by reversing the normal position of the final two words. Philippson's commentary, typically, begins by organizing the prior approaches into three groups: first, Targum Onkelos, Syriac, Saadia, Johlson; second, the Septuagint, Philo, de Wette, Zunz, Salomon; third, Aquila, Theodotion; Targum Hieros, Albo. It concludes, "But the simplest meaning of these words is 'I will be that which I will be.' "

In his Pentateuch, Samson Raphael Hirsch followed the alternate tradition of Targum Onkelos and the Amsterdam Yiddish translators and printed *Ehyeh asher Ehyeh* in Hebrew characters. Hirsch's commentary focuses not on the history of interpretation but on the significance of the *future tense* as a powerful assertion of God's freedom, which contrasts with certain unidentified "non-Jewish" views about divine freedom, human freedom, and creation. A passage towards the end of Hirsch's long excursus reads:

> *Ehe' asher Ehe'* comes crushingly against this delusion, which, with the denying of the freedom of God, has to deny the free will of Man; and by declaring the absolute freedom of God, puts the future of Man in its true perspective. . . . This [new designation of Him] expresses with absolute certainty that basic truth, the very cornerstone of all Truth and all Happiness, that the future goal of mankind is absolutely assured, and it is a call for Man to use his power to carve the immediate future, in God's service, i.e., *to make God's will* his will.[14]

Like that of Mendelssohn, Hirsch's interpretation is somewhat self-serving. Placing the emphasis on absolute futurity, on divine and human freedom, allowed Hirsch to take an utterly unorthodox approach to translating God's name: he used one German word for both the generic deity (*Elohim*) and the Tetragrammaton. In the case of *Elohim*, he wrote *Gott* like everyone else; in the case of the proper Name, he used *G o t t* with extra spaces between the letters. In the case where the two names come together, as in Genesis 2:4, he simply used the one name *Gott* because—he doesn't exactly say why. He acknowledges that the different names represented distinct, yet closely related attributes. He also notes, "the Name . . . is untranslatable."[15] He ends up arguing that the proper Name is the "inner concept" of the generic name. His commentary makes clear that a primary motive was to reject *der Ewige* as the symbol of Mendelssohn's *Be'ur* and the many cultural and religious legacies that followed from it.

Franz Rosenzweig and Martin Buber adopted capitalized pronouns, masculine when in the third person, in lieu of a single divine Name: I, YOU, HE, HIM. They rejected the premise that the Name had to designate a particular divine attribute. They made certain that God's proper Name could never become an icon, but would be present in a fluid way, as an ever-changing leitmotif. Scholem put it even more strongly: "It is one of the great paradoxes of this undertaking that in a translation which in the final analysis renders the Bible as the word of God, the name of God as such should not appear."[16] The only constant was the fact that that the Name was always in a vocative form (indicating someone who is being addressed), and always determined by the relationship of the speakers in any given moment. It was perhaps the most radical reaction against *der Ewige* imaginable. Rosenzweig noted that even Luther's *der Herr* was preferable to *der Ewige,* since that, too, is a situated name, a relational name, rather than a word that pretends to name a divine essence or attribute. Here is the Buber-Rosenzweig translation (Exod 3:14–15):[17]

> Gott sprach zu Mosche:
> **Ich werde dasein, als der ich dasein werde**.
> Und er sprach:
> So sollst du zu den Söhnen Jisraels sprechen:
> **ICH BIN DA**[18] schickt mich zu euch.
> Und weiter sprach Gott zu Mosche:
> So sollst du zu den Söhnen Jisraels sprechen:
> **ER**
> der Gott eurer Väter,
> der Gott Abrahams, der Gott Jizchaks, der Gott Jaakobs,
> Schickt mich zu euch.
> Das ist mein Name **in Weltzeit** [*sic;* not "in Ewigkeit"]
> das mein Gedenken, Geschlecht für Geschlecht.

Buber and Rosenzweig changed "Ich werde sein" (used in Luther and in the New Zurich Bible) to "Ich werde **dasein**." In common parlance, *Dasein* means existence or presence; here it is best translated as "being there" (conveyed by Everett Fox as "I will be-there howsoever I will be-there"). Symbolically, they avoided using the word *ewig* as an equivalent for "forever" in verse 15. In naming God, as in other ways, the Buber-Rosenzweig Bible sought to turn the Mendelssohn Bible on its head.

At their core, the objections and solutions of Hirsch and Rosenzweig are quite similar. Hirsch uses Mendelssohn as a straw man: " 'Eternal' is a metaphysical, transcendental conception which has scarcely any practical application to anything else, certainly not to our own lives and existence . . . The thought Eternal leaves our hearts cold, contains nothing for our lives."[19] In response, Hirsch "corrected" the Bible using only the one German word *Gott* for both biblical names to enhance the Bible's internal unity. Unity was also a priority for Buber and Rosenzweig. In "The Eternal," Rosenzweig claims that the essence of Jewish monotheism is at stake in rendering the Name correctly: "this Jewish uniting of the distant God with the near, the 'whole' with 'one's own.' Only in this fusion do we have the 'essence of Judaism.' . . . Now this union is the kernel of biblical revelation; it is what makes this book the Jewish Bible."[20] Rosenzweig also tried to argue that God was not far away, but intimately present to the reader of Scripture—a book designed to answer the innate human "longing" for eternity. Like the great philosophers, "The God of the Bible also quiets this longing—not, however, by fulfilling it or promising it fulfillment, but precisely by quieting it, by bringing it to silence . . . In the face of living time, the human desire for eternity learns to fall silent."[21]

And yet, as Andreas Losch argues, Rosenzweig's strong response to *der Ewige* must be qualified, given that the term played a central role in his own philosophical writings.[22] Rosenzweig grew up in a highly assimilated German Jewish family. He used *der Ewige* in his diaries, letters, and, most important, he wrote about eternity in *The Star of Redemption* (1919). In an oft-cited passage from that work, Rosenzweig conveys that the pathos of eternity can indeed be the very opposite of cold:

> Eternity is not a very long time, but a tomorrow that could just as well be today. Eternity is a future that, without ceasing to be a future, is nonetheless also present. Eternity is a today that is aware of being more than today. . . . [Eternity does not mean] "a very long time," but "already today."[23]

In 1929, insisting that Mendelssohn made the wrong choice, Rosenzweig not only rejected the practices of emancipated German Jewry, but also, perhaps even in the first instance, his own biography. Rosenzweig also acknowledges that Mendelssohn's *der Ewige* was an error of great significance. He concludes the essay by affirming the translator's mission—guided by Scripture itself—to extract the kernel of truth from Mendelssohn's error (and his own):

> If the Bible did not have this enigmatic power to transform our errors into its truth, then translating it would be still more risky than it already is. But it is precisely on account of this power that the risk becomes a commandment, and a goal worth any pain; for this transformational energy of the Bible is the secret of its world-historical influence.[24]

Rosenzweig was not the first to speak of Bible translation as a transformative endeavor. In a very different context, the eighteenth-century mystic Rav Nahman of Breslov wrote of the powerful impact of the Bible's stepping beyond its native Hebrew. Like the tree of knowledge of good and evil, translation might lead to enlightenment, or to deception; but translation into Aramaic, a holy vernacular already embedded in the Hebrew Bible, raised Hebrew words to a higher level, "enlightening the letters of the holy tongue."[25] The founder of Hasidism, Rabbi Israel Baal Shem Tov, also fathomed the power to enter into the letters and allow them to illuminate beyond themselves.[26] Jewish religious translators in Ashkenaz and in Germany, from Pappenheim back to Blitz, did not abide a mystical or inspirational model of translation. They aspired to the Mosaic hand: the hand that first placed (*sam*) the Torah before the nation. No antique volume: the Jewish Bible has always been a transmitted, transcribed, expounded, translated artifact. The first handprints were left by God and Moses, but many others left their mark, not to alter its essence but to safeguard it for eternity.

ACKNOWLEDGMENTS

Writing this book has been a labor of love over many years. I can only begin to convey my gratitude to the many people who contributed to my understanding of these German Jewish Bibles and who sustained me in various ways during my research.

My first thank you goes to the University of Chicago Press. Alan G. Thomas invested in this project at a very early stage and urged me to see it through—which might not have happened without the advice and ready assistance of Randolph Petilos. I thank Michael Koplow for his meticulous and generous editing of the manuscript.

I am indebted to the librarians who secured me access to the Bibles, and who made numerous accommodations to facilitate my research: Harvey Sukenic, director of the Rae and Joseph Gann Library of Hebrew College; Nell K. Carlson, curator of historical collections at Andover-Harvard Theological Library; Vardit Samuels, assistant librarian in the Judaica Division of Harvard Library; and the librarians at the Center for Jewish History and the Judaica Collection at the J. W. Goethe University in Frankfurt.

I was extremely fortunate to have fellowship support that made possible a few precious semesters of leave from teaching. Thank you to the Boston University Center for the Humanities (twice); the Leo Baeck Institute; the Center for Jewish Studies at Harvard University; and Boston University's School of Theology Religion Fellows Program.

Some years back, Katherine O'Conner and Dorothy Kelly, chairs of my former department, saw fit to advertise a dual position in Hebrew and German at Boston University; my job talk for that position contained the germ cell of this book. In this regard, and in so many ways, Boston University has been an ideal environment for teaching, learning, and scholarship. Thank you to this incredible community of colleagues, administrators, and students.

For their leadership, I thank Susan Jackson, my first friend and best advisor; Virginia Sapiro and Ann Cudd, former and current deans of the College of Arts and Sciences; J. Keith Vincent, chair of World Languages and Literatures; Stephanie Nelson, dean of the Core Curriculum; Michael Zank, director of the Elie Wiesel Center; and James Winn, former director of the Humanities Center.

In the course of my research I relied on the expertise of many scholars, including Pamela Barmash, Sacvan Bercovitch z"l, Marc Brettler, Steve Dowden, Martha Friedenthal-Haase, Rachel Greenblatt, Susannah Heschel, Judith Kates, Olga Litvak, Peter Machinist, Susan Mizruchi, Lawrence Rosenwald, Jeffrey Sammons, Ismar Schorsch, Naomi Seidman, Lisa Silverman, and Judith Wechsler. I am grateful to Erika Timm, Marion Aptroot, and Jerold C. Frakes, who educated me about the Bible in Yiddish. My conversations with Mary Bergstein, Diane O'Donoghue, and Bennett Simon enriched my understanding of the Philippson Bible (and Freud's Bible) immeasurably. Special thanks to Michael Zell for advising me about Jewish culture in Amsterdam and Rembrandt's mother; Sigalit Davis, for sharing her knowledge of Hebrew prosody; Ursula Mangoubi, for decoding Bertha Pappenheim's handwriting; and David Braun for enlightening me about Yiddish orthography and pronunciation.

At critical junctures, Margery Sokoloff and Leslie Cohen helped me to think through and develop the book's overall argument and structure; I cannot thank them enough for their wisdom and enthusiasm. Ellen K. Meisel's conscientious assistance with acquiring permissions and preparing the manuscript in the end stages was invaluable.

My best sister Debby supported and nurtured me in countless ways. Debby—your enthusiasm for this project has kept me going, and I can't thank you enough.

My understanding of what it means to translate, not just the Hebrew Bible, but also the Torah, drew upon skills and experiences from all stages of my life. I first learned how to read and interpret the Torah from my parents, Sarah Fisher Gillman and Neil Gillman. My grandmother Rose Kerstein Fisher taught me Yiddish and enticed me with stories about the multilingual world (French, Flemish, German) whence she came. Among many inspiring teachers, Rabbi Yaakov Bieler and Mrs. Rachel Taub-Weinstein challenged me to engage with biblical and rabbinic texts at the highest level and ignited my passion for studying them. Jim and Elana Ponet pushed me to think about Jewish texts and ideas with greater depth than I had thought possible.

My husband Michael Prince remains my model of intellectual acuity and scholarly integrity. Michael—thank you for all the gifts and giftlets. I simply could not have done it without you. To you, and to our children, family, and friends: I am so grateful for your love and encouragement. You are my ideal readers and my true blessings.

I dedicate this book to my parents, who anticipated its publication even more fervently than I. May you enjoy it in good health for many years to come.

A. G. 28 May 2017

Portions of chapter 2 first appeared in earlier form as "The Jewish Quest for a German Bible: The Nineteenth-Century Translations of Joseph Johlson and Leopold Zunz" in the Society of Biblical Literature's online journal *SBL Forum* (Summer 2009). Parts from chapters 1 and 4 appear in the essay "'Not like Cherries, but like Peaches': Mendelssohn and Rosenzweig as Translators of Hebrew Poetry" in the forthcoming *The German-Hebrew Dialogue*, edited by Rachel Seelig (Walter De Gruyter, 2017). I thank the editors for allowing me to rehearse some of my ideas first in these contexts.

NOTES

PREFACE

1. Mahler, *Das Lied von der Erde,* final song ("Der Abschied").

2. Propp suggests that the "persistent aspiration to know God" is really Moses's; and furthermore, "the divine name functions as a shibboleth . . . not among the characters, but between text and reader . . . a text not speaking in Yahweh's name might be discarded and ignored." Propp, *Exodus 1–18,* 223.

3. That translating Scripture and expounding Scripture were considered synonymous is in itself an indicator of the closeness of ideas of polysemy and polyglossia in Ancient Judaism. Seidman, *Faithful Renderings,* 26.

4. Plaut, *German Jewish Bible Translations,* 11. Regarding the number sixteen: aside from inconsistencies in the accounts, it is hard to obtain an exact figure, since many were subsequently revised or retranslated. A bibliography of Moses Mendelssohn's works lists eight subsequent editions of his Bible before the editor admits that he stopped counting. The "final" edition was published in Warsaw in 1888.

5. Richard I. Cohen draws the analogy between European Jewry's "repossession" of the Hebrew Bible and their emergence into the urban public sphere. Cohen, "Urban Visibility and Biblical Visions."

6. Shavit and Eran, *The Hebrew Bible Reborn* 1.

7. Shavit and Eran, *The Hebrew Bible Reborn,* 19.

8. Rosenzweig, "'The Eternal,'" 115.

9. Meschonnic, *Poètique du traduire,* 11.

10. Weintraub, *Targume Hatorah Lelashon Hagermanit.*

11. Bechtoldt, *Jüdische deutsche Bibelübersetzungen.*

12. Störig, *Das Problem des Übersetzens,* 17–18. Störig includes essays by Buber and Rosenzweig.

13. Berman, *The Experience of the Foreign,* 33. Of the translators I discuss, Berman mentions only Rosenzweig (and Mendelssohn in a footnote).

14. Seidman, *Faithful Renderings,* 153–98.

15. Plaut's "birth-death" trajectory echoes Gershom Scholem's speech at the ceremony upon the completion of the Buber-Rosenzweig Bible in Jerusalem in 1961, in which

he spoke of it as the "parting gift" from Jews to Germans, a book whose intended readership had been decimated in the interim.

16. Gillman, "Between Religion and Culture: Mendelssohn, Buber, Rosenzweig, and the Enterprise of Biblical Translation."

17. Heller, "Review of *Zeenah u-Reenah*."

18. Mosse, *German Jews beyond Judaism*.

19. "The German language lacks 'culture,' and to acquire it, it must go through a certain *expansion*, which presupposes translations marked by fidelity. For in what respect could a translation that mirrors the 'French manner' expand the horizon of the language and the culture?" Berman, *The Experience of the Foreign*, 36.

20. Berman, *The Experience of the Foreign*, 35.

21. Cohen describes the rabbinic character of German Jewish scholarship across all schools, Reform, Historical, Orthodox, in these terms. "What should never be overlooked is that for all their break with traditional methods and perspectives, each of the great scholars was simultaneously representing his school as the most authentic link in the chain of *rabbinic* tradition. They all remained to the last proud *rabbis*." Cohen, "German Jewry as Mirror of Modernity" (XXVII).

22. Olga Litvak elaborates on the Romantic character of the Haskalah: "The return to Hebrew 'excellence' and the attempt to fashion a classical, which is to say, normative, Hebrew vocabulary and syntax, the obsession with grammar, the emergence of literary criticism—all these are evidence of the Romantic attempt to construct a system of literary values in opposition to the realities of Jewish vernacular literacy." Litvak, *Haskalah*, 43.

23. Midrash Tanhuma (Buber edition), Yitro:16. Cited in Bialik and Ravnitzky, eds., *The Book of Legends*, 449.

INTRODUCTION

1. Letter to Buber, 29 July 1925, GS, 1: 1056.

2. Copeland, *Rhetoric, Hermeneutics, and Translation*, 222.

3. BT Kiddushin 49a.

4. Tractate Soferim 1.

5. See the sources assembled in Leibowitz, *Die Übersetzungstechnik*, 382–84.

6. Leibowitz, *Die Übersetzungstechnik*, 383. "One who reads the Torah [in synagogue] should read not less than three verses, and he should not read to the translator more than one verse [at a time]. In a prophet, however [he may give him] three at a time." BT Megillah 23b–24a.

7. BT Megillah 3a.

8. "R. Simeon b. Gamaliel says that books [of the Scripture] also are permitted to be written only in Greek. R. Abbahu said in the name of R. Johanan: The *halachah* follows R. Simeon b. Gamaliel. R. Johanan further said: What is the reason of R. Simeon b. Gamaliel? Scripture says, *God enlarge Japheth, and he shall dwell in the tents of Shem*; [this means] that the words of Japheth shall be in the tents of Shem. But why not say [the words of] Gomer and Magog (i.e. other sons of Japheth)? —R. Hiyya b. Abba replied: The real reason is because it is written, Let God enlarge [Yaft] Japheth: implying, let the chief beauty [Yafyuth (i.e. the Greek language)] of Japheth be in the tents of Shem." BT Megillah 9b.

9. Seidman, *Faithful Renderings*, esp. 25–26.

10. BT Berachot 8a.

11. The custom connects with the greater idea that Torah study is an end in itself. One does not engage in study in order to know; rather, learning has its own merits and its own rewards. Similarly, one is commanded to observe the rules and perform one's obligations as a Jew, regardless of intent.

12. *Shulhan Arukh*, Orah Hayyim 85:2; Mishnah Brurah 285:6.

13. The ritual of public reading of the Torah involves chanting from an animal-skin Torah scroll according to prescribed musical notation; public correction of any mispronunciations; choreographed removal of the scrolls from the ark; and processing, pointing, blessing, kissing, raising the scrolls, and bowing. These are permitted only in the presence of a quorum in the synagogue.

14. Leibowitz writes that there existed, alongside the print translations, "eine ununterbrochene tradition einer nicht nur einzelne worte glossierenden, sondern vollständigen mündlichen übersetzung mit wort- und silbentreuem charakter . . ." Leibowitz, *Die Übersetzungstechnik*, 388.

15. The vocabulary of these oral Yiddish translations became an integral part of children's mother tongue, shaping the vocabulary of average Jews. See Timm, "Der Einfluss der aschkenasischen Bibelübersetzungstätigkeit auf die jiddische Gemeinsprache."

16. "Zweimal im urtext, aus liebe zur thora, den alles was einem lieb ist, wird zweimal gelesen, und einmal im targum, um die frauen und die unkundigen die worte der thora hören zu lassen, damit die gottesfurcht in ihr herz dringe. Und so ist's auch brauch der Franzosen (sc. franz. Juden) den wochenabschnitt sonnabends zweimal im urtext und einmal fremdsprachlich in der sprache des landes durchzugehen." Cited in Leibowitz, *Die Übersetzungstechnik*, 389.

17. Baumgarten, *Introduction to Old Yiddish Literature*, 72–73. In the following section, I draw from Baumgarten; Staerk and Leitzmann, *Die jüdisch-deutschen Bibelübersetzungen*; and the articles by Timm, Turniansky, and Aptroot in Berger, *The Bible in/and Yiddish*.

18. Baumgarten, *Introduction to Old Yiddish Literature*, 86.

19. Three of the characteristics were reproduction of the Hebrew word order, often resulting in the repetition of the subject; the use of prepositional phrases with *fun* (of) where this was not the appropriate preposition according to Yiddish usage; the translation of all Hebrew affixes, sometimes resulting in constructions with an indirect object where the Yiddish verb calls for a direct object.

20. Timm, "Die Bibelübersetzungssprache," 95.

21. On the publication history of this work, see Baumgarten, *Introduction to Old Yiddish Literature*, 99n38. For a visual impression, see Timm, "Der Einfluss der aschkenasischen Bibelübersetzungstätigkeit," 28.

22. Cited in Timm, "Die Bibelübersetzungssprache," 93.

23. Cited in Baumgarten, *Introduction to Old Yiddish Literature*, 100.

24. Turniansky, "Reception and Rejection," 16.

25. Turniansky, "Reception and Rejection," 16.

26. Kearney, "The Torah of Israel in the Tongue of Ishmael."

27. Berger, in "An Invitation to Buy and Read," explicates the sociological dynamics that shaped Yiddish paratexts.

28. Baumgarten, *Introduction to Old Yiddish Literature*, 91.

29. Baumgarten, *Introduction to Old Yiddish Literature*, 106.

30. Baumgarten, *Introduction to Old Yiddish Literature*, 108–9.

31. Berger, "An Invitation to Buy and Read," 38. Turniansky, *Between the Holy and the Profane*, 61–76. See also Weissler, "Traditional Piety," and Seidman, "Engendering Audiences" 16–19.

32. Baumgarten, *Introduction to Old Yiddish Literature*, 98–99.

33. Baumgarten, *Introduction to Old Yiddish Literature*, 87.

34. Baumgarten, *Introduction to Old Yiddish Literature*, 86.

35. Sheehan, *The Enlightenment Bible*, 225–26.

36. Legaspi, *The Death of Scripture and the Rise of Biblical Studies*.

37. Sheehan, *The Enlightenment Bible*, 228.

38. John Holloran, "What Is the Enlightenment Bible?" Review of Jonathan Sheehan, *The Enlightenment Bible*, 1.

39. Shavit and Eran, *The Hebrew Bible Reborn*, 44.

40. Schorsch, "Myth of Sephardic Supremacy," 71; see also Richard I. Cohen, *Urban Visibility and Biblical Visions*, 40–61.

41. Turniansky, "Nusach ha-Maskili," 836.

42. The question "why the *bet* and not the *alef*?" is posed in the Midrash Genesis Rabbah I: 9–11. Many answers are given, among them, the answer of Rabbi Elazar b. Abinah in the name of R. Aha, which is rendered in the *Tsene-Rene* as follows: "God appeased the offended letter [alef], assuring it that the Ten Commandments given on Mt. Sinai would begin with the word *anochi* ("I") which begins with an *alef*." Zakon, *The Weekly Midrash*, 17.

43. Copeland describes similar shifts in the Christian Middle Ages. "In ancient Rome, the dominant critical discourse was rhetoric, and the ideal of translation carried an explicit agenda of rivalry with the source through the force of rhetorical invention. But in the Middle Ages, the dominant discourse has become hermeneutics—which, in the absence of a strong rhetorical practice—has assumed the rhetorical function of a productive application to discourse" namely,—the power to discover and elucidate new meanings in the inherited texts. Copeland, *Rhetoric, Hermeneutics, and Translation*, 222.

44. As Timm notes, the author of the *Mirkevet ha-Mishneh* reports that his book contains much learned from his teacher and the commentaries, and nothing of his own. "Der Einfluss der aschkenasischen Bibelübersetzungstätigkeit," 31.

45. Buber titled a lecture in November 1926 "Der Mensch von heute und die jüdische Bibel."

46. Blitz, *Bible: In the Yiddish Language*, 1678. See fig. 1.1

CHAPTER ONE

1. Witzenhausen, "Translator's Apology," 13–15.

2. Aptroot, "Bible Translation as Cultural Reform," 329.

3. Naphtali Herz Wessely's paean to Mendelssohn, cited in Mendelssohn, JubA 20,1: 328.

4. Edward Breuer's *The Limits of Enlightenment: Jews, Germans, and the Eighteenth-Century Study of Scripture* has contributed a great deal to my own thinking.

5. In "German Jewry as a Mirror of Modernity," Gerson Cohen writes, "Mendelssohn was but a mild symptom of a process, not its architect or advocate" (22). Feiner, *The Jewish Enlightenment* (2003); Feiner, *Haskalah and History* (2002); Litvak, *Haskalah*.

6. See Weinberg, "Einleitung," and Sorkin's chapters on "Psalms" and "The Pentateuch." Sorkin describes many features I highlight in this chapter, though he frames the overall significance of the *Book of the Paths to Peace* with regard to "three central themes: the Bible as a source of practical knowledge, literal meaning as the focus of exegesis, and the use of history." *Moses Mendelssohn and the Religious Enlightenment*, 55.

7. Breuer, "The Early Modern Period," groups Blitz and Witzenhausen with the *tatysh* translations of 1540 and 1544. Breuer, "The Jewish Enlightenment," discusses "Mendelssohn's Bible project."

8. Shmeruk, *Illustrations in Yiddish Books*.

9. Mühlen, *Die Bibel und ihr Titelblatt*.

10. Cohen, *Jewish Icons*, 96.

11. Cohen, *Jewish Icons*, 96.

12. Cohen, *Jewish Icons*, 97.

13. Aptroot, "Bible Translation as Cultural Reform," 345–46.

14. http://www.bijbelsdigitaal.nl/view/?mode=1&bible=luthv1648&part=1

15. Wiesemann, *Kommt heraus und schaut*, 88; also 91.

16. http://www.raremaps.com/gallery/detail/30060?view=print. In that edition, Moses and Aaron have switched sides (Gans, *Memorbook*, 141), as they do in the 1712 version, which replaced Moses at the burning bush (drawn from Merian's depiction) for the upper image in the exhibition catalogue. Wiesemann, *Kommt heraus und schaut*, 100.

17. The Sulzbach Haggadah copied illustrations and other features from the Amsterdam Haggadah such as the commentary of Abarbanel and the Yiddish translation of Passover songs. Inexpensive facsimiles of the Sulzbach Haggadah are reprinted annually for free distribution around Passover.

18. In the top strip of the title page of the Dutch States Bible, the Divine Name in Hebrew letters and an open book with printed verses from Psalms appears on the left, and Peter on the right.

19. Cohen, *Jewish Icons*, 97.

20. Gans, *Memorbook*, 140.

21. See the title page of the biblical commentary known as *Keli yakar* (Żółkiew: Aharon and Gershon Segal, 1763), reproduced in Gries, "Printing and Publishing."

22. Aptroot, "Biblical Translation as Cultural Reform," 351.

23. Excerpts from both are included in Frakes, *Early Yiddish Texts*, 713–19. See also Staerk and Leitzmann, *Die jüdisch-deutschen Bibelübersetzungen*.

24. Timm, "Blitz and Witzenhausen," 1993; Aptroot, "Bible Translation as Cultural Reform"; Aptroot, "Yiddish Bibles in Amsterdam."

25. Excerpted in Frakes, *Early Yiddish Texts*, 692–702. See also Frakes, *Early Yiddish Epic*, 181–237.

26. Timm, "Blitz and Witzenhausen," 52.

27. Blitz's at http://sammlungen.ub.uni-frankfurt.de/jd/content/titleinfo/1698613, and Witzenhausen's at http://sammlungen.ub.uni-frankfurt.de/jd/content/titleinfo/1699188.

28. Aptroot, "Bible Translation as Cultural Reform," 346.

29. Turniansky, "Reception and Rejection," 12.

30. Frakes, *Early Yiddish Texts*, 713–14.

31. "Of great importance also are the *haskomes* ('approbations') and copyrights in both books. Blitz's translation boasts *haskomes* of the Portuguese and Ashkenazic authorities of Amsterdam, as well as copyrights from the king of Poland. Witzenhausen's translation contains *haskomes* of the Council of the [Four] Lands . . . as well as copyrights from the States of Holland and West-Friesland." Aptroot, "Bible Translation as Cultural Reform," 346.

32. Although an older Dutch Bible dates back to 1522.

33. http://www.bijbelsdigitaal.nl/statenvertaling-1637/

34. Timm, "Blitz and Witzenhausen," 50.

35. Timm, "Blitz and Witzenhausen," 50–51.

36. Timm, "Blitz and Witzenhausen," 52.

37. Aptroot, "Yiddish Bibles in Amsterdam," 55–56.

38. Timm, "Blitz and Witzenhausen," 62.

39. Aptroot, "Biblical Translation as Cultural Reform," 120–78; Timm, "Blitz and Witzenhausen," 62.

40. Aptroot, "Biblical Translation as Cultural Reform," 331; also 329–36.

41. Aptroot, "Biblical Translation as Cultural Reform," 331.

42. Timm, "Blitz and Witzenhausen," 57–59.

43. Baumgarten, *Introduction to Old Yiddish Literature*, 127.

44. Sorkin, *Moses Mendelssohn*, 54. For a summary of this position, see Grossman, *The Discourse on Yiddish*, 75–82.

45. Despite the existence of an edition dated 1687, there is clear evidence that title pages were doctored so as to create an illusion of a second printing that never took place. Aptroot, "Yiddish Bibles in Amsterdam," 51.

46. English translation in Gottlieb, *Moses Mendelssohn, Writings*, 195–96. JubA 9: 1, 55–56.

47. Aptroot, "Bible Translation as Cultural Reform," 362.

48. Zinberg, *A History of Jewish Literature*, vol. 1, 137.

49. Herder, quoted in Robinson, *Western Translation Theory*, 208.

50. Berman, *Experience of the Foreign*, 43.

51. Berman, *Experience of the Foreign*, 11–12.

52. Letter to Henning, 29 June 1779, cited in Altmann, *Moses Mendelssohn*, 344, and in German in Kayserling, *Moses Mendelssohn*, 522. See inter alia Sorkin, *Moses Mendelssohn and the Religious Enlightenment*, Weinberg, "Language Questions," Bourel, *Moses Mendelssohn*, and Gillman, "Mendelssohn, Buber, Rosenzweig, and the Enterprise of Biblical Translation."

53. Kearney, "The Torah of Israel in the Tongue of Ishmael."

54. Sorkin, *Moses Mendelssohn and the Religious Enlightenment*, 68.

55. Tov, *Textual Criticism*, 149.

56. Lowenstein, "The Yiddish Written Word," 188.

57. Weinberg, "Word List," 281.

58. By reading the Aramaic translation of the Torah in Ashurite script, they would accustom themselves to this language, which had fallen into oblivion until Ezra's time, and they would also become reacquainted with Hebrew script. BT Sanhedrin 21b.

59. It is not only a matter of vocabulary or word choice. In the case of Genesis 30:38, a notoriously difficult verse (mistranslated by Luther and Blitz and also by Targum Onkelos), the *Be'ur* called attention to the accents, or notes for chanting (*te'amim*) printed above and below the Hebrew words. In fact, it reprinted the difficult verse twice, once with the correct notes, another time with alternate notation, to explain why the others got it wrong and also to demonstrate how one could use those notes for chanting to unlock the sense.

60. Reprinted in its entirety in JubA, vols. 15–19.

61. Tov, *Textual Criticism*, 65.

62. According to Jordan S. Penkower, the addition of the apparatus to the page symbolized the larger ways in which the editor of the second edition of the Rabbinic Bible, Jacob ben Hayyim Ibn Adoniyahu, improved upon the first (1517). Ben Hayyim was a Jewish scholar with a kabbalistic (Jewish mystical) background; even the most minor corrections and textual variants were of special importance for a mystic. "The Kabbalists envisaged the Torah text as the name(s) of God, and any variant would thus cause damage to the name. Therefore, they venerated the work of the Masoretes in preserving the accurate text." His Christian publisher, Daniel Bomberg, a Hebraist and convert to Christianity, was also interested in promoting Kabbalah for Christians. Penkower summarizes: "RB 1525 together with its Masoretic apparatus became the standard for the accurate Bible text for the next four centuries." It is also reputed to be the source for the King James Bible. Penkower, "The Development of the Masoretic Bible," 2082–83.

63. Altmann, *Moses Mendelssohn*, 373.

64. Altmann, *Moses Mendelssohn*, 406.

65. On the *Be'ur* displacing Rashi, see Katz, *Out of the Ghetto*, 129–30.

66. Altmann, *Moses Mendelssohn*, 69. Altmann describes other experiences with Nicolai, Ramler, and Lessing. Mendelssohn wrote to Lessing on 2 August 1756: "Who knows whether I shall not one day write verse? Madame Metaphysics may forgive me. . . . Your friendship and Nicolai's has tempted me to withdraw part of my love from that venerable matron and to give it to belles-lettres . . ." (Ibid., 66). In 1756–57 he sent samples of verse to Lessing. "Mendelssohn did not take his versifying too seriously" (Ibid., 67). Yet he translated some synagogue hymns and composed a "Friedenspredigt" in 1763, as well as other German poems on patriotic occasions. Ramler and Mendelssohn both composed odes when Frederick II returned to his capital on 30 March 1763.

67. Jonathan Karp reads *Kohelet Musar* as a work of eighteenth-century aesthetics rather than philosophy. Karp, "The Aesthetic Difference."

68. Sorkin, *Moses Mendelssohn and the Religious Enlightenment*, 59–60; Rawidowicz, "The Psalms Translation of Mendelssohn," 283.

69. By way of comparison: in the last decade of his life, Rosenzweig first translated liturgical texts, then Jehuda Halevi's poetry; then the Hebrew Bible.

70. "Elegie an die Burg Zion gerichtet" appeared in Müchler's *Beschäftigungen*, vol. 2 no. 2: 111–14, 115–18 (reprinted in JubA, 6: 425–35). Müchler reprinted it in his edition of Mendelssohn's *Kleine philosophische Schriften*.

71. JubA, 4: 20–62. On Lowth, see Kugel, *The Idea of Biblical Poetry.*

72. The hypothesis of Adam Shear, Gad Freudenthal, and others is that Mendelssohn studied the *Kuzari* with his teacher Israel Zamosc in the 1740s and '50s. Zamosc publish his commentary, *Otzar Nechmad,* in 1795. Mendelssohn quotes from the *Kuzari* in *Qohelet Mussar* and incorporates Halevi's theories about the origins of the Hebrew language on the very first page of "Or LaNetivah." Andrea Schatz argues that Mendelssohn's evolving understanding of the role of Hebrew in the bilingual diaspora—an understanding with direct relevance to translation—was influenced by the *Kuzari.* Andrea Schatz, *Sprache in der Zerstreuung,* 255–59.

73. Werner Weinberg believes that Mendelssohn copied the poem from a book of *qinot* from 1696. See Bourel, *Moses Mendelssohn,* 145–46. It is also possible he knew it in Yiddish from the *qinot* books of 1698 and 1718.

74. See Werner Weinberg's introductory remarks in JubA 10: 1, lxxiii–lxxix.

75. I include here the first eight lines in Hebrew and in Nina Salaman's English translation from the *Selected Poems of Jehudah Halevi* (1928) followed by Mendelssohn's rendering of those lines in German and in English translation.

76. "Bethel" appears in Halevi's ninth line: "My heart to Bethel and Peniel yearneth sore" (Salaman).

77. According to Wolfgang Kayser, it was Friedrich Klopstock who first wrote German verse in free rhythms in the 1750s, in particular for poems such as the famous ode "Frühlingsfeier" (Spring Storm, 1759) which addressed God within nature. Kayser, *Geschichte des deutschen Verses,* 53.

78. See his explanation in JubA 14: 368. "Reader, do not be surprised that two stanzas were not translated. This was not due to the translator's fatigue, but rather, because the poet (*meqonen* = writer of the *qinah*) skipped from topic to topic. He began comparing Israel to a herd of sheep, then spoke of them as grasping the edge of the garment, leaving the initial image."

79. "Da in dem ersten Buche sehr wenig Poesie vorkömmt; so wird es dem Leser vielleicht nicht unangenehm seyn, am Ende dieser Vorrede das *Siegeslied der Deborah,* aus dem vierten Kapitel der *Richter,* von dem Herrn Mendelssohn übersetzt zu finden, um sich daraus von der Art und Weise, wie er die poetischen Stellen der H.S. übersetzt hat, einen Begriff zu machen. Kenner der Grundsprache werden einige schwierige Stellen in demselben bemerken, die der Übersetzer, meines Erachtens, glücklich erklärt hat, und wodurch dieses Gedicht ein schönes Ganze geworden ist." *Die fünf Bücher Mose, nach der Uebersetzung des Herrn Moses Mendelssohn,* x–xi. Also cited in JubA 10: 1, lxvi. See also Altmann, *Moses Mendelssohn,* 389.

80. Sorkin, *Moses Mendelssohn and the Religious Enlightenment,* 51–52.

81. Mendelssohn to Michaelis, 13 March 1770, Cited in Bourel, *Moses Mendelssohn,* 453; JubA 12: 1, 217

82. Bourel, *Moses Mendelssohn,* 452–55.

83. Cited in Bourel, *Moses Mendelssohn,* 454. A further letter from Nicolai to Michael Denis states, "Mr. Mendelssohn . . . is working on a book about Hebrew lyric poetry . . . in particular, many Psalms in translation will be supplied there. Those which I have seen are superior." Ibid., 452–53.

84. Numerous editions followed with the German Targum transcribed into Hebrew letters: Berlin (1785–90) in four parts, Livorno (1793), Vienna (1800), Prague (1801), Offenbach (1804–5), Fürth (1804).

85. Bourel, *Moses Mendelssohn*, 457.

86. "An den Leser," *Die Psalmen*, JubA 10: 1, 6.

87. "ohne alle 'kritische Rücksicht.' . . . Kurz: ich glaube, ohne kritische Vorurtheile übersetzt zu haben; wünsche ohne kritische Vorurtheile gelesen und beurtheilt zu werden, und verspreche, ohne kritischen Eigensinn, Belehrung anzunehmen." JubA 10: 1, 6–7.

88. For an abridged English translation of the excurses on biblical poetry, see Gottlieb, *Moses Mendelssohn*, 211–15.

89. Altmann, *Moses Mendelssohn*, 410–12.

90. Gottlieb, *Moses Mendelssohn*, 212; JubA 16: 125.

91. Gottlieb, *Moses Mendelssohn*, 212; JubA 16: 125.

92. Gottlieb, *Moses Mendelssohn*, 214; JubA 16: 126.

93. Gottlieb, *Moses Mendelssohn*, 215; JubA 16: 127.

94. Examples from Psalms 12, Psalms 101 and Exodus 15 show that first verses use short phrases with two feet, and subsequent verses have longer lines. The Song of Songs uses this pattern of short/long to awaken love: *ana halach dodech* = 3 / *hayafa banashim* = 2. Lamentations uses it to arouse pity: *ani hagever ra'ah oni* = 4 / *beshevet evrato* = 2.
JubA 16,1: 128–31.

95. Sheehan, *The Enlightenment Bible*, 62.

96. Sheehan, *The Enlightenment Bible*, 57.

97. Sheehan, *The Enlightenment Bible*, 57.

98. "Perhaps the ultimate proof that the Pentateuch translation could not have been intended as a textbook for the German language, is the fact that Mendelssohn's German was much too highbrow, too sophisticated to be considered of any pedagogical value for teaching the language to beginners. If we want to ascribe to Mendelssohn a possible pedagogical-linguistic intention, we must limit this either to Jewish non-speakers of German who were exceptionally motivated and gifted individuals, or to German-speaking Jews, whom he wished to lead toward a higher level of the language than they were accustomed to." Weinberg, "Language Questions," 208.

99. JubA 9: 1, 55.

100. Leibniz, "Enriching the German Language" from "Impartial Thoughts Concerning the Use and Improvement of the German Language," 1697, cited in Robinson, *Western Translation Theory*, 184. These features go back to classical linguistics and were debated during the Renaissance.

101. Spalding, "Toward a Modern Torah," 67.

102. Sheehan, *The Enlightenment Bible*, 122. Luther, and following him the two Yiddish Bible translators, kept it simple: they used *wüst und leer* (desolate and void). Mendelssohn clearly wanted to make a bold statement with *unförmlich und vermischt* (unformed and mixed up).

103. Mendelssohn seems to allude to Schmidt in his comment on the verse, offering the alternative, "*ein starker Wind wehend*," alongside many others, such as Rashi's

"chair of glory" (*kise hakavod*). But he himself chose "der göttliche Geist," on the basis of Halevi's Kuzari.

104. Sheehan, *The Enlightenment Bible*, 124–25.

105. Sheehan, *The Enlightenment Bible*, 129.

106. Sheehan, *The Enlightenment Bible*, 129.

107. Spalding, "Toward a Modern Torah," 72. Examples include *Mizrajim* and *mizrisch* (instead of *Egypten* and *egyptisch*); *Iwrim* and *Iwrisch* (instead of *Ebräer* and *ebräisch*); *Noach* (instead of *Noah*); and *Jischmael* (instead of *Ismael*).

108. Gutzen, "Bemerkungen zur Bibelübersetzung," 72; also 71–78.

109. He was consistent: he chose *wandelnd* for *hithalech* also in Gen 3:8. "Da hörten sie die Stimme des ewigen Wesens, Gottes, wandelnd zur Seite des Tages . . ." The Hebrew verb is in a durative conjugation.

110. Schmidt (in German): "Von disem Noach ist zu merken, dass er wider die Gewohnheit seiner Zeit ein frommer Mann war, welcher einen unstraflichen und heiligen **Wandel** führte."

111. On translating *toldot*, compare the approaches to Gen. 2:4 above.

112. "Heb. *Dor* in common with its Sem. cognates, signifies 'duration, age span'; the meaning 'generation' . . . is secondary." Speiser, *Genesis*, 51; note to Gen 6:9.

113. In 1758, he published "Considerations of the Sublime and the Naïve in the Fine Sciences" anonymously in *Library of Fine Sciences and Fine Arts*.

114. Schmidt wrote, "Korb von Binsen" (basket of rushes). Luther uses "Schilfmeer." Spalding, "Toward a Modern Torah," 73.

115. Schmidt translates, "Da kam die königliche Prinzessin und ging in den Fluß hinein."

116. Luther: Und da das Kind groß war, brachte sie es der Tochter Pharaos, und es ward ihr Sohn, und hieß ihn Mose; denn sie sprach: Ich habe ihn aus dem Wasser gezogen.

117. Brettler, *Biblical Hebrew*, 174.

118. Michaelis is more radical: he uses lines to mark the end of the verse, but otherwise does not retain verse divisions when creating German sentences: "Bald nachher erschien ihm Jehova von neuen unter den Terebinthen Mamre. Abraham saß um die Zeit des Tages da es schon heiß war, vor der Thür seines Gezelts, | und da er seine Augen aufhob, sahe er drey Männer nicht weit von ihm stille stehen: und so bald er ihrer gewahr ward, lief er ihnen von der Thür seines Gezelts entgegen, warf sich zur Erde nieder, | und sagte."

119. David Braun, personal communication to the author, 16 May 2017.

120. Mendelssohn, commentary to Gen 3:21, Gen 3:7, Ex 12:1.

121. Mendelssohn: Und Adam mit seiner Frau verkrochen sich vor dem Ewigen Wesen Gottes.

122. Where Hebrew has "made," Mendelssohn invents a fancy phrase *entstehen lassen*, meaning "allowed to come into existence." *Entstehen* is also used in Genesis 2:4.

123. Luther: Und weil die Wehmütter Gott fürchteten, baute er ihnen Häuser.

124. He begins by rejecting Rashbam's interpretation that it was Pharaoh's punishment for the midwives. Rashi, Ibn Ezra, and Radak interpret it as praise, but there is a problem: How does it connect to the previous verse that describes the people multiplying?

125. Drazin, *Targum Onkelos*, 148.

126. "Usually the name 'Shimon' will be untranslated, but the etymology (in this case, 'hearing') will be translated. The principle is simple and there is agreement in all languages; so that anyone who translates a book will translate every single word from the topics and stories and general names, except for personal names of human beings which will in no case be translated, but will record the names that were originally given. That is what Onkelos and other targumim did. They did not translate 'Moshe,' only they did translate 'drew him out of the water'. . . . The relationship [between name and etymology] in Aramaic is not there, as it is in Hebrew." Mendelssohn's commentary to Exodus 2:10. JubA 16: 16.

127. He also finds evidence in other translations of Moses: Latin = Mosis; Arabic: Musa. They all appear to come from the Hebrew Moshe and alter it slightly based on the accent. Mendelssohn concludes, "I have more to say about this, and to add to the teaching of Abarbanel that pertains to the translation of proper names which I wrote [about] in my preface." JubA 16: 16–17.

128. Ex 16:15. "Man hu." It is Egyptian language. In that language they were accustomed to say it like "ma." Moshe wrote it in that language that they used, to explain why they called it 'man'. . . . also *Yigar Sahaduta* and *hipil pur* (i.e., other Fremdwörter).

129. "What emerges from all that has been written by translators and commentators to know the stones of the breastplate and their names is that it is impossible for us to 'stand on them in explanation' and we have nothing but flimsy and weak speculations from the instructions of the names, which agree only occasionally with a known precious stone. The commentators will say that that is it. And it is known that these proofs are not definitive because for one stone the name is intransitive and for many the names are transitive. And who will tell us which name is appropriate to which stone? And regarding this, we have seen that all of the translators in other languages, early and later translators, explained the names of these gems according to their opinions, even the translators into Aramaic, Onkelos and Jonathan ben Uzziel and [*Targum Yerushalmi*], did not translate them using one method. Thus, the exegetes who wanted to rely on them, like the Chizkuni and Bachya and the author of Shiltei Giborim of the many words, after he himself admitted that silence is better than invalid speech, they would give their own gems (ideas) that they reached with no help and to no purpose. So the German translator did well not to translate them at all, except for Saphire and Jasper, gems which are known to this day—though even in the case of Saphire there is some doubt (see above 24:10)." Mendelssohn's commentary on Exodus 28: 17–20. JubA 16: 285.

130. Propp, *Exodus 19–40*, 439, note to Ex 28:17.

131. Timm, "Die Bibelübersetzungssprache," 102.

132. Aptroot, "Bible Translation as Cultural Reform," 333.

133. The phrase is popularly known from the liturgy of the Torah service: "It is a tree of life to all who hold fast to it, and all of its supporters are happy; its ways are ways of sweetness, and all its paths are peace." In their original context these lines are part of a paean to wisdom/*hokhma* (Proverbs 3:17–18),

134. Equally multivalent is Mendelssohn's "light." In the preface, Mendelssohn likens those who read the Bible without a proper translation to "blind people tapping in the darkness." "Light for the Path" does double duty as reference to the preface and the translation, but also to the rabbinic authors of the Oral Torah, to whom Mendelssohn

repeatedly pays tribute. His improvisation of the famous verse (Psalm 36:9) "In *their* light, we will see the light" serves his agenda perfectly by obscuring the distinction between translation and exegesis.

135. "The final and normative solution to the problem of the authority of the Mishnah worked out in the third and fourth centuries produced the myth of the dual Torah, oral and written, which formed the indicative and definitive trait of the Judaism that emerged from late antiquity." Neusner, *The Talmud*, 146.

136. In BT Eruvin 54b, Rav Chisda comments, "Torah is acquired only through *Simanim* (schemes to remember)," in answer to the question of how Moses, Aaron, and the Elders studied the Torah.

137. We learn that the children of Israel had been living in Egypt since the arrival of Joseph and his brothers back at the end of Genesis; within a few verses, the family of seventy swells to become a numerous tribe. When a new king arises "who knew not Joseph," the Hebrew nation loses its protection. Despite Pharaoh's instructions to kill first-born sons, the midwives deceive Pharaoh and heroically resist, and are rewarded by God. The stage is thereby set for the birth and rescue of Moses, which symbolizes the imminent birth of the Jewish nation out of the Egyptian exile.

138. See Gillman, "From Myth to Memory."

139. The line is in fact a pastiche of Numbers 9:13 and Deuteronomy 4:44.

140. Why didn't he write about himself using the first person? Some say that God dictated the text to Moses, word for word, with Moses repeating the words before writing them; the final eight verses were written in tears, rather than ink. Mendelssohn even includes the Kabbalistic view that Torah was composed of black fire written on white fire.

141. JubA, 9: 1, 35.

142. Timm, "Blitz and Witzenhausen," 59–66, esp. 65–66.

143. Berman, *Experience of the Foreign*, 31.

144. Berman, *Experience of the Foreign*, 32.

145. Does the translator know what the text means? Or is it acceptable to demonstrate that meaning is uncertain, that this does not diminish the authority of the translation? Is commentary a necessary part of the Jewish Bible—which is another way of asking, is the meaning, the teaching, intellectual or religious content, internal to or outside of its language? Do the words of Torah have a fixed meaning or many possible meanings? Do men and women need different Torot? Does the Torah have "seventy faces," or is its meaning infinite and unique to each individual?

146. Berman, *Experience of the Foreign*, 85.

147. Luther, "Circular Letter on Translation," 79.

148. Witzenhausen, "Translator's Apology," 13–14; this passage corresponds to the first tenth of the apology as whole.

149. Mendelssohn, "Or Lanetiva," 58.

150. Mendelssohn, "Or Lanetiva," 56.

151. Mendelssohn, "Or Lanetiva," 59–60.

152. Mendelssohn, "Or Lanetiva," 57.

153. The phrase is found in the commentary to Exodus 21 introducing a long pericope of laws and statutes. Mendelssohn opens with a long quotation from the French medieval exegete named Rashbam, grandson of Rashi, stressing the tension between *pshat* and *hala-*

kha (law). He first comments that he will reside in the shadow of the wings of this great eagle and will not budge from the *pshat*, neither to the right nor to the left. Mendelssohn, JubA 16: 198.

154. JubA 16: 198–99

155. Berlin and Brettler, *The Jewish Study Bible*, 328.

156. Kugel, *The Bible as It Was*, 483.

157. "In the Bible, Balaam steadfastly refused to say anything not authorized by God, repeatedly scorning the pleadings of royalty and the promises of certain gain that stood behind them. What is more, Balaam's words were unequivocally favorable to Israel, and he even predicted the coming of their long-awaited messiah." Kugel, *The Bible as It Was*, 482.

158. Turniansky, "Reception and Rejection," 15.

159. Zinberg, *A History of Jewish Literature*, 139.

160. Aptroot, "Yiddish Bibles in Amsterdam," 59–60.

161. "Bible Translation," JewishEncyclopedia.com. "Only a few of Mendelssohn's followers can be mentioned here. His translation of the Song of Solomon was published after his death by Joel Löwe and Aaron Wolfson. The first of these also published a translation of Jonah (Berlin, 1788); while the second translated Lamentations, Esther, and Ruth (Berlin, 1788), Job (*ib.* 1788; Prague, 1791; Vienna, 1806), and Kings (Breslau, 1809). Isaac Euchel translated Proverbs (Berlin, 1790; Dessau, 1804), introducing, however, philosophical expressions into the text, thereby often clouding the meaning."

162. Cited in Ben-Chorin, "Jüdische Bibelübersetzungen in Deutschland," 311.

163. Cited in Ben-Chorin, "Jüdische Bibelübersetzungen in Deutschland," 311–12.

164. Cited in Weinberg, "Einleitung," JubA 15: 1, xc–xci.

165. Fishman, *Yiddish: Turning to Life*, 41.

166. Goldschmidt, *The Legacy of German Jewry*, 185.

CHAPTER TWO

1. See Lowenstein, "The Readership of Mendelssohn's Bible Translation." The *Be'ur* went through "twenty editions by the middle of the nineteenth century." Cohen, "Urban Visibility and Biblical Visions," 45.

2. 10 November 1836, cited in Glatzer, *Leopold and Adelheid Zunz*, 96.

3. Cohen, "Urban Visibility and Biblical Visions," 45.

4. On periodization, see Goldschmidt's chapter on "Historical Stages" in *The Legacy of German Jewry*, 49–55.

5. Plaut, *The Rise of Reform Judaism*, xix–xx.

6. Liberles, *Religious Conflict in Social Context*, 67.

7. Petuchowski, *Prayerbook Reform in Europe*, 50.

8. AZdJ 2 no. 4 (1837). Cited in Philipson, *The Reform Movement in Judaism*, 54–55; see also 44–50.

9. Meyer, "Jewish Communities in Transition," 90 ff.

10. Cited in Plaut, *The Rise of Reform Judaism*, 38.

11. Cited in Plaut, *The Rise of Reform Judaism*, 43–44.

12. Schorsch, *From Text to Context*, 183–84.

13. Schorsch, *From Text to Context*, 184.

14. Goldschmidt, *The Legacy of German Jewry*, 150.

15. Liberles, *Religious Conflict in Social Context*. 15.

16. Meyer, "Jewish Communities in Transition," 114.

17. Liberles, *Religious Conflict in Social Context*, 16.

18. Wealthy Jewish children, exposed to foreign languages and secular studies by private tutors, did not receive an enlightened Jewish education; moreover, upper-class Jews (bankers, traders, pawnbrokers), who numbered approximately three thousand in Berlin in 1815, "sent their children to non-Jewish schools and frequently had them baptized for the sake of their careers." Meyer, *The Origins of the Modern Jew*, 149.

19. Residency requirements were changed early on because large sections of the Jewish ghetto had been destroyed during the French occupation of 1796.

20. Schlotzhauer, *Das Philanthropin*, 9–10.

21. Schlotzhauer, *Das Philanthropin*, 7–13.

22. Schorsch, *From Text to Context*, 311. In 1837, faculty initiated an ecumenical periodical devoted to "unbiased discussion of religious events and issues in Protestantism, Catholicism, and Judaism," of which 104 numbers were published, titled *Unparteiische Universal-Kirchenzeitung für die Geistlichkeit und die gebildete Weltklasse des protestantischen, katholischen, und israelitischen Deutschlands.*

23. The school is called the I. E. Lichtigfeld Schule im Philanthropin.

24. Meyer, "Jewish Communities in Transition," 116, also 111–19.

25. Sheehan, *The Enlightenment Bible*, 62–64.

26. "The *Biblia pentapla* could conceivably become the perfect translation, one that would, as Glüsing put it, 'serve as a perfect replacement of the Greek original text.' In effect, then, the *Biblia pentapla* was to provide an exact substitute for the original text. It would provide its readers with a transparent view of God's Word, one unobstructed by human ignorance." Sheehan, *The Enlightenment Bible*, 63.

27. Marchand, *German Orientalism*, 103.

28. Marchand, *German Orientalism*, 106.

29. Telling details: Mendelssohn began translating the Psalms in 1770, and dedicated the book to Karl Wilhelm Ramler, a poet and translator of classical poetry. Michael Sachs, who was inspired by Ewald's Psalms translation, dedicated his own Psalms translation to Friedrich Rückert, poet and Oriental philologist.

30. Cohen, "Urban Visibility and Biblical Visions," 45.

31. Unpublished letter of Ewald to Sachs, 17 December 1835, cited in Lucas and Frank, *Michael Sachs*, 44n23.

32. Sachs to Zunz, 14 December 1835, in Elbogen, *Aus dem Briefwechsel von Michael Sachs und Leopold Zunz*, 9.

33. "The period of the Mendelssohnian biurists may be fittingly said to end with the Bible published by Moses Landau [20 parts, Prague, 1833–37 . . .]. Of this work the translations of the Pentateuch, Psalms, and Five Scrolls were those of Mendelssohn; the translations of the other books were contributed by Moses Landau, J. Weisse, S. Sachs, A. Benisch, and W. Mayer; and the Minor Prophets were reprinted from the edition of Dessau, 1805." Toy and Gottheil, "Bible Translations."

34. Rosin, "Die Zunz'sche Bibel," 505–6. This tribute was published in 1894 in honor of Zunz on his one-hundredth birthday.

35. Ehrenberg refers to Schalom Kohen's *Die ganze heilige Schrift im Originaltext mit einer deutscher Übersetzung* (The entire Holy Scripture in its original text with a German translation), and to the fact that Jeremiah Heinemann published Mendelssohn's translation with his own commentary for students, titled *Bi'ur la-Talmid* (1831–33). Glatzer, *Leopold and Adelheid Zunz*, 372.

36. Letter of 17 January 1835, in Glatzer, *Leopold and Adelheid Zunz*, 86.

37. Letter of 6 August 1835, in Geiger, *Michael Sachs und Moritz Veit*, 2.

38. Salomon, *Denkmal der Erinnerung*, 40.

39. Herxheimer, *Die vierundzwanzig Bücher der Bibel*, iv

40. Herxheimer, *Die vierundzwanzig Bücher der Bibel*, vi.

41. Letter of 22 September 1833, in Lehranstalt, *Berichte*, 20.

42. Johlson, *Lehrbuch der Mosaischen Religion.* The third edition was published with two strong endorsements by government officials. Schlotzhauer, *Das Philanthropin*, 32.

43. The catechism—despite its emphasis on dogma and Christian foundation—"became a leading pedagogical tool in early nineteenth century liberal Judaism." Ken Koltun-Fromm, *Abraham Geiger's Liberal Judaism*, 124. See also Petuchowski, "Manuals and Catechisms," 47–64.

44. "On Circumcision in its Historical and Dogmatic Perspective" (Ueber die Beschneidung in historischer und dogmatischer Hinsicht), Frankfurt, 1843. Controversy over circumcision erupted that year when the Health Department of Frankfurt took steps to regulate the practice, and in so doing, empowered the more radical reformers to express their opposition to the religious rite. (See Liberles, *Religious Conflict in Social Context*, 52–61.) Johlson, who was not a radical reformer, recommends the creation of an egalitarian rite of entry for boys and girls called "the Sanctification on the Eighth Day."

45. Johlson, *Toldot Avot*, v.

46. Meyer, *The Origins of the Modern Jew*, 147–48.

47. Meyer, *The Origins of the Modern Jew*, 148.

48. Meyer, *The Origins of the Modern Jew*, 160.

49. In distinguishing the goals of the Wissenschaft from those of the Enlightenment, many cite the extreme position of Eduard Gans. In attempting to explain the rise of nationalism and reactionary legislation in Germany, Gans framed current events as an inevitable backlash against the "atomization" advocated by the Haskalah. They viewed the main accomplishment of the Haskalah as "negation"; it was a "break with the intimacy (*Innigkeit*) of the old existence . . . but no new enthusiasm has broken forth, no new set of relationships has been built" (Gans, cited in Meyer, *The Origins of the Modern Jew*, 167). Meyer explains: "For Gans the romantic reaction and its Jew-hatred was in larger perspective simply a necessary response to the one-sidedness of the Enlightenment; in its turn it would produce the new form of a culturally integrated, but not monolithic Europe" (ibid.). Hermann Levin Goldschmidt points out the irony in Gans's embrace of Hegelianism. "The vibrant activity of Jewish scholars contradicted Hegel's doctrine—then at the peak of its influence—that every world-historical people could be called to lead or share leadership in the march of world history but a single time. Hegel's system implied that modern Jews had no choice but to become Germans, and thereby merge with the German tide of history if they were ever to amount to anything." Goldschmidt, *The Legacy of German Jewry*, 70.

50. Johlson explains that the first number corresponds to the biblical chronology from Exodus 12: 40–41, and the second is the view of the rabbis.

51. Johlson, *Die fünf Bücher Mose*, v.

52. Johlson, *Die fünf Bücher Mose*, vi.

53. Johlson, *Die fünf Bücher Mose*, ix–x. Goethe, "Translations," 65.

54. In Johlson's translation, Genesis 4:23–24, beginning "Adah und Zilla, höret meine Stimme! / Ihr, Weiber Lamech's, horchet meiner Rede!," are formatted as three verse couplets.

55. Sheehan, *The Enlightenment Bible*, 159.

56. Cited in Sheehan, *The Enlightenment Bible*, 159.

57. Sheehan, *The Enlightenment Bible*, 159.

58. See Robert Alter on the "heresy of explanation." Introduction, *The Five Books of Moses*, xvi.

59. On this difficult pericope, see Pardes, *Countertraditions of the Bible*, 71–74.

60. In this respect, Johlson anticipates Alter: "Biblical Hebrew . . . has a distinctive music, a lovely precision of lexical choice, a meaningful concreteness, and a suppleness of expressive syntax that by and large have been given short shrift by translators with their eyes on other goals." Alter, *The Five Books of Moses*, xlv.

61. Rosin, "Die Zunz'sche Bibel," 511.

62. Elbogen, *Aus dem Briefwechsel von Michael Sachs und Leopold Zunz*, 3.

63. Sachs, *Die Psalmen*, vi.

64. Sachs, *Die Psalmen*, x.

65. Elbogen, *Aus dem Briefwechsel von Michael Sachs und Leopold Zunz*, 9. Zunz's review appeared in Abraham Geiger's *Wissenschaftliche Zeitschrift für jüdische Theologie* 3 (1836): 499–504.

66. Rosin, "Die Zunz'sche Bibel," 509.

67. Zunz to Veit, 14 March and 4 April 1836, in Geiger, *Michael Sachs und Moritz Veit*.

68. Arnheim translated the Pentateuch, Joshua, Judges, Samuel I and II, Isaiah, Joel, Amos, Habakkuk, Zephaniah, Haggai, Malachi, Song of Songs, Lamentations, Psalms. (According to one review in *Der Orient*, Arnheim translated the first four Pentateuchal books.)

69. "Über die Orthographie der Namen, über Beibehaltung gewisser Hebräismen z.B. des . . . . *v'haya* in der Erzählung—u. dgl. sehe ich gleichfalls Ihrer Entscheidung entgegen." Sachs to Zunz, 18 February 1835, in Elbogen, *Aus dem Briefwechsel von Michael Sachs und Leopold Zunz*, 11.

70. Veit to Sachs, 13 May 1837, in Elbogen, *Aus dem Briefwechsel von Michael Sachs und Leopold Zunz*, 5–6.

71. Rosin, "Die Zunz'sche Bibel," 511.

72. The designated *haftarah* (prophetic reading) for a normal Sabbath is listed in small print at the appropriate place in the text itself; hence, no special index is needed. But for holidays, new moons (months), and special Sabbaths, such a list had to be included.

73. The presence of a second title page (Berlin: Verlag von Veit und Comp, 1839) suggests that the *Zeittafel* was also published separately.

74. Schorsch, *From Text to Context*, 152.

75. A clause beginning with a subordinating conjunction (*als*, "when") requires the form *ausging* in place of the normal *ging aus*, in the case of verbs with separable prefixes (e.g., *aus-gehen*).

76. Bunsen, "Vorerinnerungen zu seinem Bibelwerk," xvii, cited in Rosin, "Die Zunz'sche Bibel," 512.

77. Geiger, "Johlson's Bibelwerk."

78. Gen 2:7.

79. Gen 1:20.

80. Gen 21:11.

81. Gen 41:40.

82. Letter of 12 February 1837, in Glatzer, *Leopold and Adelheid Zunz*, 98–99.

83. Heß, "Bemerkungen," 549.

84. Heß, "Bemerkungen," 550.

85. Heß, "Bemerkungen," 549–50.

86. Rosin, "Die Zunz'sche Bibel," 512.

87. Rosin, "Die Zunz'sche Bibel."

88. Plaut, *German Jewish Bible Translations*, 12.

89. Adorno, *Minima Moralia*, 125.

90. Goldschmidt, *The Legacy of German Jewry*, 186.

91. Sussman, "Another Look at Isaac Leeser," 159.

92. Sussman, "Another Look at Isaac Leeser," 175.

93. Skreinka, "Bemerkungen," 468.

94. Moses Philippson, Joseph Wolf, Gotthold Salomon, Israel Neumann, and J. Löwe translated the Minor Prophets (Dessau, 1805) under the title *Mincha Tehora* (*Pure Gift*), stereotyped as early as 1837.

95. Translation plays an important role in the story of the new temple. Felix Mendelssohn-Bartholdy was invited to compose a choral setting of Psalm 100 in honor of the inauguration ceremony. He wanted to use Luther's translation of the Psalm, but the Temple asked him to use Moses Mendelssohn's version, and he refused. See the correspondence between Mendelssohn-Bartholdy and Maimon Fränkel (1788–1848), Salomon's close friend and collaborator. Werner, "Felix Mendelssohn's Commissioned Composition," 57.

96. P. Philippson, *Biographische Skizzen*, 124. Philippson believes these songs lacked the naïveté of church hymns—they were *Gedankenlieder* (125).

97. P. Philippson, *Biographische Skizzen*, 124.

98. P. Philippson, *Biographische Skizzen*, 125.

99. P. Philippson, *Biographische Skizzen*, 126–27.

100. Plaut, *German Jewish Bible Translations*, 11.

101. P. Philippson, *Biographische Skizzen*, 127.

102. Salomon, *Denkmal der Erinnerung*, 40.

103. Heß, "Bemerkungen zur Salomon'schen"; Schott, "Israelitische Volksbibeln."

104. Mendelssohn and Zunz translate "Der Stein aber auf der Mündung des Brunnens war groß," following the Hebrew word order: "The stone on the mouth of the well was large" (JPS). Salomon 'improves' the verse at the expense of literality: "ein grosser Stein

aber lag auf der Mündung des Brunnens" [= a large stone, however, lay on the mouth of the well].

105. Salomon translates Joseph's name "Fürst der Heeresmacht" or "Prince of military forces"! Ibn Ezra refers to the Targum, "A man who reveals mysteries." Mendelssohn also follows the Targum, using parentheses: "Zafnat Paneach (einer der die verborgenste Dinge weiß)." Zunz retains the original Hebrew (or Egyptian).

106. Salomon, "Erinnerungen," 341. This verse is normally mistranslated (Mendelssohn, Zunz) to reflect Jewish law. Salomon did not go along.

107. Compare: Zunz: "Nicht soll mein Geist walten in dem Menschen für immer." Luther: "Mein Geist soll nicht immerdar im Menschen walten." Mendelssohn: "Da sprach der Ewige, mein Geist wird nicht immer in dem Menschen streiten."

108. The saucer bears this inscription: "To His Reverence Herr Doctor Herxheimer on his birthday, from his grateful students (*Schülern und Schülerinnen*)." Wischnitzer-Bernstein, "Vom jüdischen Familienporzellan," 7.

109. See Jonathan Hess's analysis of Oppenheim's "readers" in "Reading and the Writing of German-Jewish History," 119–23. Hess does not discuss the mother—a figure related to the old woman who graces the cover of the present volume and about whom I write in chapter four.

110. A complete bibliography is included in Faber, *Salomon Herxheimer*, 81–94.

111. The region included Bernberg, Ballenstedt, Gernrode, Herzgerode, Hovn, Gross-Mühlingen, and Coswig. In 1854, the Bernberg Jewish community had 246 members. Most were merchants. By 1857, the number of Jewish in the district totaled 726 (of 60,000 residents).

112. Cited in Salfeld, *Dr. Salomon Herxheimer*, 12.

113. Herxheimer, *Jessode HaTorah: Israelitische Glaubens und Pflichtenlehre* (Foundations of the Torah: Israelite guide to belief and duties, 1831).

114. "*v* [Heb.]: und (hier so wohl als nämlich) fast bei jeder Satzverbindung ist das Kindliche und einfache der Sprache." Note to Genesis 1:2.

115. Herxheimer, preface, iv.

116. Herxheimer, preface, vi.

117. Herxheimer does credit Mendelssohn's Genesis commentary with establishing a scholarly, i.e., grammatical-historical, Bible interpretation for German Jewry.

118. Among them: Niebuhr, *Reisebeschreibung nach Arabien*; Michaelis, *Mosaisches Recht*; Eichhorn, *Einleitung in das alte Testament* and *Jerusalem*; Gesenius, *Hebräisch-deutsches Handwörterbuch*, Fürst, *Concordanz über die Bücher des A. T.*; Ranke, *Untersuchungen für den Pentateuch aus dem Gebiete der hoheren Kritik*.

119. Salfeld notes that German Jewish sermons were first published in 1808 by Joseph Wolf. See Kayserling, *Bibliothek jüdischer Kanzelredner*. Jewish preachers modeled themselves on German preachers.

120. Herxheimer's preface to the revised edition cited positive reviews by Franz Delitzsch; the *Magazin für die Literatur des Auslands* 40 (1863); and the *Israelitischer Volkslehrer*.

121. Based on Faber, *Salomon Herxheimer*, 58–59.

122. [Fürst], "Herxheimer's Pentateuch," 190.

123. Fürst, "Empfehlung der Israelitischen Bibel von Herxheimer," 30.

124. *Der Orient* 4, no. 19 (9 May 1843): 148.

125. See Steinschneider, *Hebräische Bibliographie*, 1: 2, 33, cited in Salfeld, *Dr. Salomon Herxheimer*, 16.

126. "Dieses Bibelwerk entsprach seinerzeit durch seine klare, verständliche, traditionsgemäße Übersetzung, durch eine vielseitige, gewissermaßen den Extrakt aller früheren Kommentare bearbeitenden Erklärung, durch seine knappen, gedankenreichen, homiletischen Anmerkungen und andere Vorzüge einem langgefuhlten Bedürfnis. Es ist ein Werk, das über den Parteien stand, von Juden und Christen gleich günstig beurteilt wurde, von Konsistorien den Pfarrern empfohlen wurde und in den meisten Universitätsbibliotheken Deutschlands zu finden ist. Und dennoch konnte es sich nicht den Bahn brechen und, bis auf den Pentateuch, nicht den Weg in das Publikum finden." Löwenstein, "Ein Vorkämpfer des modernen Judentums," 2.

127. Meyer, *The Origins of the Modern Jew*, 145.

128. Meyer, *The Origins of the Modern Jew*, 145.

CHAPTER THREE

1. Also published in AZdJ 3, no. 9 (19 January 1839): 433, without the illustration.

2. Erlin, "Luxury Editions," 30.

3. The paintings were published 1799–1800 in Cassas, *Voyage Pittoresque*.

4. IB, 1: 292.

5. Hirsch, *The Nineteen Letters*, 14–15. See also Grunfeld, "The Historical and Intellectual Background of the Horeb."

6. For context, see Smith, *The Total Work of Art*.

7. Neusner, *First Principles of Systemic Analysis*, 35–36, cited in Zahavy, "Rhetoric of Rabbinic Ritual," http://www.tzvee.com/Home/the-rhetoric-of-rabbic-ritual.

8. Zahavy, "Rhetoric of Rabbinic Ritual."

9. Berman, *Experience of the Foreign*, esp. "Herder: Fidelity and Expansion," 35–41.

10. First used in 1808; cited in Tatlock, Introduction to *Publishing Culture*, 1.

11. Tatlock, Introduction to *Publishing Culture*, 1.

12. Tatlock, Introduction to *Publishing Culture*, 6.

13. This well-known publisher, Friedrich Arnold Brockhaus, published not only the *Conversations-Lexicon* (1809–11, 5th ed. 1818–20), but a series of journals, such as *Deutsche Blätter*, providing timely reports about the Wars of Liberation, and *Isis, oder enzyklopädische Zeitung von Oken*, devoted to general knowledge as well as political writing.

14. Tatlock, Introduction to *Publishing Culture*, 12.

15. Belgum, "Documenting the Zeitgeist," 89.

16. Belgum, "Documenting the Zeitgeist," 89–90.

17. Sheehan, *The Enlightenment Bible*, 73.

18. Sheehan, *The Enlightenment Bible*, 75.

19. Marchand, *German Orientalism*, 40.

20. Marchand, *German Orientalism*, 102–5.

21. See Marchand, *German Orientalism*, 106–9.

22. AZdJ 42 (1879), 770, and 43, 1.

23. AZdJ 43 (1879), 418 f.

24. "Nicht bloss faßlich, sondern auch anziehend, der Geist erhebend und erwärmend sein, der ganze gelehrte Apparat jedoch fern bleiben." AZdJ 42 (1878), 770.

25. Marchand summarizes the position Philippson and Hirsch rejected: "The *Wissenschaft des Judentums* had religious-reformist ambitions to be sure—but much of its scholarship was just as deeply historicist, positivist, and philologically informed as that of Christian contemporaries, as just as deeply devoted to that supremely important liberal-rationalist virtue: *Wissenschaftlichkeit.* To gain the respect of their liberal Christian peers without becoming apostates, the *Wissenschaft des Judentums* in this era sought to go beyond religious polemics by engaging in uncontroversial *Wissenschaft* (the model for which was, of course, classical philology). The intellectuals who founded *Der Orient* in 1840 did not envision having to give up their Jewishness to be scientific: 'Science is a free gift,' wrote editor (and Leipzig *Privatdozent*) Julius Fürst in the first issue, 'like the love of life, which we breathe, like the rays of the sun, which warm us; science does not discriminate according to confessions, but between truth and lies.'" Julius Fürst, "Vorwort," *Der Orient* 1 (1840): vii; Marchand, *German Orientalism*, 114–15.

26. Abraham Geiger was an exception. See Heschel, *Abraham Geiger and the Jewish Jesus*.

27. Marchand, *German Orientalism*, 115.

28. Hermann, "Translating Cultures and Texts," 178–79.

29. Graetz's introduction to his *History of the Jews*—anticipating Erich Auerbach's "Odysseus' scar"—sought to make the case that European culture was rooted in Hebraism and Hellenism. Marchand, *German Orientalism*, 116; Skolnik, *Jewish Pasts, German Fictions*.

30. Hess, *Middlebrow Literature*.

31. Tasch, *Samson Raphael Hirsch*, 268–69.

32. Hirsch, "Speech Delivered at . . . Schiller Festival," in Shapiro, "Rabbi Samson Raphael Hirsch and Friedrich von Schiller," 182.

33. See the cogent description of these positions in Hoffman, "Analyzing the Zeitgeist," 109–10.

34. AZdJ 19 (1855), 1–3. The lead editorial recounts a meeting with an official in the manner of Nathan the Wise meeting Saladin. He asks: What kind of Jew are you? I know of only two sorts: reform and orthodox. Philippson replies: I am neither, I am a "historical Jew" (*geschichtlicher Jude*).

35. Shavit and Eran, *The Hebrew Bible Reborn*, 74.

36. M. Philippson, *Twelve Minor Prophets*, 1805. Moses was a self-taught Maskil, a biurist with an excellent German prose style, and cofounder and teacher of the Dessau school, who remained a traditional Jew. He published a reader for youth and "lovers of Hebrew." See Salomon, *Lebensgeschichte des Herrn Moses Philippson*.

37. L. Philippson, *Ezekiel des Jüdischen Trauerspieldichters Auszug aus Egypten und Philo des Aelteren Jerusalem*.

38. J. Philippson, "Ludwig Philippson und das Allgemeine Zeitung des Judentums," 104.

39. Horch, *Auf der Suche nach der jüdischen Erzählliteratur*, 17.

40. J. Philippson, "Ludwig Philippson," 106.

41. J. Philippson, "Ludwig Philippson," 166.

42. Tasch, *Samson Raphael Hirsch*, 42–48.

43. On its reception, see Grunfeld, "The Historical and Intellectual Background of the Horeb," xxxii–xxxvi.

44. Grunfeld, "The Historical and Intellectual Background of the Horeb," xli.

45. Graff, "Samson Raphael Hirsch," 49.

46. *Jeschurun: ein Monatsblatt zur Förderung jüdischen Geistes und jüdischen Lebens in Haus, Gemeinde und Schule* (a monthly paper for the promotion of Jewish Geist and Jewish life in the home, synagogue, and school).

47. Hirsch, "Vorwort," vi.

48. Hirsch, "Vorwort," vi.

49. Revived in 2010 as an Orthodox Jewish anti-Zionist webnewspaper, at http://www.derisraelit.org/.

50. AZdJ 23, no. 13 (1859): 183–85.

51. Philippson, *Schulmagazin* 1 (1 January 1834): 12–13. Philippson notes a more hopeful trend in southern Germany—in Bavaria, Vienna, Prague, Teplitz. Among the positive changes Philippson notes are sermons given in German; choral settings of the so-called *niggunim*, orderly singing, and the establishment of a proper relationship between cantor and the congregation. However, the critical need facing a community in which children are sent to Christian schools is for the right kind of teachers. In Philippson's view, the ideal teacher is also a *deutscher Redner*, a German orator: one who knows how to speak with *Kraft, Weihe, Eindringlichkeit* (force, devotion, urgency). The ideal teacher will be true to the Jewish past and faithful to modern values: he will combine the "historical basis" of Judaism with the "higher" need for religious knowledge and honor.

52. Kayserling, *Ludwig Philippson*, 337.

53. IB, 3: 43, section on "translations."

54. AZdJ 42 (1878): 770, cited in Hermann, "Translating Cultures and Texts," 172.

55. Hirsch, *The Nineteen Letters*, 118.

56. Hirsch, *The Nineteen Letters*, 118.

57. As if not to give fodder to his critics, the much-maligned sixteenth-century legal code, the *Shulhan Arukh*, is not even named, but only referred to as a book that became only partially known and was mostly caricatured.

58. Hirsch, *The Nineteen Letters*, 125

59. Hirsch, *The Nineteen Letters*, 123. "His followers contented themselves with developing the study of the Bible in the philological-aesthetical sense, with studying the *Moreh* [Maimonides's *Guide of the Perplexed*] and yet pursuing and spreading the humanities. But Judaism, Bible, and Talmud were neglected. Even the most zealous study of the Bible was of no avail for the proper understanding of Judaism, because it was not treated as the authoritative source of doctrine and instruction, but only as a beautiful poetic storehouse from which to draw rich supplies for the imagination" (123–24).

60. Hirsch, *The Nineteen Letters*, 127.

61. Hirsch, *The Nineteen Letters*, 127.

62. Hirsch, *The Nineteen Letters*, 127–28.

63. IB, 1: vii–viii.

64. Hebrew *Chamisha Chumshei Torah* (The Five Books of the Torah), German *Der Pentateuch*, and *Die fünf Bücher Moscheh.* By contrast, only two Hebrew words needed to appear on Hirsch's title page: *Sefer Bereshit* (The book of Genesis).

65. Klaus Hermann notes that Philippson's preface imitated that of Wilhlem Ernst Hengstenberg. Hermann, "Translating Cultures," 179.

66. IB, 1: 294.

67. IB, 1: 331.

68. Und es soll nur angedeutet werden: daß die Weigerung Pharaoh's im Plane Gottes und mit den Zwecken Gottes übereinstimmend geschah . . . weil nähmlich Gott hierbei in einer steigenden Reihe von wunderbaren Geschehnissen die Gemüther der Israeliten zur Offenbarung vorbereiten, ihnen und auch den Aegyptern die Vorstellung von Gottes allmächtiger Wunderkraft nahe bringen wollte (IB 1: 330–31).

69. Ana-Maria Rizzuto, *Why Did Freud Reject God?*, Diane O'Donoghue, "Mapping the Unconscious" and "Moses in Moravia," and Mary Bergstein, "Long Ago and Far Away."

70. Bergstein, "Long Ago and Far Away," 1.

71. IB, 1: 49.

72. Rizzuto, *Why Did Freud Reject God?*, 118. See also Pfrimmer, *Freud*, 220, 372–73.

73. IB, 1: 174–75.

74. IB, 1: 26 (1858), cited in Bergstein, "Long Ago and Far Away," 1.

75. IB, 1: 755.

76. IB, 1: 322–24.

77. Liss, "Entkontextualisierung als Programm," 6.

78. IB, 1: 361–62. "So gleichklingend auch das griechische ὕσσωπος mit dem hebr. אזוב *Ezov* ist, so daß man es gewöhnlich mit hyss. Officinalis erklärt, einer auf Schutt und Mauern wachsenden Pflanze (I Kings 5, 13), mit lanzetförmigen Blättern, 1 bis 1½ Fuß hohem Stengel, blauer Blume: dit Trad. (Pesach 11.7) [fol. 118.1] unterscheidet dennoch den Hysop des Gesetzes ausdrücklich vom röm. Und griech. Hysop, Rambam und Saad. geben es mit dem arab. צעתר. Welches صعتر Origanum (Dosten), eine aromatische Pflanze mit 1 Fuß hohem geradem Stengel und vielen wolligen Blättern, bezeichnet, die in Palästina, Syrien, Aeg. und Arab. sehr häufig wächst. Eine ganz andere Deutung versuchte man in Phytolacca decandra, die bei Aleppo und in Abyssinien häufig gefunden wird, mit langem und gestrecktem Stiele, und eine ungemeine Menge salziger Theile enthält. (Vgl. Ps 51, 9). –Nach der Tradit. (Parah 11, 9) gehören zu einem Bündel drei Stengel, nach Rambam (Pyrke Aboth 3.) was man mit einer Hand faßt."

Contrast this treatment with the scene as Cecil B. DeMille depicts it: the Hebrews huddling together in their homes, the bloody door-posts, the Angel of Death moving through the streets, and the Egyptians' screams of horror in the background.

79. Hirsch/Levy 2: 146–47.

80. Hirsch/Levy 2: 150.

81. Mendelssohn takes up the difficulty as well, in the end following Ibn Ezra ("after he had been caught in the hedges"), although noting that the *ta'amim* (cantillation notes) argue *against* that reading and suggesting instead that *achar* is an adjective describing the ram, rather than a conjunction.

82. Hirsch/Levy 1: 375.

83. Hirsch/Levy 4: 12.

84. Hirsch/Levy 1: 4–5.

85. Hirsch/Levy 1: 4–5.

86. Hirsch/Levy 1: 3.

87. Hirsch/Levy 2: 138–39.

88. I compare other translations of Exodus 12–13 in Gillman, "From Myth to Memory."

89. Hirsch/Levy 1:vi.

90. Clark, *Etymological Dictionary of Biblical Hebrew*, xi–xii. Hirsch sought to attach a distinct meaning or association to individual consonants, and to relate the meanings of words that have similar consonants, regardless of the order of the letters. He created five categories of interchanging consonants that he organized by level of intensity. He created a separate category for roots whose second and third letters were identical, but whose nuances changed. He went further to create ten types of expansion of roots by the addition of additional letters. The basis of these categories are "abstract, conceptual relationships between seemingly unrelated ideas" (Clark, 299): plants and joy; pain and cords; plants and vegetations and thinking and speaking; underground water sources and investigation. Separation and distinctiveness connect with being independent, being similar is equated with emptiness and nothingness; woven cloth connects with liquids. Words can have oppositional character; words designating people also explain the nature of their interpersonal relationships or social roles.

91. Clark, *Etymological Dictionary of Biblical Hebrew*, 293. But the historical fall into many languages going back to the Tower of Babel hinges also on the translation of *balal*—the punishment imposed on the tower-builders. If "all the earth was one language and words," this must be because all words came from the same source. When God decides to punish the tower builders, however, He does not "mix their dialects," diluting Hebrew among a multiplicity of languages, but He loosens the binds between human and God. "Hirsch explains that *navla* (from the root N-V-L) means 'withering,' not 'mixing.' In other words, the connection to God and His language withered, causing each group to create its own vocabulary and language. But that original universal language was the language of *maamad har sinai* and the giving of the Torah to the People of Israel." Ibid., x.

92. "This combination of the scientific and Romantic, the scientific predominating in theory, the Romantic in practice, is characteristic of the nineteenth century: one of the fascinating things about Hirsch is indeed how he was both soaked in Jewish tradition and also so much of his particular place and time. The result of this is a work which is philologically questionable, but retains its place as a religious classic." Lesser, "Samson Raphael Hirsch's Use of Hebrew Etymology," 277–78.

93. Lesser, "Samson Raphael Hirsch's Use of Hebrew Etymology," 271. The notion that language has a divine origin stems from German Romanticism; it was put forth by the Christian theologian Johann Peter Süssmilch, adopted by Herder and then Hamann who used it for nationalist, *völkisch* ends.

94. Commentary to Exodus 21:2. Hirsch/Levy 2: 286–87.

95. Anonymous, *Fackel der Wahrheit: Eine kritische Beleuchtung des Philippson'schen Bibelwerkes von einem orthodoxen Bibelfreunde*, vol. 1.

96. Philippson, "Einige Pamphlete," AZdJ 24, no. 17 (24 April 1860): 1.

97. Ismar Elbogen's speech in honor of Philippson's one-hundredth birthday in the Generalversammlung der Gesellschaft zu Berlin, 3 January 1912.

98. They used J. Z. Mecklenburg's *Ha-Ketav v'ha-Kabbalah* (Leipzig, 1839) as the basis of the Hebrew text. "And so, a movement for the publication of a Bible, in German

translation with commentary, both faithful to tradition, was initiated by Wolf Feilchenfeld and vigorously supported by Hildesheimer. However, it was not easy to enlist other leading Orthodox rabbis and scholars in this undertaking. Apparently no agreement could be reached over the execution of a work that was to do justice both to tradition and to scholarship. Feilchenfeld and Hildesheimer were thinking of a 'new translation that would morally recommend our side in the circles of *Wissenschaft*.' The memory of the controversy over Mendelssohn's *Biur* may have played a part among those who were reluctant. At last the project was started, but only the translation; the controversial commentary was dropped." Breuer, *Modernity within Tradition*, 184–85.

99. Lehmann, "Die Bibelanstalt für die Anhänger des traditionellen (orthodoxen) Judenthums," 274.

100. "Although [Hirsch] had given the assurance that he would not object publicly, he apparently wanted to have nothing to do with a Bible undertaking that, in his view, did not distance itself sufficiently from the faction identifying itself with universal *Wissenschaft*." Breuer, *Modernity within Tradition*, 185.

101. Bamberger, Adler, and Lehmann, *Übersetzung der fünf Bücher Moses von der orthodox israelitischen Bibelanstalt*.

102. The OBS had no problem rendering Genesis 8:21 "And God smelled the pleasing aroma . . ." (Und der Ewige roch den lieblichen Duft), adding a footnote explaining the metaphor ("D.H. Gott nahme das Opfer mit Wohlgefallen an" = which means, God accepted the sacrifice with pleasure), whereas Hirsch eliminated the image altogether: "Da nahm *G o t t* den Ausdruck der Willfahrung wahr" (Hirsch/Levy: "And God noted the expression of compliance").

103. Hirsch/Levy, 1: 55.

104. The notes in German: IB: "Radak giebt hier sprachgebrauchwidrig dem Worte *Vayishalchu* die Bedeutung, sie hätten den Rock mit einem Schwerte zerschnitten (von Shelach)." Hirsch: "Sie schickten den Rock nicht direkt, sondern ließen ihn durch andere erst in andere Häuser und dann erst zum Vater kommen." OBS: "Nach andren: und sie durchschnitten, nach Analogie von. Job 36, 12, um ihre Behauptung, dass er von einem wildern Thiere zerrissen worden sei, zu beklagen."

105. AZdJ 53, no. 2 (10 January 1889): 24.

106. The community was led by the Breuers, Hirsch's son-in-law and then grandson, who transplanted it to Washington Heights, New York, after 1939. The community retained the insistence on stringent Orthodoxy and are known to oppose Zionism and the State of Israel.

107. Meyer, *Response to Modernity*, 108.

108. Horch, "Auf der Zinne der Zeit."

109. *Biblia Gallia-La Sainte Bible*. Mühlen, *Die Bibel und ihr Titelblatt*, 138.

110. Diane O'Donoghue has written about the steel engraving of Moses that served as frontispiece to the second edition, and has also speculated on how such images of topoi, ruins, and classical scenes most likely glimpsed for the first time in this book, influenced his discursive language, which, as we know, was saturated with topographical and archaeological metaphors. O'Donoghue, "Moses in Moravia." Ana-Maria Rizzuto argues that the extensive collection of (mostly) Egyptian figurines that sat on Freud's desk and populated his office—a passion begun only after his father died—replicated or

re-created the images and icons in the pages of the Philippson Bible, the book that had connected Freud to his father. Rizzuto draws from Theo Pfrimmer, *Freud*. Rizzuto, *Why Did Freud Reject God?*

CHAPTER FOUR

1. Originally titled *Die Schrift*. Zu verdeutschen unternommen von Martin Buber gemeinsam mit Franz Rosenzweig. *Die fünf Bücher der Weisung.*

2. Rosenzweig, "afterword," in Galli, *Franz Rosenzweig and Jehuda Halevi*, 173.

3. Rosenzweig, "afterword," 173.

4. Szondi, *Theorie des modernen Dramas*, 116–17.

5. Important works include Rosenwald, "On the Reception of Buber and Rosenzweig's Bible" and "Buber and Rosenzweig's Challenge to Translation Theory"; Fox, "Franz Rosenzweig as Translator"; Askani, *Das Problem der Übersetzung*; Benjamin, *Rosenzweig's Bible*; Levenson, *The Making of the Modern Jewish Bible*; Seidman, *Faithful Renderings*; Krochmalnik and Werner, *50 Jahre Martin Buber Bibel.*

6. Also needed is an up-to-date reception history. Who reads the Buber-Rosenzweig Bible in Germany after 1961, and who uses it today?

7. Unless otherwise indicated, all citations from letters come from the Correspondence with Bertha Pappenheim located in the Martin Buber Archives, Department of Manuscripts and Archives, The Jewish National Library and University Library, Jerusalem (Arch. Ms. Var. 350/568). All translations are my own.

8. Today, Buber's former house is occupied by the Center for the International Council of Christians and Jews.

9. She and her mother moved to be with her mother's family in Frankfurt in 1888 after her father's death. The wealthy Goldschmidt family had resided there since the seventeenth century.

10. The journal, published 1916–24, was one of many initiatives Buber undertook to promote cultural Zionism and religious renewal, and to respond to the crisis facing European Jewry during the war. On the scope and agenda of *Der Jude*, see "introduction," in Buber, *The Jew.*

11. "Diese Dinas, die die gleichen sind . . . in Lemberg, auf dem Rathausplatz in Tarnopol, in Kiev, in Odessa, in Lodz, in Wilna, in Berlin, Wien, London, in Telawiw—diese Dinas sind der Ruin unseres Volkes." Pappenheim to Buber, 28 May 1916.

12. Colin, "Bertha Pappenheim Establishes the Jewish Women's Federation," 266.

13. In 1903, she had traveled to some of the poorest Jewish communities in Galicia and written up her findings in a report that "established her reputation as an expert on the social welfare of Eastern European Jewry." She later visited sites of pogroms in Russia, as well as New York's Lower East Side. An extended trip in 1911–12 took her through Eastern Europe and the Balkans, as well as to Palestine, Egypt, and Turkey. The chronicle of these trips was published a decade later under the title *Sisyphus-Arbeit*.

14. See Loentz, *Let Me Continue to Speak the Truth*, 195–271.

15. For an analysis of Pappenheim's oeuvre, including a critical survey of her reception and bibliography, see Loentz, *Let Me Continue to Speak the Truth.*

16. Heuberger, *Rabbi Nehemiah Anton Nobel*, 43–49.

17. Konz, *Bertha Pappenheim*, 216.

18. Berthold, "Frauenfrage und Frauenberuf im Judenthum," in Kugler and Koschorke, *Bertha Pappenheim*, 36. "The first commandment for an educated woman is to learn to accept that she has a duty to help, where help is needed." Ibid., 37. "Women with means must stop living mindless lives, and instead, view themselves as obligated to use their time and their intellect in the service of the general welfare."

19. Letter to Buber, 17 May 1918.

20. In her attacks on Zionism, she argued for a simpler criterion of Jewish peoplehood: anyone who "knows that the ten commandments and the command to love one's neighbor are Jewish values." Elsewhere: "*Nächstenliebe* is the foundation of the Jewish religion, equally important to men and women." Pappenheim, "Die Frau im kirchlichen und religiösen Leben."

21. Letter to Buber, 12 June 1935.

22. Letter to Buber, 13 June 1935.

23. Pappenheim was drawn to creative imitation. In 1934 she rewrote Lessing's "Ring Parable" from *Nathan the Wise*, but in a feminist vein, calling her parable "The Genuine Ring," using German (Lessing) and Jewish (Shechinah) imagery.

24. "Wissen Sie mir Jemanden zu nennen, der o. die meine *Maase-Buch* auf 'Einheitlichkeit' durchsehen könnte? . . . - Rabbi, Rabi—Rawa? Tefillah—Thefila, Tanoh—Thanno u.s.w." Letter to Buber, 14 May 1929.

25. Letter to Buber, 18 January 1936.

26. Letter to Buber, 7 June 1935.

27. Karminski, "An die fernen Freunde," 8.

28. Cited in Loentz, *Let Me Continue to Speak the Truth*, 185n113.

29. Buber, *Tales of the Hasidim*, 210.

30. Rosenzweig, *On Jewish Learning*, 98.

31. The term was popularized at the turn of the century by Langbehn's *Rembrandt als Erzieher* (1895).

32. Friedenthal-Haase, "Martin Buber im androgogischen Gespräch," 21.

33. A recent edited volume was devoted to Buber's contributions to *Erwachsenbildung* based on lectures in Jena and Marburg. See Friedenthal-Haase and Koerrenz, *Martin Buber.*

34. Konz, *Bertha Pappenheim.*

35. Pappenheim, "Die jüdische Frau," 97–98.

36. *Jüdische Rundschau* 43–44 (30 May 1933): 227, English translation cited in Colodner, *Jewish Education in Germany*, 41.

37. It is told that Buber began attending (and preaching) in the Heppenheim synagogue after 1933. Mendes-Flohr, "Martin Buber's Reception Among Jews."

38. Pappenheim, "Der Einzelne und die Gemeinschaft," *Blätter des Jüdischen Frauenbundes* 9:6 (June 1933):6.

39. Stahl, "Bertha Pappenheims erzieherisches Konzept," 15–16.

40. In her letter about Pappenheim's last days, Hannah Karminski reports that Pappenheim's last night in the home was Passover eve, April 1936. Against her doctor's wishes, she attended the seder, which was being run by a young male visitor. Karminski reports, "She kept interrupting him to ask him to translate or explain something to the children, or to add her own commentary. When they mentioned *Frohnarbeit* (slavery,

forced labor), she commented: 'I imagine it this way. What made the work in Egypt unbearable was the lack of Shabbes [Sabbath]. There was no Shabbes yet. Any kind of difficult labor is bearable if one has Shabbes to look forward to.'" Karminski, "An die fernen Freunde," 2–3.

41. Rosenzweig to Margrit Rosenstock, letters of 25 April 1920 and 10 December 1920, in GS, 1: 858.

42. Rosenzweig, "Upon Opening the Jüdisches Lehrhaus," 98.

43. Glatzer, *Franz Rosenzweig*, 77–78.

44. "In his own time, Rosenzweig thus claimed, neither the orthodox nor the liberal forms of Judaism set out a path of Jewish study and practice that was *livable*. Rosenzweig's educational program made the re-discovery of one's own personal Jewish life, or the renewed commitment to one's own Jewishness the starting point of the path of Jewish learning, and thereby sought to ensure that whatever was learned, whatever practices were taken on, would become part of a living Judaism." Pollock, "Franz Rosenzweig."

45. Rosenzweig, "Upon Opening the Jüdisches Lehrhaus," 98–99.

46. Rosenzweig, "Upon Opening the Jüdisches Lehrhaus," 98.

47. Konz, *Bertha Pappenheim*, 139.

48. Pappenheim, *Gebete*. Cited in Loentz, *Let Me Continue to Speak the Truth*, 193–94.

49. Feuilleton, *Frankfurter Allgemeine Zeitung*, 23 September 1953.

50. For detailed studies of Rosenzweig's career as a translator, see Askani, *Das Problem der Übersetzung*; Benjamin, *Rosenzweig's Bible*; and Galli, *Franz Rosenzweig and Jehuda Halevi*. Each has a different emphasis, and all have contributed to my understanding of Rosenzweig's vocation as a translator.

51. Groundbreaking editions included Rabbi Michael Sachs's 1845 collection, *Die religiöse Poesie der Juden in Spanien* (2nd ed. Berlin 1901), and the first German collection of Halevi's poetry with the name *Divan*: Abraham Geiger's *Divan des Castilliers Abu'l-Hassan Juda ha-Levi* of 1851. The roster of works noted in Dr. Heinrich Brody's preface to *Die neuhebräische Dichterschule der Spanish-Arabischen Epoche* (Leipzig 1905) mentions pioneering studies by Delitzsch, Dukes, Zunz, Kaempf, and Sulzbach. In the early twentieth century, the journal of the Hevra Mekitzei Nirdamim (Society to Awaken the Sleepers) in Berlin, *Schriften des Vereins Mekize Nirdamim*, published Brody's edition of the complete "Diwan des Abu-l-Hasan Jehuda Halevi."

52. Grace after Meals ("Tischdank"), Kaddish d'Rabanan ("Lernkaddish"), Kol Nidre, and the Sabbath liturgy for Friday night ("der Häuslichen Feier"). Mach, "Franz Rosenzweig als Übersetzer jüdischer Texte."

53. "The German language has become, in these three names [Notker, Luther, and Hölderlin], a Christian language. Whoever translates into German must to some degree translate into a Christian [idiom]. To what extent does not depend on him, but rather (especially when he translates well) exclusively on that which is translated." GS, 1: 698. Cited in Mach, "Franz Rosenzweig als Übersetzer jüdischer Texte," 255.

54. Ben-Chorin, "Jüdische Bibelübersetzungen in Deutschland," 327. Before the war, Buber had considered other collaborators such as literary writers Moritz Heimann and Efraim Frisch.

55. This edition can be viewed at https://archive.org/details/jehudahalevizwei oojudauoft.

56. Rosenzweig grouped the poems in four categories of his own devising: *Gott, Seele, Volk, Zion*, rather than by genre. He assigned each poem a German title that reflected his understanding of its central idea; Hebrew titles (first lines) were given in the notes and in a second index in back, with pagination from right to left. Like every anthologist of Halevi, Rosenzweig references the editions of Luzatto and Brody.

57. Rather than the customary philological comments and biblical references, the notes resemble prose poems or philosophical aphorisms, along the lines of Benjamin's *Passagenwerk*, Nietzsche's *Die Fröhliche Wissenschaft*, or even Adorno's *Minima Moralia*. Many relate to the poems as tangents, touching upon an essential matter but ultimately moving in unexpected, Rosenzweigian directions. The complex interconnection and idiosyncratic arrangement of the three components of the book—undone in the GS and even in the 1933 Schocken edition of twenty poems—is a fascinating topic in its own right.

58. See my forthcoming essay, "'Not like Cherries, but like Peaches': Mendelssohn and Rosenzweig as Translators of Hebrew Poetry," in Rachel Seelig, ed., *The German-Hebrew Dialogue*.

59. Rosenzweig, "Afterword," in Galli, *Rosenzweig and Halevi*, 174.

60. GS 1: 963n2.

61. Rübner and Mach, *Briefwechsel*, 87.

62. Rübner and Mach, *Briefwechsel*, 87.

63. GS, 1, no. 2: 878.

64. Cohn (1881–1948) was a rabbi and literary writer, author of the play *Letter of Uriah*. He emigrated to the U.S. in 1939.

65. Rosenzweig's cavalier attitude to prior translators of the "Ode to Zion," which he called "Zionide," comes through in another letter (15 May 1924): "Ich vergass, Sie um Herders, Mendelssohns und Bialiks Zioniden zu bitten; ich kenne sie alle nicht. Vor allem Herders." GS, 1: 961.

66. Ironically, Cohn too believed he was "correcting" a long tradition of bad translations; in his preface, he states that he began the twelve-year process translating the Diwan in the manner of "freie Nachdichtung," but eventually concluded that rather than use the poetry to inspire his own creativity, he would use translation to try to do justice to the medieval singer (*diesem Sänger selbst zum Rechte zu verhelfen*), given the inadequacy of all extant translations. Cohn, *Ein Diwan*, 139.

67. Rosenzweig, "Afterword," in Galli, *Rosenzweig and Halevi*, 169.

68. "Alle jüdische Dichtung im Exil verschmäht es, dieses ihr Im-Exil-Sein zu ignorieren." Rosenzweig, afterword to *Jehuda Halevi*, 161.

69. Rosenzweig, afterword to *Jehuda Halevi*, 167. The idea recalls Elizabeth Barrett Browning: "How do I love thee? Let me count the ways."

70. Mara Benjamin views Halevi's intellectual appeal to Rosenzweig in this way. Rosenzweig believed that Halevi enacted, in poetic language, a great inversion, whereby the evocation of a biblical world overcame, or interpreted, the exilic condition instead of being assimilated into it. Benjamin, *Rosenzweig's Bible*, 80–83.

71. "Thus traces of the storyteller cling to the story the way the handprint of the potter clings to the clay vessel." Benjamin, "The Storyteller," 92.

72. Buber, foreword, *Tales of Rabbi Nachman*, 1; in German, *Die Geschichten des Rabbi Nachman*, 3.

73. Buber, introduction, *For the Sake of Heaven*, ix.

74. Buber, introduction, *For the Sake of Heaven*, vii.

75. Rosenzweig to Buber, 25 January 1925, in GS, 1: 1021.

76. "Was wir privat machen könnten, wäre nur ein eigenes, also selbstkommentierendes Übersetzen," Rosenzweig to Buber, beginning of May 1925, in GS, 1: 1034. In his 1961 remarks to Buber, Gershom Scholem expressed it thus: "For your translation is not merely a translation; without adding a word of explanation per se it is also a commentary." Scholem, "At the Completion of Buber's Translation of the Bible," 316.

77. Torczyner, *Die heilige Schrift, neu ins Deutsch übertragen* (Berlin, 1937).

78. Schaeder, "Martin Buber: A Biographical Sketch," in *The Letters of Martin Buber*, 47; Schneider, *Rechenschaft über vierzig Jahre Verlagsarbeit.*

79. Buber, "From the Beginnings of our Bible Translation," 177.

80. Cited in Scholem, *Briefe I*, 397n.4.

81. Buber, "From the Beginnings of our Bible Translation," 178; Buber, "Zu einer neuen Verdeutschung der Schrift," 39.

82. They did retain the very first "und" in Genesis 1:2. See Rosenzweig, *Sprachdenken*, 3.

83. "Es ist ja erstaunlich deutsch; Luther ist dagegen fast jiddisch. Ob nun zu deutsch??" Letter to Buber, 19 June 1925. Cited in Rosenzweig, *Sprachdenken*, xiii.

84. Raphael Breuer attacked Buber on these grounds in 1931. Breuer, "Offene Anfrage an Martin Buber."

85. Pappenheim, *Die Memoiren der Glückel von Hameln*. Glückel wrote between 1699 and 1719, and the *Memoiren* was first published in German in 1892. David Kauffmann (1852–99) published a German translation in 1896.

86. Weissler, *Voices of the Matriarchs*, 41. This book was first published in Hebrew in 1602 (Basel). A subsequent Yiddish translation had enormous influence on Yiddish narrative prose style. Pappenheim translated the Amsterdam Yiddish edition of 1723, calling it *Allerlei Geschichten: Maasse-Buch: Buch der Sagen und Legenden aus Talmud und Midrasch nebst Volkerzählungen in jüdisch-deutscher Sprache* (All Kinds of Stories, or A Potpourri of Tales: Book of Legends from the Talmud and Midrash Including Folk Tales in Yiddish).

87. Wie sie die Vorkämpferin für die Rechte der jüdischen Frau geworden ist, so will sie mit diesem Buche der jüdischen Frau und Mutter einen alten Schatz jüdischen Gemütslebens wiedergeben, damit sein Gehalt auf die Verinnerlichung und Vertiefung des religiösen und sittlichen Lebens unserer und der kommenden Tage wirke!

88. Turniansky, "Reception and Rejection," 17.

89. See Weissler's interrogations of this category in *Voices of the Matriarchs*, 38–44.

90. Weissler, *Voices of the Matriarchs*; Marion Kaplan writes, "Both the *tkhines* and the *Tsenerene* maintained their popularity well into the twentieth century." Kaplan, *The Making of the Jewish Middle Class*, 65. See also Weissler, "The Traditional Piety of Ashkenazic Women," and Schwab, *Jewish Rural Communities in Germany*, 49.

91. Aptroot and Gruschka, *Jiddisch*, 74–75.

92. Turniansky, "Reception and Rejection," 17.

93. KJV: Now the serpent was more subtil than any beast of the field which the LORD God had made. Luther: Und die Schlange war listiger denn all Tiere auf dem Felde,

die Gott der Herr gemacht hatte. BR: Die Schlange war listiger als alles Lebendige des Feldes, das Er, Gott, gemacht hatte.

94. BR: Das Weib sprach zur Schlange: / Von der Frucht der Bäume im Garten mögen wir essen, /Aber von der Frucht des Baums, der mitten im Garten ist, hat Gott gesprochen. / Eßt nicht davon und rührt nicht daran, sonst müßt ihr sterben. (3:2–3). Luther: Da sprach das Weib zu der Schlange: Wir essen von den Früchten den Bäumen im Garten, aber von den Früchten des Baumes mittem im Garten hat Gott gesagt: Esset nicht davon, rühret's auch nicht an dass ihr nicht sterbet.

95. Pappenheim, *Zeenah u-Reenah*, 20–23.

96. Weissler, *Voices of the Matriarchs*, 42.

97. Zakon, *The Weekly Midrash / Tz'enah Ur'enah*, vol. 1, 154–55.

98. Schultz, introduction, in Hurwitz, *Ze'enah U-Re'enah*, ii.

99. "The literacy of both men and women made the Torah accessible to them, but men actively *studied* Torah, while women read Bible stories in Yiddish out of the *Tseina Ur'eina* on their own. Study of Torah was a prestigious activity through which men fulfilled a religious obligation. Women, by contrast, read the *Tseina Ur'eina* as an optional act of devotion that was of a far lower status than Torah study." Parush, *Reading Jewish Women*, 59.

100. Parush, *Reading Jewish Women*, 64.

101. Badt-Strauß [Bath-Hillel], "Die Zenne-Renne," 57. She quotes here from Lessing's play *Nathan the Wise*, just prior to the parable of the rings.

102. Loentz locates eight reviews of her *Maasse-Buch*, ten of the *Zeenah u-Reenah*, and one review of the Glückel memoir (published privately). Loentz, *Let Me Continue to Speak the Truth*, 44. See 47–53 for a summary of reviews.

103. Heller, review of *Zeenah u-Reenah*, 312.

104. J. Posen, review of *Allerlei Geschichten*, literary supplement of *Der Israelit* 42 (17 October 1929): 2.

105. Susman, review of *Zeenah u-Reenah*, 455.

106. Susman, review of *Zeenah u-Reenah*, 455.

107. Susman, review of *Zeenah u-Reenah*, 456.

108. "The memoirs from the nineteenth century are full of accounts telling of the profound effect that reading popular Yiddish novels was having on women. Under its sway they slowly began to switch perspectives, becoming, at times unconsciously, accelerants of the changes taking place in contemporary Jewish society." Parush, *Reading Jewish Women*, 154–55.

109. Parush bases these findings on memoir literature and fiction, such as I. L. Peretz's stories "The Reading Woman" and "Sorele the Perfect." She emphasizes that the similarity in tone between religious and secular literature facilitated this evolution of women's reading, leading to a "pact" between early popular Yiddish authors and their female readers. Parush, *Reading Jewish Women*, 141–42.

110. In his memoir *The Life of Jews in Poland before the Holocaust*, Ben-Zion Gold writes that he envied his sisters' education: learning in yeshiva perpetuated immaturity, while his sisters acquired languages and knowledge that lead to employment and independence.

111. "The *Tseina Ur'eina* really opened my eyes. As I noted above, in the heder I studied only discontinuous sections of the Five Books, with no relation or connection be-

tween them. Through the *Tseina Ur'eina* a complete and elaborate picture from the lives of our ancestors was disclosed to me, a picture seasoned with fine and wonderful *Aggadot* [legends], which captured my heart." From the 1947 memoir of Buki ben Yogli [pseud. Yehuda Leib Benjamin Katzenelson], cited in Parush, *Reading Jewish Women*, 66.

112. Buber, "On Word Choice in Translating the Bible," 73.

113. Pappenheim, 5 December 1923, cited in Edinger, *Bertha Pappenheim*, 141.

114. See my discussion of the modernist *Erlebnis* in Gillman, *Viennese Jewish Modernism*.

115. Buber, "The How and Why," 219.

116. Buber, "People Today and the Jewish Bible," 4–5.

117. Buber, "People Today and the Jewish Bible," 7.

118. Buber, *I and Thou*, in Herberg, *The Writings of Martin Buber*, 61.

119. Gillman, *Sacred Fragments*, 180.

120. Gillman, *Sacred Fragments*, 180–81.

121. Rosenzweig, "Bible," cited in Glatzer, *Franz Rosenzweig*, 275.

122. Letter to Buber, 18 March 1936.

123. Vogelaar and Korevaar, *Rembrandt's Mother*, 112. See also 110–20. These features include oriental or exotic clothing and headgear, and the illumination of the book, rather than the model's face. Many other painters painted widows, who were numerous in Leiden, in this pose of piety, praying or bent over the Bible. Widows are most often singled out in the Bible as those who are without means and who rely on God to protect and provide for them. Rembrandt liked to paint older people, preferring older beauty to younger.

124. Letter to Dozent Josef Wohlgemuth, end of January 1926, in Buber and Rosenzweig, *Scripture and Translation*, 198.

125. "Aber die Bibel müßte den Juden—auch den einfältigen—so nahe gebracht werden, daß sie lieben und hassen lernen (was ja dasselbe ist) sonst nichts." Letter to Buber, 18 March 1936.

126. Parentheses in Old Yiddish Bibles (as well as in the Amsterdam Yiddish Bible of Yekutiel Blitz) set off Hebrew words. Mendelssohn used them to eliminate ambiguity in the source text, and to deflect the exegetical impulse. Johlson used parentheses with the opposite motive in mind: in order to open up nuances in the Hebrew. In a 1927 edition of the *Tsene-Rene* published in New York in two-column format, parentheses function like quotation marks to set off excerpts from biblical verses.

127. "The success of Pappenheim's translation lay, in the eyes of her German Jewish critics, in her ability to create an 'old-new language,' a watered-down Pseudo-Yiddish that was accessible to German Jews who could not read the original Yiddish without sacrificing the 'folksiness' [*Volkstümlichkeit*] associated with it. Ironically, Pappenheim's invented language resembles another invented language, namely the *Mauscheln* attributed to Jews by antisemites." Loentz, *Let Me Continue to Speak the Truth*, 52.

128. Lowenstein, "The Complicated Language Situation," 180–81. Yiddish texts played different and shifting roles within the modern cultural polysystem. Standardized literary Yiddish was no longer viable in Germany after 1780. Rather, Yiddish dialects were phonetically reproduced in Hebrew or Latin (Gothic) letters. In nineteenth-century Germany, four different types of "transitional" writing were common: old literary Yiddish;

Jüdisch-Deutsch (High German written in Hebrew script, as in the Mendelssohn *Be'ur*); Yiddish dialect in Hebrew script; and Yiddish dialect in German script. These languages were used for different audiences and different purposes. Works written in literary Yiddish continued to be printed in Yiddish, but they sometimes added German titles pages with intermixtures of Hebrew words.

129. One of her stories, "The Redeemer," features a debate between an Eastern European Jew and a Zionist, with the former lamenting that he had only a "hodgepodge" of languages, but no mother tongue. When the Zionist argues that the appropriate language for Jews is, of necessity, either Hebrew or Jargon (a derogatory term for Yiddish), his interlocutor makes the case that it would be more "practical" to "really master a language that is both a living language and a language of culture." Cited in Loentz, *Let Me Continue to Speak the Truth*, 54.

130. Loentz, *Let Me Continue to Speak the Truth*, 60.

131. Benjamin, *Rosenzweig's Bible*, 148, 149,150; see also 146–54.

132. Buber, "*Leitwort* and Discourse Type: An Example," 143.

133. Buber, "*Leitwort* Style in Pentateuch Narrative," 116.

134. Goethe, "Translations," 65.

135. Olga Litvak notes, "In the decades prior to the publication of the *Biur*, there were a score of new editions of the *Tsene-rene* . . . it was reprinted only three times in the seventeenth century; between 1700 and 1775, however, it was reissued at least ten times, primarily in German-speaking lands." Litvak understands the *Be'ur* as a direct response to the "provoking popularity" of the Yiddish women's Bible: "it was a precedent-setting text in the romantic 'system of defenses against the new power of reading' that motivated the maskilic recovery of the Bible against the eighteenth-century dispersion of Jewish knowledge." Litvak, *Haskalah*, 42.

136. Benjamin, *Rosenzweig's Bible*, 72.

137. See Hanna Liss's insightful essay, "Keine Heilige Schrift? Anfragen an Martin Buber's Prinzip der Oralität."

138. Levenson, *The Making of the Modern Jewish Bible*, 88.

139. Rosenzweig, "Scripture and Luther," 56.

140. Buber, "The How and Why," 219.

141. "The great work of the human mind and spirit inscribed upon the waxen surface is named *history*; but the name of the original text is *the book*. To the former belongs the honor of having gathered humanity around the book; to the latter, however, belongs the right, in a late and necessarily reflective moment of that history, to be discovered and contemplated by that humanity." Buber, "On Word Choice in Translating the Bible," 89.

142. "The translator must elicit from the letter of the Hebrew text its actual auditory form; he must understand the writtenness of Scripture as for the most part the record of its spokenness—which spokenness, as the actual *reality* of the Bible, is awakened anew wherever an ear biblically hears the word or a mouth biblically speaks it." Buber, "On Word Choice in Translating the Bible," 75.

143. Buber, "On Word Choice in Translating the Bible," 89.

144. Buber, "The How and Why," 207.

145. Buber, "The How and Why," 207–8.

146. "ein Weg . . . zu wem? Zu Gott, nicht zu IHM."

147. Rosenzweig, "The Eternal," 105.

148. Pappenheim, *Zeenah u-Reenah*, xi.

149. By contrast, in the memoir authored by a women, which Pappenheim translated in 1910, she did find exemplary womanhood. Her preface closes as follows: "Glückel von Hameln gebührt ein Platz unter denjenigen Frauen, die bescheiden und unbewußt das beste und wertvollste eines Frauendaseins vekörperten." Pappenheim, *Die Memoiren der Glückel*, iii.

150. "Nur aus der Tradition, ohne sie zu kennen, soll die jüdische Frau die Lehre leben, ein eigenartiges Verhalten, das seine verhängnisvollen Schatten bis in die heutige Zeit wirft." Pappenheim, *Zeenah u-Reenah*, xi.

151. Baumgarten, *Introduction to Old Yiddish Literature*, 119.

152. Cited in Edinger, *Bertha Pappenheim*, 117.

153. Hannah Karminski "had entrusted the Pappenheim documents to Swiss friends in Berlin, but they were destroyed in the Allied bombings." Loentz, *Let Me Continue to Speak the Truth*, 202.

154. See Loentz's chapter on "Bertha Pappenheim's biographers," which surveys the many ways that Pappenheim's biographers, even feminist ones, "have used her life story to tell their own." Loentz, *Let Me Continue to Speak the Truth*, 195. Even those who take seriously Pappenheim's "female-Jewish project of modernity" (Konz) neglect the significance of her translations. See Brenner, *The Renaissance of Jewish Culture in Weimar Germany*; Boyarin, "Retelling the Story of O., Or, Bertha Pappenheim, My Hero"; Colin, "Bertha Pappenheim Establishes the Jewish Women's Federation," 266; Konz, *Bertha Pappenheim*.

155. http://www.neu-isenburg.de/erlebniswelt/kultur/seminar-und-gedenkstaette-bertha-pappenheim.

156. See Rosenwald, "On the Reception of Buber and Rosenzweig's Bible," and the essays collected in *Die Schrift und ihre Verdeutschung*, 1936, translated as Buber and Rosenzweig, *Scripture and Translation*.

EPILOGUE

1. Hirsch criticized the term in his commentary on Genesis 2:4 (1867–78). Rosenzweig devoted an entire essay to the problem, " 'Der Ewige': Mendelssohn und der Gottesname," and he praised Mendelssohn for designating Exodus 3:14 (rather than Genesis 2:4) as the "primal scene," even though he made the wrong choice. Rosenzweig, "The Eternal."

2. "This word [Adonai] occurs in the Masoretic text 315 times by the side of the Tetragram YHWH (310 times preceding and five times succeeding it) and 134 times without it. Originally an appellation of God, the word became a definite title, and when the Tetragram became too holy for utterance Adonai was substituted for it, so that, as a rule, the name written YHWH receives the points of Adonai and is read Adonai, except in cases where Adonai precedes or succeeds it in the text, when it is read Elohim. The vowel-signs *e*, *o*, *a*, given to the Tetragrammaton in the written text, therefore, indicate this pronunciation, Aedonai, while the form Jehovah, introduced by a Christian writer about 1520, rests on a misunderstanding. The translation of YHWH by the word Lord in the King James's and in other versions is due to the traditional reading of the

Tetragrammaton as Adonai, and this can be traced to the oldest translation of the Bible, the Septuagint. About the pronunciation of the Shem ha-Meforash, the "distinctive name" YHWH, there is no authentic information." Kohler, "Adonai."

3. Bail et al., *Bibel in gerechter Sprache*, 16–17.

4. Benno Jacob writes that biblical critics notoriously misunderstood the Judaic conception of the divine Name. In Ancient Egypt, knowing the secret name of Ra gave one magic power. But the name of the Israelite God was no magic spell; it is not used, for example, during the showdown with Pharaoh. The power was wholly confined to God's Being. Jacob, *The Second Book of the Bible: Exodus*, 67.

5. "Wir hätten nichts als *Shmot*, die inneren Wahrheiten der Dinge. Unser ganzes Gott-Bewußtsein besteht aus *shmotav shel hakavah*." Hirsch, *Pentateuch*, commentary to Ex 3:13.

6. The KJV's "I AM THAT I AM" is based on the Greek version. Ostensibly, the fact that Hebrew has no copula in the present tense made it possible for the ancient Greek translator to render "I will be" as "I am."

7. English translation cited in Rosenzweig, "The Eternal," 102–3. For a lengthier English excerpt see Gottlieb, *Moses Mendelssohn*, 217–18.

8. BT Berakhot 9b.

9. In a letter to his research assistant Nahum Glatzer, Rosenzweig writes that he was "shocked" to discover this prior use of the word. "Eben erfahre ich zu meinem Schreck, daß in französich reformierten Bibeln des 19. Jahrhunderts der Gottesname durchweg mit LÉternel wiedergegeben wird! Wie alt ist das? Es werden doch französische Bibeln des 17. und 18. Jahrhunderts auf der Bibliothek sein." Letter to Glatzer, 27 June 1929, in GS, 1: 1220.

10. Rosenzweig, "The Eternal," 105.

11. Johann Lorenz Schmidt translates (Ex 6:3): "Jehova / a thing that can make the possible real (*ein Ding, welches das Mögliche wirklich machen kann*)." Johann David Michaelis also used Jehova in his *Deutsche Uebersetzung des Alten Testaments, mit Anmerkungen für Ungelehrte*, and explained that the context called for a *nomen proprium*, rather than a translation.

12. Rosenzweig, "The Eternal," 103.

13. Johlson, *Die Heiligen Schriften der Israeliten*.

14. Hirsch/Levy, 2: 31.

15. Hirsch/Levy, 1: 51.

16. Scholem, "At the Completion of Buber's Translation of the Bible," 317.

17. Buber and Rosenzweig, *Die fünf Bücher der Weisung*, 10th ed.

18. A number of recent German Bibles, including the *Einheitsübersetzung* and the *Gute Nachricht Bibel* (1997), use Buber's "Ich bin da" (sometimes with hyphens). *Gute Nachricht* combines "Er-ist-da" with "Herr":

> Gott antwortete: »Ich bin da«, und er fügte hinzu: "Sag zum Volk Israel: 'Der Ich-bin-da hat mich zu euch geschickt: der HERR! Er ist der Gott eurer Vorfahren, der Gott Abrahams, Isaaks und Jakobs.' Denn 'HERR' (Er-ist-da) ist mein Name für alle Zeiten. Mit diesem Namen sollen mich auch die kommenden Generationen ansprechen, wenn sie zu mir beten."

https://www.die-bibel.de.

19. Commentary on Gen 2:4, in Hirsch/Levy, 1: 49.

20. Rosenzweig, "The Eternal," 108.

21. Rosenzweig, "The Eternal," 112.

22. Losch, " 'Der Ewige' als Synthese des Stern." See also Liss, "Entkontextualisierung als Programm."

23. In German: "Ewigkeit ist nicht eine sehr lange Zeit, sondern ein Morgen, das ebensogut Heute sein könnte. Ewigkeit ist eine Zukunft, die, ohne aufzuhören Zukunft zu sein, dennoch gegenwärtig ist. Ewigkeit ist ein Heute, das aber sich bewußt ist, mehr als Heute zu sein." Losch concludes: "Ganz kurz gefasst bedeutet Ewigkeit 'nicht "sehr lange," sondern "heute schon."' " Rosenzweig, *Der Stern der Erlösung*, 250, 261, cited in Losch, " 'Der Ewige' als Synthese des Stern," 205.

24. Rosenzweig, "The Eternal," 113.

25. Shimon Gershon Rosenberg, "On Translation and the Proliferation of Worlds" (Hebrew), 96–97. I am grateful to Yishai Mevorach for directing me to these Hasidic ideas about translation.

26. He saw a deeper meaning in God's commandment to Noah, "you shall make a skylight to the ark," as the Hebrew word for ark, *tevah*, can also mean "word." The earliest source for this idea in the name of Rabbi Israel Baal Shem Tov is found in the corpus of teachings attributed to the Maggid of Meziritsh and first printed in the collection *Zava'at Ha-Rivash* in 1793.

BIBLIOGRAPHY

Adorno, Theodor W. *Minima Moralia: Reflections from Damaged Life*. Translated by E. F. N. Jephcott. New York: Verso, 2006.

Alter, Robert. *The Five Books of Moses: A Translation with Commentary*. New York: W. W. Norton, 2008.

Altmann, Alexander. *Moses Mendelssohn: A Biographical Study*. Philadelphia: Jewish Publication Society of America, 1973.

Anonymous. *Fackel der Wahrheit: Eine kritische Beleuchtung des Philippson'schen Bibelwerkes von einem orthodoxen Bibelfreunde*. Vol. 1. Würzburg: J. M. Richter, 1860.

Aptroot, Marion. "Bible Translation as Cultural Reform: The Amsterdam Yiddish Bibles." PhD diss., Oxford University, 1989.

Aptroot, Marion. "Yiddish Bibles in Amsterdam." In *The Bible in/and Yiddish*, edited by Shlomo Berger, 42–60. Amsterdam: Menasseh Ben Israel Institute for Jewish Social and Cultural Studies, 2007.

Aptroot, Marion, and Roland Gruschka. *Jiddisch: Geschichte und Kultur einer Weltsprache*. Munich: C. H. Beck, 2010.

Ascheim, Steven, Richard L. Cohen, Jonathan Frankel, and Stefani Hoffman, eds. *Insiders and Outsiders: Dilemmas of East European Jewry*. Oxford: Littman Library of Jewish Civilization, 2010.

Askani, Hans-Christoph. *Das Problem der Übersetzung: dargestellt an Franz Rosenzweig*. Tübingen, Ger.: J. C. B. Mohr (Paul Siebeck), 1997.

Badt-Strauß, Bertha [Bath-Hillel]. "Die Welt des Maasse-Buches." *Der Morgen* 6, no. 1 (April 1930): 103–4.

Badt-Strauß, Bertha [Bath-Hillel]. "Die Zenne-Renne." *Neue Jüdische Monatshefte* 2–4 (1919–20): 55–59.

Bail, Ulrike, Frank Crüsemann, Marlene Crüsemann, et al., eds. *Bibel in gerechter Sprache*, 3rd ed. Gütersloh: Gütersloher Verlagshaus, 2007.

Bamberger, S. B., A. Adler, and M. Lehmann, eds. *Übersetzung der fünf Bücher Moses von der orthodox israelitischen Bibelanstalt*. Frankfurt am Main: Commissions-Verlag der J. Kauffmann'schen Buchhandlung, 1880/1881.

Bath-Hillel. *See* Badt-Strauß, Bertha.

Batnitzky, Leora. "Translation as Transcendence: A Glimpse into the Workshop of the Buber-Rosenzweig Bible Translation." *New German Critique*, no. 70, special issue on Germans and Jews (Winter 1997): 87–116.

Baumgarten, Jean. *Introduction to Old Yiddish Literature*. Translated by Jerold C. Frakes. Oxford: Oxford University Press, 2005.

Bechtoldt, Hans-Joachim. *Jüdische deutsche Bibelübersetzungen vom ausgehenden 18 bis zum Beginn des 20 Jahrhunderts*. Stuttgart: Kohlhammer, 2005.

Belgum, Kirsten. "Documenting the Zeitgeist: How the Brockhaus Recorded and Fashioned the World for Germans." In *Publishing Culture and the "Reading Nation": German Book History in the Long Nineteenth Century*, edited by Lynne Tatlock, 89–117. Rochester, NY: Camden House, 2010.

Ben-Chorin, Schalom. "Jüdische Bibelübersetzungen in Deutschland." *Leo Baeck Institute Yearbook* 4 (1959): 311–31.

Benjamin, Mara H. *Rosenzweig's Bible: Reinventing Scripture for Jewish Modernity*. New York: Cambridge University Press, 2009.

Benjamin, Walter. "The Storyteller." In *Illuminations*, translated by Harry Zohn, 83–110. New York: Schocken Books, 1968.

Berger, Shlomo, ed. *The Bible in/and Yiddish*. Amsterdam: Menasseh Ben Israel Institute for Jewish Social and Cultural Studies, 2007.

Berger, Shlomo. "An Invitation to Buy and Read: Paratexts of Yiddish Books in Amsterdam, 1650–1800." *Book History* 7 (2004): 31–61.

Bergstein, Mary. "Long Ago and Far Away: Origins of the Ancient and Oriental World in the Philippson Bible." Unpublished manuscript.

Berlin, Adele, and Marc Zvi Brettler, eds. *The Jewish Study Bible*. New York: Oxford University Press, 2004.

Berman, Antoine. *The Experience of the Foreign: Culture and Translation in Romantic Germany*. Translated by S. Heyvaert. Albany: State University of New York Press, 1992.

Berthold, P. [pseud. of Bertha Pappenheim]. "Frauenfrage und Frauenberuf im Judenthum." *Allgemeine Zeitung des Judentums* 61, no. 41 (October 8, 1897): 484–85.

Bialik, Hayim Nahman, and Yehoshua Hana Ravnitzky, eds. *The Book of Legends/Sefer Ha-Aggadah: Legends from the Talmud and Midrash*. Translated by William G. Braude. New York: Schocken Books, 1992.

Blitz, Jekuthiel b. Isaac. *Bible: In the Yiddish Language* [*Torah Nevi'im u'Khtuvim: bilshon Ashkenaz*]. Amsterdam: Uri Phoebus Ben-Aharon Halevi, 1678.

Bourel, Dominique. *Moses Mendelssohn: La naissance du judaïsme modern*. Paris: Gallimard, 2004.

Boyarin, Daniel. "Retelling the Story of O., Or, Bertha Pappenheim, My Hero." In *Unheroic Conduct: The Rise of Heterosexuality and the Invention of the Jewish Man*, 313–59. Berkeley: University of California Press, 1997.

Brann, Ross, and Adam Sutcliff, eds. *Renewing the Past: Reconfiguring Jewish Culture from al-Andalus to the Haskalah*. Philadelphia: University of Pennsylvania Press, 2004.

Brenner, Michael, Stefi Jersch-Wenzel, and Michael A. Meyer. *Emancipation and Acculturation: 1780–1871*. Vol. 2 of *German-Jewish History in Modern Times*, edited by Michael A. Meyer and Michael Brenner. New York: Columbia University Press, 1996.

Brenner, Michael. *The Renaissance of Jewish Culture in Weimar Germany*. New Haven, CT: Yale University Press, 1996.

Brettler, Marc Zvi. *Biblical Hebrew for Students of Modern Israeli Hebrew*. Yale Language Series. New Haven, CT: Yale University Press, 2001.

Breuer, Edward. *The Limits of Enlightenment: Jews, Germans, and the Eighteenth-Century Study of Scripture*. Cambridge, MA: Harvard University Press, 1996.

Breuer, Mordechai. "The Early Modern Period." In *German-Jewish History in Modern Times*, edited by Michael A. Meyer and Michael Brenner. New York: Columbia University Press, 1996–98.

Breuer, Mordechai. "The Jewish Enlightenment." In *German-Jewish History in Modern Times*, edited by Michael A. Meyer and Michael Brenner. New York: Columbia University Press, 1996–98.

Breuer, Mordechai. *Modernity Within Tradition: The Social History of Orthodox Jewry in Imperial Germany, 1871–1918*. New York: Columbia University Press, 1992.

Breuer, Mordechai, and Michael Graetz. *Tradition and Enlightenment: 1600–1780*. Translated by William Templer. Vol. 1 of *German-Jewish History in Modern Times*, edited by Michael A. Meyer and Michael Brenner. New York: Columbia University Press, 1996.

Breuer, Raphael. "Eine Offene Anfrage an Martin Buber." *Nahalath Zwi* 1 (1930/31): 308–18.

Brody, Heinrich, ed. "Diwan des Abu-l-Hasan Jehuda Halevi." *Schriften des Vereins Mekize Nirdamim* vol. 3. Berlin: H. Itzkowski, 1902–11.

Brody, Heinrich, and K. Albrecht. *Die neuhebräische Dichterschule der spanisch-arabischen Epoche*. Leipzig: J.C. Hinrich, 1905.

Buber, Martin. *For the Sake of Heaven: A Chronicle*. Translated by Ludwig Lewisohn. New York: Athenaum, 1969.

Buber, Martin. "Foreword to Tales of Rabbi Nachman." In Buber, *Tales of Rabbi Nachman*. Translated by Maurice Friedman. New York: Avon Books, 1956.

Buber, Martin. "From the Beginnings of Our Bible Translations" [1938]. In Buber and Rosenzweig, *Scripture and Translation*, 176–83.

Buber, Martin. *Die Geschichten des Rabbi Nachman*. 4th ed. Frankfurt am Main: Literarische Anstalt, 1918.

Buber, Martin. "The How and Why of Our Bible Translation" [1938]. In Buber and Rosenzweig, *Scripture and Translation*, 205–19.

Buber, Martin. *The Jew: Essays from Martin Buber's Journal, Der Jude, 1916–1928*. Edited by Arthur A. Cohen, translated by Joachim Neugroschel. Tuscaloosa: University of Alabama Press, 1980.

Buber, Martin. "Jüdische Religiosität." In *Vom Geist des Judentums*, 49–74. Leipzig: Kurt Wolff, 1916.

Buber, Martin. "*Leitwort* and Discourse Type: An Example" [1935]. In Buber and Rosenzweig, *Scripture and Translation*, 143–50.

Buber, Martin. "*Leitwort* Style in Pentateuch Narrative" [1927]. In Buber and Rosenzweig, *Scripture and Translation*, 114–28.

Buber, Martin. *Moses*. Oxford: East & West Library, 1946.

Buber, Martin. "On Word Choice in Translating the Bible" [1930]. In Buber and Rosenzweig, *Scripture and Translation*, 73–89.

Buber, Martin. "People Today and the Jewish Bible: From a Lecture Series" [1926]. In Buber and Rosenzweig, *Scripture and Translation*, 4–26.

Buber, Martin. *Tales of the Hasidim*. Translated by Olga Marx. Vols. 1 and 2. New York: Schocken Books, 1991.

Buber, Martin. "Zu einer neuen Verdeutschung der Schrift." Supplement to vol. 1 of Buber and Rosenzweig, trans. *Die fünf Bücher der Weisung*, 10th ed.

Buber, Martin, and Franz Rosenzweig, trans. *Die fünf Bücher der Weisung*. Berlin: Schocken, 1925–27.

Buber, Martin, and Franz Rosenzweig, trans. *Die fünf Bücher der Weisung*, 10th ed. [1954]. Licensed edition. Stuttgart: Deutsche Bibelgesellschaft, 1992.

Buber, Martin, and Franz Rosenzweig. *Scripture and Translation*. Translated by Lawrence Rosenwald with Everett Fox. Bloomington: Indiana University Press, 1994. Originally published as *Die Schrift und ihre Verdeutschung* (Berlin: Schocken), 1936.

Cassas, Louis-François. *Voyage Pittoresque de la Syrie, de la Phenicie, de la Palestine, et de la Basse Egypte*. Paris, 1799–1800.

Childs, Brevard S. *The Book of Exodus: A Critical, Theological Commentary*. Westminster, UK: John Knox Press, 2004.

Clark, Matityahu. *Etymological Dictionary of Biblical Hebrew: Based on the Commentaries of Rabbi Samson Raphael Hirsch*. Jerusalem: Feldheim, 1999.

Cohen, Arthur A. Introduction to Martin Buber, *The Jew: Essays from Martin Buber's Journal, Der Jude, 1916–1928*. Edited by Arthur A. Cohen and translated by Joachim Neugroschel.

Cohen, Gerson D. "German Jewry as Mirror of Modernity: Introduction to the Twentieth Volume." *Leo Baeck Institute Yearbook* 20 (1975): 9–31.

Cohen, Richard I. *Jewish Icons: Art and Society in Modern Europe*. Berkeley: University of California Press, 1998.

Cohen, Richard I. "Urban Visibility and Biblical Visions: Jewish Culture in Western and Central Europe in the Modern Age." In *Cultures of the Jews*, vol. 3, edited by David Biale, 9–74. New York: Schocken Books, 2002.

Cohen, Shalom ben Jacob. *Mikra Kodesh: kolel kol sifre Torah Nevi'im u-Ketuvim 'im targum Ashkenazi = di heilige schrift*. 3 volumes. Hamburg: Yazef Ernst, 1823–24.

Cohn, Emil. *Ein Diwan*. Berlin: E. Reiss, 1921.

Colin, Amy. "Bertha Pappenheim Establishes the Jewish Women's Federation." In *Yale Companion to Jewish Writing and Thought in German Culture, 1096–1996*, edited by Sander Gilman and Jack L. Zipes. New Haven, CT: Yale University Press, 1997.

Colodner, Solomon. *Jewish Education in Germany under the Nazis*. New York: G.M.T. Typographic, 1964.

Copeland, Rita. *Rhetoric, Hermeneutics, and Translation in the Middle Ages: Academic Traditions and Vernacular Texts*. Revised ed. Cambridge: Cambridge University Press, 1995.

Delitzsch, Franz. *Zur Geschichte der jüdischen Poesie: vom Abschluss der heiligen Schriften Alten Bundes bis auf die neueste Zeit*. Leipzig: Karl Tauchnitz, 1836.

Dietz, Feike, Adam Morton, Lien Roggen, Els Stronks, and Marc Van Vaeck, eds. *Illustrated Religious Texts in the North of Europe, 1500–1800*. Surrey, UK: Ashgate, 2014.

Dov Baer of Meseritz ("Maggid"). *Zava'ot me-Rivash*. [Zolkiew], 1793.

Drazin, Israel. *Targum Onkelos to Exodus: An English Translation of the Text with Analysis and Commentary*. Jersey City: Ktav, 1990.

Dubbini, Renzo. *Geography of the Gaze: Urban and Rural Vision in Early Modern Europe*. Translated by Lydia G. Cochrane. Chicago: University of Chicago Press, 2002.

Edinger, Dora. *Bertha Pappenheim: Leben und Schriften*. Frankfurt am Main: Ner Tamid Verlag, 1963.

Elbogen, Ismar. *Aus dem Briefwechsel von Michael Sachs und Leopold Zunz*. "Sonderdruck aus der Festschrift für Dr. Jakob Freimann." Berlin: n.p., 1937.

Elbogen, Ismar. "Ludwig Philippson 28 Dez. 1811–28 Dez. 1911." Speech in honor of Philippson's hundredth birthday. Generalversammlung der Gesellschaft zu Berlin, 3 January 1912. Leipzig: Fock, 1912.

Ellenson, David. *Rabbi Esriel Hildesheimer and the Creation of a Modern Jewish Orthodoxy*. Tuscaloosa: University of Alabama Press, 2011.

Epstein, Isadore, ed. *Hebrew-English Edition of the Babylonian Talmud*. Translated by J. Rabbinowitz. London: Soncino Press, 1984.

Erlin, Matt. "Luxury Editions." In *Publishing Culture and the "Reading Nation": German Book History in the Long Nineteenth Century*, edited by Lynne Tatlock, 25–54. Rochester, NY: Camden House, 2010.

Faber, Rolf. *Salomon Herxheimer, 1801–1884: Ein Rabbiner zwischen Tradition und Emanzipation*. Wiesbaden, Ger.: Heimat- und Verschönerungsverein Dotzheim, 2001.

Faur, Jose. "*Ribbono shel 'Olam* / God, *Dominus*: What Does It Mean?" In *Tiferet Leyisrael: Jubilee Volume in Honor of Israel Francus*, edited by Joel Roth, Menahem Schmelzer, and Yaacov Francus, 13–29. New York: Jewish Theological Seminary of America, 2010.

Feiner, Shmuel. *Haskalah and History: The Emergence of a Modern Jewish Historical Consciousness*. Translated by Chaya Naor and Sondra Silverston. Oxford, UK: Littman Library of Jewish Civilization, 2001.

Feiner, Shmuel. *The Jewish Enlightenment*. Translated by Chaya Naor. Philadelphia: University of Pennsylvania Press, 2004.

Fishman, Joshua A. *Yiddish: Turning to Life*. Amsterdam: John Benjamins, 1991.

Fox, Everett, ed. and trans. *The Five Books of Moses*. The Schocken Bible vol. 1. New York: Schocken Books Inc., 1995.

Fox, Everett. "Franz Rosenzweig as Translator." *Leo Baeck Institute Yearbook* 34 (1989): 371–84.

Frakes, Jerold C., ed. and trans. *Early Yiddish Epic*. Syracuse, NY: Syracuse University Press, 2014.

Frakes, Jerold C., ed. *Early Yiddish Texts 1100–1750*. Oxford: Oxford University Press, 2004.

Friedenthal-Haase, Martha. "Martin Buber im androgogischen Gespräch," *Martin Buber: Bildung, Menschenbild und Hebräischer Humanismus*, edited by Martha Friedenthal-Haase and Ralf Koerrenz, 19–54. Paderborn, Germany: Ferdinand Schöningh, 2005.

Fürst, Julius. "Empfehlung der Israelitische Bibel von Herxheimer." *Der Orient* 4, no. 4 (24 January 1843): 29–30.

[Fürst, Julius]. "Herxheimer's Pentateuch." *Der Orient* 1, no. 12 (21 March 1840): 190.

Galli, Barbara Ellen. *Franz Rosenzweig and Jehuda Halevi: Translating, Translations, and Translators*. Montreal: McGill-Queen's University Press, 1995.

Gans, Mozes Heimen. *Memorbook: History of Dutch Jewry from the Renaissance to 1940, with 1100 Illustrations*. Baarn, Netherlands: Bosch and Keuning, 1972.

Gaskell, Philip. *A New Introduction to Bibliography*. 2nd ed. Oxford: Oxford University Press, 1985.

Geiger, Abraham. *Divan des Castilliers Abu'l-Hassan Juda Halevi*. Breslau, 1851.

Geiger, Abraham. "Johlson's Bibelwerk." *Wissenschaftliche Zeitschrift für jüdische Theologie* vol 3 (1837): 121–22.

Geiger, Abraham. *Urschrift und Übersetzungen der Bibel: In ihrer Abhängigkeit von der innern Entwicklung des Judentums* [1857]. 2nd ed. Frankfurt am Main: Verlag Madda, 1928.

Geiger, Ludwig, ed. *Michael Sachs und Moritz Veit: Briefwechsel*. Frankfurt am Main: J. Kauffmann, 1897.

Gesenius, Heinrich Friedrich Wilhelm. *Hebräisch-deutsches Handwörterbuch über die Schriften des Alten Testaments*. 2 vols. Leipzig: F. C. W. Vogel, 1810–12.

Gillman, Abigail. "Between Religion and Culture: Mendelssohn, Buber, Rosenzweig, and the Enterprise of Biblical Translation." In *Biblical Translation in Context*, edited by Frederick W. Knobloch, 93–114. Bethesda: University Press of Maryland, 2002.

Gillman, Abigail. "From Myth to Memory: A Study of German-Jewish Translations of Exodus 12–13:6." In *Exodus in the Jewish Experience: Echoes and Reverberations*, edited by Pamela Barmash and W. David Nelson, 191–212. Lanham, MD: Lexington Books, 2015.

Gillman, Abigail. "The Jewish Quest for a German Bible: The Nineteenth-Century Translations of Joseph Johlson and Leopold Zunz." *SBL Forum* 7 (Summer 2009). http://www.sbl-site.org/publications/article.aspx?articleId=829.

Gillman, Abigail. "'Not like Cherries, but like Peaches': Mendelssohn and Rosenzweig as Translators of Hebrew Poetry." *The German-Hebrew Dialogue*, edited by Rachel Seelig. Berlin: Walter De Gruyter, 2017.

Gillman, Abigail. *Viennese Jewish Modernism. Freud, Beer-Hofmann, Hofmannsthal and Schnitzler*. University Park: Penn State University Press, 2009.

Gillman, Neil. *Sacred Fragments: Recovering Theology for the Modern Jew*. New York: Jewish Publication Society, 1990.

Gilman, Sander L., and Jack Zipes, eds. *Yale Companion to Jewish Writing and Thought in German Culture, 1096–1996*. New Haven, CT: Yale University Press, 1997.

Ginzburg, Louis. *The Legends of the Jews*. Translated by Henrietta Szold and Paul Radin. 7 vols. Baltimore: Johns Hopkins University Press, 1998.

Glatzer, Nahum N., ed. *Franz Rosenzweig: His Life and Thought*. 2nd ed. New York: Schocken Books, 1976.

Glatzer, Nahum N., ed. *Leopold and Adelheid Zunz: An Account in Letters, 1815–1885*. London: East and West Library, 1958.

Goethe, Johann Wolfgang von. "Translations" [1819]. Translated by Sharon Sloane. In *The Translation Studies Reader*, edited by Lawrence Venuti. 2nd ed., 64–66. New York: Routledge, 2004.

Goetschel, Willi, and David Suchoff. Introduction to *The Legacy of German Jewry*, by Hermann Levin Goldschmidt. New York: Fordham University Press, 2007.

Gold, Ben-Zion. *The Life of Jews in Poland before the Holocaust*. Lincoln: University of Nebraska Press, 2007.

Goldschmidt, Hermann Levin. *The Legacy of German Jewry*. Translated by David Suchoff. New York: Fordham University Press, 2007.

Gordon, Peter Eli. *Rosenzweig and Heidegger: Between Judaism and German Philosophy*. Berkeley: University of California Press, 2003.

Gottlieb, Michah. "Aesthetics and the Infinite." In *New Directions in Jewish Philosophy*, edited by Aaron W. Hughes and Eliot Wolfson, 326–53. Bloomington: Indiana University Press, 2010.

Gottlieb, Michah, ed. *Moses Mendelssohn: Writings on Judaism, Christianity, & the Bible*, translated by Curtis Bowman, Elias Sacks, and Allan Arkush. Waltham, MA: Brandeis University Press, 2011.

Graff, Gil. "Samson Raphael Hirsch: 100 Years Later." *Shofar* 7, no. 1 (Fall 1988): 48–59.

Gries, Zeev. "Printing and Publishing: Printing and Publishing before 1800." *The YIVO Encyclopedia of Jews in Eastern Europe*, translated by Jeffrey Green, 2010. http://www.yivoencyclopedia.org/article.aspx/Printing_and_Publishing/Printing_and_Publishing_before_1800.

Grossman, Jeffrey. *The Discourse on Yiddish in Germany from the Enlightenment to the Second Empire*. Rochester, NY: Camden House, 2000.

Grunfeld, Isidor. "The Historical and Intellectual Background of the Horeb." Introduction to *Horeb: A Philosophy of Jewish Laws and Observances*, by Samson Raphael Hirsch, translated by Isidor Grunfeld, xix–cxl. New York: Soncino Press, 1962.

Gutzen, Dieter. "Bemerkungen zur Bibelübersetzung des Johann David Michaelis." *Vestigia Bibliae* 4 (1982): 71–78.

Heller, Bernard. Review of *Zeenah u-Reenah: Frauenbibel*, translated by Bertha Pappenheim. *Monatschrift für Geschichte und Wissenschaft des Judentums* 78, no. 2 (1934): 312–15.

Herberg, Will, ed. *The Writings of Martin Buber*. New York: Meridian Books, 1956.

Hermann, Klaus. "Translating Cultures and Texts in Reform Judaism: The Philippson Bible." *Jewish Studies Quarterly* 14 (2007): 164–97.

Herxheimer, Salomon. *Jesode Ha-Torah: Glaubens und Pflichtenlehre für Israelitische Schulen* [1830]. 36th ed. Leipzig: Roßberg'sche Verlagsbuchhandlung, 1916.

Herxheimer, Salomon. *Die vierundzwanzig Bücher der Bibel im hebräischen Texte: Mit worttreuer Uebersetzung, fortlaufender Erklärung und homiletisch benutzbaren Anmerkungen*. 4 vols. Berlin: J. Lewent, 1841–48.

Heschel, Susannah. *Abraham Geiger and the Jewish Jesus*. Chicago: University of Chicago Press, 1998.

Hess, Jonathan M. *Middlebrow Literature and the Making of German Jewish Identity*. Stanford: Stanford University Press, 2010.

Hess, Jonathan M. "Reading and the Writing of German-Jewish History." In *Literary Studies and the Pursuits of Reading*, edited by Eric Downing, Jonathan M. Hess, and Richard V. Benson, 105–29. Rochester: Camden House, 2012.

Heß, M. "Bemerkungen über die in letztverflossenen Jahren erschienenen deutschen Bibelübersetzungen: Die Bibelübersetzung unter Redaktion des Dr. Zunz." *Der Orient* 1, no. 35 (29 August 1840): 549–53.

Heß, M. "Bemerkungen zur Salomon'schen Volks- und Schulbibel." *Israelitische Annalen*, no. 12 (22 March 1839): 92–93; no. 14 (5 April 1839): 109–10.

Heubach, Helga, ed. *Bertha Pappenheim u. a. "Das unsichtbare Isenberg." Über das Heim des Jüdischen Frauenbundes in Neu-Isenberg, 1907–1942*. Frankfurt am Main: Kulturamt der Stadt Neu-Isenberg, 1994.

Heuberger, Rachel. *Rabbi Nehemiah Anton Nobel: The Jewish Renaissance in Frankfurt am Main*. Frankfurt am Main: Societäts-Verlag, 2007.

Hirsch, Samson Raphael. *Horeb: A Philosophy of Jewish Laws and Observances*. Translated by Isidor Grunfeld. New York: Soncino Press, 1962.

Hirsch, Samson Raphael. *The Nineteen Letters on Judaism*. Edited by Jacob Breuer, translated by Bernard Drachman. New York: Feldheim, 1969.

Hirsch, Samson Raphael, trans. and comm. *Der Pentateuch*. Frankfurt am Main: J. Kaufmann, 1867–78.

Hirsch, Samson Raphael, trans. into German and comm. *The Pentateuch*. Translated into English by Isaac Levy. 2nd rev. ed. Gateshead: Judaica Press, 1982.

Hirsch, Samson Raphael. "A Speech Delivered at the Celebration of the Israelitischen Religionsgesellschaft's School in Frankfurt am Main on November 9, 1859 on Eve of the Schiller Festival." Translated by Marc B. Shapiro. In Shapiro, "Rabbi Samson Raphael Hirsch and Friedrich von Schiller" *Torah u-Madda Journal* 15 (2008–9): 172–87.

Hirsch, Samson Raphael, "Vorwort." In *Der Pentateuch*, Part 1: *Die Genesis*. 6th ed. Frankfurt am Main: J. Kauffmann, 1920.

Hirschler, Gertrude, trans. *T'rumath Tzvi: The Pentateuch with a Translation by Samson Raphael Hirsch and Excerpts from the Hirsch Commentary*. Edited by Ephraim Oratz. New York: Judaica Press, 1986.

Hoffman, Christhard. "Analyzing the Zeitgeist: Ludwig Philippson as Historian of the Modern Era." In *Mediating Modernity: Challenges and Trends in the Jewish Encounter with the Modern World: Essays in Honor of Michael A. Meyer*, edited by Lauren B. Strauss and Michael Brenner, 109–20. Detroit: Wayne State University Press, 2008.

Holloran, John. "What Is the Enlightenment Bible?" Review of Sheehan, *The Enlightenment Bible, Published on H-German* (February 2007), http://www.h-net.org/reviews/showrev.php?id=12880.

Homolka, Walter, Hanna Liss, and Rüdiger Liwak, eds., in collaboration with Susanne Gräbner and Daniel Vorpahl. *Die Tora: Die Fünf Bücher Mose und die Prophetenlesungen (Hebräisch-Deutsch) in der revidierten Übersetzung von Rabbiner Ludwig Philippson*. Freiburg/Basel, Ger.: Herder, 2015.

Horch, Hans Otto. *Auf der Suche nach der jüdischen Erzählliteratur: Die Literaturkritik des "Allgemeine Zeitung des Judentums" (1837–1922)*. Frankfurt am Main: Verlag Peter Lang, 1985.

Horch, Hans Otto. "'Auf der Zinne der Zeit': Ludwig Philippson (1811–1889)—der 'Journalist' des Reformjudentums." *Bulletin of the Leo Baeck Institute* 86 (1990): 5–21.

Horwitz, Rivka. "Moses Mendelssohns Interpretation des Tetragrammaton: 'Der Ewige.'" *Judaica* 55 (1999): 2: 2–19; 3: 132–52.

Hurwitz, Israel M., trans. *Ze'enah U-Re'enah: Book of Genesis*, by Jacob ben Isaac Ashkenazi of Janow [Hebrew]. Edited by Joseph P. Schultz. Philadelphia: Dropsie College, 1985.

Jacob, Benno, inter. *The Second Book of the Bible: Exodus*. Translated by Walter Jacob. Jersey City, NJ: Ktav, 1992.

Jasper, David, ed. *Translating Religious Texts: Translation, Transgression, and Interpretation*. New York: St. Martin's Press, 1993.

Johlson, Joseph. *'Erekh milim = Biblisch-Hebräisches Wörterbuch*. Frankfurt am Main: Andreäische Buchhandlung, 1840.

Johlson, Joseph. *Die heiligen Schriften der Israeliten, erster Theil. Die fünf Bücher Mose, nach dem masoretischen Texte worttreu übersetzt, mit Anmerkungen*. Frankfurt am Main: Andreäische Buchhandlung, 1831.

Johlson, Joseph. *Shorshe haDat. Lehrbuch der Mosaischen Religion: Nebst Anhang, Ceremonialgesetze und Gebräuche—Schulgebete und des Maimonides Abhandlung von den Sitten*. Frankfurt am Main: Andreäische Buchhandlung, 1829.

Johlson, Joseph. *Shire Yeshurun: Israelitisches Gesangbuch zur Andacht und zum Religionsunterricht*. 3rd ed. Frankfurt am Main: Andreäische Buchhandlung, 1829.

Johlson, Joseph. *Toldot Avot: Chronologisch geordnete Biblische Geschichte*. 2d ed. Frankfurt am Main: Andreäische Buchhandlung, 1837.

Kaplan, Marion A. *The Making of the Jewish Middle Class: Women, Family, and Identity in Imperial Germany*. Oxford: Oxford University Press, 1991.

Karminski, Hannah. "An die fernen Freunde von Fräulein Pappenheim." 7 June 1936. Manuscript. Leo Baeck Institute Archives. Berlin: 1936.

Karp, Jonathan. "The Aesthetic Difference: Moses Mendelssohn's *Kohelet musar* and the Inception of the Berlin Haskalah." In *Renewing the Past: Reconfiguring Jewish Culture from al-Andalus to the Haskalah*, edited by Ross Brann and Adam Sutcliff, 93–120. Philadelphia: University of Pennsylvania Press, 2004.

Katz, Jacob. *Out of the Ghetto: The Social Background of Jewish Emancipation, 1770–1870*. Syracuse, NY: Syracuse University Press, 1998.

Kayser, Wolfgang. *Geschichte des deutschen Verses*. 3rd ed. Munich: Francke, 1981.

Kayserling, Meyer. *Bibliothek jüdischer Kanzelredner: Eine chronologische Sammlung der Predigten, Biographieen und Charakteristiken der vorzüglichsten jüdischen Prediger*. 2 vols. Berlin: Springer, 1870–72.

Kayserling, Meyer. *Moses Mendelssohn: Sein Leben und seine Werke*. Leipzig: Hermann Mendelssohn, 1862.

Kayserling, Meyer. *Ludwig Philippson; eine Biographie*. Leipzig: Hermann Mendelssohn, 1898.

Kearney, Jonathan. "The Torah of Israel in the Tongue of Ishmael." *Proceedings of the Irish Biblical Association* 33–34 (2010–11): 55–75.

Knobloch, Frederick W., ed. *Biblical Translation in Context*. Bethesda: University Press of Maryland, 2002.

Koltun-Fromm, Ken. *Abraham Geiger's Liberal Judaism*. Bloomington: Indiana University Press, 2006.

Konz, Britta. *Bertha Pappenheim (1859–1936): Ein Leben für jüdische Tradition und weibliche Emanzipation*. Frankfurt: Campus, 2005.

Korn, Bertram W. "German-Jewish Intellectual Influence on American Jewish Life." B. G. Rudolph Lecture. Syracuse University, Syracuse, NY, 1972.

Kohler, Kaufmann. "Adonai" [1906]. In *Jewish Encyclopedia*. http://www.jewishencyclopedia.com/articles/840-adonai.

Krochmalnik, Daniel, and Hans-Joachim Werner, eds. *50 Jahre Martin Buber Bibel: International Symposium of the Institute of Jewish Studies in Heidelberg and the Martin Buber Society*. Berlin: Lit Verlag, 2014.

Kugel, James L. *The Bible as It Was*. Cambridge, MA: Belknap Press, 1999.

Kugel, James L. *The Idea of Biblical Poetry: Parallelism and Its History*. New Haven, CT: Yale University Press, 1981.

Kugler, Lena, and Albrecht Koschorke, eds. *Bertha Pappenheim (Anna O.): Literarische und publizistische Texte*. Vienna: Turia und Kant, 2002.

Langbehn, Julius. *Rembrandt als Erzieher, von einem Deutschen*. Leipzig: Hirschfeld, 1890.

Legaspi, Michael Chris. *The Death of Scripture and the Rise of Biblical Studies*. Oxford: Oxford University Press, 2010.

Legaspi, Michael Chris. "Reviving the Dead Letter: Johann David Michaelis and the Quest for Hebrew Antiquity." PhD diss., Department of Near Eastern Languages and Civilizations, Harvard University, 2006.

Lehmann, Markus. "Die Bibelanstalt für die Anhänger des traditionellen (orthodoxen) Judenthums." *Der Israelit* 2, no. 23 (5 June 1861): 273–74.

Lehranstalt für die Wissenschaft des Judenthums in Berlin. "Aus dem Leben von Leopold Zunz." Zwölfter Bericht. Berlin: Rosenthal & Co., 1894.

Leibowitz, Nehama. *Die Übersetzungstechnik der jüdisch-deutschen Bibelübersetzungen des XV. und XVI. Jahrhunderts dargestellt an den Psalmen*. Halle: Max Niemeyer, 1931.

Lesser, A. H. "Samson Raphael Hirsch's Use of Hebrew Etymology." In *Hebrew Study from Ezra to Ben-Yehuda*, edited by William Horbury. Edinburgh: T & T Clark, 1999.

Levenson, Alan T. *The Making of the Modern Jewish Bible: How Scholars in Germany, Israel, and America Transformed an Ancient Text*. Plymouth, UK: Rowman & Littlefield, 2011.

Liberles, Robert. *Religious Conflict in Social Context: The Resurgence of Orthodox Judaism in Frankfurt am Main, 1838–1877*. Westport, CT: Greenwood Press, 1985.

Liss, Hanna. "Entkontextualisierung als Programm: Die Bedeutung des göttlichen Namens bei Franz Rosenzweig und die pronominale, Er-Setzung' des Tetragramms." In *Judaistik zwischen den Disziplinen [Jewish Studies between the Disciplines: Papers in Honor of Peter Schäfer on the Occasion of his 60th Birthday]*, edited by Klaus Herrmann, Margarete Schlüter, and Giuseppe Veltri, 373–404. Leiden: Brill, 2003.

Liss, Hanna. "Keine Heilige Schrift? Anfragen an Martin Buber's Prinzip der Oralität." In Krochmalnik and Werner, *50 Jahre Martin Buber Bibel*, 215–30.

Litvak, Olga. *Haskalah: The Romantic Movement in Judaism*. New Brunswick, NJ: Rutgers University Press, 2012.

Loentz, Elizabeth. *Let Me Continue to Speak the Truth: Bertha Pappenheim as Author and Activist*. Cincinnati: Hebrew Union College Press, 2007.

Loewenstamm, Samuel E. *The Evolution of the Exodus Tradition*. Translated by Baruch J. Schwartz. Jerusalem: Magnes Press, Hebrew University, 1992.

Losch, Andreas. "'Der Ewige' als 'Synthese' des Stern: Der Gebrauch des Gottesnamens 'der Ewige' bei Franz Rosenzweig." *Naharaim* 9, nos. 1–2 (2015): 195–215.

Löwenstein, Berthold. "Ein Vorkämpfer des modernen Judentums." *Gemeindeblatt der israelitischen Religionsgemeinde zu Leipzig* 11, no. 2 (11 January 1935): 2.

Lowenstein, Steven M. "The Complicated Language Situation of German Jewry, 1760–1914." *Studia Rosenthaliana* 36 (2002–3): 3–29.

Lowenstein, Steven M. "The Readership of Mendelssohn's Bible Translation." *Hebrew Union College Annual* 53 (1982): 179–213.

Lowenstein, Steven M. "The Yiddish Written Word in Nineteenth-Century Germany." *Leo Baeck Institute Yearbook* 24 (1979): 179–92.

Lucas, Franz D., and Heike Frank. *Michael Sachs: Der konservative Mittelweg*. Tübingen, Ger.: J. C. B. Mohr, 1992.

Luther, Martin. "Circular Letter on Translation" [1530]. Translated by Douglas Robinson. In *Western Translation Theory from Herodotus to Nietzsche*, edited by Douglas Robinson, 84–89. 2nd ed. Manchester, UK: St. Jerome, 2002.

Mach, Dafna. "Franz Rosenzweig als Übersetzer jüdischer Texte: Seine Auseinandersetzung mit Gershom Scholem." In *Der Philosoph Franz Rosenzweig: Internationaler Kongreß, Kassel 1986*, edited by Wolfdietrich Schmied-Kowarzik, 251–71. Freiburg: Verlag Karl Alber, 1988.

Mach, Dafna. "Jüdische Bibelübersetzungen ins Deutsche." In *Juden in der deutschen Literatur*, edited by Stéphane Moses and Albrecht Schöne, 54–63. Frankfurt am Main: Suhrkamp Taschenbuch, 1986.

Marchand, Suzanne. *German Orientalism in the Age of Empire*. Cambridge: Cambridge University Press, 2010.

Mendelssohn, Moses, trans. *Die fünf Bücher Mose, nach der Uebersetzung des Herrn Moses Mendelssohn*. Vol. 1. Berlin: Friedrich Maurer, 1783.

Mendelssohn, Moses. *Gesammelte Schriften, Jubilaeumsausgabe*. Vols. 9.1, 15.1, 15.2, 16. Edited by Werner Weinberg. Stuttgart: Friedrich Frommann, 1993.

Mendelssohn, Moses. *Hebräische Schriften: Gesammelte Schriften—Jubiläumsausgabe*. Edited by Werner Weinberg. Stuttgart: Friedrich Frommann, 1990.

Mendelssohn, Moses. "On the Sublime and Naive in the Fine Sciences" [1758]. In *Moses Mendelssohn: Philosophical Writings*, translated and edited by Daniel O. Dahlstrom. Cambridge: Cambridge University Press, 1997.

Mendelssohn, Moses. *Sefer Netivot HaShalom . . . im Targum Ashkenazi*. Berlin: George Friedrich Starcke, 1783.

Mendes-Flohr, Paul. "Martin Buber's Reception among Jews." *Modern Judaism* 6, no. 2 (May 1986): 111–26.

Meschonnic, Henri. *Poètique du traduire*. Paris: Verdier, 1999.

Meyer, Michael A. "Jewish Communities in Transition." In vol. 2, *Emancipation and Acculturation: 1780–1871*, of *German Jewish History in Modern Times*, edited by Michael A. Meyer and Michael Brenner, 90–127. New York: Columbia University Press, 1996–98.

Meyer, Michael A. *The Origins of the Modern Jew: Jewish Identity and European Culture in Germany, 1749–1824*. Detroit: Wayne State University Press, 1972.

Meyer, Michael A. *Response to Modernity: A History of the Reform Movement in Judaism*. Detroit: Wayne State University Press, 1995.

Meyer, Michael A., and Michael Brenner, eds. *German-Jewish History in Modern Times.* 4 vols. New York: Columbia University Press, 1996–98.

Michaelis, Johann David. *Deutsche Uebersetzung des Alten Testaments, mit Anmerkungen fur Ungelehrte: Der erste Theil, welcher das Buch Hiobs enthält.* Göttingen, Ger.: Johann Christian Dieterich, 1773.

Mosse, George L. *German Jews beyond Judaism.* Cincinnati: Hebrew Union College Press, 1997.

Müchler, Johann Georg Philipp, ed. *Beschäftigungen des Geistes und des Herzens.* Vol. 2. Berlin: J. C. Klüter, 1756.

Mühlen, Reinhard. *Die Bibel und ihr Titelblatt: Die bildliche Entwicklung der Titelblattgestaltung lutherischer Bibeldrucke vom 16. bis zum 19. Jahrhundert.* Würzburg, Ger.: Stephans-Buchhandlung Matthias Mittelstädt, 2001.

Neusner, Jacob. *The Talmud: A Close Encounter.* Minneapolis: Fortress Press, 1991.

Nora, Pierre. "Between Memory and History: *Les Lieux de Mémoire.*" *Representations* 26 (1989): 7–25.

O'Donoghue, Diane. "Mapping the Unconscious: Freud's Topographic Constructions." *Visual Resources: An International Journal of Documentation* 23, no. 1–2 (March–June 2007): 105–17.

O'Donoghue, Diane. "Moses in Moravia." *American Imago* 67, no. 2 (Summer 2010): 157–82.

Pardes, Ilana. *Countertraditions of the Bible.* Cambridge, MA: Harvard University Press, 1992.

Parush, Iris. *Reading Jewish Women: Marginality and Modernization in Nineteenth-Century Eastern European Jewish Society.* Waltham, MA: Brandeis University Press, 2004.

Pappenheim, Bertha. *Allerlei Geschichten: Maasse-Buch: Buch der Sagen und Legenden aus Talmud und Midrasch nebst Volkserzählung in jüdisch-deutscher Sprache.* Frankfurt am Main: J. Kauffmann, 1929.

Pappenheim, Bertha. "Der Einzelne und die Gemeinschaft." *Blätter des Jüdischen Frauenbundes* 9, no. 6 (June 1933): 6.

Pappenheim, Bertha. "Die Frau im kirchlichen und religiösen Leben." In *Der Deutsche Frauenkongreß, Berlin, 27 Feb. bis 2 März 1912: Sämtliche Vorträge,* edited by Gertrud Baümer, 237–45. Leipzig: B. G. Teubner, 1912.

Pappenheim, Bertha. "Frauenfrage und Frauenberuf im Judentum." *Allgemeine Zeitung des Judentums* 61, no. 41 (8 October 1897): 484–85. Reprinted in Lena Kugler and Albrecht Koschorke, eds., *Bertha Pappenheim (Anna O.): Literarische und publizistische Texte.* Vienna: Turia und Kant, 2002.

Pappenheim, Bertha. *Gebete/Prayers.* [1936] Edited by Elisa Klapheck and Lara Dämmig. Teetz: Hentrich and Hentrich, 2003.

Pappenheim, Bertha. "The Jewish Woman in Religious Life: A Paper Read at the Women's Congress at Munich, 1912," translated by Margery Bentwich. *Jewish Review* 3, no. 17 (January 1913): 405–14.

Pappenheim, Bertha. "Die jüdische Frau" [1934]. In *Bertha Pappenheim (Anna O.): Literarische und publizistische Texte,* edited by Lena Kugler and Albrecht Koschorke, 87–99. Vienna: Turia und Kant, 2002.

Pappenheim, Bertha, trans. *Die Memoiren der Glückel von Hameln, geboren in Hamburg 1645, gestorben in Metz 19. September 1724*. Vienna: S. Meyer und W. Pappenheim, 1910.

Pappenheim, Bertha, trans. *Zeenah u-Reenah: Frauenbibel: Bereschith. Übersetzung und Auslegung des Pentateuch von Jacob Ben Isaac aus Janow* [*Women's Bible: Genesis*]. Frankfurt am Main: J. Kauffmann, 1930.

Penkower, Jordan S. "The Development of the Masoretic Bible." In *The Jewish Study Bible*, edited by Adele Berlin and Marc Zvi Brettler, 2077–84. New York: Oxford University Press, 2004.

Petuchowski, Jakob J. "Manuals and Catechisms of the Jewish Religion in the Early Period of Emancipation." In *Studies in Nineteenth-Century Jewish Intellectual History*, edited by Alexander Altmann. Cambridge, MA: Harvard University Press, 1964.

Petuchowski, Jakob J. *Prayerbook Reform in Europe: The Liturgy of European Liberal and Reform Judaism*. New York: World Union for Progressive Judaism, 1968.

Pfrimmer, Théo. *Freud, lecteur de la Bible*. Paris: Presses Universitaires de France, 1982.

Philippson, Johanna. "Ludwig Philippson und das Allgemeine Zeitung des Judentums." In *Das Judentum in der deutschen Umwelt, 1800–1850*, edited by Hans Liebeschutz and Arnold Paucker, 243–92. Tübingen: Mohr Siebeck, 1977.

Philippson, Ludwig. *Ezekiel des Jüdischen Trauerspieldichters Auszug aus Egypten und Philo des Aelteren Jerusalem*. Berlin: J. A. List, 1830.

Philippson, Ludwig, ed. and trans. *Die israelitische Bibel: Enthaltend—Den heiligen Urtext, die deutsche Übertragung, die allgemeine, ausführliche Erläuterung mit mehr als 500 englischen Holzschnitten*. Leipzig: Baumgärtner, 1841–58.

Philippson, Phöbus. *Biographische Skizzen*. Vols. 1–3. Leipzig: Oskar Leiner, 1863–66.

Philipson, David. *The Reform Movement in Judaism*. London: Macmillan, 1907.

Plaut, W. Gunther. *German Jewish Bible Translations: Linguistic Theology as a Political Phenomenon*. New York: Leo Baeck Institute, 1992.

Plaut, W. Gunther. *The Rise of Reform Judaism*. New York: World Union for Progressive Judaism, 1963.

Pollock, Benjamin. "Franz Rosenzweig." In *The Stanford Encyclopedia of Philosophy*, edited by Edward N. Zalta. Summer 2015 ed. http://plato.stanford.edu/archives/sum2015/entries/rosenzweig/

Posen, J. Review of *Allerlei Geschichten*. "Literarische Warte." *Der Israelit* 42 (17 October 1929): 2.

Propp, William H. C. *Exodus 1–18*. New Haven, CT: Yale University Press, 1999.

Propp, William H. C. *Exodus 19–40*. New Haven, CT: Yale University Press, 2006.

Rawidowicz, Simon. "The Psalms Translation of Mendelssohn" [Hebrew]. In *Festschrift for J. Klausner in Honor of his 60th Birthday*, by Naphtali Herz Tur Sinai et al., 283–301. Tel Aviv: Va'ad ha-Yovel, 1936–39.

Rizzuto, Ana-Maria. *Why Did Freud Reject God? A Psychodynamic Interpretation*. New Haven, CT: Yale University Press, 1998.

Robinson, Douglas. *Western Translation Theory: From Herodotus to Nietzsche*. Manchester, UK: St. Jerome, 2002.

Rosenberg, Shimon Gershon. "On Translation and the Proliferation of Worlds" [Hebrew]. In *Shearit Ha-Emunah: Drashot postmoderniot l'moadei yisrael* [Remainder of faith:

postmodern sermons on Jewish holidays]. Edited by Yishai Mevorach and Eitan Abramovitz. Tel Aviv: Resling, 2014.

Rosenwald, Lawrence. "Buber and Rosenzweig's Challenge to Translation Theory." In Martin Buber and Franz Rosenzweig, *Scripture and Translation*, xxix–liv. Bloomington: Indiana University Press, 1994.

Rosenwald, Lawrence. "On the Reception of Buber and Rosenzweig's Bible." *Prooftexts* 14 (1994): 141–65.

Rosenzweig, Franz. "Afterword." Translated by Barbara Ellen Galli. In Barbara Ellen Galli, *Franz Rosenzweig and Jehuda Halevi: Translating, Translations, and Translators*, 169–84. Montreal: McGill-Queen's University Press, 1995.

Rosenzweig, Franz. *Briefe und Tagebücher*. Vols. 1 and 2. of *Der Mensch und sein Werk. Gesammelte Schriften*. Edited by Rachel Rosenzweig and Edith Rosenzweig-Scheinmann, together with Bernhard Casper. The Hague: Martinus Nijhoff, 1979.

Rosenzweig, Franz. " 'The Eternal': Mendelssohn and the Name of God." In Martin Buber and Franz Rosenzweig, *Scripture and Translation*, translated by Lawrence Rosenwald, 99–113. Bloomington: Indiana University Press, 1994. Originally published as " 'Der Ewige': Moses Mendelssohn und der Gottesname," in *Gedenkbuch für Moses Mendelssohn*. Berlin: M. Poppelauer, 1929; reprinted in Buber and Rosenzweig, *Die Schrift und ihre Verdeutschung* (Berlin: Schocken Verlag, 1936), 184–210.

Rosenzweig, Franz. *Jehuda Halevi: Zweiundneunzig Hymnen und Gedichte*. Berlin: Verlag Lambert Schneider, 1927.

Rosenzweig, Franz. *Die Schrift: Aufsätze, Übertragugen und Briefe*, edited by Karl Thieme. Frankfurt am Main: Europäische Verlagsanstalt, 1964.

Rosenzweig, Franz. "Scripture and Luther." In Martin Buber and Franz Rosenzweig, *Scripture and Translation*, translated by Lawrence Rosenwald, 47–69. Bloomington: Indiana University Press, 1994. Originally published as "Die Schrift und Luther" (1926).

Rosenzweig, Franz. *Sprachdenken: Arbeitspapiere zur Verdeutschung der Schrift*. Vol. 4 of *Der Mensch und sein Werk. Gesammelte Schriften*. Edited by Rachel Bat-Adam. Dordrecht: Martinus Nijhoff Publishers, 1984.

Rosenzweig, Franz. "Upon Opening the Jüdisches Lehrhaus." In *On Jewish Learning*, edited by N. N. Glatzer, 95–102. New York: Schocken Books, 1955.

Rosin, David. "Die Zunz'sche Bibel." *Monatsschrift für Geschichte und Wissenschaft des Judentums* 38, no. 11 (1894): 504–14.

Rübner, Tuvia, and Dafna Mach, eds. *Briefwechsel Martin Buber–Ludwig Strauß 1913–1953*. Frankfurt am Main: Luchterhand, 1990.

Sachs, Michael. *Die Psalmen: Uebersetzt und erläutert*. Berlin: Veit u. Comp, 1835.

Sachs, Michael. *Die religiöse Poesie der Juden in Spanien*. 2nd ed. Berlin, 1901.

Salaman, Nina, ed. *Selected Poems of Jehudah Halevi*. Philadelphia: Jewish Publication Society, 1928.

Salfeld, Siegmund. *Dr. Salomon Herxheimer: Ein Lebensbild*. Frankfurt am Main: F. B. Auffarth, 1885.

Salomon, Gotthold. *Denkmal der Erinnerung an Moses Mendelssohn zu dessen erster Säkularfeier im September 1829: Nebst einem Blick in sein Leben*. Hamburg: Hofmann and Campe, 1829.

Salomon, Gotthold. *Die deutsche Volks- und Schulbibel für Israeliten. Aufs Neue aus dem massoretischen Text übersetzt*. Altona: Hammerich, 1837.

Salomon, Gotthold. "Erinnerungen gegen die in No. 12, 14, 18, 19 der I. A. von M. Heß in Trier und L. Schott, Rabbine zu Randegg, gemachten Bemerkungen zu meiner Volks- und Schulbibel." *Allgemeine Zeitung des Judentums* vol. 3 no. 80 (13 July 1839): 341–44; vol. 3 no. 81 (20 July 1839): 357–59.

Salomon, Gotthold. *Lebensgeschichte des Herrn Moses Philippson, Lehrers an der israelitischen Haupt- und Freischule zu Dessau*. Dessau, 1814.

Sammons, Jeffrey. *Heinrich Heine: A New Biography*. Princeton, NJ: Princeton University Press, 1979.

Schaeder, Grete. "Martin Buber: A Biographical Sketch." In *The Letters of Martin Buber* edited by Nahum N. Glatzer and Paul Mendes-Flohr, translated by Richard and Clara Winston and Harry Zohn, 1–62. New York: Schocken Books, 1991.

Schatz, Andrea. *Sprache in der Zerstreuung: Die Säkularisierung des Hebräischen im 18. Jahrhundert*. Göttingen, Ger.: Vandenhoeck & Ruprecht, 2009.

Schlotzhauer, Inge. *Das Philanthropin 1804–1942: Die Schule der Israelitischen Gemeinde in Frankfurt am Main*. Frankfurt am Main: Verlag Waldemar Kramer, 1990.

[Schmidt, Johann Lorenz], trans. *Die göttlichen Schriften vor den Zeiten des Messie Jesus: Der erste Theil worinnen sind nach einer freyen Übersetzung welche durch und durch mit Anmerkungen erläutert und bestätiget wird*. Wertheim: Johann Georg Nehr, 1735.

Schneider, Lambert. *Rechenschaft über vierzig Jahre Verlagsarbeit. 1925–1965*. Heidelberg: L. Schneider, 1965.

Scholem, Gershom. "At the Completion of Buber's Translation of the Bible." In *The Messianic Idea in Judaism and Other Essays on Jewish Spirituality*, 314–19. New York: Schocken Books, 1971.

Scholem, Gershom. *Briefe*, vol. 1, *1914–1941*. Edited by Itta Shedletzky. Munich: C. H. Beck, 1994.

Schorsch, Grit. *Moses Mendelssohns Sprachpolitik*. Berlin: De Gruyter, 2012.

Schorsch, Ismar. "The Myth of Sephardic Supremacy." In *From Text to Context: The Turn to History in Modern Judaism*, 71–92. Hanover, NH: University Press of New England, 1994.

Schott, Leopold. "Israelitische Volksbibeln." *Israelitische Annalen* 18 (3 May 1839): 140–41; 19 (10 May 1839): 148–49.

Schwab, Hermann. *Jewish Rural Communities in Germany*. London: Cooper Book Co., 1956.

Seidman, Naomi. "Engendering Audiences: Hebrew, Yiddish, and the Question of Address." In *A Marriage Made in Heaven*, 12–39. Berkeley: University of California Press, 1997.

Seidman, Naomi. *Faithful Renderings: Jewish-Christian Difference and the Politics of Translation*. Chicago: University of Chicago Press, 2006.

Shapiro, Marc B. "Rabbi Samson Raphael Hirsch and Friedrich von Schiller." *Torah u-Madda Journal* 15 (2008–9): 172–87.

Shavit, Yaakov, and Mordechai Eran. *The Hebrew Bible Reborn: From Holy Scripture to the Book of Books*. Berlin: Walter de Gruyter, 2007.

Shavit, Yaakov, and Mordechai Eran. "A Jewish Bible in German—Simon Bernfeld's German Translation of the Bible (1903): Between 'Heretical' Scholarship and 'Conservative' Translation." *Beit Mikra* 54 (2009): 121–52.

Shear, Adam. *The Kuzari and the Shaping of Jewish Identity, 1167–1900*. Cambridge: Cambridge University Press, 2008.

Sheehan, Jonathan. *The Enlightenment Bible: Translation, Scholarship, Culture*. Princeton, NJ: Princeton University Press, 2005.

Shmeruk, Chone. *The Illustrations in Yiddish Books of the Sixteenth and Seventeenth Centuries: The Texts, the Pictures, and Their Audience* [Hebrew]. Jerusalem: Akademon, The Hebrew University, 1986.

Skolnik, Jonathan. *Jewish Pasts, German Fictions: History, Memory, and Minority Culture in Germany, 1824–1955*. Stanford, CA: Stanford University Press, 2014.

Skreinka, L. "Bemerkungen über die in letztverflossenen Jahren erschienenen deutschen Bibelübersetzungen: Die Bibelübersetzung von Dr. G. Salomon." *Der Orient* 30 (25 July 1840): 468–70; 32 (8 August 1840): 504.

Smith, Matthew Wilson. *The Total Work of Art: From Bayreuth to Cyberspace*. New York: Routledge, 2007.

Sorkin, David. *Moses Mendelssohn and the Religious Enlightenment*. Berkeley: University of California Press, 1996.

Sorkin, David. *The Religious Enlightenment: Protestants, Jews, and Catholics from London to Vienna*. Princeton, NJ: Princeton University Press, 2008.

Spalding, Paul. "Toward a Modern Torah: Moses Mendelssohn's Use of a Banned Bible." *Modern Judaism* 19, no. 1 (February 1999): 67–82.

Speiser, E. A. *Genesis: Introduction, Translation, and Notes*. Vol. 1 of *The Anchor Bible*. New Haven, CT: Yale University Press, 1964.

Staerk, Wilhelm, and Albert Leitzmann. *Die jüdisch-deutschen Bibelübersetzungen von den Anfängen bis zum Ausgang des 18. Jahrhunderts*. Frankfurt am Main: J. Kaufmann, 1923.

Stahl, Johanna. "Bertha Pappenheims erzieherisches Konzept als Heimleiterin" [1936]. In *Bertha Pappenheim u.a. "Das unsichtbare Isenberg,"* edited by Helga Heubach, 15–16. Frankfurt am Main: Kulturamt der Stadt Neu-Isenberg, 1994.

Stein, Leopold. *Die israelitische Volkslehrer*. 4 vols. Frankfurt am Main: Schmerbersche Buchhandlung, 1854.

Steiner, George. *After Babel: Aspects of Language and Translation*. London: Oxford University Press, 1975.

Störig, Hans Joachim, ed. *Das Problem des Übersetzens*. Darmstadt, Ger.: Wissenschaftliche Buchgesellschaft, 1963.

Susman, Margarete. "Review of Zeenah u-Reenah." *Der Morgen* 7, no. 5 (December 1931): 454–56.

Sussman, Lance J. "Another Look at Isaac Leeser and the First Jewish Translation of the Bible in the United States." *Modern Judaism* 5, no. 2 (May 1985): 159–90.

Szondi, Peter. *Theorie des modernen Dramas*. Frankfurt am Main: Suhrkamp, 1965.

Tanakh: A New Translation of the Holy Scriptures, according to the Traditional Hebrew Text. Philadelphia: Jewish Publication Society, 5746/1985.

Tasch, Roland. *Samson Raphael Hirsch: Jüdische Erfahrungswelten im historischen Kontext*. Berlin: Walter de Gruyter, 2011.

Tatlock, Lynne, ed. *Publishing Culture and the "Reading Nation": German Book History in the Long Nineteenth Century*. Rochester, NY: Camden House, 2010.

Tigay, Jeffrey H. "Introduction and Commentary to Exodus." In *The Jewish Study Bible*, edited by Adele C. Berlin and Marc Zvi Brettler, 102–7. Oxford: Oxford University Press, 2004.

Timm, Erika. "Die Bibelübersetzungssprache als Faktor der Auseinanderentwicklung des jiddischen und des deutschen Wortschatzes." In *Sprache und Identität im Judentum*, edited by Karl E. Grözinger, 91–109. Wiesbaden, Ger.: Harrassowitz, 1998.

Timm, Erika. "Blitz and Witzenhausen." In *Studies in Jewish Culture in Honour of Chone Shmeruk*, edited by Israel Bartal, Ezra Mendelssohn, and Chava Turniansky, 39–66. Jerusalem: Zalman Shazar Center for Jewish History, 1993.

Timm, Erika. "Der Einfluss der aschkenasischen Bibelübersetzungstätigkeit auf die jiddische Gemeinsprache." In *The Bible in/and Yiddish*, edited by Shlomo Berger, 21–41.

Torczyner, H., ed. *Die heilige Schrift, neu ins Deutsch übertragen*, 4 vols. Frankfurt am Main: 1935–37. 2nd ed., Jerusalem: Jewish Publishing House, 1954–59, by N. H. Tur-Sinai [H. Torczyner]. 3rd ed., 1993. This book refers to the third edition.

Tov, Emanuel. *Textual Criticism of the Hebrew Bible*. 2nd rev. ed. Minneapolis: Fortress Press, 2001.

Toy, Crawford Howell, and Richard Gottheil. "Bible Translations" [1906]. *Jewish Encyclopedia*. http://www.jewishencyclopedia.com/articles/3269-bible-translations.

Trepp, Leo. "Segregation or Unified Diversity: The Controversy between Samson Raphael Hirsch and Seligmann Bamberger and Its Significance." In *Bits of Honey: Essays for Samson H. Levey*, edited by Stanley Chyet and David H. Ellenson, 289–310. Atlanta: Scholars Press, 1993.

Turniansky, Chava. *Between the Holy and the Profane: Language, Education, and Scholarship in Eastern Europe*. Tel Aviv: Open University, 1994.

Turniansky, Chava. "Nusach ha-Maskili shel 'Tsene u'Réne" (A Maskilik form of the *Tsene-Rene*). *Hasifrut* 2, no. 4 (1971): 835–41.

Turniansky, Chava. "Reception and Rejection of Yiddish Renderings of the Bible." In *The Bible in/and Yiddish*, edited by Shlomo Berger, 7–20. Amsterdam: Menasseh Ben Israel Institute for Jewish Social and Cultural Studies, 2007.

Turniansky, Chava. "Translations and Adaptations of the *Tsene-Rene*" (Yiddish). In *Sefer Dov Sadan*, edited by Samuel Werses, Nathan Rotenstreich, and Chone Shmeruk, 165–90. Jerusalem: Ha-Kibbutz ha-Me'uchad, 1977.

Venuti, Lawrence, ed. *The Translation Studies Reader*. 3rd ed. London: Routledge, 2012.

Venuti, Lawrence. *The Translator's Invisibility: A History of Translation*. London: Routledge, 1995.

Vogelaar, Christiaan, and Gerbrand Korevaar. *Rembrandt's Mother: Myth and Reality*. Zwolle, the Netherlands: Waanders Publishers, 2005.

Weinberg, Werner. "Language Questions Relating to Moses Mendelssohn's Pentateuch Translation." *Hebrew Union College Annual* 55 (1984): 197–242.

Weinberg, Werner. "A Word List for Teaching Eighteenth-century Jews Some Fine Points of High German." *Leo Baeck Institute Yearbook* 29 (1984): 277–93.

Weintraub, William. *Targume Hatorah Lelashon Hagermanit* [Translations of the Torah into the German Language]. Chicago: College of Jewish Studies Press, 1967.

Weissler, Chava, "The Traditional Piety of Ashkenazic Women." *Jewish Spirituality II*, edited by Arthur Green, 245–75. New York: Crossroad Press, 1989.

Weissler, Chava. *Voices of the Matriarchs: Listening to the Prayers of Early Modern Jewish Women*. Boston: Beacon Press, 1998.

Werner, Eric. "Felix Mendelssohn's Commissioned Composition for the Hamburg Temple: 'The 100th Psalm' (1844)." *Musica Judaica* 7, no. 1 (1984): 54–57.

Wiesemann, Falk. *"Kommt heraus und schaut": Jüdische und christliche Illustrationen zur Bibel in alter Zeit*. Essen, Ger.: Klartext Verlag, 2002.

Wischnitzer-Bernstein, Rahel. "Vom jüdischen Familienporzellan." *Gemeindeblatt* (Berlin) (25 October 1936): 7.

Witzenhausen, Joseph b. Alexander. *Torah Nevi'im U'Ktuvim*. Amsterdam: Joseph Athias, 1679.

Witzenhausen, Joseph b. Alexander. "Translator's Apology." In *Torah Nevi'im U'Ktuvim*. Amsterdam: Joseph Athias, 1679.

Wollstonecraft, Mary. *Eine Verteidigung der Rechte der Frau: Mit einer kritischen Bemerkung über politische und moralische Gegenstände*. Translated by P. Berthold [pseud. Bertha Pappenheim]. Dresden: E. Pierson, 1899.

Zahavy, Tzvee. "The Rhetoric of Rabbinic Ritual." *Tzvee Zahavy*. Online publication. http://www.tzvee.com/Home/the-rhetoric-of-rabbic-ritual (accessed 27 May 2017).

Zakon, Miriam Stark, trans. *The Weekly Midrash / Tz'enah Ur'enah*, vol. 1. Brooklyn: Mesorah Publications, Ltd., 2003.

Zinberg, Israel. *Old Yiddish Literature from Its Origins to the Haskalah Period*. Edited and translated by Bernard Martin. Jersey City: Cincinnati: Hebrew Union College Press, 1975.

Zunz, Leopold, ed. *Torah Neviim Ketuvim. Die vier und zwanzig Bücher der heiligen Schrift: Nach dem masoretischen Texte*. Translated by Heymann Arnheim, Julius Furst, and Michael Sachs. Prague: Veit & Comp., 1838.

INDEX